THE SPEECHES IN ACTS

THE SPEECHES IN ACTS

Their Content, Context, and Concerns

Marion L. Soards

WESTMINSTER/JOHN KNOX PRESS
Louisville, Kentucky

Scripture quotations from the New Revised Version of the Bible are copyright © 1989 by the Division of Christian Education of the National Council of the Churches of Christ in the U.S.A., and are used by permission.

Book design by The HK Scriptorium, Inc.

Cover design by Susan Jackson

Cover illustration: Vittore Carpaccio's *Debate of Stephen.* Courtesy of Superstock

First edition

Published by Westminster/John Knox Press
Louisville, Kentucky

This book is printed on acid-free paper that meets the American National Standards Institute Z39.48 standard. ∞

PRINTED IN THE UNITED STATES OF AMERICA

9 8 7 6 5 4 3 2 1

Library of Congress Cataloging-in-Publication Data

Soards, Marion L., date.
    The speeches in Acts : their content, context, and concerns /
Marion L. Soards. — 1st ed.
        p.   cm.
    Includes bibliographical references and indexes.
    ISBN 0-664-25221-4 (alk. paper)
    1. Bible. N.T. Acts—Criticism, interpretation, etc.   2. Direct
discourse in the Bible.   I. Title.
BS2625.6.S6S63   1994
226.6'06—dc20   93-40127

CONTENTS

PREFACE

When I conceive a large musical work I always arrive at a point where I am compelled to draw upon the "word" as the bearer of my musical ideas.
— Gustav Mahler

THE FIRST TIME I set out to read the Bible through from beginning to end, I almost made it. I did not get lost at creation, in Egypt, or in the wilderness; nor did I bog down in the details of the law or the vituperations of the prophets. Of course the Gospels were easy reading, but I finally came to a halt in Acts, specifically in Acts 7. I quit squarely in the middle of Stephen's speech. Even to an untrained teenager's eye it was apparent that something beyond my ability to comprehend was taking place. Stumped by Stephen's speech I closed the Bible for a while.

My return to Acts, especially to the speeches in Acts, comes after the passage of much time. The motivation for this renewed investigation of the speeches in Acts is the result of a combination of factors. First, there is a deep personal interest in Christian preaching; I care about its contents, its style, its purposes, and its motivations. Second, there is the joy of reading and contemplating ancient historiographic literature. Third, there was and is an abiding curiosity about *what* the author of Acts was up to in the speeches in Acts. The present study is the result of much reading and reflection, and I hope the parts and the whole of this investigation will assist others who labor to appreciate Acts, especially the speeches.

My debts in relation to the production of this monograph are many, and it is my pleasure to acknowledge those to whom I am indebted. First, for study time and a sabbatical leave I must thank the trustees and faculty of Louisville Presbyterian Theological Seminary. I am especially grateful to President

John M. Mulder and Dean Louis B. Weeks for supporting my request for a sabbatical, although when I asked for this leave I had only recently joined the ranks of the faculty. To my colleagues in the biblical field who took on heavier responsibilities because of my absence I am thankful. They are Professors Johanna W. H. Bos, Virgil Cruz, and W. Eugene March.

Second, different phases of the study were supported by the Younger Scholars Programs of both The Association of Theological Schools in the United States and Canada and The Catholic Biblical Association of America. I wish to thank Dr. Gail Buchwalter King of the former and the Rev. Dr. Joseph Jensen of the latter for the assistance of their organizations. An entire year abroad in Münster, Germany, was underwritten by a fellowship from the Alexander von Humboldt-Stiftung of Bonn. The first draft of this work and much other scholarly research and writing were possible because of the generosity of the Humboldt-Stiftung. As a token of my appreciation to the entire Foundation I wish to offer a personal word of thanks to Generalsekretär Dr. Heinrich Pfeiffer and Stiftung-Präsident Prof. Dr. Reimar Lüst.

Third, my *Gastgeber* for the year in Münster was Prof. Dr. Martin Rese of the Evangelisch-Theologische Fakultät of the Westfälische Wilhelms-Universität, Münster. No Humboldtian has ever had a more personally and professionally generous host than Prof. Dr. Rese. He and his wife, Frau Dr. Margaret Rese, along with their son, Matthias, welcomed and cared for me and my family in such a way that we came to be truly *zu Hause* in Münster. I wish to thank Prof. Dr. Rese for his friendship as well as for his careful scholarship. I can only hope this study will not appear to be "too American" to him, although I am well aware that the methods and conclusions are not "typically German." *Mea culpa.* In turn, I am grateful to the other members of the Evangelisch-Theologische Fakultät for the hospitality of that institute.

I wish to thank my friends Dr. Joel Marcus, who read an early draft of chapter 1 and whose comments helped me focus my thought and research, and Dr. Thomas B. Dozeman, whose assessment of the original draft of my entire study aided me in reshaping the materials into a more coherent whole. I am grateful to my editor, Dr. Cynthia Thompson, of Westminster/John Knox Press for persuading me of the value of making this study accessible to the broadest possible readership. In accordance with her request I have included English translations of German materials while preserving the original German in footnotes. I am most grateful to my friend and colleague Dr. Darrell L. Guder, an excellent, professional translator, for rendering the German into clear and accurate English. For original Greco-Roman materials I have given the standard translations from the Loeb Classical Library. For the English versions of biblical texts I have attempted to stay as close as possible to the New Revised Standard Version translation, but at times I have been forced to alter the NRSV. Frequently the laudable concern of the NRSV to use inclusive anthropological language produces translations that completely obscure the repetitions and connections in the original Greek. Since repetition is a key factor in this study, I have given as literal a translation of the biblical texts as possible. My concern is not to preserve the masculine cast of the biblical language; rather, I have sought to facilitate the recognition of noticeable repetitions in the biblical passages.

Had I fully realized the size of the ocean of secondary literature related to the speeches in Acts, I might have been more hesitant to engage Acts and the other pertinent ancient historiographic literature treated in this study. Nevertheless, the labor of examining that secondary literature was rewarded by the joy of reading Acts, the Septuagint, Hellenistic Jewish historians, and a variety of Greco-Roman writers. The results of the study as seen in this monograph represent only a fraction of the work that had to be done to clear the brush before plowing the field. Yet two people, above all, taught me to love to work; they are my father, M. Lloyd Soards, and my Doktorvater and friend, Raymond E. Brown. It is only fitting that I dedicate this study to them.

Marion L. Soards
Ash Wednesday 1993

1 INTRODUCTION

A NYONE TURNING TO READ the Acts of the Apostles is struck by the amount of direct speech in Luke's work. Scholars routinely refer to twenty-four speeches comprising 295 verses of the approximately one thousand verses in Acts;[1] but, in fact, there are twenty-seven or twenty-eight speeches, seven or more "partial speeches," and at least three "dialogues"— which together amount to over 365 verses. Moreover, in the remaining parts of Acts there are a multitude of shorter statements cast as direct speech. The present study focuses on the speeches and partial speeches and asks about the function of these portions of Acts in the construction and operation of the total narrative. The investigation of the speech materials is done through combined comparative-historiographical and literary methods.

Gaining a Bearing

Before beginning this study, it is crucial to see where this work stands in relation to earlier research. In many previous treatments of the speeches in Acts scholars have referred to the well-known statement in Thucydides (1.22.1) which says that his method of recording speeches "has been, while keeping as closely as possible to the general sense of the words that were actually said, to have the speakers say what, in my view, was called for by each situation."[2] From this starting point, in both the precritical and the critical periods, the speeches in Acts were taken as précis of actual apostolic preaching, and they

1. E.g., G. Schneider, "Die Reden der Apostelgeschichte," in *Die Apostelgeschichte* (HTKNT 5/1–2; Freiburg/Basel/Vienna: Herder, 1980–82) 1:95–103.
2. This translation of part of Thucydides' notoriously difficult sentence is that of M. I. Finley (*Ancient History: Evidence and Models* [New York: Elisabeth Sifton Books/Viking, 1985] 14).

were analyzed in relation to the various speakers — especially Peter and Paul, but also Stephen and James — to recover the particular content of their messages. When scholars found there was a uniformity to the message, they concluded that the early Christian preaching at the time of the apostles had been cut of one cloth.[3] Clearly, no comparative element was operative in such study, though there was reference to ancient historiography.

To gain a clearer bearing it is helpful to trace major steps in the evolution of research during the past nearly two hundred years of study. A new development in critical scholarship came shortly after the beginning of the nineteenth century. At least since the time of J. G. Eichhorn there has been an interest among scholars in determining the authenticity of the speeches in Acts. In the process of attempting to identify the probable sources behind Acts, Eichhorn focused on the content and the style of selected speeches. His conclusion was as follows:

> The speeches themselves, even though they have been placed in the mouths of different persons, follow one and the same type, are of the same character, make use of one form of proof, and thus have so much in common that they present themselves thus as speeches of one and the same author.[4]

Eichhorn illustrated his observations in some detail, and the problems of interpretation that he identified have continued to be the points of debate in subsequent studies of the speeches.[5]

While recognizing the validity of many of Eichhorn's observations, W. M. L. de Wette considered the speeches in relation to Luke's use of sources in the writing of Acts. De Wette argued that there was evidence of written sources behind Acts, although these were freely reworked as their information was included in Acts. In turn, de Wette concluded: "If Luke used written sources, it is thus probable that he did not freely compose the letters and the speeches of the apostle and the others."[6] In his commentary on Acts, de Wette elaborated his position thus:

---

3. The best-known and most influential of such studies is that of C. H. Dodd (*The Apostolic Preaching and Its Developments* [London: Hodder, 1936], a work foreshadowed in Dodd's article, "The Framework of the Gospel Narrative," *ExpTim* 43 [1931–32] 396–400).

4. J. G. Eichhorn, *Einleitung in das Neue Testament* (2 vols.; Leipzig: Weidmann, 1810) 33–43, esp. 36–43; quotation from p. 38: "Die Reden selbst, ob sie gleich verschiedenen Personen in den Mund gelegt worden, folgen einem und demselben Typus, tragen einerlei Character, brauchen einerlei Beweisart, und haben unter sich so viel gemein, daß sie sich dadurch als Reden eines und desselben Schriftstellers erproben."

5. I am grateful to Prof. Dr. Martin Rese of Münster for the information that Eichhorn was the first scholar to publish the idea that the speeches in Acts were Luke's creations.

6. W. M. L. de Wette, *Lehrbuch der historisch-kritischen Einleitung in die kanonischen Bücher des Neuen Testaments* (6th rev. ed.; Berlin: Georg Reimer, 1860; 1st ed. 1826) 250–52; quotation from p. 250: "Wenn Lukas schriftliche Quellen benutzt hat, so ist wahrscheinlich, dass die Briefe und die Reden der Apostel und Anderer nicht von ihm frei zusammengesetzt sind. . . ."

Several things speak against the consistent, literal faithfulness of the speeches
of the apostles and other persons: (a) the improbability that they were written
down by their original hearers either during or immediately after their delivery;
(b) some inappropriate elements in the content . . . ; (c) thoughts and expressions
which recur in the speeches of different persons . . . ; (d) the linguistic peculiarities
of the author which are found in all the speeches. . . . However, since not only
individual thoughts (20:33ff.) but also in part the general thrust and approach
(7:2ff., 17:22ff.) are peculiar and appropriate to the persons and conditions, and
the high degree of historic art which would have inhered in the free composition
of such speeches cannot be ascribed to the simple narrator, then he must have
at least used written materials.[7]

The next major step(s) in the study of Acts, including the speeches, came
with the application of F. C. Baur's *Tendenzkritik*[8] to the book. This interpretation of Acts was carried out in two similar, but ultimately different, forms by
M. Schneckenburger and E. Zeller. Schneckenburger, whose work departed
from the "school" line of Baur and his followers understood Acts to be an essentially reliable historical work. Yet, noticing in particular the uniformity of the
style and contents of the speeches throughout Acts, he argued that the speeches
were Luke's compositions, intended to give (although inaccurately) examples
of early Christian preaching and to defend the veracity of the early Christian
proclamation of Jesus as the Christ to Gentiles as well as to Jews.[9] In reference
to Paul's speech in Pisidian Antioch, Schneckenburger wrote:

7. W. M. L. de Wette, *Kurze Erklärung der Apostelgeschichte* (2d rev. ed.; Leipzig: Weidmann,
1841) 5: "Gegen die durchgängige wörtliche Treue der Reden der Apostel und anderer Personen
spricht allerdings Manches: a) die Unwahrscheinlichkeit, dass sie von Ohrenzeugen nach-
geschrieben oder gleich hinterher aufgezeichnet worden; b) manches Unangemessene sowohl
im Inhalte . . . c) Gedanken und Wendungen, die in den Reden verschiedener Personen wieder-
kehren . . . d) die Spracheigenthümlichkeiten des Verf., die sich durch alle Reden hindurch-
ziehen. . . . Da aber nicht nur einzelne Gedanken (20,33ff.), sondern zum Theil auch Gang und
Anlage (7,2ff. 17,22ff.) eigenthümlich und den Personen und Umständen angemessen sind, und
dem schlichten Erzähler der hohe Grad von historischer Kunst, der zur freien Composition solcher
Reden . . . gehört hätte, nicht zugeschrieben werden kann: so muss er wenigstens schriftliche
Materialien benutzt haben."
8. Baur's basic position and method were first articulated in a lengthy article ("Die Christus-
partei in der korinthischen Gemeinde, der Gegensatz des petrinischen und paulinischen Christen-
thums in der ältesten Kirche, der Apostel Petrus in Rom," *Tübinger Zeitschrift für Theologie* 5
[1831] 61–206). In this discussion of the early *Tendenzkritik* of Acts, I am indebted to the lead
provided by W. W. Gasque (*A History of the Interpretation of Acts* [Peabody, MA: Hendrickson,
1989]; a rev. ed. of *A History of the Criticism of the Acts of the Apostles* [BGBE 17; Tübingen;
J. C. B. Mohr (Paul Siebeck), 1975] with an addendum originally published as "A Fruitful Field:
Recent Study of the Acts of the Apostles," *Int* 42 [1988] 117–31) in his discussion of this "school"
of thought (esp. pp. 55–72).
9. M. Schneckenburger, *Ueber den Zweck der Apostelgeschichte: Zugleich eine Ergaenzung der
neueren Commentare* (Bern: C. Fischer, 1841) 127–51.

It appears that the author by placing the Antiochene speech first intended to establish it as the primary pattern of Pauline teaching on his travels. Or will one want to assume that Luke received resources for this speech on the first missionary trip which were more accurate than for other speeches given later? To be sure, the probability of a special report is . . . to be asserted; whether this one was, however, authentic, derived directly from the missionaries, is very doubtful and improbable. . . . Let us take this speech as an example of the Pauline way of teaching: its major relationship to the speeches in the first section immediately confronts us; it is only the echo of the speeches of Peter and Stephen. . . . If we remind ourselves of the manner of teaching otherwise known to be Paul's, then we cannot avoid finding this remarkable. . . .[10]

By contrast, E. Zeller scrutinized the details of Acts and concluded that Acts was wholly unreliable, although some bare historical facts and legends may lie behind Luke's creatively composed account. The speeches, or sermons, were all Luke's creations. They were placed in the narrative sometimes in relation to vaguely remembered events and sometimes in relation to occasions Luke invented.[11] As Zeller observed,

The basic doctrines of the historical Paul are found in Acts in only a few allusions (13:38f.; 20:24) which are so weak that the author can place stronger or at least as strong statements in the mouths of Peter (15:10; 10:34) and even James (15:13ff.), the way he represents these persons.[12]

Zeller understood that the speeches were defenses of Christianity against the religious charges of Judaism and the political charges of Rome.

The next major study of Acts came with F. Overbeck's reworking of de Wette's commentary. In the course of a lengthy new introduction, Overbeck explicitly denied de Wette's contention that the speeches in Acts showed signs of the

10. Ibid., 129–30: "Es scheint, daß der Verfasser durch Voranstellung der antiochenischen sie als Muster der paulinischen Lehre auf seiner Reise überhaupt zu betrachten gibt. Oder wird man wohl für diese Rede auf der ersten Missionsreise genauere Quellen statuiren wollen, die dem Lucas zugekommen seien, als für später gehaltene Vorträge? Allerdings ist die Wahrscheinlichkeit eines Spezialberichts . . . zu behaupten; ob dieser aber ein authentischer war, von den Missionsären selbst ausgegangen, [ist] sehr zweifelhaft und unwahrscheinlich. . . . Nehmen wir mithin diese Rede als ein Muster der paulinischen Lehrweise: so springt von selbst ihre große Verwandtschaft mit den Reden des ersten Theils in die Augen; sie ist nur ein Widerhall der Vorträge des Petrus und Stephanus. . . . Vergegenwärtigen wir uns die sonst bekannte Lehrweise des Paulus, so können wir nicht umhin, es auffallend zu finden. . . ."

11. E. Zeller, *Die Apostelgeschichte nach ihrem Inhalt und Ursprung kritisch untersucht* (Stuttgart: C. Mäcken, 1854) 250–75.

12. E. Zeller, "Das Urchristenthum," in *Vorträge und Abhandlungen geschichtlichen Inhalts* (Leipzig: Fues's Verlag [L. W. Reisland], 1865) 202–66; quotation from p. 208: ". . . von [den] Grundlehren des geschichtlichen Paulus finden sich bei dem der Apostelgeschichte kaum ein paar Anklänge (13,38f. 20,24), die so schwach sind, daß der Verfasser stärkeres und ebenso starkes auch dem Petrus (15,10. 10,34), und selbst dem Jakobus (15,13ff.), so wie er diese Männer darstellt, in den Mund legen kann."

use of earlier reliable written historical sources.[13] Indeed, they are but the creations of the author of Acts. After citing the section quoted above from the earlier edition of the commentary by de Wette, Overbeck continued:

> The artfulness, which de Wette has reservations in ascribing to the author, is found precisely and most evidently in the speeches which are placed in the mouths of the major characters in the Acts, even if otherwise one regarded the author of the book as a "simple narrator." In its essence, the question of these speeches was already decided by Eichhorn. . . . Now, with even more gravity, the considerations against the genuineness of the apostolic speeches intervene, which de Wette himself offered and which must be decisively strengthened.[14]

The consensus of German critical scholarship around the turn of the twentieth century is summarized by A. Jülicher in his introduction. Regarding the speeches in Acts, he writes as follows:

> Every reader who knows Thucydides and Livy will have to regard the many speeches which "Lc" places in the mouths of his heroes, Peter, Paul in a great variety of situations, and most extensively Stephen in 7:2–55, as free inventions of the author. The fact that these speeches . . . are the creation of the author is shown clearly in the first speech, 1:16–22, where Peter tells the story of Judas in detail to the Jerusalem brethren, a story which all of them would have long since known, but which the author had to relate to his readers . . . the historian in a rhetorical work of art will want his chief characters to portray themselves and their time.[15]

---

13. F. Overbeck, *Kurze Erklärung der Apostelgeschichte* (Kurzgefasstes exegetisches Handbuch zum Neuen Testament von W. M. L. de Wette 1/4; 4th rev. ed.; Leipzig: S. Hirzel, 1870) VII–LXXI, esp. LII–LIX. Remarkably, Overbeck's introductory comments on Acts appeared in English as "Introduction to the Acts of the Apostles" in the English translation of E. Zeller's *Apostelgeschichte (The Contents and Origins of The Acts of the Apostles, Critically Investigated* [London/Edinburgh: Williams & Norgate, 1875] esp. 2–81).

14. Overbeck, *Kurze Erklärung*, LIII–LIV: "Allein die Kunst, welche *de W.* dem Verf. zuzuschreiben Bedenken trägt, liegt gerade in den Reden, welche in der AG. den Hauptpersonen in den Mund gelegt werden, am evidentesten vor, selbst wenn man sonst den Verf. des Buchs als einen 'schlichten Erzähler' gelten zu lassen hätte; und im Wesentlichen hat die Frage dieser Reden allerdings schon *Eichhorn* entschieden. . . . Mit um so unvermindeterem Gewicht treten nun gegen die Aechtheit der apostol. Reden die von *de W.* selbst angeführten und beträchtlich zu verstärkenden . . . Momente ein. . . ."

15. A. Jülicher, *Einleitung in das Neue Testament* (Grundriss der Theologischen Wissenschaften 3/1; 5th/6th eds.; Tübingen: J. C. B. Mohr [Paul Siebeck], 1913) 404–5: "Als freie Erfindungen des Vrf. wird wohl jeder mit Thucydides und Livius bekannte Leser . . . die zahlreichen Reden ansehen, die 'Lc' seinen Helden in den Mund legt, dem Petrus, dem Paulus bei den verschiedensten Gelegenheiten, die ausführlichste dem Stephanus 7.2–53. Dass diese Reden . . . Gebilde des Schriftstellers sind, zeigt sich deutlich gleich bei der ersten 1.16–22, wo Petrus den Brüdern zu Jerusalem eingehend von Judas erzählt, was jene längst wussten, was dagegen der Schriftsteller seinen Lesern erzählen musste . . . der Historiker will in einem rhetorischen Kunstwerk seine Hauptpersonen sich selbst und ihre Zeit charakterisieren lassen."

The degree to which this interpretive position had established itself is clear from the words of E. Meyer, himself a great defender of the historical accuracy and worth of Acts, who wrote, "Characteristic of the first part of the book are the long speeches which Luke presents here. . . . The speeches of the first part are almost totally free compositions of Luke."[16]

Moreover, in perhaps the standard English-language critical introduction from the early part of the twentieth century, J. Moffatt made these remarks on the speeches in Acts:

> The speeches in the earlier part may represent not untrustworthily the primitive Jewish-Christian preaching of the period. . . . This is due, not to any verbatim reports or Hellenistic versions being available, but to the excellent historical sense of the author, who, while following the ordinary methods of ancient historiography in the composition of such speeches, was careful to avoid moulding and shaping his materials with a freedom which should obliterate the special cast of their aim and temper. These materials were probably furnished in the main by oral tradition. . . . A skillful writer, having access to circles where such Jewish Christian ideas had been cherished and still lingered . . . would find little difficulty in composing discourses such as these, which would harmonise satisfactorily with the period he was engaged in depicting.[17]

Thus, one sees the small distance between major segments of critical scholarship around the turn of the century.

Against this background, the basic agenda for current study of the speeches in Acts in relation to Greco-Roman historiography was set by the seminal studies of two scholars. First came the work of H. J. Cadbury, especially in his studies related to introductory issues on Acts in 1922 and then in his work as a commentator on the book in 1933. Both of these contributions appeared in the multivolumed work *The Beginnings of Christianity: Part I, The Acts of the Apostles*.[18] Moreover, in 1927 Cadbury published his monumental monograph *The Making of Luke-Acts*,[19] which anticipated the shape and substance of his most detailed and influential work on the speeches, an essay entitled "The Speeches in Acts," which appeared in 1933.[20] After Cadbury's work came the ground-breaking work of M. Dibelius, especially in two essays: "Paul on

16. E. Meyer, *Ursprung und Anfänge des Christentums: Dritter Band, Die Apostelgeschichte und die Anfänge des Christentums* (Stuttgart/Berlin: J. G. Cotta'sche Buchhandlung, 1923) 139: "Für den ersten Teil des zweiten Buchs charakteristisch sind die großen Reden, die Lukas hier bringt. . . . Die Reden des ersten Teils dagegen sind fast alle freie Kompositionen des Lukas."

17. J. Moffatt, *An Introduction to the Literature of the New Testament* (International Theological Library; 3d rev. ed.; Edinburgh: T. & T. Clark, 1918) 305–6.

18. F. J. Foakes Jackson and K. Lake, eds., *The Beginnings of Christianity: Part I, The Acts of the Apostles* (5 vols.; London: Macmillan, 1920–33) 2:7–29 and vol. 4 passim.

19. H. J. Cadbury, *The Making of Luke-Acts* (London: Macmillan, 1927; reprint, London: S.P.C.K., 1958, 1961). In the edition from 1961 see esp. pp. 184–93.

20. Foakes Jackson and Lake, *Beginnings*, 5:402–27.

Areopagus," in 1939, and "The Speeches in Acts and Ancient Historiography," composed in 1944 and published in 1949.[21] Although Cadbury's work preceded that of Dibelius and while their positions are similar in many ways, Dibelius's essays had a determinative effect on German exegesis; and, in turn, German criticism of the speeches has largely set the agenda of subsequent studies.[22] Dibelius built on previous critical work and moved away from the non-comparative, historiographically naïve, and artificially synthetic methods of many previous studies, arguing, "The ancient historian was not aware of any obligation to reproduce only or even preferably, the text of a speech which was actually made. . . ."[23] Rather, Dibelius showed that *speech* was regarded by ancient historians as the natural complement to *deeds;* and he observed that ancient historians composed speeches in order (1) to provide insight into the total situation of the narrative, (2) to provide insight into the historical moment, (3) to provide insight into the character of a speaker, (4) to provide insight into general ideas that would explain the situation, or (5) merely to serve to further the action of the account. Thus, he insisted that the real task in the study of the speeches in Acts in the context of ancient historiography is "of discovering what place the speeches in the Acts of the Apostles take among the quite varied types of speeches recorded by historians, and thus, at the same time, of determining the meaning to be attributed to the speeches in the work as a whole."[24]

21. In English translation one finds these in Dibelius's *Studies in the Acts of the Apostles* (ed. H. Greeven; New York: Charles Scribner's Sons, 1956) 26–77, 138–85.

22. There has always been a healthy dissent from the positions of most German critics and the many scholars of other nations who have come to critical biblical studies from a German point of view. Initially the protest came in the work of German scholars themselves. Important representatives of the conservative treatment include A. Harnack (*Beiträge zur Einleitung in das Neue Testament: III, Die Apostelgeschichte* [Leipzig: J. C. Hinrichs, 1908]), T. Zahn (*Die Apostelgeschichte des Lucas* [Kommentar zum Neuen Testament 5/1–2; 3d/4th ed.; Leipzig: Deichert, 1922–27]), and E. Meyer (*Ursprung*). Moreover, British scholarship has almost always tended toward the conservative side in the treatment of Acts as a historical document. See, e.g., W. M. Ramsay, *The Cities of St. Paul: Their Influence on His Life and Thought: The Cities of Asia Minor* (London: Hodder & Stoughton, 1907) esp. 299–300; and his *St. Paul the Traveller and the Roman Citizen* (London: Hodder & Stoughton, 1895; 14th ed. 1920) 1–14, 144–51. More recently one sees Acts appraised conservatively in the work of F. F. Bruce ("The Acts of the Apostles: Historical Record or Theological Reconstruction?" *ANRW* 2.25.3 [1985] 2569–2603, esp. 2582–88; and "The Speeches in Acts" in his *The Acts of the Apostles: Greek Text with Introduction and Commentary* [3d rev. ed.; Grand Rapids: Eerdmans; Leicester: Apollos, 1990] 34–40) and B. Gärtner (*The Areopagus Speech and Natural Revelation* [ASNU 21; Lund: C. W. K. Gleerup, 1955]). Strikingly, of late in some circles of German scholarship there has also been a strong reaction to the positions of Dibelius and his followers (e.g., M. Hengel, *Acts and the History of Earliest Christianity* [Philadelphia: Fortress, 1979] 3–68, esp. 59–68; and most recently, C.-J. Thornton, *Der Zeuge des Zeugen: Lukas als Historiker der Paulusreisen* [WUNT 56; Tübingen: J. C. B. Mohr (Paul Siebeck), 1991]).

23. Dibelius, *Studies*, 139.

24. Ibid., 145.

In the essay "The Speeches in Acts and Ancient Historiography," Dibelius treated the addresses in Acts in groups by distinguishing "speeches" from "sermons." He regarded certain of the addresses as speeches (those in Acts 7; 11; 17; 20; and 22) and took them to be almost completely analogous to speeches in ancient works of history. These speeches are located at important turning points in the narrative and function as speeches in Greco-Roman historiography do, that is, to illuminate events and to emphasize special times and places — especially by justifying the pertinent events and giving their cause. For Luke this meant their *theological* cause. In turn, Dibelius focused on the addresses that are known to critics as the missionary sermons (or discourses) — the addresses in Acts 2; 3; 5; 10; and 13, where the speakers preach the gospel and call for repentance and conversion. Through careful analysis of these sermons Dibelius found that they were uniform in *form* and *content* regardless of the speaker or audience. Moreover, he contended that these sermons were composed using a literary technique different from that found in ancient histories. Thus, he argued that Luke was primarily an evangelist[25] (and so, only secondarily a historian); Luke's subject was not politics but preaching and teaching, and he sought "to instruct the reader and to proclaim the message of salvation to him anew."[26] Inherent in Luke's program was the desire to make it clear to the reader of Acts, particularly through the illumination provided by the speeches, that the *cause* of the move of Christianity away from Judaism was an act of God.[27] In both the speeches and the sermons (as Dibelius distinguished them) Dibelius argued that Luke demonstrated literary creativity. First, Luke freely composed all the addresses (speeches and sermons); and, second, he actually introduced or invented a new form of speech, the missionary sermon, in the writing of history.

Perhaps the main point picked up from Dibelius by subsequent scholarship was that the speeches in Acts were Luke's own compositions.[28] From this

25. Dibelius understood the form and content of the missionary sermons to be derived from sermons typical of Luke's own day, ca. 90 C.E.

26. Dibelius, *Studies,* 166.

27. Dibelius's work has undergone attack in two basic ways: On the one hand, scholars have argued that Luke was *not* so creative as Dibelius maintained (see the works of Bruce and Gärtner listed in n. 22 above; and E. Plümacher, *Lukas als hellenistischer Schriftsteller: Studien zur Apostelgeschichte* [SUNT 9; Göttingen: Vandenhoeck & Ruprecht, 1972]); on the other hand, scholars have concluded that Luke was even *more* creative than Dibelius suggested (see U. Wilckens, *Die Missionsreden der Apostelgeschichte: Form- und traditionsgeschichtliche Untersuchungen* [WMANT 5; Neukirchen-Vluyn: Neukirchener Verlag, 1961; rev. 1963 and 1974; subsequent references are to the 3d ed.).

28. The finest example of a complete interpretive program for Acts that is worked out from this perspective is the commentary by E. Haenchen (*The Acts of the Apostles: A Commentary* [Philadelphia: Westminster, 1971; from the 14th German ed., 1965; German original, 1956]). Of course, many have debated the validity of this contention. For an overview of the extensive scholarly discussion and for a summary of the position of those both in agreement and in disagreement with the contention that the speeches in Acts were Luke's own compositions, see the thorough survey of the history of interpretation of Acts by Gasque (*History*).

starting point a remarkable amount of tradition-historical analysis of the speeches has been done in an effort to determine what traditions and models were employed by Luke in the process of composing the speeches in Acts. This tradition-historical work, though variegated in terms of results that are often at odds, has been valuable in showing that Luke very likely drew on a striking variety of information that was available to him for the composition of the speeches in Acts.[29] But the consistent concern of these studies with questions of tradition history has caused the analysis of the speeches to fall into exclusive or fragmented, and thus reductionistic categories—literary, historiographic, or theological—for assessing "the meaning to be attributed to the speeches in the work as a whole." For example, one-sided interpretations include the following:

1. *The speeches are a literary device.* G. H. R. Horsley studies both the frequency and the patterns of the speeches and argues that Luke's primary motive for "use of direct discourse in Acts is likely to be due to the author's stylistic concern to lighten the narrative, and vivify it."[30] That is, the speeches are a stylistic convention for *variatio.* Likewise, W. C. van Unnik can relate the speeches to Luke's following one of the "rules" of Hellenistic historiography— for example, the author wanted to give his narrative a stamp of "vividness" (ἐνάργεια).[31]

2. *The speeches are a convention of historiography.* Van Unnik interprets the introduction and styling of speeches in Acts as (mere) evidence that "Luke new [sic] the rules of the game [of history writing] and was capable of applying them with propriety."[32] Similarly H. Conzelmann states: "Luke follows the general example of ancient historiography by inserting 'speeches' into his narrative. These serve to instruct, but also seek to please the reader; the latter is a conscious goal of historiography."[33] Dibelius also saw this dimension of the meaning of the speeches in Acts.[34]

29. Gasque's survey is helpful here. Although he accurately reports the work of others, he is not without strong bias. He has himself regularly and vigorously defended the historical authenticity of the speeches in Acts, though not uncritically; see, e.g., W. W. Gasque, "The Speeches of Acts: Dibelius Reconsidered," in *New Dimensions in New Testament Study* (ed. R. N. Longenecker and M. C. Tenney; Grand Rapids: Zondervan, 1974) 232–50.

30. G. H. R. Horsley, "Speeches and Dialogue in Acts," *NTS* 32 (1986) 609–14; quotation from p. 613.

31. W. C. van Unnik, "Luke's Second Book and the Rules of Hellenistic Historiography," in *Les Actes des Apôtres: Traditions, rédaction, théologie* (ed. J. Kremer; BETL 48; Gembloux: Duculot; Leuven: Leuven University Press, 1979) 37–60; on "vividness," see esp. pp. 55–57.

32. Ibid., 59.

33. H. Conzelmann, *Acts of the Apostles* (Hermeneia; Philadelphia: Fortress, 1987; trans. 2d ed. 1972; German original, 1963) xliii.

34. Dibelius, *Studies,* 166–75.

3. *The speeches are a theological (or ideological) device.* Dibelius could say, "the book has a theme [theological causality in the developments within early Christianity] and the speeches play their part in developing it."[35] In this line G. Schneider writes, "The speeches of Acts are not directed to the hearers in the presupposed situation but from Luke to the readers of his book." The speeches are "thus for the readers of the book."[36]

In its own way each of these observations is correct. Yet they all fall short — even taken in sum — of the kind of interpretation for which Dibelius called, namely, "the meaning to be attributed to the speeches in the work as a whole." Perhaps Dibelius merely meant "the meaning of each speech given its place in the whole of Acts," but his phrase is suggestive for holistic interpretation.

In order to move to a more comprehensive level of interpreting the speeches, it is instructive to notice two things: First, Acts comprises, at base level, much highly diverse material. The action takes place in different geographical locations: sometimes Palestine, sometimes Asia Minor, sometimes Greece, sometimes the Mediterranean, and sometimes Italy. The primary characters in the story change: most often we see Peter or Paul, but on other occasions we are concerned with Jesus, the Jerusalem "church," Barnabas, Stephen, Philip, James, and others. The ethnic makeup of the communities where the action is located changes: sometimes being Jewish, sometimes Gentile, and sometimes a combination.

Second, both in the description of the act of speaking and in the elements comprised by the speeches, Acts is highly repetitive. (A) Scholars have often counted, catalogued, and described the speeches — most often the so-called missionary sermons — always finding five to nine formal elements within the speeches that are a regularly repeated general speech scheme. Dibelius's work directed the attention of interpreters to the patterns of repetition in some of the speeches by pointing to their recurring (1) situational introductions; (2) kerygma of Jesus' life, passion, and resurrection; (3) emphasis on the disciples as witnesses, (4) evidence from scripture; and (5) exhortation to repentance.[37] In turn, E. Haenchen, E. Schweizer, U. Wilckens, and H. Conzelmann (and others) have offered refinements of the repeated elements, suggesting that there is *a* regularly repeated pattern underlying the *Missionsreden* in Acts.[38] Conzelmann's listing of these "persistent elements" is perhaps the norm;[39] he charts them as follows:

35. Ibid., 175.

36. Schneider, *Apostelgeschichte*, 1:97 and 102 respectively: "Die Reden der Apostelgeschichte sind nicht an Hörer der vorausgesetzten Situation gerichtet, sondern von Lukas an die Leser seines Werkes." The speeches are "also für die Leser des Werkes."

37. Dibelius, *Studies*, 165.

38. Haenchen, *Acts*, 104 n. 1, 185–86; E. Schweizer, "Concerning the Speeches in Acts," in *Studies in Luke-Acts* (ed. L. E. Keck and J. L. Martyn; London: S.P.C.K., 1968) 208–16; Wilckens, *Missionsreden*, esp. 32–55; Conzelmann, *Acts*, xliii–xlv.

39. Conzelmann, *Acts*, xliv. A longer, but similar, list of nine elements present in the mis-

1. An appeal for a hearing, which parallels appeals in the Old Testament prophets and Hellenistic trial hearings.
2. Making a connection between the situation and the speech — moreover, the situation may be reflected in the course of the speech.
3. The body of the speech — which frequently begins with a scriptural quotation.
4. Christological kerygma.
5. A scriptural proof of the kerygma's veracity.
6. The offer of salvation, with repentance the condition for salvation (where appropriate).
7. Occasionally the speaker is interrupted, but only after everything essential has been stated.

Nevertheless, all such outlines are artificial, as should be apparent to anyone who studies these lists carefully. Materials in the speeches must be juggled and rearranged, and frequently the critics are forced to admit that one (or more) of the regularly repeated elements simply does not occur in a particular speech. These observations do not mean that there are no discernible patterns in the speeches; rather, one cannot think or speak of a single form that is repeated consistently, nor can one easily and accurately compartmentalize the speeches into distinct types. Indeed, the proposed elements or patterns for the so-called *Missionsreden* of Acts characterize Paul's "defense speech" in Acts 26 as much as the group of "missionary speeches."

(B) Furthermore, beyond the creation of lists of the "persistent" elements, several scholars have also noticed the recurrence in certain speeches of the theme of resurrection presented with a particular negative force; that is, the resurrection is portrayed as a divine repudiation of those who reject Jesus as Lord and Messiah.[40] (Although, at other times the declarations of resurrection have no negative tone.) Further, still other scholars have identified Greek rhetorical forms (manner of address, method of formulating a defense, etc.) that occur repeatedly in the speeches.[41]

Taking a New Direction

Having observed (1) the diverse nature of the Acts material and (2) the highly repetitive character of the speeches in terms of their occurrence and

---

sionary discourses is offered by Schweizer, who suggests that "with due recognition of differences in context" these items reveal "a far-reaching identity of structure" ("Speeches," 210).

40. Above all, C. F. Evans, "'Speeches' in Acts," in *Mélanges bibliques en hommage au R. P. Béda Rigaux* (ed. A. Descamps and R. P. A. de Halleux; Gembloux: Duculot, 1970) 287–302.

41. Ibid., 292–96; and Dibelius, *Studies*, 138–45; Haenchen, *Acts*, passim; Conzelmann, *Acts*, xliii–xliv, et passim; but, above all, Plümacher, *Lukas als hellenistischer Schriftsteller*, 10–13, 32–78, and 137–39.

contents, one may turn to an observation about Acts by E. Haenchen, who wrote, "The spread of Christianity was no such simple process as the reader of Acts must at first impression be given to believe. . . . It is not the oft-broken line of the mission's evolution that Luke traces — but its ideal curve."[42] The thesis of the current study is that the speeches are a crucial factor in the coherence of the Acts account. The speeches in Acts are more than a literary device, or a historiographic convention, or a theological vehicle — though they are all of these; they achieve the unification of the otherwise diverse and incoherent elements comprised by Acts. Through the regular introduction of formally repetitive speeches, Luke unified his narrative; and, more important, he unified the image of an otherwise personally, ethnically, and geographically diverse early Christianity. This is no mean feat: Luke crafted from events and words a history that was coherent and, moreover, ideologically pointed — a history that could, in turn, move through the future selectively preserving the tradition it repeated and thereby deliberately advancing its causes.

Through the repetition of speech Luke created the dynamic of *analogy*, which unifies his presentation. Precisely because there are so many speeches in Acts, one is able to compare and contrast the different speeches with each other to notice where and how language, motifs, and patterns are reiterated and varied. As J. Van Seters has observed in relation to Old Testament materials and Greco-Roman historiography, "Analogy may be indicated by the balancing of units opposite each other or by the repetition of the same words in two different and widely separated contexts. The external structural device complements the internal thematic one."[43] The creation of analogy through repetition is a deliberate, selective process that gives clues to the real meaning of a narrative. H. R. Immerwahr found the unity and the meaning of Herodotean parataxis through the recognition of this phenomenon.[44] M. Noth interpreted the Deuteronomistic History in a similar manner by correlating the elements of the "great speeches" of Moses, Joshua, and Samuel to view the Deuteronomistic History as a unified and purposeful whole.[45] More recently R. Alter has focused on the repetitions of *Leitwörter*, motifs, themes, sequences of actions, and type-scenes in biblical literature, especially the Hebrew Bible, to show that "there is a supreme confidence in an ultimate coherence of meaning through language that informs the biblical vision. . . . It is the inescapable tension between human freedom and divine historical plan that is brought

42. Haenchen, *Acts*, 103.

43. J. Van Seters, *In Search of History: Historiography in the Ancient World and the Origins of Biblical History* (New Haven/London: Yale University Press, 1983) 36.

44. H. R. Immerwahr, *Form and Thought in Herodotus* (APAMS 23; Cleveland: Western Reserve University Press, 1966) esp. 42.

45. M. Noth, *The Deuteronomistic History* (JSOTSup 15; Sheffield: JSOT Press, 1981; trans. of German 2d ed., 1957) 1–110, esp. 34–35, 39, 42–45.

forth so luminously through the pervasive repetitions of the Bible's narrative art."[46]

The importance of the repetitiveness of the speeches has, however, often been unrecognized;[47] for the majority of past studies have either (1) treated individual speeches in isolation, focusing on one or another of the major speeches (e.g., Peter's Pentecost speech, Stephen's speech, Paul's speech at Antioch of Pisidia, Paul's speech on the Areopagus, or Paul's farewell speech to the Ephesian elders at Miletus), or (2) focused on the several speeches attributed to Peter or to Paul, or (3) divided the speeches into stylistic categories and worked with one group in isolation from the others (e.g., missionary speeches [sometimes divided into speeches to Jews and speeches to Gentiles], defense speeches, farewell speeches, and even prayer speeches), or (4) separated speeches by Christians from speeches by non-Christians. One should not deny the value of the detailed study of individual speeches or of clusters of speeches, but one should recognize that simply treating the speeches in this manner turns the Acts account into a series of episodes. If Acts is viewed in this way, it is indeed a peculiar narrative. The major figures who dominate the scenes of the early portion of the work play minimal roles in the middle part of the story and are completely gone at its end. The ending itself is a strange, ungratifying (non-)conclusion to the account, for it leaves unresolved a major issue dealt with through the last several chapters of Acts, namely, Paul's fate in the law courts of Rome. Furthermore, to examine the speeches merely in isolation or in clusters invites an endless search for sources that are thought to be useful for reconstructing beliefs and events behind the Acts account; but here the speeches are chiefly valuable only when they are disassembled and used as parts of a whole that is something other than Acts.

The Aim and the Method of the Study

The following investigation seeks to comprehend *the role of the speeches in the Acts of the Apostles.* This goal means that this study is concerned with both the part the speeches play as a whole in the work as a whole and the place of Acts itself in the ancient world. To these ends, more specifically, the

---

46. R. Alter, *The Art of Biblical Narrative* (New York: Basic Books, 1981) 88–113, esp. 112–13.

47. Recent literary criticism, especially related to modern writings of fiction, works with repetitions — verbal and episodic — as *a key* to the meaning of the texts as whole entities. The insightful study by J. H. Miller (*Fiction and Repetition: Seven English Novels* [Cambridge, MA: Harvard University Press, 1982] esp. 1–21, 233–35) demonstrates the value of analysis of repetition. Miller distinguishes two forms of repetition: repetition of verbal elements and repetition of events or scenes. He concludes "that each form of repetition calls up the other as its shadow companion" (p. 16). In the present study all forms of repetition are taken together as a single phenomenon, although there are clearly major and minor elements that are recurrent in the speeches.

work falls into three parts: The first major section of the study will analyze
the speeches one by one. An introductory note will identify the setting of the
speech in Acts, the speaker, and any items or features that are necessary for
a full appreciation of the particular speech. Then the speech will be outlined;
and, finally, the contents of the speech will be described and analyzed in
recognition of prominent elements of the speech and points of contact with
the other speeches in Acts. Instead of viewing speeches in isolation or in
clusters, the following analysis works with the speeches as a whole.[48] In two
important essays P. Schubert began to move in this direction, but even in those
studies limits were imposed that restricted the number of speeches that were
treated.[49] The investigation of the speeches that follows attempts to analyze
the utterances in the sequence of their occurrence, noting points of connection between the speeches as they are encountered in each address. When
one views the speeches together, one observes a remarkable coherence. The
consistency occurs in terms of the forms and the contents of the speeches.
There are (1) regularly repeated elements — for example, the manner of address,
the tendency to speak beyond the immediate situation, the declaration of truth
claims, the use of the past in explanation or support of the claims made, and
the act of offering God's now-available salvation to the hearers for acceptance

48. The advantage of this approach may not be immediately apparent, and there are certain
liabilities of which one must be aware in conducting the research. As F. F. Bruce warns, "Each
speech calls for individual study; features then emerge which might be overlooked in an overall
survey of the speeches in Acts, and generalizations about the speeches as a whole are seen to
be at times superficial" (*Acts*, 38).

49. P. Schubert, "The Place of the Areopagus Speech in the Composition of Acts," in *Traditions in Biblical Scholarship* (ed. J. C. Rylaarsdam; Essays in Divinity 6; Chicago: University of
Chicago Press, 1968) 235–61; idem, "The Final Cycle of Speeches in the Book of Acts," *JBL*
87 (1968) 1–16.
Early in the second of these essays Schubert wrote, "Further research has led me to under-
take a literary analysis of the speeches of Acts and to the conclusion that all the speeches of
Acts, not just the traditionally so-called 'missionary speeches' . . . are vital and prominent parts
of Luke's theology based on the 'proof-from-prophecy.'" Regardless of one's assessment of the
validity of Schubert's thesis that Luke's theology is best understood as "proof-from-prophecy"
or "divine fulfillment," Schubert's perception of the coherence of the speeches is an insight that
has been too little appreciated and has had too little affect on scholarship.
In the first essay Schubert claimed to deal with the speeches from chaps. 1–15, the Areopagus
speech, and Paul's farewell speech in Acts 20; but of the speeches in Acts 1–15 Schubert actually
considered Peter's speech at Matthias's election (1:16–22), the Pentecost speech (2:14–36, 38–40),
Peter's speech in the Temple (3:12–26), a series of statements in chaps. 4–5 (4:1–12, 19–20,
24–30; 5:38–39), Stephen's speech (7:2–53, 53b, 59b) [Schubert's citation], Peter's speech to
Cornelius and his household (10:34–43); Paul's speech at Pisidian Antioch (13:16–41), the speech
of Barnabas and Paul at Lystra (14:15–17), and the speeches of Peter (15:7–11) and James
(15:13–21) at the Apostolic Council. In the second article Schubert modified his approach and
treated Acts 21–28 by focusing on "the major scenes of this narrative and their contents" (p. 5).
Thus, he touched on selected elements of the speech materials at will and did not analyze the
speeches in sequence or in detail.

or rejection; (2) regularly repeated motifs—for example, divine necessity, a christological contrast scheme, the Holy Spirit, the early Christian witness, and salvation; and (3) regularly repeated basic vocabulary. This approach necessarily means there will be some repetition (as there is in Acts), but it is important to notice the recurrence of language and themes.[50] By considering *all* the speeches in Acts together one may understand and interpret the book along these lines—diverse personalities, ethnic groups, communities, geographical regions, and historical moments are *unified* in Acts largely through the repetitive occurrence, form, and contents of the speeches.[51] Thus, when one asks, What is "the meaning to be attributed to the speeches in the work as a whole"? one finds that the speeches unify the Acts account, and through them Luke advances his theme of divinely commissioned unified witness to the ends of the earth.

The second major section of the study will compare the form, style (language and rhetoric), content, and function of the speeches in Acts with selected documents from the period roughly contemporaneous with the composition of Acts. This comparative work will describe how the speeches in Acts are similar and dissimilar to analogous materials in the other writings. Past studies have tended to argue that the discernible historiographic dimensions of Acts were essentially Hellenistic *or* Jewish, but not both.[52] This dichotomy is, however, artificial; the Jewish writings of the Hellenistic period reveal the profound influence of Hellenism. Thus, through careful form-critical comparison of the speeches in Acts with both Hellenistic historiography and Jewish religious writings of the Hellenistic period (including the Septuagint), one discovers that the form and the use of speeches in Acts and certain elements of their content(s) are similar to Hellenistic historiography. But one also finds that the speeches in Acts are like certain speeches in the Septuagint; and, in turn, they share characteristics with the Jewish religious literature of the

50. The approach suggested here finds partial confirmation in the observation of B. R. Gaventa, who calls for more inclusive analysis of Acts, although she issues well-heeded words of caution concerning past studies of the speeches that have sought to identify the theology of Acts ("Toward a Theology of Acts: Reading and Rereading," *Int* 42 [1988] 146–57). These studies, however, even when they claimed to be exhaustive, typically dealt with subgroups of the speeches, not with the entire body of addresses in Acts.

Furthermore, see F. F. Bruce, "The Significance of the Speeches for Interpreting Acts," *Southwestern Journal of Theology* 33 (1990) 20–28.

51. J. B. Tyson also notices this *diversity*, but he goes on to speak of the dynamic, changing character of the church as Acts portrays early Christianity moving from place to place, group to group, and form to form ("The Emerging Church and the Problem of Authority in Acts," *Int* 42 [1988] 132–45).

52. Hellenistic: Dibelius, *Studies;* Conzelmann, *Acts;* Plümacher, *Lukas.* Jewish: Gärtner, *Areopagus Speech;* similarly J. W. Doeve, *Jewish Hermeneutics in the Synoptic Gospels and Acts* (Van Gorcum's Theologische Bibliotheek 24; Assen: Van Gorcum, 1954); and J. W. Bowker, "Speeches in Acts: A Study in Proem and Yelammedenu Form," *NTS* 14 (1967–68) 96–111.

Hellenistic period, for example, the references to and repetitions of Jewish (and early Christian) history, the Septuagintal language and flavor of words and phrases, the statements of a religious claim as truth, and the tendency to make an appeal for repentance or affirmation of the validity of the claims. Thus, one sees the complex, hybrid nature of the speeches in Acts.

The third major section of the work will focus on particularly prominent elements and themes in the speeches in Acts. These include: the worldview assumed and articulated, the notion of the βουλὴ θεοῦ ("plan of God") declared to be fulfilled in Jesus Christ, the various uses of the past in the course of events reported in Acts for assessing situations, the crucial nature of "witness," and other items. This study suggests that the intended purpose and the intended audience of Acts are perhaps most similar to the purpose and audience of the Hellenistic Jewish religious writing, that is, edification of those already sympathetic to the claims of the religious movement from which the writings stem. Through the speeches, Acts articulates a worldview. In common with both Hellenistic historiography and Jewish religious literature there is an overarching belief in "providence." Yet, in distinction from the other writings, one finds in Acts the claim that "God's plan" has been brought to fruition or completion or fulfillment in the person — life, work, passion, resurrection, and exaltation — of Jesus Christ. Above all else this claim unifies a remarkably diverse early Christianity. One sees this diversity in the Acts account in relation to personalities, ethnic groups, geographical locations, and to some extent theological persuasions. Through the speeches, especially in their christological claims of theological realization, Luke shows the reader of Acts the essential unity of early Christianity.[53]

53. It will be evident to some that there are interpretive concerns which the present study does not address, for example, questions of sources, methods of composition, and the issue of historicity. Some may find the omission of these matters inexcusable, so let me state plainly why I have not dealt with these problems. It is my firm *opinion* that such questions have been raised (correctly) without ever having been clearly answered, because given our resources it is finally impossible to produce definitive answers. For example, on the issue of Luke's creativity in composing the speeches, responsible critics have drawn remarkably different conclusions. While no one thinks the speeches are verbatim records of early Christian declamation, many scholars are actually not far from such an idea, themselves believing that Luke always offers a valid summary of actual addresses. Luke, Thucydides, Polybius, Lucian, and others are read as is necessary to support this contention. Other scholars, however, interpret the same ancient writers to indicate that Luke had a free hand in composing the speeches, even perhaps reporting speeches when none were made. The fact is, we do not know. I have a *suspicion* about how Luke wrote, as do others who have labored long over his writings and those of other ancient authors. The most thoroughgoing and disciplined effort to separate tradition and redaction in the speeches is probably the work of K. Kliesch (*Das heilsgeschichtliche Credo in den Reden der Apostelgeschichte* [BBB 44; Cologne/Bonn: Peter Hanstein, 1975]). Any reader profits from an encounter with this careful study. Yet, in the end, after Kliesch separates tradition and redaction with surgical precision and then comments on early Christian thought and Luke's contribution to it, one has the impression that the parts impart a vision much reduced from the complex of the whole.

Long ago Henry Cadbury wrote, "without more knowledge of the sources than is available to us in the case of Acts, it is impossible to know just how far this or any other ancient writer is writing his speeches 'out of his own head.' Perhaps a single author is not always consistent" ("Speeches," in *Beginnings*, 5:405). Nevertheless, Cadbury went on to write: "Even though devoid of historical basis in genuine tradition the speeches in Acts have nevertheless considerable historical value. . . . Like Thucydides and the other best composers of speeches he attempted to present what the speakers were likely to have said. . . . They indicate at least what seemed to a well-informed Christian of the next generation the main outline of the Christian message as first presented by Jesus' followers in Palestine and in the cities of the Mediterranean world. They attest the simple theological outlook conceived to have been original by at least one Christian of the obscure period at which Acts was written" ("Speeches," in *Beginnings* 5:426–27). Anyone who has read at length in Cadbury's work on Luke-Acts can have nothing but admiration for his sanity and judiciousness; nevertheless, I refuse to marshal still another case in defense of my own *speculation*. We have Acts — as it is — before us, and in it there is plenty to engage and to reward the interpreter.

2 ANALYSIS
OF THE SPEECHES

T HE INVESTIGATION of the speeches will proceed in two steps. First, it is necessary to determine exactly what material will be examined. Second, having identified the particular speeches that are to be analyzed, I shall treat them one by one in the order of their occurrence in the narrative. Each speech will be introduced so that its context in Acts is clear. Next, the speech will be outlined so that its overall structure and contents are in view at once. Then I shall describe and comment on the contents of the various portions of the speech in relation to the other speeches. In the final chapter of this study I shall return to the observations made here in order to state the conclusions drawn in relation to this analysis.[1]

Identifying the Speeches

Deciding to study the speeches in Acts does not provide one with a ready-made body of materials for investigation. A survey of previous treatments reveals that scholars are not in full agreement concerning the identity of speeches in Acts. In part this lack of consensus is the result of the different angles from which critics approach the materials. To illustrate, consider the following three programs: First, M. Dibelius recognizes twenty-four speeches, viewing them in relation to the speakers: (1) Christian speakers: (a) Peter (eight speeches), 1:16–22; 2:14–36, 38–39; 3:12–26; 4:8–12, 19–20; 5:29–32; 10:34–43; 11:5–17; 15:7–11; (b) Paul (nine speeches), 13:16–41;

1. In large measure I owe the inspiration for this pattern of analysis to the careful investigation of the "three great speeches" in Josephus's *Jewish War* by H. Lindner (*Die Geschichtsauffassung des Flavius Josephus im Bellum Judaicum: Gleichzeitig ein Beitrag zur Quellenfrage* [AGJU 12; Leiden: Brill, 1972] esp. 21–48).

14:15–17; 17:22–31; 20:18–35; 22:1–21; 24:10–21; 26:2–23, 25–27; 27:21–26; 28:17–20; (c) Stephen, 7:2–53; and (d) James, 15:13–21; (2) non-Christian speakers: (a) Gamaliel, 5:35–39; (b) Demetrius, 19:25–27; (c) the Ephesian town clerk, 19:35–40; (d) Tertullus, 24:2–8; and (e) Festus, 25:24–27.[2]

Second, G. A. Kennedy, who is interested in the rhetorical dimensions of the speeches, discusses twenty-five speeches;[3] but several of the speeches are not exactly the same as those cited by Dibelius. Moreover, even when Kennedy refers to a speech treated by Dibelius, he does not always cite the same verses for the speech that Dibelius did. Kennedy explains that he identified the speeches by considering addresses "consisting of four or more verses."[4] He moves through Acts, commenting on the speeches as he encounters them: (1) speech of Peter, 1:16–22; (2) speech of Peter, 2:14–36, 38–39, 40b; (3) speech of Peter, 3:12–26; (4) speech of Peter, 4:8–12; (5) the apostles' prayer, 4:24–30; (6) speech of Peter and the apostles before the council, 5:29–32; (7) speech of Gamaliel to the council, 5:35–39; (8) speech of Stephen before the council, 7:2–53; (9) speech of Peter, 10:34–43; (10) speech of Peter, 11:4–18; (11) speech of Paul, 13:16–41; (12) speech of Peter, 15:7–11; (13) the compromise of James, 15:12–21. After surveying these thirteen addresses, Kennedy suggests that "Acts 1:1–15:35 seems to be a compositional unity and could be read as a complete work. . . . Acts 1:1–15:35 may represent a compositional unit which was all that was originally intended to be added to Luke's Gospel."[5] He remarks further:

> If in fact the second half of Acts is Luke's version of Paul's travels, conceived as a separate entity and based on Timothy's account filled out by Luke for those periods Timothy did not witness . . . [then,] the result would have been a loosely connected corpus in three parts: the Gospel, the activities of the disciples from the ascension to the meeting in Jerusalem, and the missions of Paul.[6]

Then Kennedy continues his analysis by discussing the following speeches: (14) Paul's Areopagus speech, 17:22–31; (15) speech of the town clerk of Ephesus, 19:35–40; (16) Paul's farewell address at Miletus to the elders of Ephesus, 20:18–35; (17) speech of the brethren to Paul in Jerusalem, 21:20–25; (18) Paul's speech to the Jews of Jerusalem, 22:3–22; (19) speech of Tertullus to Felix, 24:2–8; (20) Paul's defense before Felix, 24:10–21; (21 and 22) addresses of Festus to Agrippa, 25:14–21 and 24–27; (23) Paul's defense before Agrippa, 26:2–23; (24) Paul's prophecy on shipboard, 27:21–26; and (25) Paul's address to the Jewish leaders of Rome, 28:17–20.

2. M. Dibelius, "The Speeches in Acts and Ancient Historiography" in *Studies in the Acts of the Apostles* (ed. H. Greeven; New York: Charles Scribner's Sons, 1956) 138–85.

3. G. A. Kennedy, *New Testament Interpretation through Rhetorical Criticism* (Chapel Hill/London: University of North Carolina Press, 1984) 114–40.

4. Ibid., 116.

5. Ibid., 127–28.

6. Ibid., 128.

Third, G. Schneider discusses the speeches in Acts in the introductory portion to his commentary.[7] He also identifies twenty-four speeches and analyzes them form-critically to categorize them as "missionary speeches," *Missionsrede* (M); "missionary speeches to Jews," *Missionsrede vor Juden* (Mj); "missionary speeches to Gentiles," *Missionsrede vor Heiden* (Mh); "farewell speeches," *Abschiedsrede* (A); and "defense speeches," *Verteidigungsrede* (V). Schneider's list of speeches matches that of Dibelius exactly, but in the form-critical analysis he attempts to add precision to the manner in which Dibelius viewed the materials: 1:16–22 (Peter, unclassified); 2:14–36, 38–39 (Peter, Mj); 3:12–26 (Peter, Mj); 4:8–12, 19–20 (Peter, Mj); 5:29–32 (Peter, Mj); 5:35–39 (Gamaliel, unclassified); 7:2–53 (Stephen, [V])[8]; 10:34–43 (Peter, M[j]); 11:5–17 (Peter, [V]); 13:16–41 (Paul, Mj); 14:15–17 (Paul, Mh); 15:7–11 (Peter, unclassified); 15:13–21 (James, unclassified); 17:22–31 (Paul, Mh); 19:25–27 (Demetrius, unclassified); 19:35–40 (Ephesian town clerk, unclassified); 20:18–35 (Paul, A); 22:1–21 (Paul, V); 24:2–8 (Tertullus, unclassified); 24:10–21 (Paul, V); 25:24–27 (Festus, unclassified); 26:2–23 (25–27) (Paul, V); 27:21–26 (Paul, unclassified); and 28:17–20 (Paul, [V]). In addition, Schneider recognizes seven "partial speeches" (5:3–4; 5:8–9; 6:2–4; 13:46–47; 18:14–15; 27:33–34; 28:25–28) and three "dialogues" (19:2–4; 23:1–6; 26:25–27, 29).

The Path of the Present Analysis

Because this investigation is concerned with the range of relationships among the speeches and with recognizing and interpreting their coherence even more than their particularity, it is best to be as inclusive as possible in identifying the speeches to be analyzed. Thus, concerns about the speakers, the length of the addresses, and their form-critical categories fall into the background of the work. Instead, the properties of *context* and *audience* set the standards whereby the speeches are recognized; thus, the idea of "speech" that guides the identification of materials is this: A speech is a deliberately formulated address made to a group of listeners. This definition excludes from the following analysis reports of statements such as the conference of the Jewish authorities about the fate of Peter and John (4:16–17), or Peter's remarks to Ananias (5:3–4) and Sapphira (5:8–9), or the report of the privately communicated promise of "the Lord" to Paul that the latter would give testimony to him in Rome (23:11), or even (perhaps the most questionable omission of all) the statements by the leaders of the Roman Jews to Paul (28:21–22) after he

---

7. G. Schneider, *Die Apostelgeschichte* (HTKNT 5/1–2; Freiburg/Basel/Vienna: Herder, 1980–82) 1:95–103.

8. Brackets around the symbol for the form-critical classification indicate less than certainty about the categorization of the speech.

initially addressed them (28:17c-20) and before they heard him out (28:25b–28). One seemingly private remark does appear in the following list of speeches in Acts, namely, Festus's original comments to King Agrippa (25:14b–21) prior to Festus's bringing Paul before Agrippa, Bernice, and an assembly (25:23–26:32). The reason for the inclusion of this address is simple; the substance of this private communication is presupposed by the subsequent speech by Festus to King Agrippa and the others who gathered to listen to Paul's self-defense (25:24–27), so that a thorough consideration of Festus's speech requires the analysis of the previous statement.

For the convenience of the reader, in order that the portions of Acts to be studied in the following analysis may be seen in a single viewing, I shall list the speeches before engaging in their analysis:

1. The words of the risen Jesus and the angels to the apostles (1:4b–5, 7–8, 11)
2. Peter's speech and the disciples' prayer prior to the enrollment of Matthias (1:16–22, 24b–25)
3. Peter's speech at Pentecost (2:14b–36, 38–39, 40b)
4. Peter's speech in Solomon's portico of the Temple (3:12–26)
5. Peter's speech to the Jewish authorities after his and John's arrest (4:8b–12, 19b–20)
6. The prayer of the apostles' and their friends (4:24b–30)
7. The speech of Peter and the apostles to the council (5:29b–32)
8. Gamaliel's speech to the council (5:35b–39)
9. The speech by the Twelve prior to the appointment of the Seven (6:2b–4)
10. Stephen's speech (7:2–53, 56, 59b, 60b)
11. Peter's speech in Cornelius's house (10:28b–29, 34b–43, 47)
12. Peter's speech to the circumcision party (11:5–17)
13. Paul's speech at Antioch of Pisidia (13:16b–41, 46–47)
14. The speech of Barnabas and Paul at Lystra (14:15–17)
15. Peter's speech at the Jerusalem gathering (15:7b–11)
16. James's speech at the Jerusalem gathering (15:13b–21)
17. Paul's speech in the middle of the Areopagus (17:22–31)
18. Paul's speech to the Corinthian Jews (18:6b–d)
19. Gallio's speech to the Corinthian Jews (18:14b–15)
20. Demetrius's speech (19:25b–27)
21. The speech of the Ephesian town clerk (19:35b–40)
22. Paul's speech to the Ephesian elders (20:18b–35)
23. Agabus's speech in Caesarea (21:11b–c)
24. Paul's speech to the disciples in Caesarea (21:13b–c)
25. The speech of James and the Jerusalem elders (21:20b–25)
26. The speech of the Jews from Asia (21:28)
27. Paul's speech to the Jerusalem Jews (22:1, 3–21)
28. Paul's speech before the council (23:1b, 3, 5, 6b)

29. The Pharisees' speech in the council (23:9c–d)
30. Tertullus's speech (24:2b–8)
31. Paul's speech before Felix (24:10b–21)
32. Paul's speech before Festus (25:8b, 10b–11)
33. Festus's speech (25:14c–21, 24–27)
34. Paul's speech before King Agrippa (26:2–23, 25–27, 29)
35. Paul's speech(es) during the sea voyage to Rome (27:10b, 21b–26, 31b, 33b–34)
36. Paul's speech to the Roman Jewish leaders (28:17c–20, 25b–28)

Analysis[9]

The Words of the Risen Jesus
and the Angels to the Apostles (1:4b–5, 7–8, 11)

After the prologue (1:1–2)[10] Luke reports the interaction between Jesus and the apostles during the forty days after the resurrection and up to the ascension. The focus is telescopic. Luke refers to Jesus' appearance ἐν πολλοῖς τεκμηρίοις ("by many convincing proofs"); he reports that the risen Jesus spoke to the apostles τὰ περὶ τῆς βασιλείας τοῦ θεοῦ ("[the things] about the kingdom of God"); and he recalls that Jesus told them not to leave Jerusalem but to wait for τὴν ἐπαγγελίαν τοῦ πατρός ("the promise of the father"). Then Luke moves into direct discourse, quoting Jesus in vv. 4–5. In v. 6 a question by the disciples solicits the final words of Jesus in vv. 7–8.[11] Finally, in vv. 9–11 one reads of the ascension and the promise by the ἄνδρες δύο . . . ἐν ἐσθήσεσι λευκαῖς ("two men in white robes") — surely angels[12]—that Jesus would come

9. For each of the following segments of Acts there is an enormous bibliography of general studies, monographs on one or more of the speeches, and articles. This literature is surveyed in a comprehensive manner by both Schneider (*Apostelgeschichte*) and R. Pesch (*Die Apostelgeschichte* [EKK 5/1–2; Zurich/Einsiedeln/Cologne: Benziger; Neukirchen-Vluyn: Neukirchener Verlag, 1986]). The literature is covered for the period through 1984.

10. Over against E. Haenchen (*The Acts of the Apostles: A Commentary* [Philadelphia: Westminster, 1971; from the 14th German ed., 1965; German original, 1956] 135–39), H. Conzelmann (*Acts of the Apostles* [Hermeneia; Philadelphia: Fortress, 1987; trans. 2d ed., 1972; German original, 1963] 3–4), J. Roloff (*Die Apostelgeschichte* [NTD 5; 17th ed.; Göttingen: Vandenhoeck & Ruprecht, 1981] 18–19), and G. Krodel (*Acts* [Augsburg Commentary on the New Testament; Minneapolis: Augsburg, 1986] 53–55), who regard 1:1–2 as the prologue or proem, Schneider (*Apostelgeschichte*, 1:197–99) and Pesch (*Apostelgeschichte*, 1:59–64) view 1:1–3 as a complete introductory statement.

11. D. Hill studies the relationship of v. 6 to vv. 7–8 to show how the Spirit works through the church in missions ("The Spirit and the Church's Witness: Observations on Acts 1:6–8," *IBS* 6 [1984] 16–26). The emphasis on the priority of the Spirit in such work is part of the theological conviction that God has and exercises ultimate authority.

12. Compare the description of the two men at the empty tomb in Luke 24:4.

again as he departed. E. Haenchen and H. Conzelmann refer to Jesus' statements as a "farewell speech."[13] Since the angelic figures speak of and for the now-ascended Jesus, it is best to understand their statements in this context as a complement to, and even as a part of, Jesus' speech.[14]

The speech combines *epideictic* and *deliberative* rhetoric, urging in the present with regard to the future, although Jesus' reply in v. 7 has shades of *judicial* rhetoric as it refutes the disciples' question.[15] The assembled elements of these statements may be outlined as follows:

1.0 Jesus' Promise of the Holy Spirit (vv. 4–5)
2.0 Jesus' Teaching about the Future (vv. 7–8)
    2.1 God's Authority (v. 7)
    2.2 Another Promise of the Spirit with the Charge to be Jesus' Witnesses (v. 8)
3.0 The Promise of Jesus' Return (v. 11)

Analysis. (1.0) The initial promise of the Holy Spirit, made here by Jesus, ties the notion of the apostles' being baptized with and empowered by the Holy Spirit into the larger framework of Luke-Acts. In Luke 3:16 words quite similar to those attributed to Jesus here are spoken by John the Baptist. In turn, as Peter explains his missionary work among Cornelius and the members of his household (11:5–17), in the course of his speech he recalls and quotes the word of the Lord, perhaps in a verbatim repetition.[16] Moreover, the recognition that John's ministry marked a moment of importance in relation to the time of Jesus' own work occurs in four other speeches in Acts—those of Peter prior to the enrollment of Matthias (1:22), in Cornelius's house (10:37), to the circumcision party (11:16), and that of Paul at Antioch of Pisidia (13:24–25).

---

13. Haenchen, *Acts,* 135–47; Conzelmann, *Acts,* 5–7.

14. This understanding finds indirect support in the recent suggestion by R. J. Dillon that the preaching of the disciples in Acts is cast as eschatological prophecy comparable to or equatable with the voice of the risen Christ ("The Prophecy of Christ and his Witnesses according to the Discourses of Acts," *NTS* 32 [1986] 544–56).

15. Kennedy offers the following concise definitions of the species of rhetoric: "The species is judicial when the author is seeking to persuade the audience to make a judgment about events occurring in the past; it is deliberative when he seeks to persuade them to take some action in the future; it is epideictic when he seeks to persuade them to hold or reaffirm some point of view in the present, as when he celebrates or denounces some person or quality" (*Interpretation,* 19).

16. The word order in 11:16 is Ἰωάννης μὲν ἐβάπτισεν ὕδατι, ὑμεῖς δὲ βαπτισθήσεσθε ἐν πνεύματι ἁγίῳ; whereas for the statement in 1:5 one finds Ἰωάννης μὲν ἐβάπτισεν ὕδατι, ὑμεῖς δὲ βαπτισθήσεσθε ἐν πνεύματι ἁγίῳ in p[74] ℵc A C E et al. and Ἰωάννης μὲν ἐβάπτισεν ὕδατι, ὑμεῖς δὲ ἐν πνεύματι βαπτισθήσεσθε ἁγίῳ in ℵ* B 81 and a few others. For a discussion of the problem and its possible solutions, see Schneider, *Apostelgeschichte,* 1:200–201.

(2.1) The stern teaching in v. 7 is Luke's version of a Synoptic logion not found in Luke's Gospel (see Mark 13:32 and Matt 24:36). By comparison with the versions of this saying in Mark and Matthew, there is an amplified emphasis on the controlling authority of God as Luke records this word from Jesus in Acts.[17] Repeatedly in the speeches in Acts, one finds this emphasis concerning God's priority in and even control of past, present, and future events. This accent appears in a variety of ways, the best-known of which is through explicit reference to ἡ βουλὴ τοῦ θεοῦ ("the plan of God"; see 2:23; 4:28; 13:36; 20:27).

(2.2) Likewise, the promise of the Spirit in v. 8 reiterates in direct speech the indirect report of v. 4 and the direct statement of v. 5, both of which fall under the rubric of "the promise of the Father," so that one learns that the gift of the Spirit is given at the discretion of God.[18] In turn, the reference to "power" (δύναμις) in this declaration provides insight into the source of the disciples' "confidence" or "boldness," which is both reported by Luke in the narrative (παρρησία, "boldness," in 4:13, 31; 28:31; παρρησιάζεσθαι, "to speak boldly," in 9:27, 28; 13:46; 14:3; 18:26; 19:8) and referred to by various speakers in their addresses (παρρησία, "boldness," in 2:29; 4:29; and παρρησιάζεσθαι, "to speak boldly," in 26:26). This received power makes the disciples Jesus' "witnesses" (μάρτυς[19] — used here for the first time in speech, the word recurs in speech [1:8, 22; 2:32; 3:15; 5:32; 10:39, 41; 13:31; 22:15, 20; 26:16] and narrative [6:13; 7:58]);[20] that is, divine empowerment focuses the lives of the disciples on Jesus.[21] Thus, again one sees that God's will and purposes determine the outcome of events. Finally, in one way or another the geographical references in v. 8 are programmatic for development of the story in the rest of Acts.[22] Implicit here is the recognition of the universal

17. F. F. Bruce argues for translating οὓς ὁ πατὴρ ἔθετο ἐν τῇ ἰδίᾳ ἐξουσίᾳ in this way "as the Father has appointed by his own authority" (The Acts of the Apostles: Greek Text with Introduction and Commentary [3d rev. ed.; Grand Rapids: Eerdmans; Leicester: Apollos, 1990] 103).

18. For a brief interpretation of the significance of the Holy Spirit in the various passages, see H. Giesen ("Der Heilige Geist als Ursprung und treibende Kraft des christlichen Lebens: Zu den Geistaussagen der Apostelgeschichte," BK 37 [1982] 126–32), who shows the authoritative guidance of the Spirit as expressed in Acts.

19. See the informative discussion by R. P. Casey ("Note V. Μάρτυς," in The Beginnings of Christianity: Part I, The Acts of the Apostles (ed. F. J. Foakes Jackson and K. Lake; 5 vols.; [London: Macmillan, 1920–33] 5:30–37).

20. The word group to which μάρτυς belongs colors the speeches and the narrative of Acts in a deep hue: μαρτυρεῖν (6:3; 10:22, 43; 13:22; 14:3; 15:8; 16:2; 22:5, 12; 23:11; 26:5, 22); μαρτυρία (22:18); μαρτύριον (4:33; 7:44); μαρτύρεσθαι (20:26; 26:22); and διαμαρτύρεσθαι (2:40; 8:25; 10:42; 18:5; 20:21, 23, 24; 23:11; 28:23).

21. On the idea that God's Christ reigns in and through the work of the faithful disciples, see D. L. Tiede, "The Exaltation of Jesus and the Restoration of Israel in Acts 1," HTR 79 (1986) 278–86.

22. Scholars have long debated whether the places named in v. 8 indicate a scheme for the ministry in two, three, four, or more parts. For a report on this debate, see G. Krodel, Acts (Proclamation Commentaries; Philadelphia: Fortress, 1981) 1–11. Krodel makes a sensible case for

significance of the message of God's salvation which is established in Jesus Christ.

(3.0) In v. 11 the angelic figures speak for the now-ascended Jesus.[23] At least five items in their statement to the apostles are noteworthy. First, the compound address ἄνδρες Γαλιλαῖοι ("Men, Galileans") addresses the hearers and identifies them with a geographical designation. This manner of address, coupling ἄνδρες ("men") with a local or ethnic term, occurs in 1:11; 2:14, 22; 3:12; 5:35; 13:16; 17:22; 19:35; and 21:28. Second, the question posed to the disciples addresses the immediate situation, although this situational question is but a stepping stone to the statement of information that follows and is not so pronounced a feature as the situationally oriented beginnings of subsequent speeches (see below on 2:15). Third, the reference to Jesus' ascent εἰς τὸν οὐρανόν ("into heaven") locates the ascended Jesus. That Jesus is raised and ascended into heaven is presupposed by elements in several subsequent speeches, for example, Stephen's speech (7:56); Paul's speech at Pisidian Antioch (13:33–37); Paul's Areopagus address (17:31); Paul's speech to the Jerusalem Jews (22:6–8); Paul's speech before Agrippa (26:13–15). Fourth, the identification of the manner of Jesus' future coming as being the same

viewing Acts, after the introductory events in chap. 1, as a two-part narrative (Part 1 = The Witness in Jerusalem, Judea, and Samaria: 2:1–9:43; Part 2 = The Witness unto the End of the Earth: 10:1–28:28). Against the "programmatic" understanding of v. 8, see D. R. Schwartz ("The End of the ΓΗ [Acts 1:8]: Beginning or End of the Christian Vision?" *JBL* 105 [1986] 669–76), who relates the verse to Matt 10:23 and interprets γῆ to mean "land" = "Israel."

Commentators frequently suggest that the phrase ἕως ἐσχάτου τῆς γῆς refers either to Rome, since Acts stops with Paul's imprisonment there, or to an unlimited geographical space. In a careful study W. C. van Unnik showed, however, that an ancient reader of Acts would have understood "daß der befragte Ausdruck immer eine geographische Bedeutung hatte und dabei nicht unbestimmt eine weite Ferne andeutete, sondern sehr bestimmt auf das Ende, die äußerste Grenze der Welt hinweis.... Für den antiken Menschen lagen diese Grenzen beim Atlantik, bei den Germanen, Skythen, Indiern und Äthiopiern" ("Der Ausdruck 'ΕΩΣ 'ΕΣΧΑΤΟΥ ΤΗΣ ΓΗΣ [Apostelgeschichte I.8] und sein alttestamentlicher Hintergrund," *Studia Biblica et Semitica: Theodoro Christiano Vriezen dedicata* [1966] 335–49; reprinted in *Sparsa Collecta: The Collected Essays of W. C. Van Unnik. Part One: Evangelia, Paulina, Acta* [NovTSup 29; Leiden: Brill, 1973] 386–401).

Most recently, E. E. Ellis has argued against associating this phrase with Rome; rather, he suggests that the western edge of "the end of the earth" would have been taken by first-century Mediterranean people to mean western Spain, more specifically, the city of Gades ("'The End of the Earth' [Acts 1:8]," *Bulletin for Biblical Research* 1 [1991] 123–32). Ellis's further suggestion, however, that locating "the end of the earth" beyond Rome indicates a date of composition for Acts prior to 68 c.e. is wishful thinking.

23. The analysis of Luke 24 and Acts 1 by M. C. Parsons combines textual criticism, form analysis, source analysis, and narrative criticism to explore the full literary dimensions of the ascension narratives (*The Departure of Jesus in Luke-Acts: The Ascension Narratives in Context* [JSNTSup 21; Sheffield: JSOT Press, 1987]). In this work Parsons is particularly interested in patterns and intertextual relations, and though his approach to repetition in narrative is different from that employed in the present study, his attempt to create a synthesis of methods in order to get at the meaning of the whole through its facets is quite stimulating, as are his results.

way that the apostles saw him depart ("[he] will come in the same way" [οὕτως ἐλεύσεται ὃν τρόπον]) refers immediately to v. 9, which itself recalls linguistically the prediction by Jesus in Luke's Gospel of the coming of the Son of Man (see Luke 21:27). Fifth, the idea of Jesus' ascension-and-parousia occurs implicitly in Peter's speech in the Temple portico in 3:21.

Peter's Speech and the Disciples' Prayer
Prior to the Enrollment of Matthias (1:16-22, 24b-25)

After the apostles observe the ascension and encounter the angels, they return to Jerusalem and rejoin the other disciples, who are the women (γυναῖκες αἱ συνακολουθοῦσαι αὐτῷ ἀπὸ τῆς Γαλιλαίας, "women who had followed him from Galilee," Luke 23:49) and certain members of Jesus' family. Luke reports that this group was united in prayer (1:12-14). Then the reader learns that in an atmosphere of reverent harmony Peter arose among the members of the group, who are numbered at about 120 (1:15-26). The subsequent report of the disciples' prayer is closely related to Peter's speech, so it is considered here.

The use of a phrase to designate the time (ἐν ταῖς ἡμέραις ταύταις, "in these days," or ἐν ταῖς ἡμέραις ἐκείναις, "in those days") occurs both in speeches (2:18; 7:41) and in the narrative of Acts (1:15; 9:37; 11:27), and the verb for Peter's opening action as an orator (ἀναστάς, "rising")[24] subsequently describes the initial action of Gamaliel (5:34), Paul (13:16), and Peter (15:7) in giving speeches. Luke also regularly locates a speaker ἐν μέσῳ ("in the middle") of a group or place (see Luke 2:46; 8:7; Acts 1:15; 2:22; 17:22; 27:21). Moreover, the pleonastic line leading into the words of the prayer (καὶ προσευξάμενοι εἶπαν, "and they prayed and said") is similar in form to the even more elaborate line introducing the prayer of the community in 4:24a (οἱ δὲ ἀκούσαντες ὁμοθυμαδὸν ἦραν φωνὴν πρὸς τὸν θεὸν καὶ εἶπαν, "when they heard it, they raised their voices together to God and said").

The substance of Peter's speech falls into two parts, which are discernible in relation to the two citations of scripture in v. 20. In general, this may be classified as a piece of *deliberative* rhetoric.[25] The speech may be outlined in the following way:

1.0 The Fate of the Betrayer (vv. 16-20a)
    1.1 Opening Address (v. 16a)
    1.2 Correlation of Scripture and Judas (vv. 16b-17)

---

24. As Conzelmann notes, here and elsewhere in relation to the description of the action of a speaker, this is a pleonastic construction (*Acts*, 10).

25. Kennedy, *Interpretation*, 116.

      1.3 Report about Judas's Actions and His Death (vv. 18–19)
      1.4 Citation of Scripture (v. 20a)
    2.0 The Necessity of Replacing Judas (vv. 20b–22)
      2.1 Citation of Scripture (v. 20b)
      2.2 Stipulation of Criteria for Judas's Replacement
          2.2.1 Necessity of Observing (vv. 21–22a)
          2.2.2 Necessity to Testify (v. 22b)

The prayer is shaped in this fashion:

    1.0 Address (v. 24b)
    2.0 Ascription (v. 24b)
    3.0 Petition (vv. 24c–25)

Analysis of the speech. (1.1) The speech opens with Peter's compound address, ἄνδρες ἀδελφοί ("Men, brothers"). This particular form of salutation occurs in the speeches in 1:16; 2:29, 37; 7:2; 13:15, 26, 38; 15:7, 13; 22:1; 23:1, 6; 28:17.[26] In 1:11 there was a related style of compound address.[27]

    (1.2) After the initial address, the first part of the speech begins with Peter's statement relating Judas's actions and death to scripture. The way in which life and text are correlated includes a number of striking items. First, the use of the verb δεῖ ("it is necessary")[28] (and, here, again at v. 21) indicates that

---

26. Bruce (*Acts*, 108) reports the work of F. H. Chase (*The Credibility of the Book of the Acts of the Apostles* [London: Macmillan, 1902] 123) wherein the only example of the address ἄνδρες ἀδελφοί outside Acts was said to be in 4 Macc 8:19.

27. For further discussion, see Schneider, *Apostelgeschichte*, 1:216, 267.

28. There is a text-critical problem related to the use of this verb, which occurs either in the present (δεῖ) or imperfect (ἔδει). In this same speech, in v. 21, the verb is clearly present. The imperfect is to be preferred, despite its peculiarity in Lukan usage, for, as commentators regularly remark, the verb here relates to the first-cited psalm text in v. 20, which is in reference to a past event, but the use of the verb in v. 21 refers back to the second-quoted passage, which relates to the future, not to the past.

This seemingly small problem is connected with a major interpretive debate, however, over the function of the Old Testament citations in Luke-Acts. An apparent majority of scholars, e.g., P. Schubert ("The Structure and Significance of Luke 24," in *Neutestamentliche Studien für Rudolf Bultmann zu seinem siebzigsten Geburtstag am 20. August 1954* [ed. W. Eltester; BZNW 21; Berlin: A. Töpelmann, 1954] 165–86), insist that Luke's theology is characterized by a linear prophecy-and-fulfillment scheme. The citations of the scriptures are the references to divine predictions which were brought to realization in accordance with the divine will. Yet other scholars, most notably M. Rese (*Alttestamentliche Motive in der Christologie des Lukas* [SNT 1; Gütersloh: G. Mohn, 1969), deny that the linear prophecy-and-fulfillment scheme is the correct understanding of the correlation of scripture and events in the treatment in Acts of the life of Jesus and the early church; instead, Rese argues that the citations are hermeneutical devices which allow one to understand correctly the meaning of events.

The ambiguous orientation of the scripture citations in this speech to the past and the future (or present) shows that this is no easy matter. The whole debate has been taken up recently with vigor by D. L. Bock, who champions the cause of the prophecy-and-fulfillment interpretation

events transpired by divine necessity.[29] This verb occurs in a number of the
speeches, sometimes clearly indicating "divine necessity" (1:16, 21; 3:21; 4:12;
5:29; 27:24), sometimes probably having that sense (20:35; 26:9; 27:21, 26),
and at times seemingly indicating nothing more than practical necessity (19:36;
24:19; 25:24). Second, the reference to the Holy Spirit in this speech is typical
of many of the speeches (1:5, 8, 16; 2:17, 18, 33, 38; 4:25; 5:32; 6:3; 7:51;
10:38; 11:12, 15, 16; 15:8; 20:22, 23, 28; 21:11; 23:9 [?]; 28:25). Third, and
similarly, the mention of David is a familar feature of several speeches (1:16;
2:25, 29, 34; 4:25; 7:45; 13:22 (2x); 13:34, 36; 15:16). One should notice the
idea expressed here that the Holy Spirit spoke through David, for exactly the
same claim is made in 4:25. Fourth, the description of Judas as the leader
of the group that arrested Jesus is consistent with the portrait of him in Luke's
passion narrative (Luke 22:47), and this depiction anticipates the first quotation of the Psalm text in v. 20.

(1.3) The report about Judas's fate in vv. 18–19 seems cast as part of the
speech, but it is most likely a Lukan editorial remark.[30] This understanding
is prompted by (A) the statement that the event was renowned, but only a
few weeks had past since Judas's death took place; and (B) the explanation
that Ἀχελδαμάχ meant "Field of Blood." (Who, hearing Peter, needs this
clarification? Is the language someone else's [τῇ ἰδίᾳ διαλέκτῳ αὐτῶν, "in their
own language"] or Peter's and the disciples' own?)

(1.4) The citation of Ps 68:26 LXX in v. 20a appears to be a free rendering
of the Septuagint which makes the original statement applicable to Judas.[31]
The introductory phrase γέγραπται γάρ ("for it is written") relates to v. 16,
which provides an explanation, as the γάρ ("for") indicates. Further, the
reference to "what is written," indicating scripture, occurs regularly in the
speeches (1:20; 7:42; 13:29, 33; 15:15; 23:5; 24:14). Notice that this first Psalm
text is concerned with the fate of Judas, a past event, whereas the next citation calls for the forthcoming (or future) replacement of Judas among the
twelve. The citation of scripture is but one form of the *use of the past* by the

---

(*Proclamation from Prophecy and Pattern: Lucan Old Testament Christology* [JSNTSup 12; Sheffield:
JSOT Press, 1987]). Throughout the speeches one finds the citation of scripture. I shall observe
the phenomenon when it occurs and, for now, refer to it simply as a citation or quotation of
scripture, or as a "use of the past." Later, in drawing conclusions from the analysis of the speeches
I shall address this important issue more directly.

29. See the succinct discussion of δεῖ by W. Popkes, who correctly relates the occurrences
of this verb throughout Luke-Acts to "Der göttliche Plan, der in Jesu Tod, Auferstehung, Erhöhung
kulminiert, bietet dem Glauben Gewißheit" (*EWNT* 1:668–71).

30. Even Bruce, who takes the speech as historical, sees that vv. 18–19 go beyond the possible historical situation of the speech (*Acts*, 109).

31. For a concise discussion of the changes from the LXX to this citation, see Schneider,
Apostelgeschichte, 1:214, 218.

speakers in Acts in relation to past, present, and future events.[32] Beyond the regular citation of scripture, other uses of the past include referring to personal experience (e.g., 2:32), quoting John the Baptist (13:25), and citing pagan poets (17:28). This feature of the speeches will be noted and described at the point of the various occurrences.

(2.1) The second portion of the speech continues the citation of scripture with the quotation of Ps 108:8 LXX. The manner in which this text is employed points to the "divine necessity" of certain events transpiring.[33] Thus, one should understand the subsequent action by the community to be in compliance with the direction of the psalm text.[34]

(2.2) Following the citation the speech articulates the qualifications necessary for the one to replace Judas.[35] (2.2.1) As vv. 21–22a reveal, Judas's successor had to be an eyewitness of the full course of Jesus' ministry.[36] Moreover, the terms defining the eyewitness "match fully the other clear statement of 10:39–42."[37] One should also notice the points of connection between these verses and 1:5; 10:37; 11:16; 13:24–25, and especially the focus on the "beginning" (ἀρξάμενος—here and in 10:37).

---

32. Bruce observes: "It is not necessarily implied that the primary reference of the two passages quoted is to Judas. Insofar, however, as the character of Judas corresponded to the descriptions in Pss. 69 and 109, these passages could be applied to him" (*Acts*, 110). This observation undermines a simply linear prophecy-and-fulfillment interpretation of the function of the cited psalm texts. Moreover, one should notice that the first text actually refers to "the Field of Blood" and only indirectly to Judas, and the second text refers to Judas's place among the Twelve.

33. P. Schubert, "The Place of the Areopagus Speech in the Composition of Acts," in *Traditions in Biblical Scholarship* (ed. J. C. Rylaarsdam; Essays in Divinity 6; Chicago: University of Chicago Press, 1968) 239.

34. The attempt of F. Manns ("Un midrash crétien: le récit de la mort de Judas," *RSR* 54 [1980] 197–203) to read 1:16–20 as "midrash" complexifies the interpretation of these verses without accounting for the actual complexity of relationships between events and scriptures as presented in the portion of Acts.

35. I do not care to dwell on one item among the stipulated characteristics, namely, that the successor to Judas had to be a man. This is not merely a matter of translation, for the specific employment of the male-specific word ἀνδρῶν (from ἀνήρ) rather than the generic ἀνθρώπων (from ἄνθρωπος) indicates the male-dominant bias of the early church. I have no wish to defend either this language or the bias it represents, nor do I wish to attempt to minimize the matter, as is occasionally done, by pointing out that women found higher standing in early Christian congregations than most other places in Palestinian Judaism. The past is the past, and some things are to be left behind. Furthermore, there is no point in reiterating these observations each time the matter occurs. Two instances of such usage, in 1:11 and 16, have already been passed over without comment; and the remainder will be also, for in its masculinity this language does nothing to help us perceive the unity of the speeches in Acts.

36. Schubert contends that this requirement defines "the eyewitness character of the college of the twelve" ("Place," 239). It is clear that the Twelve play a special role in Acts; yet one should notice in examining the speeches that it is not the Twelve alone who give eyewitness testimony of some kind.

37. Schubert, "Place," 239.

(2.2.2) Then, v. 22b states plainly the expectation that Judas's replacement will serve as a "witness" (μάρτυς) to the resurrection.[38] This is the second of eleven occurrences of μάρτυς ("witness") in the speeches. Earlier the risen Jesus spoke of the apostles as witnesses.[39] Here Peter employs this designation, as he will five more times; subsequently the term is used by Paul four times. The activity and identity of early Christians as witnesses are crucial concepts in Acts. Moreover, the witness to be borne by Judas's successor is most particularly to the resurrection, although the requirement that the one replacing Judas must have observed the entire ministry of Jesus implies that while the resurrection is the ultimate point of the testimony the ministry is at least of penultimate interest. In forthcoming speeches one reads repeatedly of God's raising Jesus (ἐγείρειν, "to raise up," in 3:15; 4:10; 5:30; 10:40; 13:30, 37; ἀνιστάναι, "to raise," in 2:24, 32; 3:26 [?]; 10:41; 13:33, 34; 17:31), of Jesus' resurrection (ἀνάστασις, "resurrection," in 1:22; 2:31; 26:23), and of God's raising the dead (ἐγείρειν, "to raise up," in 26:8; ἀνάστασις, "resurrection," in 23:6; 24:15, 21). Moreover, in narrative summaries of the content of the teaching and preaching of both the apostles and Paul one reads about resurrection (ἀνάστασις, 4:2, 33; 17:18, 32; ἀνιστάναι, "to raise," in 17:3). In a variety of ways the speeches refer to the ministry of Jesus.

Analysis of the prayer. (1.0) The prayer begins with a compound vocative address, σὺ κύριε ("You, Lord"). The early Christians address the "Lord" with κύριε in both prayer-speeches and reports of prayerful conversation in speeches in Acts (1:24; 4:29; 7:59, 60; 11:8; 22:8, 10, 19; 26:15). (2.0) An ascription is coupled with this salutation, giving poetic expression to the community's conviction concerning the Lord's intimate knowledge of all humanity (καρδιο-γνώστης, "knower of hearts").[40] Peter describes God in 15:8 with exactly the same aorist participle. (3.0) The petition that follows employs the striking verb ἀναδεικνύναι ("to designate clearly"); this word occurs otherwise in the New Testament only in Luke 10:1, when Jesus "appoints" and sends forth thirty-five or thirty-six[41] pairs of disciples. The prayer goes on to ask the Lord to

---

38. J. Guillet argues vigorously and persuasively that the mention of the resurrection in Acts implicitly issues a call to repentance ("Die Bezeugung der Auferstehung nach der Apostelgeschichte," *Internationale Katholische Zeitschrift/Communio* 11 [1982] 21–31). The essential transforming power of God was shown in the resurrection, and it was made active in the witness to the event.

39. See the analysis of 1:8 for the specific references.

40. J. B. Bauer points out that in addition to emphasizing God's knowledge and foreknowledge, this term may also have the sense that God actually determines the destiny of the human ("das Herz auch Sitz der schichsalhaften Bestimmung des Menschen ist, des ihm persönlich zugeteilten Loses") ("Καρδιογνώστης, ein unbeachteter Aspekt [Apg 1,24; 15,8]," *BZ* 32 [1988] 114–17). He argues persuasively for this third sense in the uses of καρδιογνώστης in Acts.

41. The ambiguity is the result of the textual problems in Luke 10:1 and 10:17. Did Jesus select and send seventy or seventy-two followers?

show whom he has "chosen" (ἐξελέξω from ἐκλέγεσθαι). This combination forms a request that implicitly assumes the providential guidance of human events through divine direction of human decision. The prayer is, therefore, related to the idea of "divine necessity." In two other speeches ἐκλέγεσθαι ("to choose") refers to divine calling or choice (13:17; 15:7); and it is noteworthy that in 15:7–8 ἐκλέγεσθαι and καρδιογνώστης ("knower of hearts") occur in close proximity, as they do here.

Peter's Speech at Pentecost (2:14b–36, 38–39, 40b)

Acts 2 is a neatly structured unit of material that is practically self-contained. Verses 1–13 locate the early Christian community in time and place and recount the Pentecost miracle. The story is peculiar, for sometimes one seems to encounter a miracle of speech in unstudied languages and sometimes a miracle of hearing in one's own tongue, despite the original diction. Whatever the original form or forms of this story, Luke offers an account of the spread of the gospel as the result of an eschatological (miraculous) act of God. Verses 14–40 are the speech by Peter on Pentecost (with some interaction with the crowd). Verse 41 rounds off the speech scene by providing a conclusion, and vv. 42–47 summarize the situation in Jerusalem in the earliest days.[42]

The speech is clearly structured with its parts marked by Peter's repeated addresses to the crowd (vv. 14, 22a, 29a) and narrative remarks that report the reaction of the crowd (v. 37) and summarize the content and tone of Peter's speech (v. 40a). The first continuous portion of the speech is *judicial* rhetoric, combining *refutation* (vv. 14–21) and *indictment* (vv. 22–36). The final two brief remarks (vv. 38–39, 40b) are *deliberative* rhetoric.[43] The entire speech is unified, despite its complexity, by the way in which the closing line briefly returns to the language and thought of the material from Joel in the first part of the address.[44]

The speech is longer and more complex than the previous addresses, as is evident from its outline:

42. Recently, M. A. Co examined the vocabulary, patterns, and repetitions in these summary statements to argue for Lukan authorship of the summaries ("The Major Summaries in Acts: Acts 2,42–47; 4,32–35; 5,12–16: Linguistic and Literary Relationship," *ETL* 68 [1992] 49–85). Her interest in authorship essentially precluded her consideration of the function of the repeated summaries. Yet Co's research helps one to see that in their repetitiveness the summaries in Acts form a parallel to the speeches in Acts.

43. Kennedy, *Interpretation*, 116–18.

44. Schneider notes three pairs of complementary elements which give the speech real coherence: (1) To be baptized "in the name of Jesus Christ" (v. 38) refers to "to call upon the name of the Lord" (v. 21). (2) The promise of receiving the Holy Spirit (v. 38) is supported by the promise of vv. 17–18. (3) The imperative formula in v. 40b expresses the conclusion of the Joel quotation (v. 21) (*Apostelgeschichte*, 1:264).

1.0 Peter's Refutation of the Crowd's Conclusions (vv. 14–21)
    1.1 Opening Address (v. 14)
    1.2 Explanation of the Situation (vv. 15–16)
    1.3 Citation of the Prophet Joel (vv. 17–21)
2.0 Peter's Evolving Christological Argument (vv. 22–36)
    2.1 Initial Remarks (vv. 22–28)
        2.1.1 Second Address (v. 22a)
        2.1.2 Christological Kerygma (vv. 22b–24)
        2.1.3 Correlated Scriptural Argument (vv. 25–28)
    2.2 Peter's Explanation of the Evidence (vv. 29–36)
        2.2.1 Third Address (v. 29a)
        2.2.2 Exegesis of Previous Scripture Citation (vv. 29b–31)
        2.2.3 Christological Kerygma (vv. 32–33)
        2.2.4 Exegesis and Another Quotation (vv. 34–35)
        2.2.5 Explicit Kerygma and Accusation (v. 36)
3.0 Directions and Promises to the Crowd (vv. 38–39)
    3.1 Call to Repentance and Baptism (v. 38a)
    3.2 Promise of the Holy Spirit (v. 38b)
    3.3 Explanation of the Promise (v. 39)
4.0 Final Exhortation (v. 40b)

Analysis. Prior to Peter's opening address one reads that he "stood" (σταθείς) and "lifted up his voice" (ἐπῆρεν τὴν φωνὴν αὐτοῦ). The stance is that of a Greek orator,[45] and speakers assume such a position in 2:14; 5:20; 11:13; 17:22; 25:18; 27:21. Indeed, σταθείς ("standing") occurs in 17:22 and 27:21. Having positioned himself, Peter speaks. (1.1) The opening address, ἄνδρες Ἰουδαῖοι ("Men, Jews"), is similar to the address noted in 1:11.[46] The call for a hearing, γνωστὸν ἔστω ("let it be known to you"), is in speeches or remarks in 2:14; 4:10; 13:38; 28:22, 28.

(1.2) The first topic of this speech takes up the situation of misunderstanding. This manner of beginning an address occurs in 2:15; 3:12; and 14:15. Peter's point about the time of day falls away as he refers to the prophet Joel. There are explicit references to the prophets in the speeches in 2:16, 30; 3:18, 21, 24, 25; 7:42, 48, 52; 10:43; 13:27, 40; 15:15; 24:14; 26:22, 27; 28:25.

(1.3) The quotation from Joel is a freely cited version of the Septuagint tailored to fit the act of Christian proclamation at Pentecost.[47] (A) The reference to "visions" (ὁράσεις) in the lines from Joel (2:17) finds complements in the reports of visions (ὅραμα) in later speeches (11:5; 22:17–18) as well

---

45. Haenchen, *Acts*, 178.

46. See the analysis of 1:11 for the full list of such addresses.

47. Haenchen points out correctly that the Joel text is not cited in explanation of the miracle of language (which is not mentioned in Joel) but in explanation of the verb προφητεύειν (*Acts*, 178).

as in the event of the narrative (9:10; 10:3, 11, 17, 19; 16:9–10; 18:9). (B) The mention in v. 19 of τέρατα, "portents/wonders" (in Joel), and σημεῖα, "signs" (not in Joel but added here by Luke), is echoed subsequently in speeches in 2:22; 7:36; 4:30 (though there σημεῖα καὶ τέρατα, "signs and wonders") and in the narrative in 2:43; 5:12; 6:8; 14:3; 15:12. (C) The ambiguous declaration ὃς ἂν ἐπικαλέσηται τὸ ὄνομα κυρίου σωθήσεται ("everyone who calls on the name of the Lord shall be saved") emphasizes the universal character of the gospel and thus anticipates the incorporation of the Gentiles into the Christian community in the dramatic episodes of the remainder of Acts (see 10:1–11:18 and 15:1–35, especially the speeches in these sections).[48]

(2.1.1) The second part of the speech opens with the address ἄνδρες Ἰσραηλῖται ("Men, Israelites"), which is found in 2:22; 3:12; 5:35; 13:16; 21:28.[49] Then there is an appeal for a hearing (ἀκούσατε, "listen"), a feature of speeches in 2:22; 7:2; 13:16; 15:13; 22:1; 26:3.

(2.1.2) From this opening the speech continues by delivering christological kerygma. The focus is set with a reference to Ἰησοῦς ὁ Ναζωραῖος ("Jesus the Nazorean"). This manner of naming Jesus occurs in speeches in 2:22; 4:10; 22:8; 26:9. Similarly, in Tertullus's speech (24:5) the disciples are called "the sect of the Nazoreans" (τῆς τῶν Ναζωραίων αἱρέσεως, "the sect of the Nazoreans"). Several specific items in this part of the speech are important: First, Jesus is referred to as "a man" (ἀνήρ) in 2:22 and 17:31. Second, the speech states explicitly that Jesus was attested to those hearing Peter by the mighty works, wonders, and signs that God did through him. The language echoes the modified quotation of Joel in v. 19 and is linguistically related to the other reference to τέρατα ("wonders") and σημεῖα ("signs") in the speeches (see v. 19). Moreover, by declaring that God attested to Jesus, the speech implies that the Christian witness borne to Jesus, by Jesus' own command and in the power of the Holy Spirit (1:8), is activity expressive of the very will and work of God.[50] Thus, the precedent for the testimony given in the speeches in Acts was set by God, so that one may conclude that the testimony is part of God's plan and transpires by divine necessity. This understanding becomes clear in v. 24. Third, the reference to Jesus' ministry has points of contact with the stipulation that Judas's replacement necessarily had to have observed the whole of

---

48. H. van de Sandt demonstrates the programmatic character of the citation from Joel for the entire Acts account ("The Fate of the Gentiles in Joel and Acts 2: An Intertextual Study," *ETL* 66 [1990] 56–77). Throughout the analysis of the speeches that follows I shall point out echoes of the language and thought of Joel in the speeches.

49. Haenchen suggests that this form of address is a more intimate salutation than the initial address (*Acts,* 179).

50. On God's initiative and role in the bearing of "witness," see the especially incisive article by B. R. Gaventa ("'You Will Be My Witnesses': Aspects of Mission in the Acts of the Apostles," *Missiology* 10 [1982] 413–25), wherein the crucial nature and function of "witness" in Acts are explicated in relation to the central themes of the book, especially the active role of God.

Jesus' work (1:22) and with the similar reference in Peter's speech in Cornelius's house (10:38). Fourth, in v. 23 one encounters the phrase τῇ ὡρισμένῃ βουλῇ καὶ προγνώσει τοῦ θεοῦ ("the definite plan and foreknowledge of God"), which is the first explicit reference in Acts to the important idea of ἡ βουλὴ τοῦ θεοῦ, "the plan of God" (2:23; 4:28; 13:36; 20:27). The qualifying of ἡ βουλὴ τοῦ θεοῦ ("the plan of God") with the participial form of ὁρίζειν ("to decide" or "to determine") emphasizes God's control in determining events, especially the future. This same emphasis occurs in speeches in 2:23; 10:42; 17:26, 31 through further uses of ὁρίζειν ("to determine"). Thus, the cross is not cast as a scandal,[51] for the crucifixion of Jesus at the hands of the lawless is viewed as part of the fulfillment of God's plan.[52] This idea colors statements made in 2:23; 3:18; 13:27–29; 26:23, and the report of Paul's teaching in 17:3 communicates the same thought. Fifth, one hears in 2:23; 3:13; and 13:28–29 that χειρὸς ἀνόμων ("the hand of the lawless") did the will of the Jerusalem Jews by crucifying Jesus.[53] Sixth, the kerygmatic material is stated in a "style using the relative pronoun";[54] this style occurs in kerygmatic reports in 2:23–24; 3:13, 15; 4:10; 5:30; 10:38–39; 13:31, 37; 14:15, 16. Seventh, at least since the time of H. J. Holtzmann interpreters have commented on the sharp juxtaposition of the human and divine actions in vv. 23–24, προσπήξαντες ἀνείλατε, ὃν ὁ θεὸς ἀνέστησεν ("crucifying you killed the one whom God raised").[55] Several speeches express this acute contrast using synonymous verbs

---

51. Haenchen, Acts, 180.

52. Schneider has a helpful discussion of the relationship of the idea expressed here in Acts and the Lukan passion narrative (Apostelgeschichte, 1:272).

53. In the discussion of whether Acts is anti-Jewish, the helpful study by J. R. Wilch ("Jüdische Schuld am Tode Jesu—Antijudaismus in der Apostelgeschichte," in Wort in der Zeit: Neutestamentliche Studien. Festgabe für Karl Heinrich Rengstorf zum 75. Geburtstag [ed. W. Haubeck and M. Bachmann; Leiden: Brill, 1980] 236–49; Eng. trans.: "Jewish Guilt for the Death of Jesus—Anti-Judaism in the Acts of the Apostles?" Lutheran Theological Journal 18 [1984] 49–58) shows through exegesis of Acts 2:22–23, 36; 3:13–15; 4:10; 5:30; 7:52; 13:27–28; 10:39; 4:27–28 that the mention of the death of Jesus has no inherent anti-Jewish element.

Furthermore, with clarity and insight, F. J. Matera demonstrates that the declarations in the speeches concerning the Jewish responsibility for Jesus' death are not anti-Jewish; rather, they function in the Acts account as calls to repentance ("Responsibility for the Death of Jesus according to the Acts of the Apostles," JSNT 39 [1990] 77–93). Matera argues correctly that anti-Jewish uses of these passages are serious abuses of the texts.

54. Conzelmann, Acts, 20.

55. H. J. Holtzmann, Die Apostelgeschichte (3d ed.; Hand-Commentar zum Neuen Testament 1/2; Tübingen/Leipzig: J. C. B. Mohr [Paul Siebeck], 1901) 34–37. On Acts 2:23 Holtzmann observed, "Wenn irgendwo, so reichten sich hier menschliche Freiheit und göttliche Nothwendigkeit die Hand: dies die einfachste und wohl auch älteste Form, sich mit dem paradoxen Schicksal des Messias auszusöhnen; s. zu Lc 24.26." This point is debated; see especially the article by M. Rese, which argues persuasively that the formula is not primitive, but is a Lukan formulation ("Die Aussagen über Jesu Tod und Auferstehung in der Apostelgeschichte—Ältestes Kerygma oder lukanische Theologumena?" NTS 30 [1984] 335–53).

(2:23–24; 3:15; 4:10; 5:30; 10:39–40; 13:28–30; see also 13:33–34; 17:31).[56] Eighth, the kerygma ultimately stresses Jesus' resurrection, the point to which Peter's previous address said the apostles were to be witnesses.[57]

(2.1.3) Following the christological kerygma, Ps 15:8–11 LXX is cited on the assumption that it is a report by David of the words of the Messiah.[58] This use of the past is the same as that observed in Peter's previous speech; and, as becomes apparent, the speeches frequently quote psalm texts (1:20; 2:25–28, 34–35; 4:24 [?]; 4:25–26; 13:33, 35; 14:15 [?]). Indeed, in 13:35 a portion of this same psalm is quoted again in a slightly different manner, but seemingly to make the same point.[59]

(2.2.1) The second part of the speech continues with the address Ἄνδρες ἀδελφοί ("Men, brothers"), using this salutation in the second of its thirteen occurrences in Acts.[60] (2.2.2) Peter declares his confidence[61] as he sets about the interpretation of the psalm. The explanation that David died and was buried, so that this psalm cannot be about him, is given in both instances in which this psalm is quoted (2:29; 13:36). Moreover, as Haenchen observes, after the reference in v. 30 to David's prophetic identity, one naturally expects the prophecy of vv. 31–32 to follow immediately; but instead the thought concerning the promise to David of an heir on the throne intervenes.[62] It is, therefore, noteworthy that in the course of the proclamation concerning the resurrection in 13:30–37 Paul cites not only Ps 15:10 but also Ps 2:7, which originally referred to divine blessing at the coronation of the king. Thus, in both speeches when the resurrection is considered in relation to God's promise that the Anointed One would not see corruption, one observes a tendency to blend thinking about enthronement into the interpretation.[63] Finally, David is cast as an authority on the Messiah here (2:25, 29, 34), in 4:25, and implicitly in 13:34–35.[64]

56. More recently L. Schenke has focused on the briefest form of the contrast scheme, relating it to 2:22–24; 2:36; 3:13–15; 5:30; 10:39–40; 13:28–30 in the perspectives of tradition history and literary criticism to argue that 4:10b shows clearly that "Lukas . . . eine formelhafte, geprägte Wendung übernommen hat" ("Die Kontrastformel Apg 4,10b," BZ 26 [1982] 1–20; quotation from p. 12). Thus, one sees that after nearly a century of study, scholars still wrestle with whether Luke had a tradition and, if so, what form it possessed.

57. See the analysis of 1:22b for the list of occurrences of this feature in the speeches.

58. R. P. C. Hanson, The Acts (New Clarendon Bible; Oxford: Clarendon, 1967) 68.

59. There is an ongoing debate about the interpretation of exactly what the use of this psalm means. For a brief survey of the problem, see Conzelmann, Acts, 105 n. 28; and for a report on more recent reflection on the use of this text, see Schneider, Apostelgeschichte, 2:138–39.

60. See the analysis of 1:16 for the list of occurrences.

61. In discussing Jesus' promise of the power of the Holy Spirit I noted this feature of forthcoming speeches (παρρησία, 2:29; 4:29; and παρρησιάζεσθαι, 26:26).

62. Haenchen, Acts, 182.

63. On the complex nature of the christological interpretation in Acts 2:25–26; 13:32–37, see R. F. O'Toole, "Luke's Understanding of Jesus' Resurrection-Ascension-Exaltation," BTB 9 (1979) 106–14.

64. Similarly, in 1:16 he was cast as an authority on the life of the Christian community.

(2.2.3) Verses 32–33 turn back to direct assertion of christological kerygma, and in the most explicit fashion possible Peter says that God raised Jesus and that he and the others are witnesses to God's act. The idea of resurrection is expanded in these verses by the introduction of the idea of God's exalting Jesus. This seemingly new element may, however, be an interpretation of the last portion of v. 28, πληρώσεις με εὐφροσύνης μετὰ τοῦ προσώπου σου ("you will make me full of gladness with your presence"). Here Peter declares (A) that Jesus is exalted at the right hand of God, (B) that he received the Holy Spirit from God, (C) that from his exalted position and in possession of the Spirit he bestowed the Spirit on the disciples, and (D) that the marvelous events transpiring before the crowd are now evidence to them of Jesus' resurrection, exaltation, and bestowal of the Spirit. The "evidence" of the veracity of this argument is the Holy Spirit. In several speeches one observes the tendency to understand the Holy Spirit as the ultimate "evidence" or "witness" to God's will and work (2:33; 5:32; 7:51 [?]; 11:15–17; 15:8; 20:23 [?]; 21:11).

(2.2.4) In vv. 34–35 Ps 109:1 LXX comes into the speech in relation to the idea of Jesus' being exalted to the right hand of God. As before (vv. 25–28) the psalm provides David's authoritative word about Jesus' fate. The logic matches the previous pattern of interpretation: it is not about David, but about Jesus. As the outpouring of the Spirit on the disciples demonstrates the reality of Jesus' resurrection and exaltation, so now this psalm text documents the truth of Peter's claims that God raised Jesus and exalted him.[65]

(2.2.5) The interpretation of the citation, however, does not stop at the level of relating the text to Jesus' resurrection and exaltation. From the occurrence(s) of κύριος ("Lord") in the psalm,[66] the speech then explicitly declares that God made "Lord" and "Christ" the same Jesus whom the Jerusalem Jews crucified.[67] Thus, the third part of the speech ends with (A) a

65. See the insightful discussion of the place and function of Ps 109:1 LXX by D. M. Hay (*Glory at the Right Hand: Psalm 110 in Early Christianity* [SBLMS 18; Nashville: Abingdon, 1973] 70–72). Hay notes the interplay between the themes of the coming of the Spirit and the resurrection-exaltation of Jesus in this speech and argues that while the psalm text explains the Spirit's appearance, the main theme of the speech itself is that Jesus of Nazareth is the savior to whom all must turn.

66. R. N. Longenecker notes that the title "Lord" in the psalm text describes the early Christian consciousness of Jesus' lordship which "rested upon their assurance regarding his resurrection and present exaltation" (*The Christology of Early Jewish Christianity* [SBT 2d ser. 17; London: SCM, 1970] 131).

67. Conzelmann carefully explains that Luke does not offer an adoptionist scheme in this passage, for there is no reflection in the speech concerning the time of Jesus' installation (*Acts,* 21). The titles derive from the scriptural texts: Messiah or Christ comes from Psalm 15, and Lord comes from Psalm 109. On this subject, Rese writes: "daß Jesus der Messias ist, erweist das Zitat aus Ps 16, durch das die vom Zwölferkreis bezeugte Auferweckung zum schlagenden Beweis für die Messianität Jesu wird; daß Jesus der Herr ist, geht aus Ps 110,1 hervor, der die von allen Zuhörern gesehene und gehörte Geistausgießung als Tat des erhöhten Jesus, dem vom Vater Stellung und Name gegeben ist, erkennen lehrt" (*Motive,* 65–66).

declaration of who Jesus is in the construction of God's plan and (B) an assertion of the guilt of the crowd. One encounters such declarations about the
identity of Jesus in many of the speeches (2:36; 3:13, 14, 15, 20, 22, 26; 4:10;
5:31; 7:52, 56; 10:36, 42; 13:23, 33 [?]; 22:8 [?]; 22:14; 26:15 [?]; 26:23), and
in several of the addresses one also observes the speaker confronting the
members of the audience with their guilt, often implicitly by the mention of
repentance and forgiveness (2:23, 36; 3:13–15; 4:10–11; 5:30; 7:51–53; 10:43
[?]; 13:27–29 [?], 46; 14:17 [?]; 17:30 [?]).

In v. 37 a cry from the crowd breaks into the speech. Other speeches in
Acts are interrupted (3:26/4:1; 7:53/7:54; 7:56/7:57; 10:43/10:44; 17:31/17:32
[?]; 22:21/22:22; 26:23/24; 26:27/28).

(3.1) After the "interruption"[68] (v. 38) comes a call to the crowd to repent
and to be baptized in the name of Jesus Christ for the forgiveness of their
sins (μετανοήσατε, [φησίν,] καὶ βαπτισθήτω ἕκαστος ὑμῶν ἐπὶ τῷ ὀνόματι Ἰησοῦ
Χριστοῦ εἰς ἄφεσιν τῶν ἁμαρτιῶν ὑμῶν, "Repent, and be baptized every one
of you in the name of Jesus Christ so that your sins may be forgiven").[69] Echoes
of these directions occur in elements of various speeches:[70] (A) the need for
repentance (2:38; 3:19; 5:31 [implicitly]; 14:15; 17:30; 20:21 [implicitly]; 26:20
[implicitly]; and compare 8:22);[71] (B) the call to baptism (2:38; 10:47 [implic-
itly]; 22:16; and compare 8:36); (C) the name of Jesus (2:38; 3:16; 4:10, 12;
10:43; 21:13);[72] and (D) the forgiveness of sins (2:38; 3:19; 5:31; 10:43; 13:38;
22:16; 26:18). (3.2) These directions are coupled with a promise: Peter tells
the listeners that as they do these things they will receive the gift of the Holy
Spirit. This promise is supported by and consistent with vv. 17–18.[73] While
this promise is not reiterated in another speech, Peter defends himself before

68. Haenchen observed that this was one of the few times in the Acts account when Luke
wove a short dialogue into the story (Acts, 183). Conzelmann designated this feature "a literary
device" (Acts, 22). G. H. R. Horsley has perhaps paid the most attention to this feature; his
suggestion, however, that there are interruptions at 13:42 and 20:36 seems doubtful ("Speeches
and Dialogue in Acts," NTS 32 [1986] 609–14, esp. 610).

69. The seeming linearity of this call is interpreted by B. Sauvagnat as the normative course
of conversion to Christianity ("Se repentir, être baptisé, recevoir l'Esprit, Actes 2,37ss.," Foi et
Vie 80 [1981] 77–89). But, as Krodel observes, "For Luke, repentance, Baptism, forgiveness,
and the gift of the Spirit form a unity rather than a series of three or four successive experiences,
or stages of one's spiritual journey" (Acts, 90).

70. Bruce compares the substance of this speech with "substantially the same pattern . . . in
the kerygmatic speeches of 3:12–26; 5:30–32; 10:36–43; 13:16–41" (Acts, 120). As should be
clear from the present analysis, this is an artificially limited field of comparison.

71. Dibelius listed also 10:42–43 (Studies, 165); but he seems to read this into the text rather
than out of it.

72. On the association of the "name of Jesus" in Acts with baptism, proclamation, healing,
and the Lord—not merely with a replacement motif—see J. A. Ziesler, "The Name of Jesus in
the Acts of the Apostles," JSNT 4 (1979) 28–41. On the sense of "the name," see S. New, "Note
XI. The Name, Baptism, and the Laying on of Hands," in Beginnings, 5:132–34.

73. See above n. 44.

his critics from the circumcision party by referring to God's giving "the same gift" (τὴν ἴσην δωρεὰν ἔδωκεν αὐτοῖς ὁ θεός, "God gave them the same gift"), namely, the Holy Spirit, to Cornelius and the members of his household (11:17). Moreover, the same words used in making this promise occur in 10:45 in the narrative portion of the Cornelius episode (ἡ δωρεὰ τοῦ ἁγίου πνεύματος, "the gift of the Holy Spirit").

(3.3) The final line of the third section of the speech (v. 39) comes as a word of explanation to the Jerusalem Jews in Peter's audience, but implicit in this statement is a foreshadowing of the time when the promise will be realized in relation to the Gentiles. As should be apparent, the language of this statement resounds that already encountered in v. 21, and now it goes on to complete the quotation from Joel (3:5b), which was left incomplete in the previous citation.

(4.0) Prior to the final imperative in v. 40b, Luke reports that Peter spoke more than is recorded in this speech. A similar report occurs in Luke 3:18.[74] The statement in v. 40b with its strong call to "be saved" (σώθητε) reflects v. 21 (σωθήσεται, "to be saved"),[75] and it relates to speech-statements about Jesus as "savior" (σωτήρ) in 5:31 and 13:23 as well as to speech-statements about "salvation" in 4:12 (ἡ σωτηρία), 28:28 (τὸ σωτήριον), and "being saved" in 15:11 (σωθῆναι).[76]

Peter's Speech in Solomon's Portico of the Temple (3:12–26)

After the events of Pentecost, one reads of the idyllic life of the early Jerusalem congregation. In an atmosphere of charity and growth, which Luke attributes to the work of the Lord, we find the Jerusalem disciples regularly engaging in public worship and private gatherings. In Acts 3 Luke tells of a memorable experience in the Temple that involved Peter and John. The first verses of the chapter (vv. 1–12a) narrate the healing of a man that was χωλὸς ἐκ κοιλίας μητρός ("lame from birth") and then report the amazement of πᾶς ὁ λαός ("all the people") and how they gathered around Peter, John, and the healed man. In the brief statement of Peter to the lame man prior to the subsequent speech one reads that the healing takes place ἐν τῷ ὀνόματι Ἰησοῦ Χριστοῦ τοῦ Ναζωραίου ("in the name of Jesus Christ the Nazorean"). As was observed, Ἰησοῦς ὁ Ναζωραῖος ("Jesus the Nazorean") occurs in

74. Dibelius noted this feature and compared it with analogous phenomena in Xenophon, Polybius, Appian, and Josephus (*Studies*, 160–61).

75. The interpretation of 2:40 by E. Lövestam gets lost in looking for a background against which to view this statement and misses the plain theological nature of the declaration ("Der Rettungsappell in Ag 2,40," *ASTI* 12 [1983] 84–92).

76. Schneider, *Apostelgeschichte*, 1:277.

speeches in 2:22; 4:10; 22:8; 26:9; and references to "the name of Jesus" are in 2:38; 3:16; 4:10, 12; 10:43; 26:9. This remark, which is not a speech, anticipates a part of the forthcoming speech (3:16) and echoes portions of several others; the result is that the narrative building up to Peter's speech is itself coherent with this and other speeches in Acts.

With the crowd assembled, Peter speaks. Kennedy suggests that this speech combines *judicial* (vv. 12–18) and *deliberative* (vv. 19–26) rhetoric.[77] Again, the repeated addresses to the crowd mark the sections of the speech, so that in outline it appears as follows:

1.0 Peter's Explanation of the Healing (vv. 12b–16)
    1.1 Address with Leading Situational Question (v. 12b)
    1.2 Christological Kerygma (vv. 13–15a)
    1.3 Confirmations of Kerygma (vv. 15b–16)
        1.3.1 Apostolic Witness (v. 15b)
        1.3.2 Evidence of the Healing (v. 16)
2.0 Peter's Appeal for Repentance (vv. 17–26)
    2.1 Address with Recognition of Crowd's Ignorance (v. 17)
    2.2 Declaration of God's Work in Christ (v. 18)
    2.3 Call for Repentance and Two Promises (vv. 19–21a)
        2.3.1 Exhortation to Repent (v. 19a)
        2.3.2 Promise of Forgiveness (v. 19b)
        2.3.3 The Enigmatic Explanation of the Meaning of Forgiveness (vv. 20–21)
    2.4 Scriptural Explanations of Theological Dimensions of the Situation (vv. 22–25)
        2.4.1 God's Action and Its Negative Significance (vv. 22–23)
        2.4.2 The "Time" and Its Positive Significance (vv. 24–25)
    2.5 Closing Declaration of God's Work for Repentance (v. 26)

Analysis. (1.1) The opening address ἄνδρες Ἰσραηλῖται ("Men, Israelites") is the second occurrence of this salutation, which first appeared at 2:22.[78]

---

77. Kennedy suggests an outline different from that proposed here (*Interpretation*, 118–19). He writes: "The first section (3:12–18) is judicial and seeks to explain what has happened, attributing it to God, and by contrast indicting the Jews for the death of Jesus. . . . The judicial section functions as a proem and narration for the deliberative speech . . . the proposition (19–21), proof based on Scripture (22–25), and epilogue (26)." Many outlines are possible. Schneider posits an introduction and three parts to the speech (v. 12a + vv. 12b–16, 17–21, 22–25 + 26) (*Apostelgeschichte*, 1:313). Both Pesch (*Apostelgeschichte*, 1:149–50) and Krodel (*Acts*, 99–108) recognize the same two broad sections of the speech designed above, although they suggest ways of viewing the materials in each of the parts that differ from the divisions given here.

78. I shall avoid the wholesale repetition of lists of verses in the speeches by simply referring to the place where the list has already been given in the analysis of a speech; and I shall refrain from freighting the text with footnotes by pointing out here, and not subsequently, that one may find the lists of parallels by turning to the places in the previous analyses to which statements

Peter's rhetorical question attributes misunderstanding to the crowd. The situation of misunderstanding invites an explanation as it did in 2:15 and will in 14:15.

(1.2) The speech is immediately kerygmatic.[79] Peter begins to clarify the circumstances of the healing by speaking of ὁ θεὸς 'Αβραὰμ καὶ [ὁ θεὸς] 'Ισαὰκ καὶ [ὁ θεὸς] 'Ιακώβ, ὁ θεὸς τῶν πατέρων ἡμῶν ("the God of Abraham, the God of Isaac, and the God of Jacob, the God of our fathers"), which some interpreters understand to be an allusion to Exod 3:6, 15;[80] whatever the source of this statement, a very similar designation for God occurs in 7:32.[81] This God ἐδόξασεν τὸν παῖδα αὐτοῦ 'Ιησοῦν ("glorified his servant Jesus"). The use of παῖς ("servant") is one of the many statements in the speeches concerning Jesus' identity.[82] This general phenomenon was noted at 2:36. This specific title, παῖς, is repeated in the closing line of the speech (v. 26) and later in 4:27, 30. The Greek word παῖς is, however, ambiguous[83] and may at times be understood to mean "child" or "son."[84] Should the latter be the sense

---

in subsequent analyses refer; that is, for the list of the five occurrences of ἄνδρες 'Ισραηλῖται please consult the analysis of 2:22.

79. Schubert calls the kerygmatic section at the beginning of the address a "short summary of the Pentecost speech" ("Place," 240).

80. Haenchen declares: "The designation of God derives from Exodus 3.6, 15" (Acts, 205). Schneider is more reserved, referring to this phrase as "[die] Anlehnung an biblische Ausdrucksweise" (Apostelgeschichte, 1:317). Bock argues strongly for understanding this as an allusion that "place[s] the speech in a promise context . . . with the reference to Abrahamic covenant" (Proclamation, 243–44; see also pp. 20, 282 n. 3).

81. This is but one parallel noticed by E. J. Richard, who lists nineteen linguistic and content parallels between Peter's speech in Acts 3 and Stephen's address in Acts 7 (Acts 6:1–8:4: The Author's Method of Composition [SBLDS 41; Missoula, MT: Scholars Press, 1978] 256).

82. M. D. Hooker comments that should this designation relate to the specific concept of Second Isaiah, one must note the limited way in which the sense of that title functions in Acts (Jesus and the Servant: The Influence of the Servant Concept of Deutero-Isaiah in the New Testament [London: S.P.C.K., 1959] 110). Only "delivering up" and exaltation come into play; the servant's sufferings and their atoning value are not elements of Acts' perspective.

83. See the discussion of παῖς by J.-A. Bühnen (EWNT 3:11–14).

84. Haenchen is typical of those who see in the use of παῖς an unambiguous sense of "servanthood" (Acts, 205), so that designating Jesus here as God's servant is a reference to Isa 52:13. From the connection of this "title" with Isaiah, some scholars (e.g., J. Jeremias, "παῖς θεοῦ," TDNT 5:677–717) contend that the Christology of this portion of Acts is primitive, suggesting the vintage character of the speech and its theology. See also Bruce, Acts, 139–40. H. J. Cadbury recognized the hopelessly circular logic in arguments from the speeches about the primitive character of the theology they express ("The Speeches in Acts," in Beginnings, 5:402–27). As he observed, "There is a danger of arguing in a circle . . . our ideas of early Christianity, with which the speeches in Acts are said to conform so exactly, are derived in large part from those very speeches" (p. 416). Jeremias's contentions have undergone rigorous criticism from M. Rese ("Nachprüfung einiger Thesen von Joachim Jeremias zum Thema des Gottesknechts in Judentum," ZTK 60 [1963] 21–41); and Bühnen describes the problem succinctly, writing, "In der Missionsrede Apg 3 is VV. 13.26 der π.-θεοῦ-Titel mit Auferstehung und Verherrlichung Jesu; hier ist der [Zusammenhang] nicht so deutlich von DtJes her geprägt, da Auferstehung nicht Erhöhung nach einer Zeit der Niedrigkeit

intended here, then this use of a title would have implicit connections with 13:33 as well. Whether the language designating God and Jesus here is derived from the Septuagint or simply "sounds like" the Septuagint, this speech uses language strongly associated with the past to advance its argument. Moreover, the manner in which the speech begins to refute the crowd's supposed misunderstanding, by naming God dramatically and declaring that God glorified Jesus, who is also referred to in a striking way, shows the ultimate conviction that God's authority prevails and that the most crucial point of God's authoritative activity is the work in relation to Jesus.

This kerygmatic section continues with a reference to the guilt of Peter's hearers for their rejection of Jesus. The mention of Pilate and his decision to release Jesus is consistent with elements of the Lukan passion narrative (see Luke 23:1–22). Pilate is mentioned in two other speeches in Acts (4:27; 13:28), and in 13:28 one again finds the idea that Pilate served the will of the Jerusalem Jews in executing Jesus. In the current context, however, recalling that episode underscores the pernicious nature of the rejection and thereby heightens the contrast scheme: what God did versus what the Jerusalem Jews did (v. 13). This contrast is made even more pointed by a second statement of the contrast scheme: what the Jerusalem Jews did versus what God did (vv. 14–15a). This scheme first occurred in 2:23–24.

Inherent in this contrast is the declaration that God raised Jesus, but as noted in 1:22 this idea appears in speeches outside the contrast scheme. Moreover, stating this contrast confronts the members of the audience with their guilt (see 2:36). Furthermore, one should notice that the contrast scheme employs the kerygmatic relative clause style already seen in 2:23–24. Finally, the cluster of titles found here is a prominent example of the declarations about the identity of Jesus in the speeches, a phenomenon first observed in 2:36. The designation ὁ δίκαιος occurs in 3:14; 7:52; 22:14 (compare Luke 23:47).

(1.3) In vv. 15b–16 there are two kinds of confirmation for the kerygmatic claims. (1.3.1) First, Peter declares οὗ ἡμεῖς μάρτυρές ἐσμεν ("to this we are witnesses"). Whether in context this statement means Peter and John only or refers to the larger group of disciples, this declaration is the fourth of eleven references to the early Christians as "witnesses" (see 1:8). (1.3.2) The second verification of the kerygma is the evidence of the healing which had just taken place in the name of Jesus—that is, by faith in Jesus' name.[85] The form of Peter's argument is similar to the reference in the Pentecost speech to the effects of the Holy Spirit on the disciples as evidence of the truth of kerygmatic

---

bedeutet, ja hier christologische Vollmacht und Niedrigkeit unter den Menschen nicht korrelieren, sondern Ablehnung durch Gott sich antithetisch gegenüberstehen" (*EWNT* 3:13).

85. See the careful exposition of the speech by D. Hamm ("Acts 3:12–26: Peter's Speech and the Healing of the Man Born Lame," *Perspectives in Religious Studies* 11 [1984] 199–217), which interprets the entire speech in relation to its christological/theological claims.

42   THE SPEECHES IN ACTS

claims (see 2:33); that a remarkable event validates a statement or conclusion is also seen in 10:47.

(2.1) In the second part of the speech Peter addresses the crowd as ἀδελφοί ("brothers"). This simple salutation occurs in 3:17; 6:3; 23:5. Before this form of address, however, one finds the rhetorical transition καὶ νῦν ("and now"), which appears in speeches in 3:17; 7:34; 20:22, 25; 22:16; 26:6 and in smaller statements in 10:5; 13:11; 23:21; moreover, a related form, καὶ τὰ νῦν ("and now"), occurs in 4:29; 5:38; 20:32; 27:22. As the ἀδελφοί ("brothers") are addressed, Peter informs them of his awareness that their actions and the actions of their rulers against Jesus were done in ignorance. Speakers recognize the ignorance of the hearers at 3:17; 13:27; 14:16 (implicitly); and 17:30.

(2.2) Remarkably in v. 18 one learns that God acted through the ignorance of the Jerusalem Jews to "fulfill" (ἐπλήρωσεν) ἃ προκατήγγειλεν διὰ στόματος πάντων τῶν προφητῶν [concerning] τὸν Χριστὸν αὐτοῦ ("what he foretold through the mouth of all the prophets [concerning] his Christ"). The declaration that God "fulfilled" what God "previously announced" reflects the idea of "the plan of God," which one can recognize implicitly or explicitly in every speech analyzed to this point. The general reference to the prophets without a specific quotation is repeated in this speech and elsewhere (3:18, 21, 24; 10:43; 26:22, 27; see also 2:16).

(2.3) Verses 19–21a call the crowd to repentance, promise them forgiveness, and comment on the meaning of forgiveness. (2.3.1) The call to repentance is a feature of the speeches noted at 2:38, but the double demand here (μετανοήσατε . . . ἐπιστρέψατε, "repent . . . turn") is striking and similar to the twofold call to repentance in 26:20. (2.3.2) Following the exhortation to "repent" and to "turn" is a promise of forgiveness, which is stated metaphorically as εἰς τὸ ἐξαλειφθῆναι ὑμῶν τὰς ἁμαρτίας ("so that your sins may be wiped out"). The promise of forgiveness appeared in 2:38, where it was coupled with the call to repentance as it is here and in 26:18. The passive form of the verb points to God as the actor in the work of forgiveness, as becomes clear in the closing line of the speech (v. 26); nevertheless, (2.3.3) the second promise issued speaks of the nature of the benefits of forgiveness for humans. P. Schubert describes v. 20 as an "eschatological-apocalyptical affirmation."[86] Whatever this peculiar statement intends to describe, four dimensions of the declaration are noteworthy: (A) The time of refreshment (or recovery) is sent by God. (B) This time is christologically qualified and focused. (C) God will send Christ. (D) This time anticipates God's completion of God's work. In brief, God is at work completing God's plan, and the work is being done through God's Christ.

(2.4) The next segment of the speech, vv. 22–25, offers a scriptural explanation or argument concerning God's work and the necessity of repentance.

---

86. Schubert, "Place," 240.

(2.4.1) The statements begin with a quotation of Moses' revelatory remarks about the future work of God. The lines appear to be an abbreviated version of Deut 18:15–20 with a mixture of elements from Lev 23:29.[87] Thus, we find another use of the past in the speeches, again the citation of scripture. Furthermore, the first part of v. 22 is repeated in 7:37, where Jesus is again cast as the "prophet like Moses."

The pattern of thought in this section builds a contrastable pair of contrast schemes. Verses 22–23 tell of God's positive action in raising up a prophet like Moses and the threat it poses to those who do not heed the prophet. These lines specify the peril of the members of the crowd, who rejected Jesus, echoing vv. 13–15. (2.4.2) Then, vv. 24–25 form a statement (A) recognizing the time of the speech as the time of God's fulfillment of what was announced previously, echoing v. 18, and (B) reminding the hearers they are οἱ υἱοὶ τῶν προφητῶν καὶ τῆς διαθήκης ("the sons of the prophets and of the covenant"). The force of these lines is positive, so that the solution to the dilemma of the crowd (from vv. 22–23) is inherent in the promise of God recalled in v. 25. The line may cite Gen 22:18; 26:4. The mention here of "covenant" is one of only two occurrences of this word in Acts (3:25; 7:8). The idea of God's granting the covenant is merely registered here, but in Stephen's speech (7:2–16) the theme is "the God of the covenant."[88] Furthermore, the temporal reference, τὰς ἡμέρας ταύτας ("these days"), echoes both the καὶ νῦν ("and now") of v. 17 and the language and thought of the citation of Joel in Peter's earlier address (see 2:17), and there is a reference to the prophets without a citation.

(2.5) The speech concludes with a final statement about God's work for repentance (v. 26). This single sentence reiterates the theme of God's raising Jesus (3:15; see 1:22), but there is no statement of the guilt of the crowd. Rather, now one learns that God raised Jesus to bring about the necessary repentance to which Peter has called the crowd. The thought here is related to God's working out the divine plan; and the manner of speaking about God's activity (ὑμῖν πρῶτον ἀναστήσας ὁ θεὸς τὸν παῖδα αὐτοῦ ἀπέστειλεν αὐτὸν εὐλογοῦντα ὑμᾶς ἐν τῷ ἀποστρέφειν ἕκαστον ἀπὸ τῶν πονηριῶν ὑμῶν, "When God raised up his servant, he sent him first to you, to bless you by turning

---

87. Haenchen points to an interpretive challenge inherent in the employment of this citation in this context, namely: "The difficulty of this verse consists in the fact that although certain prophecies are specified, they refer not to the second but to the first coming of Jesus" (Acts, 209). Elaborate source-critical theories have done little to alleviate this problem (see Schneider, Apostelgeschichte, 1.323–27, for a discussion of the problem and an overview of the many suggestions in relation to the interpretation of this verse). But other critics (e.g., Bruce, Acts, 144–45) apparently perceive no problem, since there is no discussion of the seemingly awkward fit of this citation with the content of the promise issued here. Nevertheless, Bruce summarizes much of the discussion, although he primarily focuses on arguments for the primitive character of the theology of this verse.

88. Schubert, "Place," 240.

each of you from your wicked ways") portrays God as taking the inititative in transforming humans. Notice again the crucial christological dimension of the realization of God's blessing the hearers.

Peter's Speech to the Jewish Authorities
after His and John's Arrest (4:8b–12, 19b–20)

After the conclusion of Peter's speech in Acts 3, one learns that certain Temple officials came upon the apostles as they were speaking and arrested them. The point concerning the apostles which Luke says annoyed the officials was their teaching about Jesus and the resurrection. As R. Pesch notices, however, when the apostles are subsequently brought before the council, the officials inquire not about what they said but about the cause of the healing that had transpired.[89] In the course of the story of the hearing in the council, the issue of the apostles' teaching appears only after Peter speaks the first time. Then the concern of the leaders becomes refocused on the apostles' teaching in the name of Jesus.

Kennedy suggests that Peter's speech (vv. 8–12) is a "very short version of what Peter has said in the previous two speeches." He understands the situation and the rhetoric of the speech to be *judicial* with *deliberation* merely implied by the statement in v. 12.[90] While Kennedy does not include vv. 19b–20 in his analysis of Peter's speech, these lines clearly continue the *judicial* rhetoric and function as an *epilogue* to the first part of the speech.

As Luke narrates the situation leading up to Peter's speech, one learns that when questioned by the council, Peter answered πλησθεὶς πνεύματος ἁγίου ("filled with the Holy Spirit"). Other speeches are made by Spirit-filled speakers (2:4; 4:8; 4:31; 13:9), and all such declarations should be viewed as both fulfillments of the promise of Jesus to his disciples in Luke 12:11–12 and as demonstrations of the power foretold at Acts 1:8. One may outline this particular pneumatically inspired speech in the following way:

1.0 Peter's Explanation of the Healing of the Man (vv. 8–12)
    1.1 Address (v. 8b)
    1.2 Statement Recognizing the Situation (v. 9)
    1.3 Christological Kerygma (vv. 10–12)
        1.3.1 Healing by Jesus' Name (v. 10)
        1.3.2 Correlated Scriptural Explanation (v. 11)
        1.3.3 Explicit Kerygma (v. 12)

89. Pesch, *Apostelgeschichte*, 1:162.
90. Kennedy, *Interpretation*, 119.

After deliberation, the council members order the apostles to desist from speaking and teaching in Jesus' name. Then, apparently in unison as if they were a chorus in a Greek drama, Peter and John speak:

2.0 The Apostles' Response to the Charge to Silence (vv. 19b–20)
   2.1 A Challenging Retort (v. 19b)
   2.2 Declaration of the Compulsion to Speak (v. 20)

Analysis. (1.1) The address ἄρχοντες τοῦ λαοῦ καὶ πρεσβύτεροι ("rulers of the people and elders") is unique in Acts. Later, when Paul appears before essentially the same group (22:30–23:10), he addresses them twice with the seemingly standard salutation ἄνδρες ἀδελφοί, "Men, brothers" (23:1, 6; see 1:16a). The special terminology of Peter's address recognizes the high social and religious standing of the council members and in doing so functions as a *captatio benevolentiae,* although implying neither reticence nor obsequiousness as the remainder of the speech shows.

(1.2) Verse 9 speaks to the situation, a manner of commencing several speeches, although in this instance there is no misunderstanding (see 2:15). Peter recognized that he and John are "being examined" (ἀνακρίνειν, a verb used in relation to similar situations in other speeches [4:9; 24:8; 28:18]; compare ἀνάκρισις in 25:26).

(1.3) Then, with v. 10 Peter begins to deliver his daring answer, which is essentially christological kerygma. He opens with the commanding words γνωστὸν ἔστω ("let it be known to you"), previously encountered in 2:14 and occurring hereafter twice. (1.3.1) What the hearers are to know is that the healing took place ἐν τῷ ὀνόματι Ἰησοῦ Χριστοῦ τοῦ Ναζωραίου ("by the name of Jesus Christ the Nazorean").[91] This form of Jesus' name first occurred in 2:22, and concern with "the name of Jesus" appeared in 2:38. Peter's kerygmatic answer continues by declaring the familiar christological contrast scheme (see 2:23–24). As is often the case, this contrast scheme is stated in a style designated "kerygmatic" because of the employment of relative pronouns (see 2:23–24). Inherent in this contrast is the assertion that God raised Jesus (Ἰησοῦ Χριστοῦ τοῦ Ναζωραίου . . . ὃν ὁ θεός ἤγειρεν, "Jesus Christ the Nazorean . . . whom God raised"), a familiar feature of the speeches (see 1:22). Moreover, the reference to the man's being healed is an indirectly stated but clearly understood verification of the content of the christological contrast scheme. Thus, G. Krodel suggests that there is an implicit call to repentance in this proclamation of the contrast of human and divine actions,[92] though there is

___

91. C. K. Barrett shows that the "name" in this speech stands for Jesus himself, as is confirmed in Acts 5:41 ("Salvation Proclaimed: XII. Acts 4:8–12," *ExpTim* 94 [1982] 68–71).
92. Krodel, *Acts,* 110.

no overt call.[93] If this is correct, then one may understand this line to be related to the explicit calls to repentance (e.g., 2:38).

(1.3.2) Verse 11 offers an additional argument in support of the veracity of the contrast scheme with its claim that God raised Jesus. The line is an allusion to Ps 117:22 LXX.[94] This use of the past is striking in that the logic of the allusion matches that of the contrast scheme—that is, divine reversal of human action that brings honor to an originally rejected object. Furthermore, from Col 1:18; 2:10; 2:19; Eph 1:22; 4:15; 5:23 (?) one sees that κεφαλή ("head") became a titular designation for Jesus in portions of the early church. Whether that level of development is to be presupposed for this allusion is uncertain, but should the allusion intend to use κεφαλή ("head") as a title, then this reference would be another of the many overt declarations about the formal theological identity of Jesus (see 2:36). Yet, even when one attributes no technical sense to κεφαλή ("head") here, the allusion should still be understood to speak about Jesus' identity.[95]

(1.3.3) The final line of the first part of the speech concludes the christological kerygma with another reference to the name of Jesus (v. 10) and an avowal of its[96] universal significance for salvation. Peter speaks about σωτηρία ("salvation") rather than about the forgiveness of sins. Speeches refer to "salvation" in 4:12; 7:25; 13:26, 47; 27:34; 28:28; and a brief statement in 16:17 states that the disciples proclaimed ὁδόν σωτηρίας ("a way of salvation"). The combination of δεῖ ("it is necessary") and σωθῆναι ("to be saved") indicates that "salvation" and "being saved" are to be understood in relation to the theme of divine necessity. The important verb δεῖ ("it is necessary") first occurred at 1:16; and σῴζειν ("to save") appeared in Peter's Pentecost address as well as earlier in the current speech (meaning "to heal"). Σῴζειν ("to save") recurs frequently in speeches (2:21, 40; 4:9, 12; 11:14; 15:11; 27:31) and in shorter statements (16:30, 31), and it is noteworthy that all of these usages are in the passive voice and that all except σέσωται ("[he] has been healed") in 4:9 mean "be saved" rather than "be healed." The close proximity of the uses of σῴζειν

93. Roloff is more cautious, writing, "Zumindest implizit wird damit eine Warnung ausgesprochen" (*Apostelgeschichte*, 82).

94. The LXX of Ps 117:22 reads, λίθον, ὃν ἀπεδοκίμασαν οἱ οἰκοδομοῦντες, οὗτος ἐγενήθη εἰς κεφαλὴν γωνίας; whereas Acts 4:11 reads, οὗτός ἐστιν ὁ λίθος ὁ ἐξουθενηθεὶς ὑφ᾽ ὑμῶν τῶν οἰκοδόμων, ὁ γενόμενος εἰς κεφαλὴν γωνίας. As Bock comments, "Peter's explanation to the council that the lame man of Acts 3 was healed by the name of Jesus Christ includes an OT text which appears frequently in the New Testament, Ps. 118.22. The Acts 4.11 quotation is distinct from the wording of the synoptic citations of Ps. 118 as well as from the wording of the citation in 1 Peter. The text represents a summary allusion to Ps. 118.22, in that its structure does not follow either the LXX or the Masoretic text, but the key verbal terms are all drawn from that passage" (*Proclamation*, 198–99).

95. See H. J. Cadbury, "Note XXIX: The Titles of Jesus in Acts," in *Beginnings*, 5:373–74.

96. Krodel observes, ". . . salvation is totally dependent upon this Jesus and his name (v. 12). . . . this conclusion does not distinguish between the name and the person" (*Acts*, 111).

("to save" or "to heal") in vv. 9 and 12 work in tandem, so that the healing becomes evidence for the saving power of the resurrected Jesus.[97]

(2.1) The epilogue opens with the apostles challenging the council to pass judgment concerning whom they must obey. The statement underscores the judicial atmosphere in which the apostles speak. A statement that is similar in thought comes from Peter and the apostles when they next appear before the council (5:29), and one phrase of the challenge, ἐνώπιον τοῦ θεοῦ ("in God's sight"), occurs again in Stephen's speech (4:19; 7:46).

(2.2) Having demanded that the council judge the matter for themselves, the apostles state their own position, which recognizes the obligation to obey God. The phrases οὐ δυνάμεθα . . . μὴ λαλεῖν ("we cannot keep from speaking") specify the responsibility of the apostles in relation to God. The language recalls the promise of Jesus that the disciples would receive δύναμις and direction (ἔσεσθέ μου μάρτυρες, "you will be my witnesses") when the Holy Spirit came upon them. The necessity to speak of what they saw and heard (ἃ εἴδαμεν καὶ ἠκούσαμεν, "what we have seen and heard") sounds again the theme of "witness" (see 1:8)[98] and refers especially to testifying to the resurrection.[99] When the apostles appear again before the council, they make a statement that is also close to this one (4:20; 5:32).

The Prayer of the Apostles and Their Friends (4:24b–30)

After the apostles' bold words before the council, the members of the council threatened them but released them. Luke suggests that they were unable to punish Peter and John because of the enthusiasm of the crowd over the healing of the formerly lame man.

A new, related incident begins at 4:23 when the apostles go to the other disciples and report their experience before the council. Despite the new setting, however, the narrative still looks back at this point; then v. 24a moves the action forward, reporting the response of all the disciples in unified praise. The prayer-speech follows.

Kennedy contends that this prayer is best classified as *deliberative* rhetoric, because it is ultimately a prayer for help (vv. 29–30). Yet the opening verses (24b–26) are an *epideictic proem* offering praise for the greatness of God. In turn, vv. 27–28 are *narration*, which supplies background information.[100]

---

97. Roloff also makes this connection (*Apostelgeschichte*, 83).

98. Krodel sees a relationship between v. 20 and 1:8, but only at the level of "divine mandate to witness" and not in terms of the language of "power" (δυνάμεθα, v. 20; δύναμις, 1:8) (*Acts*, 113).

99. Haenchen, *Acts*, 219.

100. Kennedy, *Interpretation*, 120.

A slightly more detailed outline distinguishes further elements of the prayer. The two major parts of the prayer-speech are evident from the two salutations. The whole may be outlined in this manner:

1.0 Praise and Kerygma (vv. 24b–28)
    1.1 Opening Address (v. 24b)
    1.2 First Ascription (v. 24b)
    1.3 Second Ascription with Scripture Citation (vv. 25–26)
    1.4 Kerygmatic Christological Exegesis (vv. 27–28)
2.0 Petition (vv. 29–30)
    2.1 Second Address (v. 29a)
    2.2 The Petition (vv. 29b–30)

Analysis. (1.1) The compound address δέσποτα, σύ ("Sovereign, you" [NRSV: "Sovereign, Lord"]) is unique in Acts, although δέσποτα ("sovereign") occurs in Luke 2:29;[101] and, in form, this salutation is similar to the compound address of Acts 1:24b. This manner of salutation foreshadows the purpose of the prayer, for as Conzelmann observes, "The counterpart to δέσποτα is not παῖς, 'child, servant,' but δοῦλος, 'slave'";[102] so that the opening address anticipates the concluding petition by the δοῦλοι.

(1.2) The first ascription offers praise to God in biblical diction.[103] Commentators frequently refer to Ps 145:6 LXX[104] and Exod 20:11 LXX[105] as possible texts to which this laudatory language refers or from which it gained inspiration. The theme of the praise is "God as Creator," a subject that appears in other speeches (4:24; 14:15; 17:24). The language of praise in v. 24b finds echoes in both of the other speeches where this theme occurs.[106]

(1.3) The second ascription occurs in a form similar to the first (ὁ ποιήσας, "who made," v. 24b; ὁ . . . εἰπών, "who said," v. 25);[107] but it moves beyond pure praise to provide information[108] as it cites the words spoken by the Holy Spirit through David. Several items in vv. 25–26 are significant. (A) Again, a speaker casts David in an important role, here associated with the Holy Spirit (see 1:16). (B) The reference to David leads to a citation of Ps 2:1–2 LXX,

---

101. Bruce notes the occurrence of δέσποτα in 3 Macc 2:2 (*Acts*, 156).
102. Conzelmann, *Acts*, 34.
103. Schneider, *Apostelgeschichte*, 1:357.
104. Conzelmann, *Acts*, 34.
105. Pesch, *Apostelgeschichte*, 1:176.
106. Schubert connects the image of God as creator with the idea of God's divine plan ("Place," 242). The explicit reference to the βουλή comes in the second section of this prayer, however, so that while there is a relationship between God as Creator and God's having a plan, it may not be as immediately apparent as Schubert suggests.
107. Bruce notes the use of ὁ ποιήσας τὸν οὐρανὸν κτλ. in the exordium of prayer or thanksgiving in 2 Esdr 19:6 (*Acts*, 156).
108. Schneider labels both vv. 25–26 and vv. 27–28 "situationsfremd"! (*Apostelgeschichte*, 1:354).

a familiar manner of using the past in the speeches (see 2:25–28). (C) The use of παῖς ("servant") in relation to David anticipates the application of that "title" to Jesus in 4:27, 30—a phenomenon noted at 3:13, 26—which is one form of the many statements in speeches about Jesus' identity (see 2:36). And, (D) as Schneider observes, "The polarity of Creator-God and speaking Revealer-God occurs also at 17:24, 26, 30–31."[109]

(1.4) After this citation of scripture, the prayer-speech provides exegetical treatment of the passage.[110] The direct reference to Jesus as παῖς ("servant") employs a familiar title that is repeated in v. 30. Thus, the prayer provides information indirectly about the theological identity of Jesus (see 2:36). Jesus is further viewed in relation to the words of the psalm as the one whom God anointed ('Ιησοῦν ὃν ἔχρισας, "Jesus whom you anointed");[111] the idea of God's anointing Jesus recurs in 10:38. Furthermore, in this exegesis of the psalm one hears of Herod and Pontius Pilate, who are equated with the οἱ βασιλεῖς τῆς γῆς καὶ οἱ ἄρχοντες ("the kings of the earth and the rulers") of v. 26 — Herod, a king, and Pilate, a ruler.[112] This mention of Pilate is the second of three references to him in Acts (see 3:13); but only here in Acts (and in Luke 3:1) is he named with both names.

Beyond correlating historical figures with the categories of the psalm, the interpretation continues in v. 28 with dogmatic commentary. One learns that as the adversaries of God and God's anointed gathered—that is, as Herod and Pilate took part in Jesus' passion—God brought God's plan to realization. The striking line, ποιῆσαι ὅσα ἡ χείρ σου καὶ ἡ βουλή [σου] προώρισεν γενέσθαι ("to do whatever your hand and your plan had predestined to take place"), shows with all possible clarity the conviction that the passion transpired by divine necessity and that God works in relation to human events with final authority.[113]

(2.1) The second part of the prayer-speech begins with a new form of salutation, κύριε ("Lord"), in part, the same vocative form of prayer-address first

109. Schneider, *Apostelgeschichte*, 1:357 n. 27: "Die Polarität von Schöpfergott und sprechendem Offenbarer-Gott begegnet auch 17,24.26.30f."

110. Conzelmann remarks, "Exegetical style dominates here, rather than the style of prayer" (*Acts*, 35).

111. Conzelmann contends that the idea expressed here indicates that παῖς should be understood as "son," because the sense of the word "is determined by the reference in vs 26 and the anointing at baptism" (*Acts*, 35). Yet Roloff merely remarks, "Lukas versteht Jesu Taufe as Salbung zum messianischen Amt" (*Apostelgeschichte*, 87).

112. Haenchen suggests a more precise correlation: "Herod Antipas represents 'the kings of the earth,' Pilate 'the rulers,' the Roman soldiers the ἔθνη, and the tribes of Israel the λαοί" (*Acts*, 227). But he is doing exegesis of the exegesis here.

113. In a succinct study of this prayer B. R. Gaventa shows that in the view of Acts the ability of the church to engage in mission and to withstand oppression comes from the presence and power of God alone ("To Speak Thy Word with All Boldness: Acts 4:23–31," *Faith and Mission* 3 [1986] 76–82).

observed in 1:24b. Prior to the address, one finds καὶ τὰ νῦν ("and now"), a rhetorical device noted in relation to the similar form καὶ νῦν ("and now") in 3:17.[114]

(2.2) The petition per se comes in the elaborately formulated request of vv. 29b–30. At least five items are noteworthy. (A) The designation δοῦλοι ("servants" or "slaves") for obedient servants of God is similar to the thought expressed by the citation of Joel at 2:17, and it matches the language of a simple statement in 16:17. (B) The prayer request to speak God's word μετὰ παρρησίας πάσης ("with all boldness"), noted at 2:29 and recurring in 26:26, employs language that characteristically describes the demeanor of the disciples as they bear witness throughout Acts (see 1:8). Moreover, implicit in this request is the idea of the disciples as "witnesses" (also 1:8). (C) The reference to σημεῖα καὶ τέρατα ("signs and wonders") echoes 2:22 and anticipates 7:36; and in this context, linked overtly with εἰς ἴασιν ("to heal"), this petition refers to the preceding events and speeches of Acts 3–4.[115] (D) Again, concern is expressed for the familiar theme of the "name of Jesus" (see 2:38). And, (E) the fullest phrase employing the title παῖς, "servant" (διὰ τοῦ ὀνόματος τοῦ ἁγίου παιδός σου Ἰησοῦ, "through the name of your holy servant Jesus") occurs; so that Conzelmann remarks, "God's governance again stands out clearly."[116]

The Speech of Peter and the Apostles to the Council (5:29b–32)

Luke reports that the prayer of the assembly (4:24b–30) was answered immediately, that all were filled with the Holy Spirit and spoke τὸν λόγον τοῦ θεοῦ μετὰ παρρησίας, "the word of the Lord with boldness" (4:31). The narrative then reports the common charity practiced by the members of the Jerusalem congregation (4:32–37) and the disturbing incident of Ananias's and Sapphira's attempting to feign the same inspired generosity (5:1–11) that had brought Barnabas special recognition in the community (4:36–37). Despite this unsettling occurrence, the narrative continues by reporting that σημεῖα καὶ τέρατα πολλά ("many signs and wonders") took place (further answers to the previous prayer) and the community grew (5:12–16). Then one learns of the animosity of the high priest and the Sadducees, which led to the arrest and imprisonment of the apostles who escape from prison miraculously and return to preach in the Temple only to be arrested again and brought before

---

114. Conzelmann offers a brief, but excellent, discussion of this device in a range of ancient literature (*Acts*, 35).

115. Krodel suggests that the petition for these miraculous occurrences is a request for *evidence* of God's approval of the message of the apostles (*Acts*, 115).

116. Conzelmann, *Acts*, 35.

the council (5:17–27a). The high priest registered the official charge against the apostles: Though they had been ordered to silence, the apostles had continued teaching about Jesus, and the high priest accused the apostles of trying to bring the responsibility for Jesus' death upon the council (5:27b–28). Luke continues in 5:29a by reporting that Peter and the apostles answered. Whether this statement means a choral response or that Peter spoke for all is debated.[117]

Kennedy labels this speech *judicial* rhetoric, and he points out that the stasis is metastasis since the argument seeks to transfer the responsibility for the apostles' actions to God. The apostles merely bear witness to what God has done and is doing.[118]

The speech is brief but multifaceted. Despite the paratactic style of vv. 31–32, one may schematize the speech as follows:

1.0 The Statement of the Apostles' Position (v. 29b)
2.0 Christological Kerygma (vv. 30–31)
    2.1 Contrast Scheme (v. 30)
    2.2 God's Exaltation of Jesus and Its Purpose (v. 31)
3.0 Confirmations of the Kerygma (v. 32)
    3.1 The Witness of the Apostles (v. 32a)
    3.2 The Witness of the Holy Spirit (v. 32b)

Analysis. In its general shape and in particular items of content this speech is remarkably similar to the epilogue of the speech previously made before the council. (1.0) The opening line (v. 29b) repeats the sense, but not the vocabulary, of 4:19b.[119] The ἀκούειν ("to hear") of 4:19b is replaced by πειθαρχεῖν ("to obey"), which recurs in speeches in v. 32 and 27:21. The juxtaposition of ἄνθρωποι ("humans") and θεός ("God") in this declaration anticipates the logic of the statement that follows in v. 30.[120]

(2.1) The speech continues by stating the familiar contrast scheme (see 2:23–24) with its inherent declaration concerning God's raising of Jesus (see 1:22). The way this formula occurs in the current speech, however, has a

---

117. Haenchen holds that the entire group speaks, thus revealing divinely inspired unanimity (*Acts,* 251). Yet Roloff (*Apostelgeschichte,* 103), Krodel (*Acts,* 127), and Pesch (*Apostelgeschichte,* 1:216) are typical of the majority of commentators who understand that Peter merely speaks for all the apostles. There is no solution to this argument.

118. Kennedy, *Interpretation,* 120.

119. Practically all interpreters refer to the similarity of this statement to that of Socrates: πείσομαι δέ μᾶλλον τῷ θεῷ ἤ ὑμῖν, but I shall obey God rather than you" (Plato, *Apol.* 29d).

120. Schneider (*Apostelgeschichte,* 1:395) contends that only v. 29b responds to the accusations of the high priest, but he fails to see that both the christological kerygma and the ensuing confirmations (vv. 30–31, 32) are offered in answer to the high priest's complaint that the apostles are attempting to blame the council for Jesus' crucifixion. Indeed, in vv. 30–32 one finds a case being made that the council is at fault with regard to Jesus' death. See Krodel, *Acts,* 127.

number of noticeable features: (A) The reference to ὁ θεὸς τῶν πατέρων ἡμῶν ("the God of our fathers") echoes the language of 3:13, which is found in several speeches (3:13; 5:30; 7:32; 22:14). (B) The striking verb διαχειρίζεσθαι ("to kill") recurs in 26:21. (C) Similarly, the verb κρεμᾶν/κρέμασθαι ("to hang") occurs again in 10:39. (D) Two subsequent speeches (10:39; 13:29) refer to the cross using ξύλον ("tree"), which occurs here in the phrase κρεμάσαντες ἐπὶ ξύλου ("hanging on a tree"). And (E) the use of this phrase likely constitutes a use of the past since the line is probably an allusion to Deut 21:22–23.[121]

(2.2) Verse 31 provides crucial additional information about God's actions in relation to Jesus. First, one encounters a declaration about Jesus' theological identity (see 2:36) as ἀρχηγός ("Leader") and σωτήρ ("Savior"). The title ἀρχηγός ("Leader") occurs only here in Acts, but in 3:15 Jesus was declared to be ἀρχηγὸν τῆς ζωῆς ("Author of life"), which may explain the exact sense intended for ἀρχηγός here.[122] The reference to Jesus as σωτήρ ("Savior") occurs again in 13:23, and both of these designations relate to statements about σωτηρία ("salvation") in the speeches (see the analyses of 2:40b and 4:12). Second, the claim that God "exalted" (ὑφοῦν) Jesus echoes 2:33, and this verb again refers to the work of God in relation to Israel in 13:17. Third, one has encountered the declaration that the raised and exalted Jesus is "at the right hand of God" (τῇ δεξιᾷ τοῦ θεοῦ or τῇ δεξιᾷ αὐτοῦ) in earlier speeches, and that statement will recur (2:25, 33, 34; 5:31; 7:55, 56). Fourth, elements of the striking statement that God exalted Jesus δοῦναι μετάνοιαν τῷ 'Ισραὴλ καὶ ἄφεσιν ἁμαρτιῶν ("to give repentance to Israel and forgiveness of sins") finds a number of parallels in other speeches.[123] (A) The idea of God's giving repentance recurs in 11:18. (B) A list of the range of statements about repentance and forgiveness stands in the analysis of 2:38; but (C) *repentance* and *forgiveness* appear together in 2:38; 3:19; 5:31; 26:20. Implicit in this declaration about the work of God through the exalted Jesus are the themes of divine necessity and divine authority, for the idea of determinative divine action dominates this construction.

(3.0) In v. 32 the speech offers two kinds of confirmation of the claims of the kerygma. (3.1) First, v. 32a brings forth the witness of the apostles (see 1:8). This declaration is parallel in sense to the earlier statement before the council in 4:20, but it is different in its vocabulary. The word ῥῆμα ("word"

---

121. See the informative discussion of v. 30 in Bruce, *Acts*, 172.

122. Haenchen, *Acts*, 251; Schneider, *Apostelgeschichte*, 1:395.

123. This statement is a bit too striking for many commentators. Conzelmann is typical when he writes, "Despite the wording, Luke means the *opportunity* for repentance. He does not mean that repentance as such is a gift of God, but that God gives μετάνοια in the sense of an opportunity to repent" (*Acts*, 42). This is a dogmatic assertion, not an exegetical argument. One needs to show this point from the text, not merely to state what one believes Luke thought or meant. Such assertion of opinion causes one to run the risk of making the biblical author over in one's own image.

[NRSV: "things"]) used here as a designation for the message of God's work in Jesus for salvation (or, repentance and forgiveness) occurs in speeches in 5:32; 10:37; 11:14; 26:25 (?). Thematically this way of referring to the Christian proclamation is related to uses of λόγος ("word") to designate the same message (2:22; 4:29; 6:2, 4; 10:36; 13:26; 15:7; 20:32). (3.2) Second, v. 32b contains reference to the witness of the Holy Spirit, another familiar theme (see 2:32–33). Notice, however, the speech seems to assume a twofold testimony by the Spirit. (A) The Spirit authenticates the kerygma; (B) the Spirit vouches for the early Christian community, since God gives the Spirit to those who are obedient to God's direction (an echo of 5:29b).

Gamaliel's Speech to the Council (5:35b–39)

Luke reports that the bold words of the apostles (5:29b–32) infuriated the members of the council, who, therefore, formulated their own *plan* (ἐβούλοντο ἀνελεῖν αὐτούς, "they planned to kill them"). In the midst of the apparent commotion Gamaliel "arose" (ἀναστάς),[124] ordered that the apostles be removed from the room, and spoke to the council.

Kennedy observes the resemblance between this speech and the simple *deliberative* address in 1:16–22. Yet he notes differences. The proem of this address (v. 35b) is followed by a pair of examples (vv. 36–37) rather than by true narration.[125] Thus, vv. 38–39 offer the actual deliberation.

In outline the speech appears this way:

1.0 Opening Address (v. 35b)
2.0 Gamaliel's Warning (v. 35c)
3.0 The Lessons of History (vv. 36–37)
    3.1 Theudas (v. 36)
    3.2 Judas the Galilean (v. 37)
4.0 Gamaliel's Advice (vv. 38–39)
    4.1 Avoid the Apostles (v. 38a)
    4.2 The Potential of a Human Plan (v. 38b)
    4.3 The Surety of a Divine Plan (v. 39a)
    4.4 The Danger of Opposing the Apostles (v. 39b)

Analysis. (1.0) Gamaliel's address, ἄνδρες 'Ισραηλῖται ("Men, Israelites"), is the third of five occurrences of a salutation first observed in 2:22. (2.0) Having achieved a hearing, he warns the members of the council to be cautious

---

124. See the introductory comments to 1:16–22, 24b–25 regarding ἀναστάς as the stance of speakers.
125. Kennedy, *Introduction*, 120–21.

regarding the apostles. The call to be careful employs words also found in Paul's speech to the Ephesian elders in 20:28 (προσέχετε ἑαυτοῖς, "keep watch over yourselves"). The warning is imprecise, however, giving no reason for the caution; and so it anticipates the advice to follow in vv. 38–39, especially the statement in v. 39b.

(3.0) Before giving advice Gamaliel offers two lessons from history that demonstrate in advance the reasonable nature of the suggestion to follow. (3.1) First, one learns of the unsuccessful uprising of Theudas.[126] The manner in which Gamaliel refers to Theudas, λέγων εἶναί τινα ἑαυτόν ("claiming to be somebody"), recurs in Acts in the indirect report of the claims of Simon the magician about himself (8:9). (3.3) Second, one hears of the similar incident with Judas the Galilean. These recollections are a compound use of the past.

(4.0) The following verses (vv. 38–39) draw conclusions from these disasters and proceed to give advice. (4.1) Initially, v. 38a recommends that the council simply ignore the apostles. The turn of the speech to *deliberation* is signaled by the rhetorical phrase καὶ τὰ νῦν (see 3:17). The reason to avoid the apostles is clear, "any movement of purely human inspiration must fail of its own accord."[127] (4.2) In making this point, the speech refers to ἡ βουλὴ αὕτη ἢ τὸ ἔργον τοῦτο ("this plan or this undertaking"). The concept of a "plan" is a familiar feature of the speeches (see 1:7), and the designation "work" will refer to God's actions in Paul's speech in Pisidian Antioch (13:41). (4.3) Juxtaposed to the notion of a doomed human plan or work is the idea of a plan or work "which comes from God [that] cannot be overthrown."[128] Gamaliel warns, εἰ δὲ ἐκ θεοῦ ἐστιν, οὐ δυνήσεσθε καταλῦσαι αὐτούς ("but if it is of God, you will not be able to overthrow them"). The language of "power" (δύνασθαι),[129] here in reference to a lack of power, reflects the theme of God's ultimate authority. Indeed, the very grammar of these verses makes a case for understanding the activity of the apostles as the work of God according to the divine plan. As Conzelmann observes, "With the change from the subjunctive [ἐὰν ᾖ ἐξ ἀνθρώπων ἡ βουλὴ αὕτη, "if this (plan) is of human origin"] to the indicative [εἰ δὲ ἐκ θεοῦ ἐστιν, "but if it is of God"] . . . God has spoken his own judgment

126. There are notorious interpretive problems inherent in this mention of Theudas. Josephus writes about a false prophet named Θευδᾶς who appeared during the time when Cuspius Fadus was procurator, that is, 44–46 C.E. (*Ant.* 20.97). This Theudas led τὸν πλεῖστον ὄχλον ("the majority of the masses") on a catastrophic venture to the Jordan River. The statement in Gamaliel's speech that Theudas made pretentious claims seems close to Josephus's description, προφήτης γὰρ ἔλεγεν εἶναι ("he stated that he was a prophet"). If the Theudas of Josephus's account is the same as that of Gamaliel's speech, then one finds Gamaliel recalling Theudas about a decade before he appeared. Yet, as Bruce insists (*Acts*, 124–25), Gamaliel may be referring to still another Theudas — although one wonders how many Theudases managed to lead the Judean masses into disasters in this period.

127. Haenchen, *Acts*, 253.

128. Ibid.

129. See the analysis of 1:8 on δύναμις.

through the mouth of Gamaliel."[130] Thus, the reasoning of the argument assumes and emphasizes the conviction that God exercises determinative divine control over developments in the human sphere.

(4.4) The final statement (v. 39b) makes specific the call to caution: μήποτε καὶ θεομάχοι εὑρεθῆτε ("in that you may be found fighting against God"). Here the word θεομάχος ("opposing God") is significant, for it indicates a motif found elsewhere in ancient literature to the effect that humans set themselves up as opponents of God or of the gods.[131] This idea itself presupposes divine direction of human events. The same assumption lies behind the passive form εὑρεθῆτε ("you may be found"), which speaks of the human actions from the divine point of view.[132]

The Speech by the Twelve Prior
to the Appointment of the Seven (6:2b–4)

Luke tells the reader of Acts that the members of the council found Gamaliel's suggestion regarding the apostles acceptable, though even in taking his advice, before releasing the apostles, the council had them beaten and ordered them to cease speaking τῷ ὀνόματι τοῦ 'Ιησοῦ ("in the name of Jesus"). Yet the apostles continued their teaching and preaching in public and in private. Luke goes on to report the growth of the church (πληθυνόντων τῶν μαθητῶν, "the disciples were increasing in number") and a problem that arose between the Hellenists and the Hebrews. "The Twelve" called together the full number of the disciples and spoke to the situation.[133]

The brief speech, again cast as a group statement, is *deliberative* rhetoric. A *proem* states the apostles' position (v. 2b); v. 3 delivers a *proposition;* and v. 4 forms an *epilogue*. Viewed in more detail, the speech may be outlined in this manner:

130. Conzelmann, *Acts*, 43.
131. Pesch, *Apostelgeschichte*, 1:220.
132. Bruce (*Acts*, 175) quotes J. A. Findley (*The Acts of the Apostles* [2d ed.; London: SCM, 1936] no page given) with approval, "The doctrine preached by Gamaliel is sound Pharisaic teaching; God is over all, and needs no help from men for the fulfillment of His purposes; all men must do is to obey, and leave the issue to Him." Whether or not one may characterize this summary as "sound Pharisaic teaching," this statement is an accurate synopsis of what Gamaliel says in Acts.
133. Even with these brief lines I have leapt freely over several interpretive high hurdles that normally exercise scholars at length (e.g., the identification of the Twelve, the Hellenists, the Hebrews, and the widows, or the historical nature of the controversy and the function of the Seven, or the relationship of Christian relief to Jewish relief). But consideration of these matters does not fit the lines of the present analysis, so that despite the importance of such topics it is unnecessary to attend to them here. I shall exercise similar freedom in the following introductory summaries.

1.0 Statement of the Position of the Twelve (v. 2b)
2.0 Directions to All the Disciples (v. 3)
    2.1 Charge with Address to Select the Seven (v. 3a)
    2.2 The Qualifications of the Seven (v. 3b)
        2.2.1 "Well-attested"
        2.2.2 "Full of Spirit and Wisdom"
        2.2.3 "Whom We May Appoint . . . ."
3.0 Statement of the Apostles' Intentions (v. 4)

Analysis. (1.0) The speech opens with a statement of the opinion of the Twelve concerning their own potential involvement with the equitable distribution of provisions to those in need of relief: They did not judge it right that they take on an additional responsibility which would distract them from their teaching and preaching.[134] One item requires attention. The phrase τὸν λόγον τοῦ θεοῦ ("the word of God") denotes the ministry of preaching and teaching. The same idea occurs again in v. 4 in the phrase τῇ διακονίᾳ τοῦ λόγου ("to the ministry of the word"). A list of verses wherein λόγος ("word") refers to the gospel message appears in the analysis of 5:32. Moreover, the phrase ὁ λόγος τοῦ θεοῦ ("the word of God") occurs in the narrative of Acts in 4:31; 6:7; 11:1; 12:24; 13:5, 7; 17:13; 18:11.

(2.0) Following this opening statement, the speech turns to deliberation in v. 3. (2.1) The Twelve address the other disciples, charging them to action. The verb ἐπισκέπτεσθαι ("to select"), which appears in speeches in 6:3; 7:23; 15:14, precedes the simple address ἀδελφοί ("brothers"), which is the second of three occurrences of this salutation in the speeches (see 3:17).

(2.2) Then the Twelve describe the characteristics or qualifications that "the Seven"[135] must have. (2.2.1) They are to be "well spoken of" or "well attested." This prerequisite is expressed using the passive participle μαρτυρου-μένους ("being well attested") from the μαρτυρ- word group, which was

---

134. Other interpretations of the statement are possible, but as Roloff explains, "Gemeint ist nicht, daß die Apostel eine bisher von ihnen mit wahrgenommene Funktion wegen zunehmender Überlastung abgeben und so gleichsam aus ihrem Amt ein neues Amt ausgliedern. Vielmehr soll angedeutet werden, daß sie das nunmehr neu erforderliche Amt nicht zusätzlich übernehmen können, ohne ihren eigenen Aufgabenbereich — 'das Wort Gottes' — zu vernachlässigen" (*Apostelgeschichte*, 109). Similarly, Schneider observes, "V 4 lenkt zu V 2b zurück und zeigt, daß diese Regelung den Aposteln ermöglicht, sich 'dem Gebet und dem Dienst des Wortes' ungeteilt zu widmen. Die Rede läßt erkennen, daß das Hauptanliegen der Zwölf nicht primär darin besteht, die Armenpflege zufriedenstellend zu regeln oder einen Zwist zu beseitigen, sondern die apostolische Wortverkündigung (vgl. 4,29.31) nicht zu beeinträchtigen" (*Apostelgeschichte*, 1:425).

135. The manner of referring to Philip in Acts 21:8 (ὄντος ἐκ τῶν ἑπτά) leads interpreters to conclude that "the Seven" was a formal designation for this group; see Haenchen, *Acts*, 263. This does not, however, warrant the suggestion of B. Domagalski that despite Luke's avoidance of the noun διάκονος one should see Luke advocating the continuation of "church offices" ("Waren die 'Sieben' [Apg 6,1–7] Diakone?" *BZ* 26 [1982] 21–33).

considered in part in the analysis of 1:8. Specifically this participle comes from μαρτυρεῖν ("to bear witness"), which occurs in the speeches in both active and passive forms in 6:3; 10:43; 13:22; 15:8; 22:5, 12; 26:5, 22. The verb occurs in active and passive forms in the narrative as well (10:22; 14:3; 16:2; 23:11). In this speech the passive form reiterates only indirectly the important theme of early Christian witness, but one should not miss this oblique emphasis. (2.2.2) Moreover, the Seven are to be πλήρεις πνεύματος καὶ σοφίας ("full of the Spirit and of wisdom"). Although this is the only place in the speeches where early Christians are said to be "filled with" or "full of" certain divine qualities, the narrative of Acts, often in close proximity to speeches, reports that various disciples were πλήρης ("full") of certain divine characteristics or properties (6:5, 8; 7:55; 9:36; 11:24). On the frequent recurrence of "Spirit" in the speeches, see the analysis of 1:16; one should notice also that the combination of "Spirit and wisdom" occur early in the Stephen story (6:10, τῇ σοφίᾳ καὶ τῷ πνεύματι, "the wisdom and the Spirit"). (2.2.3) The Twelve state their purposes in relation to the Seven, saying, οὓς καταστήσομεν ἐπὶ τῆς χρείας ταύτης ("whom we may appoint to this task"). The striking verb καθιστάναι, meaning "to appoint someone" to attend to a necessity, appears a total of five times in Acts, four times in speeches (6:3; 7:10, 27, 35). Moreover, the word for "necessity" or "task," χρεία, appears in Paul's address to the Ephesian elders in 20:34.

(3.0) From the final line of the speech one learns more exactly why the Twelve did not take on the responsibility for distribution of relief items, when they say, ἡμεῖς δὲ τῇ προσευχῇ καὶ τῇ διακονίᾳ τοῦ λόγου προσκαρτερήσομεν ("while we, for our part, will devote ourselves to prayer and the ministry of the word"). This line repeats in part the concern expressed in v. 2b and expands the image of the ministry of the Twelve. Indeed, the phrase τῇ διακονίᾳ τοῦ λόγου ("the ministry of the word") stands in contrast to that which the Twelve refuse to do, that is, merely διακονεῖν τραπέζαις ("to wait on tables"). Behind this sense of necessity διακονεῖν τὸν λόγον τοῦ θεοῦ ("to serve the word of God") stands the command of Jesus in 1:8 to be his witnesses. Thus, the insistence of the Twelve that they devote themselves in an unswerving manner to the ministry of the word sounds the vital themes of "witness" and "divine necessity."

Stephen's Speech (7:2–53, 56, 59b, 60b)

Luke tells the reader that the suggestion of the Twelve to the other disciples that they select the Seven pleased the whole group; and so they chose and brought the Seven to the apostles, who blessed them for their work. In turn, Luke reports the remarkable growth of the community. One learns that one of the Seven, Stephen, was especially effective among the people, so that his activities brought him into conflict with other Hellenistic Jews who were not

Christians. Luke records that Stephen's opponents could not withstand τῇ σοφίᾳ καὶ τῷ πνεύματι ᾧ ἐλάλει ("the wisdom and the Spirit with which he spoke"), so they had some men bring public accusations of blasphemy against him. The charges agitated τε τὸν λαὸν καὶ τοὺς πρεσβυτέρους καὶ τοὺς γραμματεῖς ("the people as well as the elders and the scribes"), who then brought Stephen before the council. Luke reports that there false witnesses made specific allegations (ὁ ἄνθρωπος οὗτος οὐ παύεται λαλῶν ῥήματα κατὰ τοῦ τόπου τοῦ ἁγίου [τούτου] καὶ τοῦ νόμου· ἀκηκόαμεν γὰρ αὐτοῦ λέγοντος ὅτι Ἰησοῦς ὁ Ναζωραῖος οὗτος καταλύσει τὸν τόπον τοῦτον καὶ ἀλλάξει τὰ ἔθη ἃ παρέδωκεν ἡμῖν Μωϋσῆς, "This man never stops saying things against this holy place and the law; for we have heard him say that this Jesus the Nazorean will destroy this place and will change the customs that Moses handed on to us"), and the high priest questioned Stephen, εἰ ταῦτα οὕτως ἔχει ("Are these things so")? Stephen replied.

The speech is the longest and perhaps most perplexing address in Acts. It is complex and indeed ripe with interpretive problems. As Kennedy notes, "Rhetorically the speech is incomplete. . . ."[136] It makes no effort to explain the falseness of the charges; rather, the rhetoric is *counteraccusation*, a kind of *judicial* rhetoric. Yet the speech never offers explicit rejection or a deliberative counter proposal.[137] There is, however, an epilogue to the main address in the three statements in vv. 54–60.

By observing shifts in point of view, changes of subject, and units of parataxis, one may perceive the structure of the speech[138] as follows:

136. Kennedy, *Interpretation*, 122.
137. Ibid., 121.
138. There are, of course, other ways to outline this important address. Five other reasonable suggestions come from J. Bihler (*Die Stephanusgeschichte in Zusammenhang der Apostelgeschichte* [Münchener Theologische Studien 1/16; Munich: M. Hueber, 1963] 35): I. Die Geschichte Israels (Apg 7,2–37): V 2–8a Abrahamsgeschichte; V 8b Isaak-Jakob (Verbindungsstück); V 9–16 Joseph in Ägypten; V 17–19 Zeit der Erfüllung (Verbindungsstück); V 20–37 Mosesgeschichte. II. Israels Abfall: Götzendienst und Tempelbau (Apg 7,38–50): V 38: in der Wüste empfängt Moses 'lebendige Worte'; Aber Israel fällt ab: V 40–42 Die Väter machen sich Götter und opfern ihnen; V 42: Prophetenzitat Am 5,25–27; V 44: in der Wüste besitzen die Väter das Zelt, so wie Moses es gesehen hat. Aber Israel fällt ab: V 47f: Salomon baut das Haus; V 48bff: Prophetenzitat Is 66,1f. III. Die Schuld Israels: Die Verhärtung (Apg 7,51–53); J. Kilgallen (*The Stephen Speech: A Literary and Redactional Study of Acts 7,2–53* [AnBib 67; Rome: Biblical Institute Press, 1976] 31): The Abraham Story (vv. 2–7); A Transitional Verse (v. 8); The Joseph Story (vv. 9–16); The Moses Story (vv. 17–43); The Temple (vv. 44–50); and Conclusion of the Speech (vv. 51–53); Schneider (*Apostelgeschichte*, 1:446–47) "Am Anfang (I) steht die Abrahams- und die Patriarchengeschichte (7,2–16). Es folgt (II) ein umfangreicher Teil über Mose (7,17–29.30–43). Die beiden folgenden Teile sind bedeutend kürzer. Sie handeln (III) vom Tempelbau (7,44–50) und bieten am Schluß (IV) eine Polemik gegen die Hörer (7,51–53)"; Pesch (*Apostelgeschichte*, 1:245): "Auf . . . die *Anrede* mit der *Aufforderung zum Hören* (2b) folgt als *1. Teil:* Die *Abrahamsgeschichte* (2c-8), als *2. Teil:* Die *Josefsgeschichte* (9 bis 16), als *3. Teil,* Die *Mosegeschichte* (17–43), als *4. Teil:* Die *Geschichte von Bundeszelt und Tempel* (von Josua bis Salomo) (44–50)" and "[der] an die Hörer direkt

1.0 Stephen's Reply in Story (vv. 2b–50)
    1.1 Address and Appeal for a Hearing (v. 2b)
    1.2 God and Abraham (vv. 2c–8a)
        1.2.1 God's Call to Abraham (vv. 2c–3)
        1.2.2 Abraham's Obedience (v. 4a)
        1.2.3 God's Subsequent Actions (vv. 4b–5)
        1.2.4 God's Revelatory Statements (vv. 6–7)
        1.2.5 God's Gift of the Covenant of Circumcision (v. 8a)
    1.3 Abraham and the Patriarchs (vv. 8b–e)
        1.3.1 Abraham's Fathering and Circumcision of Isaac (v. 8b–c)
        1.3.2 Isaac's Fathering of Jacob (v. 8d)
        1.3.3 Jacob's Fathering of the Twelve Patriarchs (v. 8e)
    1.4 The Joseph Story (vv. 9–16)
        1.4.1 The Selling of Joseph (v. 9a)
        1.4.2 God's Care for Joseph (vv. 9b–10)
        1.4.3 The Famine (v. 11)
        1.4.4 Jacob, the Patriarchs, and Joseph (vv. 12–13)
        1.4.5 Jacob and Family in Egypt (vv. 14–16)
    1.5 The Time of the Promise (vv. 17–43)
        1.5.1 The People and Pharaoh (vv. 17–19)
        1.5.2 Moses' Origins (vv. 20–22)
        1.5.3 Moses at Forty (vv. 23–29)
        1.5.4 God and Moses on Sinai (vv. 30–34)
        1.5.5 God's Delivery of Israel from Egypt through Moses (vv. 35–36)
        1.5.6 Moses and the Israelites (vv. 37–38)
        1.5.7 Israel's Rejection of Moses and Their Idolatry (vv. 39–41)
        1.5.8 God's Judgment of Israel (vv. 42–43)
    1.6 From the Tent to a House for God (vv. 44–50)
        1.6.1 The Tent of Witness in the Wilderness (v. 44)
        1.6.2 The Tent from the Time of Joshua to David (vv. 45–46)
        1.6.3 Solomon's Construction of a House (v. 47)
        1.6.4 God's Regard for the House (vv. 48–50)
2.0 Stephen's Indictment of the Audience (vv. 51–53)
    2.1 The Verdict (v. 51)
    2.2 The Evidence (vv. 52–53)
3.0 Tripartite Epilogue
    3.1 Revelatory Declaration (v. 56)
    3.2 First Prayer-Petition (v. 59b)
    3.2 Second Prayer-Petition (v. 60b)

Analysis. (1.0) The speech by Stephen is the most prominent example of the use of the past in an address in the form of explicit citations of scripture. In addition to explicit quotations of scripture, there are many allusions to the stories told in scripture; and although in these allusions there is no overt citation of the text, one often finds words and phrases similar to those of particular biblical passages.[139] Comparable biblical summaries of history are found

---

adressierten[er] Schluß (51–53)"; and Krodel (*Acts*, 139): God's story with Abraham (vv. 2–8); God's story with Joseph and the patriarchs (vv. 9–16); God's story with Moses, told in three parts of forty years each (vv. 17–29, vv. 30–34, vv. 35–43); the story of the tent of witness and the Temple (vv. 44–50); the indictment of the Sanhedrin and the people of Jerusalem (vv. 51–53). One remarkable similarity of these outlines is the failure to cast the statements in 7:54–60 as an integral part of the speech. Kennedy alone remarks on the importance of these sentences as a part of the speech (*Interpretation*, 122).

139. Scholars debate how many citations of scripture there are in the speeches in Acts. The reason for the lack of unanimity is that no standard exists whereby one may determine whether biblical (i.e., LXX) words and phrases are quotations or merely employments (strictly or loosely adhering to the LXX) of language that shows that Luke had absorbed a great deal of the Septuagint into his own vocabulary and thought. As long as the discussion of this issue continues to focus on the author, we will never settle this matter; but if we ask about the first readers we may pose a different question that can be answered with full agreement by all parties. The question: Where in the speeches in Acts does the speaker signal that scripture is being quoted? The answer:

1:20	γέγραπται γὰρ ἐν βίβλῳ ψαλμῶν	Pss 68:26; 109:8
2:17–20	διὰ τοῦ προφήτου Ἰωήλ	Joel 3:1–5
2:25–28	Δαυὶδ γὰρ λέγει	Ps 15:8–11
2:30 (?)	προφήτης οὖν ὑπάρχων	Ps 131:11
2:31 (?)	προϊδὼν ἐλάλησεν	Ps 15:10
2:34–35	Δαυίδ . . . λέγει	Ps 109:1
3:22–23	Μωϋσῆς μὲν εἶπεν	Deut 18:15–20 + Lev 23:29
3:25	ὁ θεὸς . . . λέγων	Gen 22:18; 26:4
4:25–26	θεὸς/πνεύματος ἁγίου/Δαυίδ/εἰπών	Ps 2:1–2
7:3	[θεὸς] εἶπεν πρὸς [Ἀβραάμ]	Gen 12:1
7:6–7	ἐλάλησεν δὲ οὕτως ὁ θεός	Gen 15:13–14; Exod 3:12
7:27–28	ὁ δὲ ἀδικῶν τὸν πλησίον . . . εἰπών	Exod 2:14
7:32	ἐγένετο φωνὴ κυρίου	Exod 3:6
7:33–34	εἶπεν δὲ αὐτῷ ὁ κύριος	Exod 3:5, 7–8, 10
7:35	ἠρνήσαντο εἰπόντες	Exod 2:14
7:37	ὁ Μωϋσῆς ὁ εἶπας τοῖς υἱοῖς Ἰσραήλ	Deut 18:15
7:40	οἱ πατέρες ἡμῶν . . . εἰπόντες	Exod 32:1, 23
7:42–43	γέγραπται ἐν βίβλῳ τῶν προφητῶν	Amos 5:25–27
7:49–50	καθὼς ὁ προφήτης λέγει	Isa 66:1–2
13:22	ὁ θεὸς . . . εἶπεν μαρτυρήσας	Ps 88:21; Isa 44:28; 1 Sam 13:14
13:33	ἐν τῷ ψαλμῷ γέγραπται τῷ δευτέρῳ	Ps 2:7
13:34	ὁ θεὸς . . . οὕτως εἴρηκεν	Isa 55:3
13:35	ὁ θεὸς . . . ἐν ἑτέρῳ λέγει	Ps 15:10
13:41	τὸ εἰρημένον ἐν τοῖς προφήταις	Hab 1:5
13:47	οὕτως γὰρ ἐντέταλται ἡμῖν ὁ κύριος	Isa 49:6
15:16a	οἱ λόγοι τῶν προφητῶν . . . γέγραπται	Jer 12:15

in the Septuagint in Deut 6:20–24; 26:5–9; Josh 24:2–13; Neh 9:6–31; Psalms 77; 104; 105; 135; Wisdom 10; Sirach 44–50; Jdt 5:6–18.[140]

(1.1) The address, ἄνδρες ἀδελφοὶ καὶ πατέρες ("Men, brothers and fathers"), is repeated exactly in 22:1 by Paul when he stands before the council.[141] While this specific address occurs only twice, the compound form ἄνδρες ἀδελφοί ("Men, brothers") appears frequently (see 1:16). Furthermore, the appeal (ἀκούσατε, "listen") is the second of six occurrences of this form (see 2:22), and this manner of opening the speech anticipates the narrative report at the conclusion (ἀκούοντες δὲ ταῦτα διεπρίοντο ταῖς καρδίαις αὐτῶν καὶ ἔβρυχον τοὺς ὀδόντας ἐπ' αὐτόν, "when they heard these things they became enraged and ground their teeth at him," 7:54).

(1.2.1) Stephen's speech begins to narrate the story of God with Israel by referring to ὁ θεὸς τῆς δόξης ("the God of glory"), a phrase found in Ps 28:3 LXX. This line is again an anticipation of the narrative conclusion of the Stephen story, for in 7:55 one reads that Stephen gazed into heaven and saw δόξαν θεοῦ. Krodel goes so far as to argue that "the God of glory" is the central theme of the entire speech.[142] This beginning emphasizes God's divine authority as God initiates involvement with Abraham. Other speeches also begin with a statement about God's activity (3:13; 7:2; 10:34b[?]; 13:17).

The story Stephen tells is related initially to Genesis 12. The address may reflect the language of Gen 12:7, and v. 3 quotes Gen 12:1 explicitly. Abraham

---

15:16b–17b	οἱ λόγοι τῶν προφητῶν . . . γέγραπται	Amos 9:11–12
15:17c–18	οἱ λόγοι τῶν προφητῶν . . . γέγραπται	Isa 45:21
23:5	γέγραπται γὰρ ὅτι	Exod 22:27 (28)
28:26–27	τὸ πνεῦμα τὸ ἅγιον ἐλάλησεν διὰ	Isa 6:9–10
	Ἡσαΐου τοῦ προφήτου . . . λέγων	

(Compare the list compiled by M. Rese ["Die Funktion der alttestamentlichen Zitate und Anspielungen in den Reden der Apostelgeschichte," in *Les Actes des Apôtres: Tradition, rédaction, théologie* (ed. J. Kremer; BETL 48; Gembloux: Duculot; Leuven: Leuven University Press, 1979) 69 n. 31].) While this question and answer move in one way past the interpretive impass concerning the number of citations of scripture that occur in Acts, they do not solve the original problem. One sees this at 7:18, where there is no signal that scripture is being quoted, although the text of Acts matches that of Exod 1:8 LXX verbatim. Nevertheless, it is helpful to know when first readers (even more, hearers!) would have been likely to understand that they were encountering an explicit citation of scripture.

140. Krodel notes these passages and remarks, "What distinguishes Stephen's summary from its predecessors is the perspective from which Israel's history is viewed: 'As your fathers did, so do you' (Acts 7:51)" (*Acts*, 139). Conzelmann observes, "There is a long tradition behind this retelling" (*Acts*, 57); and in addition to Joshua 24; Nehemiah 9; and Psalm 104 he points to the same phenomenon in Ezekiel 20; Josephus *J.W.* 5.377–400; and Pseudo-Clementine *Recognitions* 1.22ff.

141. Bihler (*Stephanusgeschichte*, 36) cites H. Thyen (*Der Stil der Jüdisch-Hellenistischen Homilie* [FRLANT n.s. 47; Göttingen: Vandenhoeck & Ruprecht, 1955] 88–89) in regard to the elaborate address here and in 22:1, arguing that the form of this salutation is typical of the ancient Jewish style of preaching.

142. Krodel, *Acts*, 140.

comes to the fore in several of the speeches (3:13, 25; 7:2, 16, 17, 32; 13:26), and (1.2.2) here his obedience is a recognition of God's authority.

(1.2.3) The way Stephen refers to Judea in v. 4b (τὴν γῆν ταύτην εἰς ἣν ὑμεῖς νῦν κατοικεῖτε, "this country in which you are now living") seems odd, for he lives in the same place.[143] The statement creates distance between Stephen and the audience he is addressing and is the first hint of the polemical character of the address. This feature of the speech will be observed in several subsequent statements, and one observes the same tone in speeches employing the christological contrast scheme (see 2:23–24) and in polemical statements in 13:46–47; 18:6; 28:25–28.

Verse 5 continues the account of God's dealings with Abraham. The statement uses language similar to Deut 2:5 and Gen 17:8, although there is no quotation here.[144]

(1.2.4) A quotation combining Gen 15:13–14 in vv. 6–7a and Exod 3:12 in v. 7b moves the story forward.[145] The speech introduces the verb λατρεύσουσιν, "they shall worship" (from λατρεύειν, "to worship"), into the line from Exod 3:12. This manner of speaking of "worship" occurs in speeches in 7:7, 42; 24:14; 26:7; 27:23. In general one sees from the story that God is in command of the events, and God seems to be working with a "plan" which the revelatory declarations reveal to Abraham.

Verse 8 forms a transition with v. 8a concluding the story focused on God and Abraham (vv. 2c–8a) and v. 8b beginning an account focused on Abraham and the ancestors of Israel (vv. 8b–16). (1.2.5) The conclusion of the first part of the historical summary tells the story from Genesis 17 and 21. The mention of the "covenant of circumcision" (διαθήκην περιτομῆς) is noteworthy. This is the second of only two references to covenant in Acts (3:25; 7:8); and it is the only reference to circumcision in a speech, although in 21:21 there is a remark about the act of circumcising (περιτέμνειν, "to circumcise"). Above all, one should notice that God "gave" (ἔδωκεν) this covenant, so that again God's direction and authority are assumed by a statement in a speech. In turn, (1.3) the report in v. 8b–c about Abraham's fathering and circumcision of Isaac refers to the story of Genesis 21. This recollection leads to the sweeping report of v. 8d–e, which brings the story to Joseph.

(1.4) Verses 9–16 refer to selected portions of the larger story told in Genesis 37–50. The manner in which the story is told gives the narrative a

---

143. Haenchen, *Acts,* 278.

144. Conzelmann refers to part of v. 5 as "a free quotation of Gen 17:8" (*Acts,* 52), but there is nothing in the text that would signal the reader to expect a citation of scripture, free or bound.

145. J. Dupont suggests that vv. 6–7 set the structure of the major portion of the remainder of the speech ("La structure oratoire du discours d'Étienne [Actes 7]," *Bib* 66 [1985] 153–67). Verse 6 anticipates vv. 9–22; v. 7a relates to vv. 23–43; and v. 7b anticipates vv. 44–50. While this interpretation may read too much into vv. 6–7, the attempt to show the thoroughly integrated nature of this address is on the right track.

polemical tone. As Conzelmann observes, "The bearers of the promise themselves bring about the crisis (Gen 37:11, 28; 39:21) thus placing the stress
on divine guidance."[146]

(1.4.1) Haenchen identifies echoes of Gen 37:11, 28 in the language of
v. 9a.[147] The focus on Joseph occurs only here in Acts, as one sees from the
complete restriction of the use of his name to this one speech (7:9, 13 [2x],
14, 18). (1.4.2) The statements in v. 9b echoes Gen 39:10, and v. 10 recalls
the incidents of Genesis 41. E. Richard notes the contrast between the negative
actions of Israel's early ancestors and the positive counteraction of God and
argues that this episode is inherently polemical.[148] Moreover, in v. 10
καθιστάναι ("to appoint") appears for the second of four times in the speeches,
and it recurs in Stephen's speech in vv. 27 and 35 (see 6:3). Finally, the reports
concerning God's caring for Joseph, God's rescuing Joseph, and God's giving
Joseph favor and wisdom before Pharaoh so that Joseph became a powerful
figure in Egypt all emphasize both the oversight of God and that God was
the source of the developments in Joseph's life.

(1.4.3) The story of Genesis 41–42 is the subject of v. 11, that is, the famine.
The words οἱ πατέρες ἡμῶν ("our fathers") are the third of fourteen occurrences
of this phrase (3:13; 5:30; 7:11, 12, 15, 38, 39, 44, 45 [2x]; 13:17; 15:10; 22:14;
26:6). Schneider notes that the use of Χανάαν ("Canaan") in the indeclinable
form occurs here and in 13:19, but otherwise it is not in the New Testament.[149]

(1.4.4) Next, in vv. 12–13 the speech refers to the events of Genesis 42
and 45, that is, the two trips of Joseph's brothers to Egypt for provisions. Verse
12 employs ἐξαποστέλλειν ("to send forth"), a verb from Luke's preferred
vocabulary,[150] which occurs in speeches in 7:12; 13:26; 22:21 and in the narrative of Acts in 9:30; 11:22; 12:11; 17:14. This verb often connotes a commissioning by God directly or indirectly through human agents, and it assumes
God's working in relation to a "plan" and recognizes God's authority.

(1.4.5) As the speech continues v. 14 reflects information from Gen 46:27[151]

146. Conzelmann, Acts, 52.
147. Haenchen, Acts, 279.
148. E. Richard, "The Polemical Character of the Joseph Episode in Acts 7," JBL 98 (1979)
255–67. Richard observes the negative portrait in these verses of Israel's early ancestors and
notes that only Joseph appears positively (and Jacob neutrally). He goes on to relate the episode
to Stephen and his hearers in Acts, suggesting that Joseph is a kind of type for Stephen and
Joseph's brothers are typical of Stephen's murderous audience. One can recognize the important
polemical nature of this story in Stephen's speech without moving with Richard to the level of
near-allegory.
149. Schneider, Apostelgeschichte, 1:456.
150. Ibid.
151. Rather than understanding this verse primarily in relation to Gen 46:27, Bruce avers,
"The construction here is taken from Deut 10:22 LXX" (Acts, 195). Exactly what he means by
this observation is not clear, since only the exceptional manuscript of Deut 10:22 LXX reads
ἑβδομήκοντα πέντε, whereas that is the standard reading of the Septuagint manuscripts for Gen
46:27; moreover, the story line here is following the Genesis account of Joseph.

LXX¹⁵² in telling of the seventy-five persons who migrated to Egypt. The unusual verb μετεχαλέσατο (from μεταχαλεῖν, "to summon," which occurs only in Acts in the New Testament) recurs in short statements (10:32; 24:25) and the narrative (20:17).¹⁵³ In three of the four uses the "summoning" advances the action in compliance with God's purposes (24:25 seems to be the exception). Verse 15 tells of the deaths of Jacob, Joseph, and the other sons of Jacob; these are reported in Genesis 49, 50, and Exodus 1 respectively. Finally, v. 16 is a confused conflation of information from Genesis 23 and 33, and possibly Joshua 24.

(1.5) The story takes a new turn in vv. 17–43, which is signaled with the statement καθὼς δὲ ἤγγιζεν ὁ χρόνος τῆς ἐπαγγελίας ἧς ὡμολόγησεν ὁ θεὸς τῷ Ἀβραάμ ("but as the time drew near for the fulfillment of the promise that God had made to Abraham"). With this line the speech unifies the two previous major portions of the address and simultaneously resounds the crucial themes of divine necessity and control. Events now proceed in relation to God's promise(s), so that human time and life are evaluated in relation to the will and work of God.¹⁵⁴

(1.5.1) While v. 17 reflects the story of Exod 1:7, v. 18 quotes Exod 1:8 LXX exactly without signaling the reader that scripture is being cited.¹⁵⁵ In relation to v. 19 Haenchen observes, "[it] makes freer use of Exod 1:10f"¹⁵⁶ in order to report the realization of God's revelatory statement to Abraham, which was reported in 7:6.

(1.5.2) The next major figure, Moses, appears in 7:20. This is the second of fourteen references to Moses in the speeches (3:22; 7:20, 22, 29, 31, 32, 35, 37, 40, 44; 13:38; 15:21; 21:21; 26:22), and his name appears in shorter statements in 6:11, 14; 15:1, 5. There is even a mention of Moses in the narrative (28:23).¹⁵⁷ The manner in which Stephen's speech tells of Moses' origins echoes Exodus 2, which supplies the story behind vv. 20–21, but not the

---

152. The Masoretic Text says that seventy of Joseph's kindred went to Egypt.

153. W. Mundle, "Die Stephanusrede Apg. 7: eine Märtyrerapologie," *ZNW* 20 (1921) 135.

154. Schubert contends that Deut 18:15 lies behind and shapes the entirety of 7:17–44 ("Place," 241).

155. See above n. 139.

156. Haenchen, *Acts,* 280.

157. Moses was a central figure in the religious debates of the Hellenistic period concerning the validity/invalidity or superiority/inferiority of Judaism. Jewish apologists portrayed Moses as the founder of science and culture (see E. Schürer, *The History of the Jewish People in the Age of Jesus Christ* [rev. and ed. English version by G. Vermes et al.; Edinburgh: T. & T. Clark, 1979] 2:350–51), whereas pagan opponents frequently ridiculed Moses' deficiencies (see J. G. Gager, *Moses in Greco-Roman Paganism* [SBLMS 16; Nashville: Abingdon, 1972]). Moreover, T. L. Donaldson shows how Moses appears in this speech to serve a sectarian-style debate typical of Second Temple Judaism wherein different groups fought one another concerning their status as the "remnant" of Israel ("Moses Typology and the Sectarian Nature of Early Christian Anti-Judaism: A Study of Acts 7," *JSNT* 12 [1981] 27–52).

information in v. 22. In reporting *how* God regarded Moses, the speech implicitly sounds the themes of divine authority and guidance.

(1.5.3) Verses 23–29 continue to echo the story of Exodus 2. The information in v. 23 that Moses decided "to visit" (ἐπισκέπτεσθαι) τοὺς ἀδελφοὺς αὐτοῦ τοὺς υἱοὺς 'Ισραήλ ("his brothers the sons of Israel") employs a form of a rare verb used in other speeches (see 6:3), and the manner of referring to the Israelites (οἱ υἱοὶ 'Ισραήλ, "the sons of Israel") occurs in speeches in 7:23, 37; 10:36. In v. 25 σωτηρία is the second of five uses of an important word (see 4:12). Haenchen argues: "Here the killing is understood as an act of God, of which Moses is merely the agent." Further: "For the first time in the speech we hear the theme of the people's incomprehension and their failure to recognize the savior sent by God."[158] Thus, the themes of God's authority and human guilt are registered by Stephen's story at this point. Moreover, the explicit rejection of Moses reflects the motif of rejecting God's chosen one, which is a prominent element of the familiar christological contrast scheme (see 2:23–24). In turn, vv. 27–28 incorporate Exod 2:14 in reporting the retort of the Israelite man to Moses. Krodel interprets these lines, writing, "'Who made you a ruler and a judge over us?' The answer to this question, namely, that God made him a ruler and a judge (cf. v. 35), never occurred to this Israelite, a paradigm of ignorance encountered in the Jesus story (cf. 2:36; 3:17; 13:27)."[159] The implicit recognition of ignorance here is similar to the theme of ignorance encountered in speeches elsewhere in 3:17; 13:27; 14:16; 17:30.

(1.5.4) The story continues with vv. 30–34 reflecting the narrative of Exodus 3 and moving from general retelling to direct quotation of scripture. Verse 32 cites Exod 3:6, and the way of naming God echoes Peter's speech in 3:13 (see 5:30 for other references to ὁ θεὸς τῶν πατέρων, "the God of the fathers"). Then, vv. 33–34 cite Exod 3:5, 7–8, 10; and within this citation at v. 34 καὶ νῦν ("and now") occurs, a regular rhetorical feature of several speeches (see 3:17). Again, the story being told emphasizes God's initiative, which produces revelation to Moses, direction to Moses, and deliverance through Moses.

(1.5.5) As the speech tells of God's delivery of Israel from Egypt through Moses, v. 35 incorporates Exod 2:14 and, thus, repeats a portion of the words of the retort from v. 27. Now, however, the rejection is attributed to all Israel. The idea of Israel's rejection of Moses will be reiterated in v. 39, so that vv. 35 and 39 form a bracket around vv. 36–38, which report different facets of Moses' work with the Israelites. God's action in sending Moses shows divine initiative and authority. Verse 36 speaks of the departure from Egypt using the verb ἐξάγειν ("to lead out"), which recurs in similar statements in v. 40 and 13:17; and the recalling of τέρατα καὶ σημεῖα ("wonders and signs") employs this phrase

158. Haenchen, *Acts*, 281.
159. Krodel, *Acts*, 145.

for the fourth and final time in the speeches (see 2:19). (1.5.6) Verse 37 cites Deut 18:15 and so repeats the earlier statement of 3:22.[160] The language of v. 38 may reflect further portions of Deuteronomy,[161] and the mention of the angel here in relation to Mount Sinai will become even more explicit in 7:53 with the declaration that the law was delivered to Moses by angels.

(1.5.7) Verse 39 refers back to v. 35; and v. 40 incorporates Exod 32:1, 23 into the speech. Concerning "the epexegetical, demonstrative, and relative pronouns of the section [vv. 35–40]" Schubert argues that "the prophecy as quoted in Acts 3:22–23 is interpreted in great detail."[162] Together vv. 40–41 illustrate the apostasy of Israel in the wilderness. In turn, v. 41 seems to reflect Exod 32:4, 6; and the temporal marker ἐν ταῖς ἡμέραις ἐκείναις ("in those days") echoes a phrase from 2:18.

(1.5.8) The speech tells of God's judgment of Israel's apostasy by quoting a version of Amos 5:25–27 that is slightly different from the Septuagint.[163] The statement in v. 42a concerning God's act of judgment clearly declares that God possesses ultimate authority and has final say over human affairs. Verse 42b leads into the quotation from Amos by referring to what is written (here even more specifically = γέγραπται ἐν βίβλῳ τῶν προφητῶν, "it is written in the book of the prophets"); this method of signaling the citation of selected texts occurs in other speeches (see 1:20).

(1.6) The next segment of the speech, vv. 44–50, moves swiftly through the years from the time of the tent in the wilderness to the time of the Temple. (1.6.1) The story behind the report in v. 44 that ἡ σκηνὴ τοῦ μαρτυρίου ἦν τοῖς πατράσιν ἡμῶν ἐν τῇ ἐρήμῳ ("the tent of testimony was with our fathers in the wilderness") comes from Exodus, especially chapters 25 and 27. In Stephen's speech, however, this line has noticeable features. (A) The reference to "the tent of witness" both registers the important general theme of "witness" (see

---

160. J. Via argues that vv. 35–37 are related to God's raising up Jesus from the dead ("An Interpretation of Acts 7:35–37 from the Perspective of Major Themes in Luke-Acts," *Perspectives in Religious Studies* 6 [1979] 190–207). Thus, as God liberated Israel through Moses, despite Moses' being rejected by Israel, in the resurrection God overturns the crucifixion and establishes Jesus as the figure of God-ordained saving significance. Thus, vv. 35–37 are best related to *resurrection*.

161. Haenchen suggests that ἐκκλησία may reflect Deut 4:10; 9:10; 18:16; whereas λόγια ζῶντα may reflect Deut 32:45–47 (*Acts*, 283).

162. Schubert, "Place," 241.

163. On the intricate nature of the relationship between Acts and Amos, see E. Richard, who shows how Luke is at liberty to alter the Septuagint but how also the Septuagint text influences Luke ("The Creative Use of Amos by the Author of Acts," *NovT* 24 [1982] 37–53); so that "one is never quite sure whether Luke has chosen carefully his OT texts to reinforce his ideas and his view of history, or whether the composition results, in large part, from a serious reading of the Jewish scriptures and meditation upon their meaning for the spread of Christianity" (p. 52). Furthermore, Richard argues that neither *mimesis* nor *testimonium* adequately explains Luke's knowledge and use of the Old Testament.

1:8) and illustrates the point that people in former times were "not without a witness," a theme that occurs in 7:44; 14:17; 17:25b–28. (B) That this tent was made καθὼς διετάξατο ὁ λαλῶν τῷ Μωϋσῇ ποιῆσαι αὐτὴν κατὰ τὸν τύπον ὃν ἑωράκει ("as he who spoke to Moses directed to make it according to the pattern that he had seen") alludes to God's direction, authority, and plan. (1.6.2) The story in v. 45 reflects Joshua 3 and 18. The phrase οἱ πατέρες ἡμῶν ("our fathers") occurs twice in this verse, the final uses of the phrase in this speech and the ninth and tenth of fourteen employments of the phrase in the speeches (see 7:11). Another matter is less certain: With the mention of Joshua, it is hard to imagine that early readers and hearers would not naturally make a mental move from Joshua's name (Ἰησοῦς) to think about Jesus, to whom the speech has made no reference to this point. Yet the speech hurries along with the reference to David (see 1:16b–17). The language of v. 46 may echo Ps 131:5. The way the speech characterizes David (Δαυίδ, ὃς εὗρεν χάριν ἐνώπιον τοῦ θεοῦ, "David, who found favor before God") is similar to the earlier reference to Moses (see v. 20); both descriptions offer implicit recognition of God's authority, since the issue is how one appears to God. The phrase used to situate David ἐνώπιον τοῦ θεοῦ ("before God" or "in God's sight") repeats part of Peter's speech in 4:19, where he located himself, John, and the members of the council "before God." With the use of this phrase these speeches have in common the assumption that human life is lived in relation to the standards of God. Finally, the report of David's request to build "a house"[164] advances the story to a new level.

(1.6.3) With the mention of Solomon's construction of a house the story reflects 1 Kings 6–8. This is the only reference to Solomon as a historical figure in the speeches, but from 3:11 and 5:12 the reader should already associate Solomon with the Temple. (1.6.4) The following verses (48–50) become sharply polemical. The statement in v. 48 that God does not dwell in human constructions parallels the same idea in 17:24.[165] Verses 49–50 cite Isa 66:1–2

---

164. There is a serious textual problem related to David's request. By far the better textual tradition reads ᾐτήσατο εὑρεῖν σκήνωμα τῷ οἴκῳ Ἰακώβ; but a significant variant, ᾐτήσατο εὑρεῖν σκήνωμα τῷ θεῷ Ἰακώβ, is found in other manuscripts. The "better" reading makes no sense in context, whereas the "inferior" reading seems to fit the flow of thought, especially when one notices the following statement in v. 47, Σολομῶν δὲ οἰκοδόμησεν αὐτῷ οἶκον. The word αὐτῷ parallels θεῷ unless one understands that Solomon build himself a house, which makes absolutely no sense in relation to vv. 48–50. Fortunately this matter does not have to be solved here, but should it be necessary I would prefer the "inferior" reading because of the parallel with αὐτῷ and because of the nonsense of the better-attested variant. Richard comes to the same conclusion, noting furthermore that when one recognizes Luke's generally careful manner of quoting the Septuagint it is most likely that Acts 7:46 would match Ps 131:5, which reads σκήνωμα τῷ θεῷ Ἰακώβ (Author's Method, 131–32). For the opposite view, see B. M. Metzger, A Textual Commentary on the Greek New Testament: A Companion Volume to the United Bible Societies' Greek New Testament (3d ed; New York: United Bible Societies, 1971) 351–53.

165. Mundle, "Stephanusrede," 135; and almost all subsequent commentators.

explicitly (καθὼς ὁ προφήτης λέγει, "as the prophet says"). Here scripture serves as evidence of the veracity of a claim made by the speaker, a phenomenon observed frequently in the speeches in relation to kerygmatic declarations. The quotation, however, not only undergirds Stephen's point; it simultaneously declares God's freedom and ultimate authority over all creation.[166]

(2.0) The explicit statement of the guilt of the listeners in vv. 51–53 repeats a form of declaration found in several speeches (see 2:36).[167] (2.1) Stephen's language of indictment "sounds biblical," although whether it is related to the established pattern of telling Israel's story while offering negative comments (e.g., Psalm 77 LXX) is impossible to determine.[168] The mention of the Holy Spirit is a frequent phenomenon in the speeches (see 1:16b–17). Furthermore, in v. 51 (and v. 52) the reference to οἱ πατέρες ὑμῶν ("your fathers") stands in sharp contrast to the uses of οἱ πατέρες ἡμῶν ("our fathers") through the earlier portions of the speech; yet, at least as early as 7:4 (τὴν γῆν ταύτην εἰς ἣν ὑμεῖς νῦν κατοικεῖτε, the country in which you are now living") the speech anticipated the distance created by this rhetoric.[169]

(2.2) After the speech levels Stephen's charge, vv. 52–53 present argument and evidence in support of the accusation. The persecuted prophets are those who made revelatory declarations concerning God's divine purposes. This characterization once again relates to the idea of a divine plan. The one of whom the prophets spoke is ὁ δίκαιος ("the Righteous One"), a title applied to Jesus in 3:14 and which will recur in 22:14. This designation is one of the cluster of titles used by speakers to declare Jesus' theological identity (see 2:36). More specifically, the speech refers to "the Righteous One" as the one οὗ νῦν ὑμεῖς προδόται καὶ φονεῖς ἐγένεσθε ("of whom now you betrayed and have become murderers"). This line issues a now familiar charge against the audience (see 2:23–24, 36)[170] using the style of the kerygmatic relative

166. Similarly, D. D. Sylva has examined this portion of Stephen's speech, arguing with clarity that the speech indicates that God transcends the Temple, not that God has rejected the Temple ("The Meaning and Function of Acts 7:46–50," *JBL* 106 [1987] 261–75).

167. Bihler argues for the connection of this speech with the others that share this feature of accusation (*Stephanusgeschichte*, 36).

168. For a detailed analysis of the speech in relation to historical summaries in the Old Testament, especially those delivered for the purposes of edification, see P. Dschulnigg, "Die Rede des Stephanus im Rahmen des Berichtes über sein Martyrium (Apg 6,8–8,3)," *Judaica* 44 (1988) 195–213.

169. Contra Conzelmann, who writes, "The fact is that literary seams are evident, precisely at those points where transitions are made from positive biblical matters to polemics. These polemical sections can be isolated (vss 35, 37, 39–42, 48–53, perhaps 25, 27)" (*Acts*, 57). Indeed, it is impossible to find parts of the speech that are devoid of polemical elements, as one sees from the analysis done above.

170. J. J. Kilgallen shows, while pursuing the larger question of *function*, that the basic line of argument throughout this address is that through past and present Israel has resisted the will of God ("The Function of Stephen's Speech [Acts 7,2–53]," *Bib* 70 [1989] 173–93). The chief form of opposition being the rejection of Jesus.

pronoun, which is seen in the speeches that contain the christological contrast scheme (see 2:23–24). Observing the minimal amount of reference to Jesus here—life, passion, resurrection—J. Bihler suggests that a parallel exists between Stephen's speech and Paul's Areopagus address specifically in their lack of standard kerygma.[171] In turn, the issue of "law observance" (v. 53) is an explicit concern in one other speech (21:24), although in 13:38; 18:15; 21:20, 28; 22:3, 12; 23:3; 24:14 there are references to the law in speeches. There is also a mention of the law in the report of a speech in 28:23. Finally, one may or may not understand that Stephen completed his address, but the note about the audience's furor in v. 54 shifts the focus away from him. This feature of several speeches first occurred in 2:36.

(3.0) An epilogue to the main body of the speech comes in the three individual, but complementary, statements of vv. 56, 59b, and 60b. (3.1) Verse 56 makes a revelatory declaration.[172] The opening word ἰδού occurs at the beginning of direct speech (speeches and statements) in 5:25; 7:56; 8:36; 9:10; 10:19, 21. This report of Stephen's vision functions to confirm the validity of the previous speech.[173] The declaration informs the reader or hearer that Jesus is raised and exalted, thus supplying important information otherwise absent from the speech. The reference to the risen, exalted Jesus as ὁ υἱὸς τοῦ ἀνθρώπου ("the Son of Man") is unique,[174] although other singular and repeated titles are applied in speeches (see 2:36). (3.2) The compound vocative address κύριε 'Ιησοῦ ("Lord Jesus") is also unique; although κύριε occurs as a prayer address nine times (see 1:24). Implicitly the petition δέξαι τὸ πνεῦμά μου ("receive my spirit") recognizes that Jesus is σωτήρ, "savior" (5:31; 13:23) with authority over human life and death, an idea inherent in the title ὁ ἀρχηγὸς τῆς ζωῆς, "the Author of life" (3:15). (3.3) The second petition again employs κύριε ("Lord"). The request is remarkable. While nothing in Stephen's speech calls the hearers to repentance and forgiveness, this final appeal to the "Lord"

171. Bihler, *Stephanusgeschichte*, 37. Bihler also labels Stephen's speech "situationsfremd" and suggests, therefore, it is parallel to Paul's reply to charges in 22:1–21.

172. M. Rese notes that in context the statement in 7:52 finds an indirect complement in vv. 55–56, so the lines may be viewed in relationship to each other ("Aussagen," 340). But Rese insists that the connection here is too loose to view Stephen's statement in relation to other statements in speeches which explicitly and deliberately hold death-and-resurrection together. This observation means that the statements in 7:52, 55–56 have their own particular identity in relation to the range of speech-statements in Acts.

173. Krodel, *Acts*, 155.

174. The most recent discussions of the interpretive problems associated with this title comes from R. Kearns (*Das Traditionsgefüge um den Menschensohn: Ursprünglicher Gehalt und älteste Veränderung in Urchristentum* [Tübingen: J. C. B. Mohr (Paul Siebeck), 1986] 5–54), who treats Acts 7:56 briefly (p. 23) in the course of surveying the history of scholarship; and C. C. Caragounis (*The Son of Man: Vision and Interpretation* [WUNT 38; Tübingen: J. C. B. Mohr (Paul Siebeck), 1986] 1–33) who deals with Stephen's statement in the survey of scholarship and in his own subsequent interpretive work.

is for the forgiveness of those who both rejected Jesus (v. 52) and are now killing Stephen.[175] This appeal is a clear recognition of the "Lord" as the one with the power to realize forgiveness. This divinely realized forgiveness through the raised and exalted Jesus is in fact the goal of the plan of God (see 2:23–24, 38–39).

Peter's Speech in Cornelius's House
(10:28b–29, 34b–43, 47)

The speech by Stephen occupied center stage in the section of Acts running from 6:1 to 8:8. After the speech a narrative report tells about the persecution that came on a segment of the church (8:1–3). The remainder of chapters 8 and 9 tell of important developments by focusing on the missionary work of Philip (8:4–40), the conversion of Saul (9:1–31), and Peter's work as a healer in Lydda and Joppa (9:32–43). There are statements and conversations throughout this material, but there is no speech.

The next major segment of Acts is 10:1–11:18. Here there are two speeches by Peter, both of which are associated with the conversion of the Gentile centurion Cornelius σὺν παντὶ τῷ οἴκῳ αὐτοῦ ("with all his household"). In 10:1–23 one learns of a vision granted to Cornelius that directed him to send for Simon Peter and of a vision granted to Peter and a subsequent command by the Spirit that directed Peter to go with Cornelius's emissaries to visit Cornelius. The next episode contains Peter's first speech. It comes in three parts: 10:28b–29, which opens the address by stating a fact and asking a question; 10:34b–43, which comes in response to Cornelius's answer to the previous question; and 10:47, which makes a final declaration after ἐπέπεσεν τὸ πνεῦμα τὸ ἅγιον ἐπὶ πάντας τοὺς ἀκούοντας τὸν λόγον, "the Holy Spirit fell upon all who heard the word" (10:44).

Kennedy follows all other commentators by treating only 10:34–43 as Peter's speech. On these verses he observes that the speech is essentially *epideictic* rhetoric. As such it is purely kerygmatic, offering no indictment; and the speech has a relatively economical style, since the only elaborations are in v. 38, which contains an enthymeme (ὅτι ὁ θεὸς ἦν μετ' αὐτοῦ, "for God was with him"), and v. 41, which offers amplification (οἵτινες συνεφάγομεν καὶ συνεπίομεν αὐτῷ μετὰ τὸ ἀναστῆναι αὐτὸν ἐκ νεκρῶν, "we who ate and drank with him after he rose from the dead"). Kennedy also notes that the decision to baptize came

---

175. This interpretation goes beyond rather than against the usual conclusions of interpreters who simply observe "daß in der Stephanusrede dem Hohen Rat nur noch die Schuld vorgeworden wird, aber kein neues Heilsangebot an die Juden ergeht, wie wir es Apg 2,38; 3,19 finden" (F. Schnider, *Jesus der Prophet* [OBO 2; Freiburg: Universitätsverlag; Göttingen: Vandenhoeck & Ruprecht, 1973] 97).

in response to the work of the Holy Spirit, not in answer to an appeal by Peter.[176]

While these insights are correct and helpful, they are limited in their accuracy by the failure to view vv. 28b–29 and 47 as integral parts of the speech. In fact, vv. 28b–29 are *judicial* rhetoric wherein the stasis is metastasis as Peter transfers the responsibility for his seemingly unorthodox behavior to God;[177] and v. 47 is *deliberative* rhetoric aimed at Peter's Jewish-Christian companions from Joppa and the reader. By broadening the point of view to regard all of Peter's remarks to Cornelius and his household as Peter's speech, one perceives a more complex structure, which may be outlined as follows:

1.0 Initial Remarks (vv. 28b–29)

Cornelius speaks for the entire group in answer to Peter's inquiry. This reply to Peter's question is a simple answer to an individual, not a speech. The singular Greek pronouns make this point clear. One should notice, however, in Cornelius's report in direct address of his previous vision that v. 33 goes beyond the mere repetition of the earlier experience saying νῦν οὖν πάντες ἡμεῖς ἐνώπιον τοῦ θεοῦ πάρεσμεν ἀκοῦσαι πάντα τὰ προστεταγμένα σοι ὑπὸ τοῦ κυρίου ("so now all of us are here before God to listen to all that the Lord has commanded you to say"). This crucial line scores four points in familiar rhetoric: (A) The temporal marker νῦν identifies a major turning point in Acts in a manner similar to καὶ νῦν ("and now") and καὶ τὰ νῦν ("and now"); see 3:17. (B) The phrase ἐνώπιον τοῦ θεοῦ ("before God"), which was noticed in 4:19 and 7:46, sets this group squarely before God. (C) With the statement πάρεσμεν ἀκοῦσαι ("we are here to listen") Cornelius declares that this assembly is ready to do exactly what previous speeches have called for other audiences to do, that is, "to listen" (see 2:22). (D) With the words πάντα τὰ προστεταγμένα σοι ὑπὸ τοῦ κυρίου ("all that the Lord has commanded you to say") there is a clear recognition that "the Lord" is the source of the forthcoming message and the director of the events that were transpiring; implicit here is the idea that Peter is the Lord's witness.

2.0 Peter's New Opening (vv. 34b–35)
   2.1 Peter's New Perception (v. 34b)
   2.2 Statement of God's Policy (v. 35)
3.0 Christological Kerygma (vv. 36–38)
   3.1 Characteristics of God's Word (v. 36)
   3.2 Further Definition of "the Word" (v. 37)
   3.3 God's Anointing of Jesus (v. 38a–b)

---

176. Kennedy, *Interpretation*, 122–23.

177. Pesch remarks, "So übersetzt er [Peter] nun den empfangenen Gottesentscheid" (*Apostelgeschichte*, 1:341).

3.4 Jesus' Ministry (v. 38 c–d)
4.0 The Apostolic Witness (v. 39a)
5.0 Further Kerygma: Death and Resurrection (vv. 39b–40)
6.0 The Qualified Witness (v. 41)
7.0 Jesus' Commandment (v. 42)
8.0 Interpretation through Prophetic Testimony (v. 43)

After this portion of the speech the Holy Spirit falls on the hearers so that they repeat an element of the Pentecost miracle(s) by speaking in tongues and praising God. Then Peter continues to speak.

9.0 Rhetorical Epilogue (v. 47)

Analysis. (1.0) Peter's first declaration to the assembly in Cornelius's house contains four distinct items: (A) an address with a statement of Jewish policy in relation to Gentiles (v. 28b), (B) a report of God's revelation to Peter (v. 28c), (C) an account of Peter's subsequent action (v. 29a), and (D) a question to the group (v. 29b). The manner of address ὑμεῖς ("you") occurs both here and in v. 37 in this speech. In both places there is a rhetorical appeal to the "knowledge" of the hearers, ὑμεῖς ἐπίστασθε ("you yourselves know") here and ὑμεῖς οἴδατε ("you know") in v. 37. In Peter's first major address a similar rhetorical form occurred in 2:22 (καθὼς αὐτοὶ οἴδατε, "as you know"), although there the phrase was not the opening line of the address. The knowledge to which Peter appeals at this point recognizes the problematic nature of his presence in Cornelius's house, but Peter's report of God's revelation (θεὸς ἔδειξεν, "God has shown") explains why he is there in apparent defiance of Jewish practice. This report anticipates the fuller statement about God in v. 34b, though, above all, the statement recognizes the supreme authority of God.

(2.0) When Peter speaks again after Cornelius's telling answer, one reads of the solemnity of his manner in v. 34a, 'Ανοίξας δὲ Πέτρος τὸ στόμα εἶπεν ("when Peter opened his mouth he said"), a phrase leading toward direct address in 8:35 and 18:14. (2.1) Krodel compares this speech in general with Paul's Areopagus address, noting that both speeches begin with acknowledgments of the audience's piety and end with reference to Jesus as future judge; yet he finds the addresses otherwise strikingly different.[178] As Peter begins to speak, he uses the phrase ἐπ' ἀληθείας ("truly"), which occurs in speeches in 4:27 and 10:34. This declaration of truth is a theological observation in relation to the situation (vv. 34b–35). Speeches are often initially focused on the situation, but here the real concern is the statement about God which builds on v. 28 in a more explicitly theological fashion. (2.2) Moreover, in both vv. 34b–35 and v. 43 the universal character of God's salvation is

178. Krodel, *Acts*, 200.

emphasized,[179] and the same note is sounded in v. 36c with the statement that Jesus is "Lord of all." All of these statements together echo and amplify the universality implicit in the lines of the citation from Joel in 2:17–21. In vv. 34b–35, again, as is the case throughout this speech, the basic assumption is that God defines and directs reality.

(3.0) The following verses (36–38) offer christological kerygma. The grammar of these lines, especially v. 36, is difficult.[180] (3.1) Verse 36 treats the nature of God's λόγος ("word"). There may be allusions to lines from the Old Testament in this awkward statement. The idea and language of God's sending the word, τὸν λόγον ὃν ἀπέστειλεν ("the message he sent"), may employ a portion of Ps 106:20 LXX,[181] and the words εὐαγγελιζόμενος εἰρήνην ("preaching peace") may reflect Isa 52:7 LXX. Concerning the references to God's message as ὁ λόγος ("the word"), see the discussion at 5:32. One also learns that God's word was sent τοῖς υἱοῖς 'Ισραήλ ("to the sons of Israel"), the group named twice in Stephen's speech (see 7:23). God's message of peace was brought to the Israelites διὰ 'Ιησοῦ Χριστοῦ ("by Jesus Christ"). The manner of speaking casts Jesus as God's agent. Later, in v. 38d, one finds the idea that Jesus' work was the result of God's presence with him. Both statements are comparable to the declaration of 2:22 where Peter's speech plainly says that God worked through Jesus to do great things. All of these lines assume, and state, the ultimate authority of God.

Having mentioned Jesus Christ, Peter declares, οὗτός ἐστιν πάντων κύριος ("he is Lord of all"). The proclamation of Jesus as Lord occurs explicitly in 2:36 and 10:36, and implicitly in 22:8 and 26:15. This is but one form of statement about the theological identity of Jesus (see 2:36). Again, the universality of God's work and Jesus' lordship are emphasized.

(3.2) In v. 37 the address ὑμεῖς ("you") recurs.[182] The mention of John the Baptist with an emphasis on the ἀρξάμενος ("beginning") of the ministry is

179. See D. Lotz, "Peter's Wider Understanding of God's Will: Acts 10:34–48," *International Review of Missions* 77 (1988) 201–7.

180. In the following discussion I am assuming the solution to the grammatical difficulties proposed by H. Riesenfeld, who reads the initial words τὸν λόγον ὃν ἀπέστειλεν as standing in apposition to Peter's previous statement in vv. 34b–35 ("The Text of Acts 10:36," in *Text and Interpretation: Studies in the New Testament Presented to Matthew Black* [ed. E. Best and R. McL. Wilson; Cambridge: Cambridge University Press, 1979] 191–94). Riesenfeld offers this translation of vv. 34–37: "Truly I realize that God does not show partiality, but in every nation anyone who fears him and does what is right is acceptable to him; (this is) the word which he sent to the children of Israel, proclaiming good news of peace through Jesus Christ — he is Lord of all. You know what took place throughout all Judea, beginning from Galilee after the baptism which John preached. . . ." Additional support for this reading comes in the survey article by F. Neirynck ("Acts 10,36a τὸν λόγον ὅν," *ETL* 60 [1984] 118–23).

181. Bruce suggests that Ps 147:7 LXX may also stand behind τὸν λόγον ὃν ἀπέστειλεν (*Acts*, 261).

182. Krodel notes this repetition and suggests, "Peter tells the Gentiles the story of Jesus as proof of the affirmation made in . . . vv. 34–36" (*Acts*, 197).

similar to other statements in speeches (see 1:4–5). While the word ῥῆμα may mean "the occurrence" rather than "the word" in this context, ῥῆμα is closely associated with the gospel message in the speeches (see 5:32).

(3.3) The story of Jesus begins with a reference to God's anointing Jesus. The way of naming Jesus, 'Ιησοῦν τὸν ἀπὸ Ναζαρέθ ("Jesus, the one from Nazareth"), is striking, but similar to forms noted at 2:22.[183] The prayer of the Jerusalem congregation mentioned God's anointing of Jesus (see 4:27–28). Haenchen suggests that these references to God's anointing may reflect Isa 61:1, which was quoted at length in Luke 4:18.[184] In turn, one reads again of the Holy Spirit (1:16b–17) and of the important concept of "power," which is associated with divinely inspired ministry (see 1:8). Finally, one should note that this general kerygmatic report is cast in the relative pronoun style seen frequently in similar statements (see 2:23–24).

(3.4) The overt treatment of dimensions of Jesus' ministry is similar to information in speeches in 1:22 and 2:22b–24. The declaration ὅτι ὁ θεὸς ἦν μετ' αὐτοῦ ("for God was with him") is remarkably similar to the phrase in Stephen's speech which explained the rise of Joseph in Egypt (see 7:9). J. Roloff describes the idea of God's being with one as an Old Testament motif, pointing to the allusion to Gen 39:21 at Acts 7:9.[185] Furthermore, one may compare 2:22, where Peter's speech explained that Jesus' work was done as God acted through him.[186] With christological kerygma placed before the audience, (4.0) v. 39a registers the important theme of "witness" (see 1:8; 1:21–22). One should also notice that the concern with πάντων ὧν ἐποίησεν ("to all that he did") reflects the comprehensive nature of the witness anticipated in 1:21–22. As is the case throughout the speeches, kerygma and testimony operate in tandem.

(5.0) The speech issues further information about Jesus Christ in vv. 39b–40, lines cast in the familiar christological contrast scheme (see 2:23–24) but without the previously observed direct polemical tone since the composition of the audience makes such a polemic impossible. Verse 39b tells of Jesus' death. The verb ἀναιρεῖν ("to put to death") occurs in speeches in reference to the execution of Jesus in 2:23; 10:39; 13:28. Moreover, the phrase κρεμάσαντες ἐπὶ ξύλου ("hanging him on a tree") alludes to Deut 21:22–23 and so employs the verb κρεμᾶν ("to hang") for the crucifixion and the noun ξύλον ("tree") for the cross. All these phenomena occurred at 5:30. The following part of the contrast scheme (v. 40) treats God's raising of Jesus. The emphatic manner of referring to the crucified Jesus as τοῦτον—from οὗτος, "this one"—

183. Bruce judges 'Ιησοῦν τὸν ἀπὸ Ναζαρέθ and 'Ιησοῦν τὸν Ναζωραῖον (2:22) to be synonymous (Acts, 262).

184. Haenchen, Acts, 352.

185. Roloff, Apostelgeschichte, 173.

186. Schneider, Apostelgeschichte, 2:77.

appears in kerygmatic materials in 2:32; 5:31; 10:40.[187] All the references to God's raising Jesus in the speech are listed in the analysis of 1:22b, but this particular form using ἐγείρειν ("to raise up") occurs in 3:15; 4:10; 5:30; 13:30, 37. Schneider points to the similar use of διδόναι ("to give" or "to allow") in reference to God's action(s) in raising Jesus in this statement and the statements in 2:27 and 13:35, both of which are citations of Ps 15:10 LXX;[188] thus, there is the possibility that Old Testament language influenced this formulation. The formula makes the repeated point that God has the power and the authority over events in creation.[189]

(6.0) In the same way that v. 39a offered testimony concerning the kerygma of vv. 36–38, now v. 41 resounds the theme of "witness" in confirmation of the declarations of vv. 39b–40. Here, however, one encounters a new note: οὐ παντὶ τῷ λαῷ ἀλλὰ μάρτυσιν τοῖς προκεχειροτονημένοις ὑπὸ τοῦ θεοῦ, ἡμῖν . . . ("not all the people but to us who were chosen by God as witnesses . . ."). This assertion that God chose those to whom the raised Jesus appeared and made them witnesses to the resurrection makes clear that the will and the direction of God control the dissemination of the news of the resurrection. The implication of this statement is that God operates with a "plan" (compare 10:41; 22:14; 26:16).[190]

(7.0) The report of the commandment(s) of Jesus in v. 42 refers to his words to the disciples at 1:8. Several items are noticeable. First, the scheme of preaching — that is, to the Israelites first — matches the procedure articulated in 13:46. Second, the necessity "to testify" (διαμαρτύρεσθαι) resounds the witness theme (see 1:8). Third, the report that the resurrected Jesus told his "witnesses" to testify ὅτι οὗτός ἐστιν ὁ ὡρισμένος ὑπὸ τοῦ θεοῦ κριτὴς ζώντων καὶ νεκρῶν ("that he is the one ordained by God as judge of the living and the dead") contains at least three crucial points: (A) The use of ὡρισμένος, "being ordained" (from ὁρίζειν, "to determine") states God's control. (B) The same word was used in reference to God's "plan" in 2:23, and it recurs elsewhere (see 2:23). (C) In both language and thought the statement about Jesus' being appointed judge over the living and the dead has a parallel in 17:31 (there ἐν ἀνδρὶ ᾧ ὥρισεν, "by a man whom he has appointed").[191] Fourth, through these statements this report of Jesus' commandments moves beyond the simple witness motif to become kerygmatic proclamation.

187. Bruce, Acts, 263.
188. Schneider, Apostelgeschichte, 2:78.
189. Roloff states the consensus regarding this kerygmatic formulation: "Die Auferwechung am dritten Tage und die Erscheinungen des Auferstandenen. Beides ist, dem Stil des ältesten Kerygmas gemäß, als von Gott ausgehendes Geschehen verstanden (s. zu 2,24)" (Apostelgeschichte, 173).
190. Roloff, Apostelgeschichte, 173.
191. Bruce, Acts, 263.

(8.0) The speech takes its final major turn with v. 43, which offers both support for and interpretation of the foregoing declarations. One reads, τούτῳ πάντες οἱ προφῆται μαρτυροῦσιν ("all the prophets testify about him"). This statement is an example of reference to the prophets without explicit citation (see 3:18). Interpreters view the phrase "all the prophets bear witness" as a typically Lukan statement, and one may observe parallels in 3:24 and 26:22.[192] Now, even references to the prophets sound the theme of witness to Christ (see 1:8; 6:3b). Verse 43 continues, ἄφεσιν ἁμαρτιῶν λαβεῖν διὰ τοῦ ὀνόματος αὐτοῦ πάντα τὸν πιστεύοντα εἰς αὐτόν ("that everyone who believes in him receives forgiveness of sins through his name"). Here one receives interpretation of the meaning of the peace preached through Jesus and the work of God in his ministry and resurrection. The reference to "forgiveness of sins" repeats an important theme of several speeches (see 2:38); indeed the forgiveness of sins appears as a subject of prophecy in 3:18–19.[193] Moreover, saying that sins are forgiven "through the name" of Jesus emphasizes still another familiar theme (see 2:38). Although this speech neither levels a charge at the audience nor explicates the necessity of repentance, vv. 42b–43 seem at least implicitly to confront the hearers with their sinfulness and to call for their repentance.[194] The last part of the verse, "all believing in him," sounds a theme that is repeated in speeches in 10:43; 11:17; 13:39.[195]

The coming of the Holy Spirit upon the members of Cornelius's household seems to interrupt Peter's speech, although, as is usually the case with such interruptions, the speaker has come to a convenient stopping point. The device first appeared in 2:36.

(9.0) Following the report of the occurrences at the coming of the Spirit, v. 47 forms an epilogue to the speech. Peter's rhetorical query, μήτι τὸ ὕδωρ δύναται κωλῦσαί τις τοῦ μὴ βαπτισθῆναι τούτους, οἵτινες τὸ πνεῦμα τὸ ἅγιον ἔλαβον ὡς καὶ ἡμεῖς ("Can anyone withhold the water for baptizing these people who have received the Holy Spirit just as we have?"), anticipates the answer no, as is clear from the form of the inquiry (μήτι). The question is an implicit call to baptism (see 2:38). The mention of the Holy Spirit echoes v. 38 and other references to the Spirit in the speeches (see 1:16b–17). Moreover, Peter's logic, that is, understanding that an event validates a statement or conclusion, appears in other addresses (3:15b–16). Furthermore, the verb κωλύειν ("to withhold" or "to hinder") is repeated in the reference back to this event in Peter's forthcoming address (see 11:17); and finally the phrase ὡς καὶ ἡμεῖς

192. Krodel, Acts, 199; Conzelmann, Acts, 84.

193. Bruce, Acts, 263.

194. Haenchen designates vv. 42–43 a "summons to repentance" (Acts, 351); and Roloff observes, "Der Hinweis auf Umkehr und Sündenvergebung wird etwas künstlich mit dem Zeugnis der Propheten verknüpft"(Apostelgeschichte, 174).

195. Bruce points out that 14:23; 19:4 read πιστεύω εἰς; 9:42; 11:17; 16:31 read πιστεύω ἐπί; and 5:14; 8:12; 16:34; 18:8; 24:14; 26:27; 27:25 read πιστεύω with dative (Acts, 264).

("just as we [have]") appears in appropriately altered grammatical form in 11:17 (ὡς καὶ ἡμῖν), so that the universality of salvation is emphasized.

Peter's Speech to the Circumcision Party (11:5–17)

Since no one present in Cornelius's house objected to the baptism of the Gentiles upon whom the Holy Spirit had fallen, Peter called for them to be baptized ἐν τῷ ὀνόματι Ἰησοῦ Χριστοῦ ("in the name of Jesus Christ"). At the request of these new believers Peter remained among them for some days. The Jewish Christians of Judea learned of the conversion of Cornelius's household, so when Peter returned to Jerusalem οἱ ἐκ περιτομῆς ("the cirumcised") criticized his recent behavior and called for him to explain himself.

Peter's speech is a kind of *judicial* rhetoric, offering a defense through *narration* that transfers the responsibility for Peter's action to God (metastasis). Peter's "basic argument" is "that the order of God takes precedence over the law," and remarkably "no evidence is given other than Peter's own words."[196] The only argument offered in conjunction with the narration is the rhetorical question at the end of the speech.

Essentially, vv. 5–10 recount Peter's visionary experience in Joppa (10:9–16); vv. 11–12 tell of Cornelius's calling Peter to Caesarea (10:17–29); vv. 13–15 report the events in Cornelius's house (10:30–46a); v. 16 adds an explanation to the report; and v. 17 poses the question to the Jerusalem Christians that Peter previously presented to the Jewish Christians from Joppa (10:47).[197] In outline the speech appears this way:

1.0 The Story of the Vision in Joppa (vv. 5–10)
2.0 Recalling Cornelius's Summons (vv. 11–12)
3.0 The Report of the Events in Cornelius's House (vv. 13–15)
4.0 Peter's Recollection of the Lord's Word (v. 16)
5.0 Concluding Rhetorical Question (v. 17)

---

196. Kennedy, *Interpretation*, 123.

197. Schneider is typical of commentators who note that the retelling varies slightly from the original events (*Apostelgeschichte*, 2:83); for example, according to 11:15 the Spirit came on the Gentiles at the beginning of Peter's address, whereas according to 10:44 this occurred at the end of the speech. The speech also adds information not previously given: there were six Christians from Joppa; Cornelius learned in his vision that Peter's message would bring salvation to his whole household; the anointing of the Gentiles with the Spirit is clearly comparable to Pentecost; and Peter tells of his remembering the word of the Lord.

This variation is not significant, as Roloff remarks, "Doch dies ist erzählerische Technik des Lukas" (*Apostelgeschichte*, 167). Likewise, Haenchen (*Acts*, 355) cites O. Bauernfeind (*Die Apostelgeschichte* [THKNT 5; Leipzig: Deichert, 1939] 142) with approval, "He prefers a sizeable self-contradiction to a dreary self-repetition."

Analysis. Since the speech retells previous episodes of Acts, it is natural that there are parallels between elements of the speech and items in the passage where the event being reported is located. There are, however, other noticeable parallels to portions of other speeches, and these repetitions are the primary concern of the following analysis.

(1.0) The mention of the "vision" (ὅραμα) echoes the language of 2:17, where other references to visions in speeches were noted. Further, Peter's prayerful address, κύριε ("Lord"), repeats a form first noted at 1:24. Moreover, Pesch observes similarities in thought and language between the statements about God's cleansing foods (ὁ θεὸς ἐκαθάρισεν) in vv. 8–9 and about God's cleansing the hearts of humans (ὁ θεὸς . . . καθαρίσας) at 15:8–9;[198] so that one sees here God's divine authority.

(2.0) As Peter tells of Cornelius's having called him to come to Caesarea, he speaks of the revelatory direction of the Holy Spirit. The Spirit is an important theme throughout the speeches (see 1:16b–17), and the report itself emphasizes the divine direction of events according to the will of God.

(3.0) The three verses (vv. 13–15) that recall the dramatic occurrences in Cornelius's house strike a number of familiar notes. The simple report about the appearance and words of the angel to Cornelius (A) refers to the angel's "standing" (σταθέντα), which attributes to the angel a position identical to that of other speakers (see 2:14); (B) refers to Peter's "message" (ῥήματα) using familiar terminology (see 5:32); and (C) declares that Peter's ῥήματα will bring salvation to Cornelius and his whole household (σωθήσῃ σὺ καὶ πᾶς ὁ οἶκός σου, "you and your entire household will be saved"); on the verb σῴζειν, "to save," see 4:12). Moreover, F. F. Bruce notes that the phrase σωθήσῃ σὺ καὶ πᾶς ὁ οἶκός σου (without πᾶς) is repeated in a short statement in 16:31.[199]

In turn, v. 15 again speaks of the Holy Spirit, now telling how the Spirit fell on the Gentiles. Like most commentators, Conzelmann notices the difference in the temporal sequence between 10:44 and 11:15, but he observes, "The intention in both cases is the same, namely, to indicate divine initiative."[200] Furthermore, this emphasis on God's initiative in sending the Spirit upon these people brings to realization the line from Joel in 2:17.[201]

(4.0) Peter's report of recalling the words of the Lord repeats the statement of Jesus in 1:5 and harks back directly to 10:37 with the mention of John the Baptist. The report uses ῥῆμα in reference to the "word" (see 5:32). A similar phenomenon occurs in Paul's address to the Ephesian elders in 20:35, when in the speech he tells the elders to remember "the words of the Lord Jesus" (τῶν λόγων τοῦ κυρίου Ἰησοῦ) and then cites the Lord's statement. This style of using the past is striking.

198. Pesch, *Apostelgeschichte*, 1:346.
199. Bruce, *Acts*, 269.
200. Conzelmann, *Acts*, 86.
201. Pesch, *Apostelgeschichte*, 1:347.

(5.0) In the concluding line Peter poses a question that restates the earlier question from 10:47–now, however, asking for a decision from a new audience. Again there is reference to the Holy Spirit, but here in terms of the idea of the Spirit as a gift from God (see 2:38). The phrase ὡς καὶ ἡμῖν ("just as we [have]") echoes ὡς καὶ ἡμεῖς ("just as we [have]") in 10:47, and it will be resounded with καθὼς καὶ ἡμῖν ("exactly as we [have]") in 15:8. The statement αὐτοῖς . . . πιστεύσασιν ἐπὶ τὸν κύριον Ἰησοῦν Χριστόν ("them . . . having believed in the Lord Jesus Christ") resembles 10:42b–43 (see there, and the note thereto). Finally, the verb κωλύειν ("to withhold" or "to hinder") is repeated from 10:47.

In relation to v. 17 Haenchen comments, "Two ideas here flow together: 1. Who was I, to prevent God? 2. How was I in a position to prevent God?"[202] Indeed, Peter's rhetorical question is a clear recognition of the authority of God and the involvement of God directing the course of events.

Paul's Speech at Antioch of Pisidia (13:16b–41, 46–47)

Peter's speech to his critics in the circumcision party silenced them and even moved them to affirm the mission to the Gentiles. Then, in chapters 11–13 the account in Acts records further developments in the life of the church, alternating the focus from Antioch to Jerusalem and back to Antioch. One learns that Barnabas brought Paul into the work of the Antioch church; that Peter was pressured out of Jerusalem by Herod's deadly hostility; that Herod died, Ὁ δὲ λόγος τοῦ θεοῦ ηὔξανεν καὶ ἐπληθύνετο, "but the word of God continued to advance and gain adherents" (12:24); that Barnabas and Paul were divinely selected and then blessed and sent out by the Antioch congregation to do missionary work in Cyprus and portions of Asia Minor. In Pisidian Phrygia (the southern portion of the Roman province Galatia)[203] Paul and his associates (οἱ περὶ Παῦλον, "the ones around Paul") entered a synagogue on a Sabbath and there Paul delivered his first major speech in Acts. The speech is formed into two larger sections (vv. 16b–25; vv. 26–37) that are followed by a conclusion (vv. 38–41), and after further developments, there is an epilogue (vv. 46–47).

Kennedy analyzes the speech somewhat differently, since he does not take vv. 46–47 into consideration. He notes that despite the invitation to deliver an exhortation (v. 15), Paul's speech is not *deliberative* but *epideictic* rhetoric with a relatively formal *proem* (v. 16b), *narration* (vv. 17–25), *proposition* (v. 26), explanatory *proof* (vv. 27–37), and an *epilogue* (vv. 38–41).[204]

202. Haenchen, *Acts*, 355 n. 4.
203. Conzelmann, *Acts*, 103.
204. Kennedy, *Interpretation*, 124–25.

Although the speech is essentially paratactic in style, one may discern the following outline by observing the repeated addresses and the shifts in topics:

1.0 The Story of God and Israel (vv. 16b–25)
    1.1 Address and Appeal for a Hearing (v. 16b)
    1.2 God's Dealings with Israel (vv. 17–23)
        1.2.1 God's Choice and Care of the Ancestors (v. 17)
        1.2.2 God and Israel in the Wilderness (v. 18)
        1.2.3 God's Gift of the Land (vv. 19–20a)
        1.2.4 God's Gift of the Judges (v. 20b)
        1.2.5 Israel's Call for a King (v. 21a)
        1.2.6 God's Gift of Saul (v. 21b–d)
        1.2.7 God's Removal of Saul and Gift of David (v. 22)
        1.2.8 God's Gift of the Promised Savior, Jesus (v. 23)
    1.3 The Evidence from John the Baptist (vv. 24–25)
        1.3.1 John's Ministry (v. 24)
        1.3.2 John's Testimony (v. 25)
2.0 The Message of Salvation (vv. 26–37)
    2.1 Address and Declaration (v. 26)
    2.2 Christological Kerygma (vv. 27–30)
    2.3 The Evidence (v. 31)
    2.4 The Explanation through Scripture (vv. 32–37)
3.0 The Meaning of Salvation (vv. 38–39)
    3.1 Appeal and Address (v. 38a)
    3.2 Explanatory Declarations (vv. 38b–39)
4.0 A Stern Warning (vv. 40–41)

Paul's preaching aroused the curiosity of some hearers who asked him to speak to them again after a week. When Luke tells of his next address, one learns that he and Barnabas met strong opposition. We hear nothing but their final statement, which functions as a conclusion to the previous remarks. This connection is clear in the way the final warning of the major portion of the address now becomes bold confrontation.

5.0 Concluding Remarks (vv. 46–47)
    5.1 The Course of Proclamation (v. 46)
    5.2 Scriptural Explanation (v. 47)[205]

---

205. In an elaborate study of Acts 13:16–41, M. F.-J. Buss brings the material in 13:46–47 into the overall interpretation of this speech, noting especially the importance of these lines for comprehending how the plan of God traced through the earlier portions of the speech is being worked out in the context of the life of the early church (*Die Missionspredigt des Apostels Paulus im Pisidischen Antiochien: Analyse von Apg 13,14–41 im Hinblick auf die literarische und thematische Einheit der Paulusrede* [FB 38; Stuttgart: Verlag Katholisches Bibelwerk, 1980] 134–41). He points out that the apostles are sent to the Gentiles under the authority of the Holy

Analysis. Commentators regularly compare this speech to one or more of the other addresses in Acts. Haenchen notes similarities to and differences from Stephen's speech;[206] Krodel also sees a relationship between Acts 13 and Acts 7, but he treats "several parallels between Peter's Pentecost speech and Paul's speech in Antioch" in detail;[207] and Schubert went so far as to compare Paul's speech to Stephen's speech, Peter's Pentecost address, and Peter's speech in Cornelius's house.[208] The sense of this speech and the meaning of the similarities, however, are debated. Roloff and Bruce compare Paul's address to Stephen's speech and argue that the negative tone of Stephen's speech is entirely gone in Paul's address;[209] yet, making the same comparison, Krodel observes, "Looking at the speech as a whole we find a progressive intensification of the negative aspects of the people of God."[210] As will become clear through the analysis, I understand the speech as Krodel does, against the line of interpretation suggested by Roloff and Bruce.

As Paul moves to speak, he takes the stance of a Hellenistic orator, even making an orator's gesture.[211] The narrative reports similar gesturing in 12:17 and 21:40, and other speakers have and will rise (ἀναστάς) to speak (see the introductory remarks to 1:16–22, 24–25).

(1.1) Paul's address is one of the many uses of ἄνδρες (see 1:11) in salutation, and the specific form ἄνδρες 'Ισραηλῖται ("Men, Israelites") is the fourth of five uses of this greeting (see 2:22). The recognition of the God-fearers (οἱ φοβούμενοι τὸν θεόν, "others who fear God") recurs in v. 26, and both of these mentions of pious Gentiles in the synagogue anticipate the reference to πᾶς

Spirit, so that the saving power of God seen in Jesus' death and resurrection is operative in the missionary activity of the apostles. Indeed, Buss argues that the mission to the Gentiles is grounded in the resurrection itself (esp. p. 140).

206. Haenchen, *Acts*, 415.

207. Krodel, *Acts*, 232.

208. Schubert, "Place," 245–46.

209. Roloff, *Apostelgeschichte*, 202–3; Bruce, *Acts*, 303. Bruce's comments are puzzling: "Stephen's survey of his people's past was negative, emphasizing their repeated apostasy, which had recently reached its climax in their rejection of Jesus; Paul's, on the other hand, is positive, emphasizing the faithfulness of 'the God of this people' in the past and supremely in the present, through the fulfilment in Jesus of the ancient promises. Stephen holds out no hope for the Jewish nation; Paul holds out every hope for it." That God had to "put up with" Israel in the wilderness; that Israel asked for a king (effectively rejecting the kingship of God), whom God subsequently removed; that the people of Jerusalem and their leaders had Pilate kill Jesus without just cause; that Paul pointedly warned the Pisidian Jews not to scoff at God's work; and that Paul finally scolds them for rejecting the word of God — all are quite negative. Bruce is correct: God's actions are consistently positive and for Israel's good, but Israel's own initiatives are portrayed negatively. Moreover, that Stephen's final words were a prayer for the Lord not to reckon his murderers' sin against them indicates that Stephen's hope of Israel, which was real, was nothing other than the power of the Lord to forgive!

210. Krodel, *Acts*, 243.

211. See Haenchen, *Acts*, 408; Conzelmann, *Acts*, 103; and Kennedy, *Interpretation*, 124.

ὁ πιστεύων ("everyone who believes") in v. 39.[212] And, finally, the appeal ἀκούσατε ("listen") is the third of six occurrences of this exhortation (see 2:22).

(1.2) Verses 17–23 are a general retelling of events found in Genesis, Exodus 6, Deuteronomy 1 and 7, Joshua 14–17, 1 Samuel 7–10, 15–16, and 2 Samuel 7[213] and 22; and the same sweep of Israel's history from οἱ πατέρες ἡμῶν ("our fathers") to Δαυίδ ("David") is the focus of Psalm 77 LXX, which repeatedly incorporates a negative critique of the Israelites' behavior into the account of God's faithful and authoritative dealings with them. Paul's report of history, although briefer than Psalm 77, offers several details not found in the Psalm.

(1.2.1) The story begins with a reference to God's activity, a manner of beginning several speeches (see 7:2). This opening is portentous, for through-out vv. 17–23 God is clearly the dominant figure in the history, whereas other characters come and go. The verb ἐξελέξατο ("chose"), from ἐκλέγεσθαι ("to choose"), indicating a divine choice, occurs in other speeches (see 1:24b–25). The mention of οἱ πατέρες ἡμῶν ("our fathers") is the eleventh of fourteen references to this group in speeches (see 7:11). In turn, the use of the verb ὑψοῦν ("to make great") in reference to an act of God, especially in the sense of a beneficial act, occurs elsewhere (see 5:31). Finally, the verb ἐξάγειν ("to lead out") here describes God's leading Israel out of Egypt, and at 7:40 the same verb describes Moses' activity in God's behalf.

The story now moves rapidly from the wilderness to David, and with each point of the account emphasizes God's authority. (1.2.2) In both Stephen's speech (7:36) and in v. 18 there are statements about God and Israel in the wilderness. Stephen's speech elaborates the problem of Israel's apostasy, whereas the brief mention here merely reports that God ἐτροποφόρησεν (from τροποφορεῖν)—that is, God "put up with [their] moods."[214] This statement portrays God in an authoritative role in relation to the Israelites. (1.2.3) A further clear indication of God's power and authority comes in the report about the gift of the land. A similar recollection occurred in 7:45, and the use of Χανάαν ("Canaan") in the indeclinable form repeats 7:11, the only other occurrence of this convention in the New Testament. (1.2.4) God acts again in giving Israel the judges. The temporal boundary recognized by the mention of Samuel echoes the reference to him in 3:24. (1.2.5) Then the speech notes a negative moment in Israel's history, when the people called for a king. That Israel's request is not a positive development becomes clear from the fol-lowing remarks. Thus, this portion of the speech has a polemical undertone.

212. Krodel, Acts, 233.

213. For a detailed chart and discussion sketching and analyzing the thematic and verbal parallels between Acts 13 and 2 Samuel 7, see M. Dumais, Le langage de l'évangélisation: L'annonce missionnaire en milieu juif (Actes 13,16–41) (Tournai: Descleé; Montrêal: Bellarmin, 1976) 90–95.

214. Bruce, Acts, 304.

(1.2.6) God responds to Israel's initiative by giving them Saul for a king. The references to Saul in this speech are the only mention of him in Acts. (1.2.7) The authority of God is again demonstrated by God's removal of Saul and God's raising up David as Israel's king. Verse 22 is striking.[215] God testifies concerning David, and the vocabulary used in the statement (εἶπεν μαρτυρήσας, "he said, giving witness") echoes the familiar "witness" theme (see 1:8).[216] The testimony per se, however, is a conflation of Ps 88:21 LXX (εὗρον Δαυίδ, "I have found David"); 1 Kgdms 13:14 (here: ἄνδρα κατὰ τὴν καρδίαν μου, "a man after my heart"; there: ἄνθρωπον κατὰ τὴν καρδίαν αὐτοῦ, "a person after his own heart"; and Isa 44:28 (here: ὃς ποιήσει πάντα τὰ θελήματά μου, "who will carry out all my wishes"; there: καὶ πάντα τὰ θελήματά μου ποιήσει, "and he will carry out all my wishes").[217] The idea that David did all God's will recognizes not only God's authority but also that God has purposes or a plan.[218] Moreover, the mention of David per se is a frequent feature of speeches (see 1:16).

(1.2.8) Having brought the story to David, the speech bridges from David to God's act of giving Israel the promised savior, Jesus. The use of σπέρμα ("seed" [NRSV: "posterity"]) in the sense of a "descendant" occurs in speeches in 3:25; 7:5, 6; 13:23.[219] Moreover, this verse makes one of the several declarations in the speeches about the theological identity of Jesus (see 2:36); and the specific designation σωτήρ ("Savior"), appeared in 5:31 (see the discussion at 2:40b). The statement that ὁ θεὸς . . . κατ' ἐπαγγελίαν ἤγαγεν τῷ 'Ισραὴλ σωτῆρα 'Ιησοῦν ("God . . . as he promised has brought to Israel a Savior, Jesus") again indicates that God works in relation to a plan and that God is the one who possesses the power to fulfill the plan.

(1.3) Having made this theologically saturated survey of history, which ended in a christological claim, Paul's next remarks offer evidence of the veracity of his declaration that God brought forth Jesus as the savior promised to Israel. The evidence, like the foregoing survey, comes from Israel's history, specifically from John the Baptist. The use of the past in vv. 24–25 is remarkable. (1.3.1) Verse 24 recalls John's ministry to Israel prior to the coming of Jesus. His work is described as προκηρύξαντος . . . βάπτισμα μετανοίας παντὶ τῷ λαῷ 'Ισραήλ ("had already proclaimed a baptism of repentance

215. See D. Duling, "The Promises to David and their Entrance into Christianity," *NTS* 20 (1973–74) 55–77, esp. 77.

216. Citing E. E. Ellis ("Midrash, Targum and New Testament Quotations," in *Neotestamentica et Semitica: Studies in Honour of Matthew Black* [ed. E. E. Ellis and M. Wilcox; Edinburgh: T. & T. Clark, 1969] 65 [*sic;* see p. 68]), Dumais (*Langage*, 95) interprets the material here as "un exposé sur un texte dans le contexte d'autres Écritures."

217. A similar mixture occurs in *1 Clem.* 18.1, producing discussion of whether Clement knew Acts or, more likely, whether he and Luke knew a similar source or tradition.

218. Schubert, "Place," 245.

219. Schneider, *Apostelgeschichte,* 2:133 n. 60.

to all the people of Israel"). This is the fifth of five references to John in the speeches (see 1:5); but the phrase βάπτισμα μετανοίας ("baptism of repentance") occurs again in 19:4 in a short conversation between Paul and some persons who had experienced John's baptism.[220] (1.3.2) The evidence offered in support of v. 23 comes in John's testimony reported in v. 25, namely, that John was not the one Israel expected (i.e., the promised savior) but another greater one was coming after him. The statement is effectively a nontitular declaration about Jesus' theological identity similar to the many statements about him that recognize Jesus with titles (see 2:36). John functions as a "witness" in this retelling.

   (2.0) The second major portion of the speech (vv. 26–37) leaves the survey of Israel's history to focus on Jesus, especially on his execution and resurrection; but in the interpretation of the significance of these events one sees that God is still the overarching, controlling figure whose own divine purposes were accomplished through Jesus. (2.1) Verse 26 addresses the Jewish hearers with the words Ἄνδρες ἀδελφοί ("Men, brothers"; see 1:16), which is expanded through the phrase υἱοὶ γένους Ἀβραάμ ("sons of the family of Abraham"), and again recognizes the presence of the God-fearers in a fashion similar to the address in v. 16b (οἱ ἐν ὑμῖν φοβούμενοι τὸν θεόν, "others among you who fear God"). Ἄνδρες ἀδελφοί ("Men, brothers") occurs once more in v. 38 at the outset of the conclusion. The reference to the Jewish listeners as υἱοὶ γένους Ἀβραάμ ("sons of the family of Abraham") mentions Abraham for the seventh and final time in the speeches. The declaration that follows this greeting refers to the Christian message as ὁ λόγος, "the word" (see the discussion of 5:32) and stipulates the subject of the message as σωτήρια ("salvation")[221] (see 4:12). In the epilogue, in v. 47, Paul and Barnabas will refer to "salvation" as the subject or goal of their proclamation, so that in this speech one encounters the third and fourth of five occurrences of σωτήρια ("salvation") in the speeches. Finally the use of the verb ἐξαποστέλλειν ("to send out") in the sense of a divinely commissioned sending is a recurring feature of the speeches (see 7:12).

   (2.2) Verses 27–30 deliver christological kerygma. The tone of the speech becomes overtly negative at this point, although the statements about God's activity are positive. The overall pattern of these verses is that of the familiar christological contrast scheme (see 2:23–24). Initially vv. 27–29 offer an elaborate report of the guilt of the Jerusalemites for their rejection of Jesus. The hearers are not themselves confronted directly with this charge (see 2:36), although in the epilogue (v. 46) those resisting the preaching of Paul and

   220. Ibid., 2:13 n. 66; and Bruce, *Acts*, 306.
   221. R. F. O'Toole notes the correlation of proclamation to the Gentiles in vv. 44–52 and the major focus on Jesus' having been raised in vv. 30–37 to argue that the resurrection of Christ is the key to the extension of salvation to humankind ("Christ's Resurrection in Acts 13,13–52," *Bib* 60 [1979] 361–72).

Barnabas are accused directly of rejecting the message of God's work and, thereby, of being affiliated with the guilt of those who actually rejected Jesus. Several features of these verses are noteworthy: First, the reference to οἱ ἄρχοντες ("the leaders") is one of four mentions of this group in the speeches (3:17; 4:8, 26; 13:27). Second, one hears again that Jesus was rejected because of the ignorance (ἀγνοήσαντες, "did not recognize" or "did not know") of the Jerusalemites (see 3:17), specifically because of ignorance concerning the utterances of the prophets. Third, the phrase μηδεμίαν αἰτίαν θανάτου ("no cause for a sentence of death"), whereby Jesus' innocence is recognized, recurs in Paul's speech to the Roman Jews in 28:18, there in reference to Paul's own innocence.[222] Fourth, the idea that Pilate did the will of the Jerusalem Jews in permitting them to execute Jesus repeats the allegation of 3:13 exactly; and this mention of Pilate is the third of three references to him in the speeches. Fifth, the use of ἀναιρεῖν ("to put to death") occurs in other speeches in reference to Jesus' execution (see 10:39). Sixth, the explicit reference in v. 29 to "what was written" (γεγραμμένα) concerning Jesus is repeated in v. 33 (γέγραπται, "it was written") and is a feature of other speeches (see 1:20). Seventh, the word ξύλον ("tree") in reference to the cross is the third of three uses of this striking term (see 5:30). Eighth, despite the injustice of Jesus' execution, the speech casts the cross as the fulfillment of scripture rather than as a scandal (see 2:23); thus, it is clear that Jesus' death occurred in relation to the plan of God. Ninth, the statement in v. 30 that God raised Jesus is part of the larger system of synonymous declarations in the speeches (see 1:22b). The specific verb ἐγείρειν ("to raise up") occurs again in this speech as it has in previous speeches (3:15; 4:10; 5:30; 10:40; 13:30, 37); and, more specifically, ἐγείρειν ("to raise up") is linked with ἐκ νεκρῶν ("from the dead") in 3:15; 4:10; 13:30.

(2.3) After the kerygma is given, in v. 31 the speech offers evidence in support of the proclamation by referring to those to whom the raised Jesus appeared who were witnesses to the people. This simple statement employs the kerygmatic relative pronoun style[223] (see 2:23–24) to emphasize the familiar "witness" theme (see 1:8).

(2.4) In vv. 32–37 Paul's address explains the salvific meaning of the foregoing kerygma. Verses 32–33 declare that Paul and his companions "bring the good news" concerning God's fulfillment τοῖς τέκνοις ("to the children")[224] of what God promised πρὸς τοὺς πατέρας ("to the fathers"). The verb εὐαγγελίζειν ("to bring good news") occurs for the act of Christian preaching in speeches

222. Schneider, *Apostelgeschichte,* 2:135.
223. Bruce takes this line as a demonstrative rather than a relative clause (*Acts,* 308), but Conzelmann reads the statement as a relative clause (*Acts,* 105).
224. The textual problems of v. 33 are, as Haenchen observes (*Acts,* 411), most easily resolved by the reading τοῖς τέκνοις, ἡμῖν.

in 10:36; 13:32; 14:15, and the same verb appears in several narrative reports of Christian preaching (5:42; 8:4, 12, 25, 35, 40; 11:20; 14:7, 21; 15:35; 16:10; 17:18).

In demonstration of the veracity of this interpretation of the kerygma, the following verses offer an elaborate exegetical argument.[225] In both content and logic this argument is similar to the exegetical section of Peter's Pentecost speech in 2:25–36. Several specific observations are necessary: First, v. 33 cites Ps 2:7 LXX in relation to the claim that God raised Jesus.[226] The statement itself uses the word ἀνιστάναι ("to raise"), which is repeated in v. 34 and in other speeches (see 1:22b). The citation of a psalm recurs in v. 35 and is a regular phenomenon of speeches (see 2:25–28). With this citation one learns of Jesus' identity as God's Son, one of the several titles used in reference to Jesus by speakers (see 2:36). Second, v. 34 cites Isa 55:3 LXX to certify ὅτι . . . ἀνέστησεν αὐτὸν ἐκ νεκρῶν μηκέτι μέλλοντα ὑποστρέφειν εἰς διαφθοράν ("as to his raising him from the dead, no more to return to corruption"). The issue of διαφθορά ("corruption") in this verse and the subsequent three verses is similar to the focus of the comments in 2:27 and 31. The term comes into both contexts from Ps 15:10 LXX, which is cited in both passages but is not otherwise found in the New Testament.[227] Further, the citation itself refers to David, who becomes the subject of the argument in v. 36 (see 1:16). Third, as noted, v. 35 cites Ps 15:10 LXX, repeating 2:27. The use of these three Old Testament texts is striking, for originally Ps 2:7 referred to divine blessing at the coronation of the king, Isa 55:3 promised restoration to the nation of exiled Israel, and Ps 15:10 expressed personal piety precipitated by confidence in God's providence, present and future. Now, however, Paul's speech frames these texts in the context of the story of Jesus, especially in relation to his resurrection. Fifth, vv. 36–37 issue explicit explanation of the argument. The Old Testament citations were not about David but about Jesus. This logic parallels the thought of 2:29. Indeed, in v. 36 there is explicit mention of ἡ βουλὴ τοῦ θεοῦ ("the plan of God"), one of the four overt references

225. The logic of this section is to demonstrate the truth of christological claims by arguing that one finds God's promises fulfilled in Jesus and one knows this by viewing God's actions in relation to Old Testament texts. The idea of divine promise and fulfillment is itself an interpretation of Jesus' resurrection. It is quite remarkable that ἐκπληροῦν occurs only here in all of Acts. The use of the Old Testament in this context is not along the lines of a prophecy-fulfillment or a proof-from-prophecy scheme; rather the texts serve as explanations of the veracity of the promise-fulfillment interpretation of Jesus' resurrection. Contra Schubert, "Place," 244–46; and Bock, *Proclamation*, 245–49.

226. Interpreters debate whether ἀναστήσας 'Ιησοῦν here means that God brought Jesus forth as God raised up the prophets or that God raised Jesus from the dead. The statements in vv. 30 and 34 demand the latter understanding; similarly, Conzelmann, *Acts*, 105. Contra Rese, who, nevertheless, is in part correct in observing, "Die christologische Bedeutung des Zitats liegt in der Anwendung des Sohnestitels auf Jesus" (*Motive*, 81–86; quotation from p. 86).

227. Schneider, *Apostelgeschichte*, 2:138.

to God's plan (see the discussion at 1:7; see 2:23). And v. 37 occurs in the style of the kerygmatic relative pronoun (see 2:23–24).

(3.0) The concluding portion of Paul's Sabbath speech provides insight into the meaning of the salvation being proclaimed by Paul.[228] (3.1) This section opens with the words γνωστὸν οὖν ἔστω ὑμῖν, ἄνδρες ἀδελφοί ("let it be known to you therefore, men, brothers"). The admonition γνωστὸν ἔστω ("let it be known to you") occurs in other speeches (see 2:14), as do the words of address ἄνδρες ἀδελφοί ("men, brothers"; see 1:16). (3.2) Verses 38b–39 now supply the hearers with the necessary information. The idea that it is through Jesus that the hearers experience the forgiveness of their sins (διὰ τούτου ὑμῖν ἄφεσις ἁμαρτιῶν καταγγέλλεται, "through this man forgiveness of sins is proclaimed to you") points to God's divine power of forgiveness and divine control of events. The reference to forgiveness of the hearers' sins is an implicit call to repentance[229] in vocabulary that recurs in other speeches (see 2:38). In turn, the reference to the law and the mention of Moses strike notes occurring else-where (see discussion at 7:53 and 7:20 respectively). Finally, the phrase πᾶς ὁ πιστεύων ("everyone who believes") echoes 10:43 and recalls the universal-istic scope of the citation from Joel in 2:17.

(4.0) Another negative turn comes in the speech with the words of warn-ing in vv. 40–41. The reference to the prophets in v. 40 gives no name although the citation is from Hab 1:5 LXX. The same pattern occurred in 7:42, 49 and will recur in 15:15; a similar phenomenon occurs in 17:28 with a reference to unnamed pagan poets who are then quoted. Moreover, in v. 41 the men-tion of God's ἔργον ("work") echoes 5:38b.

(5.0) After the interval of a week, opposition arises as Paul and Barnabas return to speak. Yet, given the final note of the earlier address, it is as if the speech had simply continued to grow negative. The reader learns that in the face of hostility the speakers spoke with great boldness (παρρησιάζεσθαι, "to speak boldly"; see the discussion at 1:8). (5.1) The necessary sequence of the proclamation — to the Jews first (ὑμῖν ἦν ἀναγκαῖον πρῶτον λαληθῆναι τὸν λόγον τοῦ θεοῦ, "it was necessary that the word of God should be spoken first to you") — reminds one of 10:42. The designation of the message as "the word of God" is a regular reference to the Christian message (see 5:32). Further, the word for the rejection of the message, ἀπωθεῖσθαι ("to reject" or "to thrust away"), occurred in Stephen's speech in 7:27 and 39 in the sense of rejecting God's messenger Moses, whom the Israelites "thrust away."[230] (5.2) Verse 47

228. J. J. Kilgallen demonstrates that the speech is complex and subtle in what it seeks to communicate ("Acts 13,38–39: Culmination of Paul's Speech in Pisidia," *Bib* 69 [1988] 480–506, esp. 504–5). The promises to David not only find their realization in Jesus, but the benefits of God's grace are *now* being extended through the proclamation of the disciples to humanity.

229. Schneider, *Apostelgeschichte*, 2:139.

230. It may not be reading too much into this word to observe that although the Israelites thrust away Moses, he did not leave them. Rather, he suffered the rejection only to continue

cites Isa 49:6 LXX in an abbreviated form.[231] While the scripture is applied
here to Paul and companions,[232] similar language colors statements in 1:8 and
26:23b regarding the apostles and the raised Jesus. Moreover, the latter of
these statements points to the explicitly universal dimensions of the Christian proclamation. The line leading into the citation, οὕτως γὰρ ἐντέταλται ἡμῖν
ὁ κύριος ("for so the Lord has commanded us"), makes it clear that God's will
is at work directing the actions of the disciples.

The Speech of Barnabas and Paul at Lystra (14:15–17)

After the initial uproar in Antioch of Pisidia, Luke reports that the Gentile
hearers reacted positively so that "the word of God" spread abroad; but the
Jewish opposition recruited assistance and drove Paul and Barnabas out of
the region. Nevertheless, rejoicing and full of the Spirit, the disciples went
to Iconium in Lycaonia (still in the Roman province of Galatia), where they
preached in a synagogue with great success. Hostility arose, however, that
forced the disciples to flee to Lystra, where a crippled man was miraculously
healed through Paul. In an enthusiastic reaction, the crowd took Barnabas
and Paul for gods and attempted to offer sacrifices to them. The disciples stayed
the crowd with the words of a short speech.

This address is clearly *epideictic* rhetoric, since it seeks to convince the
hearers to hold a particular point of view in the present, but there are clear
judicial tones in the speech. Though brief, this speech is complex and may
be outlined as follows:

1.0 Address with Rhetorical Question (v. 15a)
2.0 The Identity and Purpose of the Disciples (v. 15b)
3.0 The Work and Ways of the Living God (v. 15c–17)
    3.1 God's Creation (v. 15c)
    3.2 God's Past Permissiveness (v. 16)
    3.3 God's Witness in Nature (v. 17)

---

to work among them. Thus, it is noteworthy that the next report of Paul's and Barnabas's preaching
locates them in a synagogue in Iconium (14:1). Thus, the statement in 14:46 cannot be understood
as an absolute turning away from the Jews.

231. Contra Haenchen, who declares that this citation is not from the Septuagint (*Acts,* 414);
but in agreement with the identification of this text as deriving from the Septuagint, see
Conzelmann, *Acts,* 106; Schneider, *Apostelgeschichte,* 2:145; Pesch, *Apostelgeschichte,* 2:46; and
Bruce, *Acts,* 314–15.

232. P. Grelot, argues, however, that the quotation from Isaiah is not transferred from Christ
to the disciples; rather, "Christ in glory" is the "light of the nations" ("Note sur Actes XIII,47,"
RB 88 [1981] 368–72). *Application* and *transferal* are not, however, necessarily the same
phenomenon.

Analysis. Interpreters regularly point to similarities between this speech and 17:22–31. Schubert describes these three verses as a "prelude to the Areopagus speech."[233] Yet the speech relates to other speeches as well, as will become clear through the analysis.

(1.0) The speech opens with the address ἄνδρες ("Men"). This simple salutation appears in speeches and statements in 7:26; 14:15; 19:25; 25:24; 27:10, 25. From the salutation, the speech takes as its opening topic the situation of misunderstanding, a topic that opens other speeches (see 2:15).

(2.0) The speech next explains that Barnabas and Paul are ἄνθρωποι ("humans"), like the people of Lystra. This clarification of the disciples' humanity parallels the words of Peter to Cornelius in 10:26 when Cornelius expressed excessive reverence for the apostle. In turn, one learns that the disciples "bring good news" (εὐαγγελίζειν), a statement made in other speeches and frequently in reports of the disciples' activities (see 13:32). The good news is explained in a striking manner as ἀπὸ τούτων τῶν ματαίων ἐπιστρέφειν ἐπὶ θεὸν ζῶντα ("to turn from these worthless things to the living God"). Implicit in ἀπὸ τούτων τῶν ματαίων ἐπιστρέφειν ("to turn from these worthless things") is a regular feature of the speeches, namely, a call to repentance (see 2:38); and with the words θεὸν ζῶντα ("living God") the speech announces the topic that dominates the rest of the address.

(3.0) The "living God" is the subject of all of the following statements. Indeed vv. 15c and 16 issue statements about God in the kerygmatic relative pronoun style (2:22b–24). (3.1) Interpreters often suggest there is an allusion to Exod 20:11 LXX in the biblical-sounding statement of v. 15c.[234] The line is even more comparable to Ps 145:6 LXX, yet it is impossible to determine if this reference to God's action is a deliberate use of the Septuagint. The praise offered here to the creator God occurred in 4:24 and will recur in 17:24.[235] The images of creation echo the universal character of the divinely achieved salvation to which the disciples are calling their hearers, and the images are a clear recognition of God's authority as Creator. (3.2) Two items in v. 16 are remarkable. The idea of God's determining the destiny of nations is similar to the thought expressed in 17:26; and the recognition that πάντα τὰ ἔθνη πορεύεσθαι ταῖς ὁδοῖς αὐτῶν ("all the nations to follow their own ways") sounds the theme of "ignorance" (see 3:17) in a fashion most comparable to 17:30. (3.3) The closing declaration is frequently compared to 17:24–31.[236] The statement employs a New Testament *hapax legomenon* (ἀμάρτυρον, "without a witness") in a phrase, καίτοι οὐκ ἀμάρτυρον αὐτὸν ἀφῆκεν ("he has

---

233. Schubert, "Place," 246.
234. E.g, Haenchen, *Acts,* 428.
235. On 14:15, especially in relation to the Areopagus address, see B. Gärtner, "Paulus und Barnabus in Lystra: Zu Apg. 14,8–15," *SEÅ* 27 (1962) 83–88, esp. 85–86.
236. E.g., Haenchen, *Acts,* 429; Conzelmann, *Acts,* 111.

not left himself without a witness"), which echoes the important "witness" theme (see 1:8); and, more specifically, it expresses the idea that God was not without a witness (see 7:44). The reference to God's doing good and supplying human needs is similar to the declaration of 17:25, and the focus on natural order, especially the "seasons" (καιρούς) is comparable to 17:26. Indeed, the implication here that humans could discern God because of the "witnesses" is similar to the notion expressed in 17:27 that humans were capable of seeking and finding God. Finally, the unusual word for "gladness," εὐφροσύνη, occurred in the citation of Ps 15:11 LXX in 2:28, but otherwise it does not appear in the New Testament.

Peter's Speech at the Jerusalem Gathering (15:7b–11)

Barnabas and Paul managed to prevent the crowd in Lystra from offering sacrifices to them. Subsequently Luke tells of the arrival in Lystra of Jews from Antioch and Iconium who convinced the people (Jews and Gentiles?) to stone Paul, who was then left for dead. He was not dead, however; and he rejoined Barnabas and the others in Lystra and then went to Derbe with Barnabas. After preaching there they visited the converts they had previously made in the cities of southern Galatia before going to still other cities. Finally they returned to Antioch, where a controversy arose when some Jewish Christians from Judea came insisting that unless Gentile converts were circumcised they could not σωθῆναι ("be saved")!

Paul and Barnabas argued against these people, so that the matter was taken to Jerusalem for discussion and a decision. This turn in the narrative emphasizes the interest of all parties in maintaining the unity of the church. In Jerusalem there was much debate and very different opinions emerged. In the process of the deliberation Luke reports a speech made by Peter. The address is, as the narrative suggests, *deliberative* rhetoric, wherein the argument advances through narration that is empirical and pragmatic.

Through observing the parataxis of vv. 7b–9 and the rhetorical elements of vv. 10–11 one may outline the speech in this way:

1.0 The Community's Knowledge of God's Work (vv. 7b–9)
    1.1 Address with Reference to Awareness (v. 7b)
    1.2 God's Choice (v. 7b)
    1.3 God's Testimony (v. 8)
    1.4 God's Nondiscrimination (v. 9)
2.0 Rhetorical Objection (v. 10)
3.0 Statement of Belief (v. 11)

Analysis. (1.0) In the line leading to the address by Peter one learns that ἀναστάς ("rising") Peter spoke to the assembly. Thus, he does what speakers often do in Acts (see the introduction to 1:16–22, 24–25). (1.1) Having arisen, Peter addressed the group with the familiar salutation ἄνδρες ἀδελφοί ("Men, brothers"; see 1:16). Then he proceeds to remind them of what they already know (ὑμεῖς ἐπίστασθε ὅτι, "you know that"). From this start, the speech continues in vv. 7b–9 to speak about God, the subject of all the verbs in these verses. By now the reader of Acts is aware that the focus on God is an established convention of the speeches.

(1.2) Verse 7b recalls that God ἐξελέξατο ("chose") Peter among the Jewish Christians to preach to the Gentiles. The verb ἐκλέγεσθαι ("to choose") is used in speeches to refer to God's act of divine decision in relation to God's own purposes (see 1:24c–25). The statement made here recalls the Cornelius episode in a general way. The reference to the message that Peter spoke to the Gentiles, τὸν λόγον τοῦ εὐαγγελίου ("the message of the good news"), is remarkable. The use of λόγος ("word") to designate the Christian message is a recurring feature of speeches (see the discussion at 5:32), but the modification of λόγος with τοῦ εὐαγγελίου ("of the good news") is unusual. The word εὐαγγέλιον ("good news") occurs in Acts only here and in a portion of Paul's speech in 20:24.[237]

(1.3) The recollection of God's bearing testimony to the Gentiles refers to the events of 10:44–47.[238] This single line contains several noticeable elements. First, the reference to God, ὁ καρδιογνώστης θεός ("God who knows the heart"), employs the word καρδιογνώστης ("knower of hearts"), which appeared earlier in the prayer-ascription of the community in 1:24b. Second, the verb ἐμαρτύρησεν ("testified"), which refers to God's activity, sounds the familiar witness theme (see 1:8) and is one of the uses of μαρτυρεῖν ("to bear witness") in speech (see 6:3); more specifically, μαρτυρεῖν with the personal dative occurs in 10:43; 13:22; 15:8; 22:5.[239] Third, the statement that God gave the Holy Spirit to the Gentiles recognizes God's authority and activity in relation to events. Fourth, the mention of the Holy Spirit in this speech is one of several references to the Spirit in speeches (see 1:16b–17). Fifth, the Holy Spirit is cited as evidence of a claim or conclusion repeatedly in speeches (see 2:32–33). Sixth, the phrase καθὼς καὶ ἡμῖν ("exactly as to us") is similar to ὡς καὶ ἡμῖν ("as also to us") in 10:47 and 11:17 and ὥσπερ καὶ ἐφ᾿ ἡμᾶς ("just as upon us") of 11:15,[240] and it recognizes the universal character of the gospel.

(1.4) The third statement about the determinative work of God is a blunt declaration that God does not distinguish between Jews and Gentiles. Thus, the universalistic tones of previous speech statements are replayed (see 2:17).

237. Schneider, *Apostelgeschichte*, 2:179; Bruce, *Acts*, 336.
238. Haenchen, *Acts*, 445.
239. Schneider, *Apostelgeschichte*, 2:180.
240. Pesch, *Apostelgeschichte*, 2:77.

Here οὐθὲν διέκρινεν ("he has made no distinction") echoes μηδὲν διακρίναντα ("not to make a distinction") in 11:12.[241] In turn, πίστις ("faith") as an absolute reference to the means of God's work is unique in the speeches, although similar uses of πίστις occur in the narrative in 6:5, 7; 11:24; 13:8; 14:22, 27; 16:5. Moreover, earlier, in 11:8–9, one heard Peter's statement about God's cleansing foods (θεὸς χαθάρισεν), and here the activity of God in cleansing human hearts (θεὸς . . . χαθαρίσας) identifies a similar divine activity; so that one perceives that true purification is the work of God.

(2.0) Verse 10 poses a rhetorical question, which functions to object to the desire of some to require the Gentile Christians to become law-observant. One recognizes a new moment in the speech with the opening νῦν ("now"), which is similar to the rhetorical devices χαὶ νῦν ("and now") and χαὶ τὰ νῦν ("and now"), which are used in speeches to refer to major moments (see 3:17). In turn, the focus of Peter's comments on οἱ πατέρες ἡμῶν ("our fathers") repeats a frequent element of other speeches (see 7:11). Finally, this seemingly negative statement about the law echoes 13:38–39.[242]

(3.0) The final line of the speech contains both unique and familiar elements. The phrase διὰ τῆς χάριτος τοῦ χυρίου 'Ιησοῦ ("through the grace of the Lord Jesus") is unparalleled, although the notion of the lordship of Jesus appears elsewhere in the speeches (see 2:36). The following phrase πιστεύομεν σωθῆναι ("we believe that we will be saved") has a Pauline ring, but the notion of "being saved" (passive form in recognition of God's ultimate authority and work) occurs elsewhere (see the discussion at 2:40b; and see the examination of σώζειν, "to save") in speeches (4:12). Finally, χαθ' ὃν τρόπον χἀχεῖνοι ("exactly as they will") echoes v. 9 and its parallels.[243]

James's Speech at the Jerusalem Gathering (15:13b–21)

As Luke continues to tell of the deliberations in the Jerusalem assembly he emphasizes the solemnity of the proceedings with the report 'Εσίγησεν δὲ πᾶν τὸ πλῆθος ("the whole assembly kept silence"), and then he recounts that Barnabas and Paul related how God had done σημεῖα χαὶ τέρατα ("signs and wonders") among the Gentiles through their ministry. Thus, Barnabas and Paul spoke in support of Peter's argument. When they concluded their report, James spoke.

The speech is further *deliberative* rhetoric, now proposing specific actions. Kennedy notes the peculiarity of the address, observing that it gives no reason for the four requirements it suggests for the Gentiles. Although "verse 21

241. Schneider, *Apostelgeschichte*, 2:180.
242. Conzelmann, *Acts*, 117.
243. Bruce, *Acts*, 337.

ostensibly gives [James's] reason . . . in fact it is not a reason why these four
requirements are the essential ones, nor does that appear from the prophecy
cited (16–18)."[244]

The speech advances in three movements, which appear as follows in
outline:

1.0 The Evidence of God's Work and Will (vv. 13b–18)
    1.1 Address with Appeal for a Hearing (v. 13b)
    1.2 Recalling Simeon's Report (v. 14)
    1.3 The Words of the Prophets (vv. 15–18)
2.0 James's Judgment (vv. 19–20)
    2.1 Not to Trouble the Gentile Converts (v. 19)
    2.2 Publishing a Statement on Restraint (v. 20)
3.0 James's Reasoning (v. 21)

Analysis. (1.1) James's speech opens with a salutation that occurs in several
other addresses, ἄνδρες ἀδελφοί ("Men, brothers"; see 1:16); and the appeal
that follows, ἀκούσατέ μου ("listen to me"), is but a slight variation of another
familiar feature of the speeches (see 2:22). From this start the speech immediately offers information that is understood to indicate God's own will concerning the matters under discussion.

(1.2) Verse 14 mentions Peter's report in the previous speech, and through
reference to it the speech recalls the entire Cornelius episode (10:1–11:18).
The assumption of this statement is that the audience has been informed about
God's activity. Several items in this reminiscence of God's action are striking.
First, the temporal qualification πρῶτον ("first") echoes a similar specifica-
tion in Peter's speech in 15:7, ἀφ᾽ ἡμερῶν ἀρχαίων ("in the early days"). Second,
the use of ἐπεσκέψατο ("visited" [NRSV: "looked favorably upon"]) in speaking
of God's "visiting" the Gentiles indicates an act of deliberate identification
that was noted at 6:3 and subsequently repeated in relation to Moses' visiting
the Israelites as God's deliverer (7:23). Bruce points out that examination of
the verb in the larger context of Luke-Acts shows that it is used of providential
visitation.[245] Moreover, in this verb Conzelmann finds an echo of ἐξελέξατο
("he chose") in Peter's speech in 15:7.[246] Third, the coupling of ἐπεσκέψατο
("he visited") and λαβεῖν ("to take") dramatizes the divine action being reported
and adds emphasis to God's action in relation to the Gentiles.[247] Fourth, the

244. Kennedy, *Interpretation*, 126.
245. Bruce, *Acts*, 339.
246. Conzelmann, *Acts*, 117.
247. N. A. Dahl, "'A People for his Name' (Acts xv.14)," *NTS* 4 (1957–58) 319–27, esp. 326–27.
More recently J. Dupont has shown the crucial role 15:14 plays in the bold sounding of a theology
of divine election ("Un peuple d'entre les nations [Actes 15.14]," *NTS* 31 [1985] 321–35).

phrase ἐξ ἐθνῶν λαὸν τῷ ὀνόματι αὐτοῦ ("but of the Gentiles a people for his name") anticipates the Old Testament citation in vv. 16b–17, which speaks of "the Gentiles who are called by my name."

(1.3) Verses 15–18 offer a pastiche of prophetic lines as further evidence of God's will in relation to Gentiles. In form, this citation is most like the similar mixture in 13:22, and the manner in which the prophets remain unnamed recalls the same manner of reference to citations in the speeches (see 13:40), as does the use of καθὼς γέγραπται ("as it is written"; see 1:20). In turn, the use of οἱ λόγοι ("the words") to designate the prophets' message reflects the tendency in speeches to use λόγος ("word") as a term for a divinely inspired declaration. The quotation per se is complex. Verse 16a comes from Jer 12:15 LXX. The focus is on a determinative act of God. Then, vv. 16b–17 cite an altered version of Amos 9:11–12 LXX. Here the mention of David echoes other speech statements (see 1:16b–17). The idea implicit in the phrase ὅπως ἂν ἐκζητήσωσιν οἱ κατάλοιποι τῶν ἀνθρώπων τὸν κύριον ("so that all other people may seek the Lord") assumes that as a result of the activity of God human beings are capable of seeking (and finding) the Lord (compare 14:17; 17:27). Verse 17 also sounds the theme of the "name of the Lord," though here the Gentiles are called by the Lord's name rather than that they are to call on the name of the Lord (see 2:38). Finally, v. 18 picks up a phrase from Isa 45:21 LXX. In conjunction with the final phrase of v. 17, λέγει κύριος ποιῶν ταῦτα γνωστὰ ἀπ᾽ αἰῶνος ("says the Lord, who has been making these things known from long ago"), this line forms a strong statement about God's active role in revealing divine purposes. Conzelmann finds still a further echo of ἀφ᾽ ἡμερῶν ἀρχαίων ("in the early days") from 15:7 in the words ἀπ᾽ αἰῶνος ("from long ago"),[248] and Bruce suggests a possible relationship between ἀπ᾽ αἰῶνος and διὰ στόματος τῶν ἁγίων ἀπ᾽ αἰῶνος αὐτοῦ προφητῶν ("long ago through the mouth of his holy prophets") at 3:21.[249]

(2.0) The speech moves from recalling evidence to recommending what James thinks most appropriate for the Gentiles in light of the evidence examined. Krodel observes that the positive (v. 19)–negative (v. 20) sequence of statements in this report of James's judgment is comparable to the sequence of Peter's conclusions in 15:10–11.[250] (2.1) Verse 19 suggests that Gentile converts should not be troubled by the Jewish Christians. The restriction of James's conclusion τοῖς ἀπὸ τῶν ἐθνῶν ἐπιστρέφουσιν ἐπὶ τὸν θεόν ("those Gentiles who are turning to God") is consistent with the later statement by James and the Jerusalem elders in 21:25. The verb ἐπιστρέφουσιν ("they turn to") sounds the language of repentance (see 2:38) and the idea ἐπιστρέφουσιν ἐπὶ τὸν θεόν ("they are turning to God") resounds the stated goal of Christian proclamation in 14:15 and will repeat in 26:20.[251] (2.2) The four recommendations[252] delineated in v. 20 recur with slight variation in 21:25.[253] The condemnation of idolatry implicit in the proscription against eating meats offered to idols[254] anticipates Paul's proclamation in 17:24–27.

(3.0) The final verse of the speech, v. 21, is an interpretive riddle.[255] The lack of a clear correlation between this verse and the rest of the speech makes the reference to Moses all the more striking, for now Peter, Stephen, Paul, and James have all spoken of Moses in one or more of their addresses (see 7:20).

Paul's Speech in the Middle of the Areopagus (17:22–31)

Luke informs the reader that the Jerusalem assembly ratified James's proposal and sent a letter to Antioch by representatives of the Jerusalem congregation along with Paul and Barnabas. The church in Antioch received the letter gladly, and Paul and Barnabas remained there working among that congregation. Later Barnabas and Paul parted ways with Paul taking on Silas as an associate for work in Syria and Cilicia. Subsequently Timothy joined them, and they went through Phrygia and Galatia but not into Asia. Through a nocturnal vision Paul understood the group to be called to Macedonia. One reads of their work in Philippi, Thessalonica, and Beroea, where they both enjoyed successes and experienced steady opposition. Eventually because of hostility in Beroea, Luke reports that Paul went alone to Athens (leaving the province of Macedonia and going into Achaia), and from there he called for Silas and Timothy to join him.

Acts 17:16–21 sets the stage for Paul's well-known Areopagus address. The reader learns that in Athens Paul's spirit παρωξύνετο . . . ἐν αὐτῷ θεωροῦντος κατείδωλον οὖσαν τὴν πόλιν ("was deeply distressed . . . [in him] to see that the city was full of idols"), so that he argued in the synagogue and the marketplace with those he encountered. A controversy arose when some Epicureans and

---

251. Schneider, *Apostelgeschichte*, 2:183 n. 86.

252. On the purpose of these four enigmatic items, see C. Perrot, who contends that the stipulations aim at a kind of secondary assimilation of Gentile Christians to Christian Israel ("Les Décisions de l'Assemblée de Jerusalem," *RSR* 69 [1981] 195–208).

253. See the extensive discussion of this verse by Bruce (*Acts*, 342–43).

254. The exact meaning of τῶν ἀλισγημάτων τῶν εἰδώλων becomes clear through the parallel use of εἰδωλόθυτον in 21:25.

255. Commentators make various attempts to relate v. 21 to vv. 15–20, vv. 15–18; vv. 16–17; vv. 19–20; v. 19; and v. 20. Haenchen makes a cogent case for understanding the line only in relation to v. 20, not the earlier verses, especially not the Old Testament materials (*Acts*, 450 n. 1). Nevertheless, D. R. Schwartz would understand James (!) to articulate Luke's own understanding that it is useless to try to require law observance of Gentiles in the Christian community since the Jews have not succeeded previously in such an effort ("The Futility of Preaching Moses [Acts 15,21]," *Bib* 67 [1986] 276–81).

Stoics heard Paul preaching τὸν Ἰησοῦν καὶ τὴν ἀνάστασιν ("Jesus and the resurrection"). The conclusion of some hearers was that Paul ξένων δαιμονίων δοκεῖ καταγγελεὺς εἶναι ("seems to be a proclaimer of foreign divinities"). (One should recall that Socrates was tried and sentenced to death for similar charges![256]) Therefore, the philosophers brought Paul to the Areopagus and demanded that he explain his new teaching; and so, Paul spoke.

The situation was *judicial*, as is the majority of the rhetoric of the speech; but Paul's purpose was ultimately *deliberative*, so there are tinges of suitable rhetoric.[257] The speech presents two broad movements,[258] which may be outlined as follows:

1.0 Paul's Refutation of the Philosophers' Charge (vv. 22b–28)
    1.1 Address (v. 22b)
    1.2 Paul's Observations (vv. 22b–23a)
    1.3 Paul's Declarations (vv. 23b–28)
        1.3.1 Statement of Purpose (v. 23b)
        1.3.2 God the Creator (v. 24a)
        1.3.3 God the Independent Lord (vv. 24b–25a)
        1.3.4 God the Source of All (v. 25b)
        1.3.5 God and Humanity (vv. 26–27)
        1.3.6 Poetic Perceptions (v. 28)[259]
2.0 Paul's Pressing of Charges (vv. 29–31)
    2.1 Identification of Faulty Logic (v. 29)
    2.2 Contrasting Times (v. 30)
    2.3 The Surety of Divine Judgment (v. 31)
        2.3.1 The Day of Appointed Judgment (v. 31a)
        2.3.2 The Evidence (v. 31b)

Analysis. In 17:20a Luke describes Paul's physical positioning prior to the outset of the speech. First, Paul is σταθείς ("standing"), the recognizable posture of a Greek orator (see 2:14); and he is located ἐν μέσῳ ("in the middle") of the Areopagus (see the introduction to 1:16–22, 24–25). Thus placed, he speaks.

(1.1) The speech opens with the address ἄνδρες Ἀθηναῖοι ("Men, Athenians"), so that once again a speaker couples ἄνδρες ("men") with a local or ethnic

256. Haenchen, *Acts*, 527.

257. Kennedy, *Interpretation*, 129–31.

258. J. Dupont divides the speech into three parts: vv. 22b–23, 24–29, 30–31 ("Le discours à l'Aréopage [Ac 17,22–31] lieu de rencontre entre christianisme et hellénisme," *Bib* 60 [1979] 530–46). He contends that the structure serves the argument of the speech against idolatry. In support of the scheme identified by Dupont, see D. Zweck, "The *Exordium* of the Areopagus Speech, Acts 17.22, 23," *NTS* 35 (1989) 94–103.

259. On the "poetic" dimension of this speech and the perspective it propagates, see J. Calloud, "Paul devant l'Aréopage d'Athènes: Actes 17,16–34," *RSR* 69 (1981) 209–48, esp. 235–48.

designation to salute the hearers (see 1:11). (1.2) Paul reports his observations and perceptions, finally referring to the altar inscription Ἀγνώστῳ θεῷ ("to an unknown God"). This reference becomes the basis of a motif that is replayed through the speech, first in v. 23b when Paul builds on the idea of "unknown" to declare his intentions, ὃ οὖν ἀγνοοῦντες εὐσεβεῖτε, τοῦτο ἐγὼ καταγγέλλω ὑμῖν ("what therefore you worship as unknown, this I proclaim to you"); and then in v. 30 when Paul refers to τοὺς . . . χρόνους τῆς ἀγνοίας ("the times of ignorance").[260]

(1.3.1) Paul's declaration of intentions leads to a series of statements about God, about both God's character (vv. 24–25) and God's dealings with humanity (vv. 26–27) — strongly indicating God's authority. Interpreters routinely suggest that the thought and language of Isa 42:5 LXX lie behind vv. 24–25.[261]

(1.3.2) Paul's speech presents to the Athenians the idea of God as Creator (v. 24a). This image of God has appeared in earlier speeches (see 4:24), and indeed in the parallel passages ὁ ποιήσας ("the one making") occurs in 4:24 and ὃς ἐποίησεν ("who made") in 14:15. In this particular context the statement may reflect Isaiah. (1.3.3) Verses 24b–25a inform the audience that God is the Lord of the created order and is not capable of being domesticated by humans. The phrase οὐκ ἐν χειροποιήτοις ναοῖς κατοικεῖ ("does not live in shrines made by hands") resounds the declaration from Stephen's speech (see 7:48) that οὐχ ὁ ὕψιστος ἐν χειροποιήτοις κατοικεῖ ("the Most High does not dwell in houses made with hands"). Moreover, the declaration that God is Lord echoes the statement of Peter in 10:36. (1.3.4) In turn, v. 25b speaks of how God gives life, breath, and everything else, so that one hears echoes of Paul's declaration at Lystra concerning God's generosity, οὐρανόθεν ὑμῖν ὑετοὺς διδοὺς καὶ καιροὺς καρποφόρους, ἐμπιπλῶν τροφῆς καὶ εὐφροσύνης τὰς καρδίας ὑμῶν, "giving you rains from heaven and fruitful seasons, and filling you with food and your hearts with joy" (14:17b–c). Again, here, the statement may reflect Isaiah.

(1.3.5) The focus shifts slightly from God's character to the manner in which God interacts with humanity in vv. 26–27. The idea that God determines the destiny of nations parallels the thought of 14:16 (see also 10:35[262]). The use of ὁρίζειν ("to allot" or "to determine") in v. 26 emphasizes God's authority and reflects the idea that God works with a plan (see 2:23), and the same verb recurs in this speech in v. 31. Furthermore, the mention of καιρούς ("times"

---

260. On 17:22b–23 Pesch remarks, "Daß er Jes 45,15 im Blick hat, ist keinesfalls unwahrscheinlich" (Apostelgeschichte, 2:136).

261. E.g., Haenchen, Acts, 522; Conzelmann, Acts, 141–42; Bruce, Acts, 382; and Schneider, Apostelgeschichte, 2:239. Compare:

Acts: ὁ θεὸς ὁ ποιήσας τὸν κόσμον καὶ πάντα τὰ ἐν αὐτῷ . . . ὑπάρχων κύριος . . . διδοὺς πᾶσι ζωὴν καὶ πνοήν. . . .

Isaiah: κύριος ὁ θεὸς ὁ ποιήσας τὸν οὐρανὸν καὶ πήξας αὐτόν . . . διδοὺς πνοήν. . . .

262. Bruce, Acts, 383.

or "seasons") echoes the language and thought of 14:17.[263] In addition, Schubert observes the similarity between the idea expressed in v. 26 and the lengthy treatments of God's dealings with Israel in its history in 7:2–53 and 13:16–25.[264] Moreover, those analyzing this passage often see in v. 26 an allusion to Deut 32:8 LXX.[265] Indeed, this statement also recalls Paul's words in 14:16–17, which imply that humans could seek and find God, as is also the case with James's remarks in 15:16b–17.[266] And finally, the idea that God is near to every human echoes Peter's statement in 10:35, so that, in general, this verse resounds the theme of God's not being without a witness in the past (see 7:44).

(1.3.6) Verse 28 takes a new direction with its citation of ὡς καί τινες τῶν καθ' ὑμᾶς ποιητῶν ("as even some of your own poets").[267] K. Lake and H. J. Cadbury explain the anonymous citation of the poets saying, "The omission of the name or names of the writers quoted is not really strange. The anonymous citation of authors was common in classical and Hellenistic writers. . . ."[268] Yet in this use of the past there is a more immediate parallel in Acts itself, for in the speeches of Stephen, Paul at Pisidian Antioch, and James before the Jerusalem assembly there are references to unnamed prophets who are subsequently quoted in the speeches.[269]

(2.0) Paul's response to the charges that he is proclaiming strange or foreign gods is complete after v. 28, and now rather than being defensive he goes

---

263. Against B. Gärtner (*The Areopagus Speech and Natural Revelation* [ASNU 21; Lund: C. W. K. Gleerup, 1955] 147–50) and with W. Eltester ("Gott und die Natur in der Areopagrede," in *Neutestamentliche Studien für Rudolf Bultmann* [2d ed.; BZNW 21; Berlin: A. Töpelmann, 1957] 202–27), who concludes, "Die Areopagrede steht als erstes Zeugnis am Anfang einer . . . Verbindung biblischen Schöpfungsglaubens und griechischer Weltfrömmigkeit im Bereich des Christentums. Daß sie ihm durch das hellenistische Diasporajudentum vermittelt worden ist, kann nach den beigebrachten Zeugnissen keine Frage mehr sein" (p. 226). See esp. pp. 206–9, where Eltester shows that "die προστεταγμένοι καιροί von Act 17.26 eine volle Parallele zu 14.17 darstellen."

264. Schubert, "Place," 255–56.

265. This recognition seems to have originated with E. Norden (*Agnostos Theos: Untersuchung zur Formengeschichte religiöser Rede* [2d ed.; Leipzig/Berlin: Teubner, 1929] 8).

266. Similarly, Schubert, "Place," 256.

267. Against the normal scholarly identifications of this reference, R. Renehan argues that Luke composed the line "in him we live and move and have our being" ("Acts 17.28," *GRBS* 20 [1979] 347–53). If this is the case one would find in this line a key for reconstructing a picture of Luke's own theology, which would appear different from that which scholars more often develop. Yet simply calling this anonymous quotation into question is not sufficient to undo the history of scholarship that has viewed this as an actual quote from Greek literature. Compare Bruce, *Acts,* 384–85.

268. K. Lake and H. J. Cadbury, *Beginnings,* 4:218. See further K. Lake, "Note XX. 'Your own Poets,'" in *Beginnings,* 5:246–51.

269. Nevertheless, the quotations in v. 28 seem to come from Epimenides (v. 28a) and Aratus's *Phaenomena* 5 (v. 28c).

on the offensive in the remainder of the speech. These three verses take up a broad range of topics.

(2.1) Verse 29 exposes the faulty logic that has led to constructing elaborate religious edifices and paying homage to mere material objects. Haenchen notes that this attack on "pagan image worship" makes intelligible the accusations of Demetrius against Paul in 19:26.[270] Moreover, the condemnation of idolatry forms an implicit parallel to the denunciation of eating meat offered to idols in 15:2; 21:25.

(2.2) The following statement in v. 30 contrasts two times, τοὺς χρόνους τῆς ἀγνοίας ("the times of ignorance") and the time μετανοεῖν ("to repent"). The statement about God's overlooking the times of ignorance recalls the theme of ignorance per se which is registered in other speeches (see 3:17).[271] Then the temporal phrase τὰ νῦν ("now") dramatizes the change of the times according to the work and will of God (see 3:17). Moreover, the mention of the need to repent sounds an important theme of many speeches (see 2:38), and the call to repentance itself is an implicit recognition of the guilt of the hearers (see 2:36). Finally, the phrase τοῖς ἀνθρώποις πάντας πανταχοῦ ("to all people everywhere") emphasizes the universal character of salvation and the Christian message noticed since the earliest speeches (see 1:8 and 2:17).[272]

(2.3) The final verse of the speech refers to the certainty of eschatological judgment. (2.3.1) Several striking items appear in v. 31a. First, Jesus is referred to as "a man" (ἐν ἀνδρί, "by a man") by whom God will execute judgment. This manner of reference repeats 2:22. Second, the use of ὁρίζειν ("to fix" or "to determine") repeats v. 26 and emphasizes God's authority and even alludes to God's "plan" (see 2:23). Third, the entire statement resembles 10:42, where Jesus was declared to be the future judge of the living and the dead, and there one found the striking participial phrase ὡρισμένος ὑπὸ τοῦ θεοῦ ("the one ordained by God"). Fourth, this comment echoes references in the speeches to a day of future judgment at 2:20; 3:19–20; 10:42;[273] and the same issue appears in the narrative in 24:25. (2.3.2) Verse 31b gives the divine evidence for the foregoing remarks. This statement assumes the resurrection *and* exaltation of Jesus (see 1:11). The explicit reference to the resurrection employs ἀνιστάναι ("to raise"; see 1:22b) and brings the notion of resurrection

270. Haenchen, *Acts*, 525.

271. T. L. Wilkinson suggests the pagans are portrayed in this speech as being *guilty* in their ignorance ("Acts 17: The Gospel Related to Paganism: Contemporary Relevance," *Vox Reformata* 35 [1980] 13–14). Similarly, H. Külling finds the Athenians' ignorance to be their distance from God, that is, their sinfulness ("Zur Bedeutung des Agnostos Theos: Eine Exegese zu Apostelgeschichte 17,22.23, *TZ* 36 [1980] 65–83). And K. Plötz shows how the speech works up to a subtle denunciation of the Athenians' idolatry ("Die Areopagusrede des Apostels Paulus: Eine Beispiel urkirchlicher Verkündigung," *Internationale Katholische Zeitschrift/Communio* 17 [1988] 111–17).

272. Similarly, Krodel, *Acts*, 338.

273. Schubert, "Place," 258.

into close proximity with the idea of judgment (compare 10:41–42). This declaration registers the second half of the familiar christological contrast scheme (see 2:23–24), which often follows the mention or implication of an audience's guilt.[274]

Finally, the end of the speech and the notice of the reaction of the hearers seem abrupt, so that the speech may be understood to have been broken into by the audience (see 2:36/37). Yet, as Haenchen remarks, "There is no hint that Paul is interrupted. . . ."[275]

Paul's Speech to the Corinthian Jews (18:6b–d)

There was a mixed reaction to Paul's proclamation of the resurrection in the middle of the Areopagus. Some converts were made, and Luke tells the reader that Paul stayed in Athens for some further time, although one cannot determine how long from the narrative. When Paul left Athens he went to Corinth, where he met Aquila and Priscilla, apparently Jewish Christians, who were also tentmakers. Paul lived and worked with this couple, and he was active in the synagogue seeking to convert Jews and Gentile God-fearers.

Eventually certain Jews stringently opposed Paul, and Luke records Paul's parting remarks to them. This short speech is essentially *epideictic* rhetoric, though there is a degree of *judicial* rhetoric as well in Paul's self-defense. The speech has three parts:

1.0 Denunciation of Opponents (v. 6b)
2.0 Declaration of Innocence (v. 6c)
3.0 Statement of Intention (v. 6d)

Analysis. In form and content this statement is comparable to 13:46–47 and 28:25b–28. Paul's shaking out τὰ ἱμάτια ("his clothes") resembles his and Barnabas's shaking the dust off their feet in protest in 13:51. Conzelmann observes that the situation and the speech fit the established pattern "to the Jews first" (see 13:46).[276]

(1.0) The overt denunciation of Jewish opponents who refuse to hear the Christian message occurs in speeches in 13:46; 18:6; 28:25b–27. The specific denunciation τὸ αἷμα ὑμῶν ἐπὶ τὴν κεφαλὴν ὑμῶν ("your blood be on your own

274. Regarding vv. 30–31, M. Dibelius observes, "In these two verses . . . past, present and future appear in close connection. . . . These concluding words consist of one sentence, the *only Christian* sentence in the Areopagus speech" ("Paul on the Areopagus," in *Studies in the Acts of the Apostles* [New York: Charles Scribner's Sons, 1956]).

275. Haenchen, *Acts*, 526.

276. Conzelmann, *Acts*, 152.

heads") is an idiom from 2 Sam 1:16 LXX, and it resembles the words of the members of the council in 5:28 when they charged the apostles with attempting to make them responsible for Jesus' death. Moreover, in 20:26 Paul informs the Ephesian elders that he is καθαρός . . . ἀπὸ τοῦ αἵματος πάντων ("innocent . . . of the blood of all") because he declared to them the plan of God. Thus, the denunciation of the Corinthian Jews seems related to their opposition to God's plan, not simply their resistance to Paul.

(2.0) The simple declaration of Paul's innocence, καθαρὸς ἐγώ ("I am innocent"), especially in close proximity to the blood metaphor, immediately reminds one of 20:26. Paul declares his innocence elsewhere in speech in 25:8, 10.

(3.0) Paul next declares his future intentions to those whom he has denounced. The speech emphasizes the dramatic moment of change with the phrase ἀπὸ τοῦ νῦν ("from now on"), which is comparable to other statements recognizing a crucial moment with the word νῦν ("now") alone or in a temporal phrase (see 3:17). Finally, Paul's intention (εἰς τὰ ἔθνη πορεύσομαι, "I will go to the Gentiles") echoes 13:46 and anticipates 28:28, and comparable statements come as reports of Paul's activity in speeches in 22:21; 26:17–18. The statement recognizes the universal relevance of the gospel.

Gallio's Speech to the Corinthian Jews (18:14b–15)

Paul left the synagogue in Corinth to continue his preaching at the house of Titius Justus, a God-fearing Gentile. One learns that despite the opposition Paul had success among the Jews, and through a subsequent nocturnal vision he was directed to continue working in Corinth, which he did for eighteen months. Eventually the Jewish resistance brought charges against Paul before Gallio the proconsul of Achaia. The aim of the charge was to have Paul convicted of propagating an illicit religion.[277]

Hearing the charge, Gallio thwarted Paul's effort at self-defense by refusing to judge the case. Luke records his brief speech to those who attempted to prosecute Paul. The setting is *judicial*, as is the rhetoric, although Gallio's remarks are more an explanation than an effort to persuade. The speech is a complex compound statement juxtaposing a contrary-to-fact condition with a condition of reality and then declaring Gallio's conclusion. In outline the speech appears as follows:

1.0 Explanation of Conditions Meriting Judgment with Address (v. 14b)

2.0 Description of Circumstance with Advice (v. 15a–b)

3.0 Statement of Gallio's Position (v. 15c)

277. On this point, however, see Conzelmann, *Acts*, 153–54.

Analysis. Paul's attempt ἀνοίγειν τὸ στόμα ("to open his mouth") almost puts him in a position similar to statements in 8:35a and 10:34a that lead toward speech, but Gallio speaks instead.

(1.0) The use of ἀδίκημα ("crime") identifies a topic that recurs in Paul's speech before Felix in 24:20. The address ὦ 'Ιουδαῖοι ("O Jews") is unique, though appropriate for the circumstances, so that one finds the act of addressing repeated, if not a specific salutation.

(2.0) Gallio's description of the actual circumstances employs words that are noteworthy. First, the use of λόγος ("word") in v. 15 may refer indirectly to the Christian message,[278] since it was for his preaching that the Corinthian Jews attempted to prosecute Paul. Second, Gallio's recognition of the Jewish law as the point of conflict parallels elements of other speeches (see 7:53).

(3.0) The simple refusal to hear the case is unique, although later the Ephesian town clerk disbands a crowd that brought accusations against the Christians in Ephesus (19:35b–40).

Demetrius's Speech (19:25b–27)

After Gallio dismissed the case against Paul, Luke informs the reader that Paul stayed some time before departing from Corinth with Priscilla and Aquila for Syria. They went to Ephesus, where Paul went into the synagogue with his message. Despite an invitation to remain, he left Ephesus and sailed to Caesarea. From there he went to Jerusalem and greeted the church, and then he went on to Antioch. Subsequently he went through Galatia and Phrygia to visit the converts.[279]

Luke shifts the focus from Paul back to Ephesus with an account of Apollos's arrival in that city and his learning the details of the gospel from Priscilla and Aquila. In turn, Apollos went to Achaia, where he proclaimed the message and debated with Jewish opponents. Although Luke refers to Apollos's eloquence, accuracy, boldness, and effectiveness as a speaker, the reader finds no speech from him. Rather, Luke returns to Ephesus, where Paul now arrives. One reads of Paul's encounter with an enigmatic group of "disciples," who in conversation with Paul come to believe, undergo Christian baptism, and receive the Holy Spirit as Paul laid hands on them, so that they spoke in tongues. Next Luke tells that Paul labored in the synagogue for three months before withdrawing to work in the hall of Tyrannus for two more years. One

---

278. Haenchen, *Acts*, 536.

279. There are notorious difficulties in attempting to correlate this travel (and other travel!) of Paul in Acts with Paul's own reports of his journeys, especially the trips to Jerusalem. On this portion of Paul's travels, see A. Suhl, *Paulus und seine Briefe: Ein Beitrag zur paulinischen Chronologie* (Gütersloh: G. Mohn, 1975) esp. 129–40.

also learns of the great works that God did through Paul and how a group of Jewish exorcists, the seven sons of the chief priest Sceva, were undone as they tried merely to use the name of Jesus in exorcism.

The success of the Christian mission finally stirred up a silversmith named Demetrius, who expressed his concern over the threat posed to the silver trade by the conversion of the residents of Ephesus and Asia. Luke reports Demetrius's speech to the other silversmiths. The address is a combination of *epideictic* and *deliberative* rhetoric, although Demetrius narrates the problem without ever proposing a solution. The speech is essentially parataxis and may be outlined as follows:

1.0 Address with Reference to Awareness (v. 25b)
2.0 Recognizing Paul's Activity (v. 26)
3.0 Declaration of the Danger (v. 27)

Analysis. (1.0) Demetrius addresses the other silversmiths simply as ἄνδρες ("men"), the third of six instances of this greeting (see 14:15). His initial remarks appeal to the knowledge of his hearers in a manner similar to the beginning of Peter's speech in Cornelius's house (10:28), Peter's speech at the Jerusalem gathering (15:7), and Paul's forthcoming speech to the Ephesian elders (20:18). (2.0) Perhaps still appealing to the awareness of the audience, Demetrius's second statement recognizes Paul's activity and success in converting people from devotion to Artemis to Christian faith. The thought and the language of the statement, especially in reporting what Paul said (οὐκ εἰσὶν θεοὶ οἱ διὰ χειρῶν γινόμενοι, "gods made with hands are not gods"), echo statements in Paul's Areopagus speech in 17:24–25, 27; and one recalls similar words from Stephen (see 7:48). (3.0) The final topic of the speech expresses concern for the temple of Artemis. While Demetrius's statement is without exact parallel in the other speeches, the themes of "Temple" and "concern for the Temple" were elements behind and in Stephen's speech and they recur in 21:28.

The Speech of the Ephesian Town Clerk (19:35b–40)

Demetrius's speech produced a reaction that set off a chain of events. The silversmiths raised a cry that threw the city into an uproar, and the citizenry assembled in the theater. Some of the Ephesians apprehended Paul's companions and brought them before the crowd. Paul himself was prevented from going into the assembly by friends. When a Jew named Alexander attempted to speak, Luke reports that the confused crowd recognized he was a Jew and cried, "Great is Artemis of the Ephesians!" for two hours.

At last the town clerk managed to silence the throng, and he spoke to them.

The speech is *deliberative* rhetoric[280] in four basic movements, which in outline are as follows:

1.0 Address with Introductory Rhetorical Question (v. 35b)
2.0 Advice for the Assembly (v. 36)
3.0 Argument in Support of the Advice (vv. 37–39)
    3.1 Recognition of the Crowd's Inappropriate Action (v. 37)
    3.2 Description of Appropriate Action (v. 38)
    3.3 Declaration of the Referral of the Matter (v. 39)
4.0 Recognition of the Crowd's Perilous Standing (v. 40)

Analysis. The speech is an economical but polished deliberation. (1.0) It opens with the address ἄνδρες Ἐφέσιοι ("Men, Ephesians"), another salutation coupling ἄνδρες ("men") with a geographical or ethnic term (see 1:11). Following this greeting there is a rhetorical question that actually narrates the religious status enjoyed by Ephesus. (2.0) On the basis of the information supplied through the question, v. 36 advises the assembly to do nothing rash. Kennedy notes the similarity of this suggestion to that of Gamaliel to the Jewish Council in 5:35, 38–39.[281] In the statement of advice the important verb δεῖ ("it is necessary") occurs, although in the context of this speech there is no emphasis on the sense of divine necessity, merely a recognition of practical exigency. (3.1) The argument in support of the advice begins in v. 37 with a denial that the Christians are guilty of blasphemy, which is exactly opposite of the statements made regarding Stephen in Acts 6–8. (3.3) In the final remark, the rare verb ἐγκαλεῖν ("bring charges against") occurs; it appears in speeches in 19:38, 40; 23:28, 29; 26:2, 7.[282] The conclusions of the town clerk are similar to those of Gallio—namely, there is in fact no legal case against the Christians and the attempt to level charges is inappropriate.

Paul's Speech to the Ephesian Elders (20:18b–35)

When the near-riot in Ephesus was quelled, Paul assembled the disciples, and after exhorting them he left for Macedonia. Having encouraged the congregations in that province, Paul went to Greece (Achaia), where after three months Jewish opponents made plans against him, so that he altered his travel plans. Eventually Paul and various companions came to Troas, where the dramatic events involving young Eutychus transpired. Paul and some associates left Troas, traveling by different routes to Assos; and from there they sailed together to Miletus en route to Jerusalem.

280. Kennedy, *Interpretation*, 132.
281. Ibid.
282. Schneider, *Apostelgeschichte*, 2:278.

From Miletus Paul sent for the elders from Ephesus, and when they arrived he spoke to them. The "farewell address" is a special, recognizable form of *epideictic* rhetoric. Yet, as Kennedy observes, "Paul's discourse here does not accord with the rhetorical conventions described by Menander Rhetor,"[283] for even the use of the past in this address is subsumed to the major concern with the future.[284] From the general beginning, the repeated temporal clauses, and shifts in point-of-view, one may discern the following outline for the speech:

1.0 Paul's Recalling of His Asian Ministry (vv. 18b–21)
    1.1 Address with Reference to Awareness (v. 18b)
    1.2 Description of the Nature and Course of the Ministry (vv. 18c–21)
2.0 Words about the Future (vv. 22–27)
    2.1 Paul's Forthcoming Experiences (vv. 22–24)
        2.1.1 The Uncertainty of Jerusalem and the Testimony of the Spirit (vv. 22–23)
        2.1.2 Paul's True Concern (v. 24)
    2.2 Information for the Ephesian Elders (vv. 25–27)
        2.2.1 Revelatory Declaration (v. 25)
        2.2.2 Testimony (vv. 26–27)
3.0 Advice for the Elders (vv. 28–31)
    3.1 Admonition (v. 28)
    3.2 Future Peril (vv. 29–30)
    3.3 Exhortation (v. 31)
4.0 Concluding Blessing and Admonition (vv. 32–35)
    4.1 Benediction (v. 32)
    4.2 Recalling Paul's Labors (vv. 33–34)
    4.3 Paul's Example and Jesus' Proverb (v. 35)[285]

---

283. Kennedy, *Interpretation*, 132–33.

284. Bruce recognizes the particularity of this speech, arguing that it "has a different quality from all the other speeches in Acts, in style and content alike" (*Acts*, 429–30). As the present analysis shows, while this "farewell address" is somewhat distinct from the other speeches, Bruce's observation is an overstatement. Nevertheless, he is correct in identifying the hortatory character of the speech and its apologetic tone.

285. H. J. Michel (*Die Abschiedsrede des Paulus an die Kirche Apg 20,17–38: Motivegeschichte und theologische Bedeutung* [SANT 35; Munich: Kösel, 1973] 26–27) rejects the suggestion of C. Exum and C. Talbert ("The Structure of Paul's Speech to the Ephesian Elders [Acts 20,18–35]," *CBQ* 29 [1967] 233–36) that the speech is formed as a chiasm, and he argues that the speech presents two parallel parts: vv. 18–24 is a personal section in four subparts, paralleled by vv. 28–35, a parenetic section in four subunits; thus, vv. 25–27 are the "Kulminationspunkt" of the address. As is evident, I have adopted neither scheme, since both impose artificial symmetry on the material which misfocuses the reading of the speech. Dibelius divided the speech into four main parts: (1) vv. 18–21; (2) vv. 22–27; (3) vv. 28–31; and (4) vv. 32–34 ("Speeches," 157). Dibelius understood

Analysis.[286] Interpreters regularly compare this farewell address to that of Samuel in 1 Sam 12:1–25 LXX, especially vv. 18 and 33 with 1 Sam 12:2–3.[287] This form of speech was well established in both Gentile and Jewish literature of Luke's day.[288]

(1.1) The simple beginning ὑμεῖς ("you [yourselves]") recalls the way Peter initially spoke to the assembly in Cornelius's house, although in that context there was a lack of familiarity whereas here the lack of a formal address may suggest some intimacy. The immediate appeal to the knowledge or awareness of the listeners (ἐπίστασθε, "you know") occurs in 10:28; 15:7; 19:25; 20:18; and in this speech the same manner of appeal recurs in vv. 31 and 34. (1.2) From the reference to the knowledge of the audience the speech moves to recount aspects of Paul's ministry in Asia. Verse 19 makes clear that Paul worked in service τῷ κυρίῳ ("to the Lord"), so that the ultimacy of divine authority is recognized before more is said about Paul's work.[289] The statement in v. 20 about Paul's lack of hesitation in preaching focuses on a crucial activity, as one sees from the repetition of this comment in v. 27. In turn, v. 21 employs the verb διαμαρτύρεσθαι ("to bear witness" or "to testify"), which occurs twice more in this speech in vv. 23–24. This striking verb is part of the vocabulary of the speeches related to the "witness" theme (see 1:8); this verb is in Acts 2:40; 8:25; 10:42; 18:5; 20:21, 23–24; 23:11; 28:23.[290] Verse 21 makes explicit mention of Paul's proclamation of τὴν εἰς θεὸν μετάνοιαν ("repentance toward God"), and implicit in this statement is the recognition of the need to repent (see 2:38). Conzelmann regards v. 21 as a summary statement of the gospel message in Acts, pointing to similar summaries in 14:15; 26:18, 20.[291]

---

v. 35 to be a word of confirmation concerning the fourth part of the speech.

Still other proposals are possible. See F. Prast, *Presbyter und Evangelium in nachapostolischer Zeit: Die Abschiedsrede des Paulus in Milet (Apg 20,17–38) im Rahmen der lukanischen Konzeption der Evangeliumsverkündigung* (FB 29; Stuttgart: Katholisches Bibelwerk, 1979) 49–50.

286. The careful exegetical section in Prast's study (*Presbyter*, 50–156) is a gold mine of earlier interpreters' opinions. Though Prast's concern is broader than mine in the current analysis, his work was most helpful in checking my own observations and understanding of the text.

287. E.g., Conzelmann, *Acts*, 173, 176.

288. For a brief discussion of the literary genre of *testament* with references to a representative body of such writings in classical Greek literature; the Old Testament, canonical and apocryphal; the pseudepigrapha; and the New Testament, canonical and apocryphal, see M. L. Soards, *The Passion according to Luke: The Special Material of Luke 22* (JSNTSup 14; Sheffield: JSOT Press, 1987) 55, 143–44.

289. See F. Zeilinger, "Lukas, Anwalt des Paulus: Überlegungen zur Abschiedsrede von Milet Apg 20,18–35," *BLit* 54 (1981) 167–72.

290. E. Plümacher, *Lukas als hellenistischer Schriftsteller: Studien zur Apostelgeschichte* (SUNT 9; Göttingen: Vandenhoeck & Ruprecht, 1972) 48.

291. Conzelmann, *Acts*, 174.

(2.0) The speech turns from the past to the future in the following verses. (2.1.1) The words καὶ νῦν ("and now") signal a dramatic shift in Paul's speaking, a convention repeated two more times in this speech and several other times in speeches (see 3:17). Paul's comment concerning his uncertainty regarding the forthcoming visit to Jerusalem because of the certainty of the testimony of the Spirit pairs dramatically contrasting ideas, which together point to the superior role of the divine in divine–human relations. The reference to the Holy Spirit is a regular element of speeches (see 1:16b–17), as is the understanding of the Holy Spirit as evidence or a witness of God's intentions (see 2:32–33). (2.1.2) In v. 24 Paul's declaration of his lack of concern with himself because of his ultimate concern for the gospel contains three conspicuous items. First, one again encounters διαμαρτύρεσθαι ("to testify") in this speech; second, τὸ εὐαγγέλιον ("the good news") appears for the second of only two uses in Acts (see 15:7); and third, the recognition of God's authority inherent in the qualification of the gospel in terms of τῆς χάριτος τοῦ θεοῦ ("of God's grace") recurs in v. 32.

(2.2.1) Another striking turn comes in the speech with Paul's informing the Ephesian elders they will not see him again. The shift is again emphasized with the words καὶ νῦν ("and now"; see v. 21 and 3:17). Moreover, the phrase κηρύσσων τὴν βασιλείαν ("proclaiming the kingdom") in reference to Paul's proclamation occurs again in the last verse of Acts (28:31) in the narrative report of Paul's preaching in Rome. (2.2.2) From this combined revelation-recollection the speech delivers "testimony" in vv. 26–27. Here μαρτύρεσθαι ("to witness" [NRSV: "declare"]) sounds the theme of "witness" directly (see 1:8). The statement in v. 26 declaring Paul's "innocence" (καθαρός εἰμι, "I am innocent") makes further use of the blood metaphor (ἀπὸ τοῦ αἵματος πάντων, "of the blood of all") and recalls 5:28 and more so 18:6, where these ideas occurred together. Verse 27 refers explicitly to ἡ βουλὴ τοῦ θεοῦ ("the plan of God"; see the discussion of 1:7; see also 2:23), the phrase that above all others indicates God's authority and purposefulness along with the conviction that events occur because of divine necessity. Moreover, this striking statement both refers to Jesus' passion as the point of God's work of salvation and recognizes Jesus' theological identity.

(3.0) In the next portion of the speech, the Ephesian elders receive advice for their future ministry. (3.1) Paul's admonition προσέχετε ἑαυτοῖς ("keep watch over yourselves") repeats the words Gamaliel spoke to the members of the Jewish Council in 5:35b. In turn, the statement that the Holy Spirit gave the elders their charges recognizes divine initiative and authority in selection of church leadership (see 1:16–22, 24b–25; 6:2b–4).[292] The declaration that

---

292. G. Schneider focuses on this statement and argues strongly against the label "Früh-katholizismus," which is often used to depreciate Acts' view of church offices ("Die Entwicklung kirchlicher Dienste in der Sicht der Apostelgeschichte," *TPQ* 132 [1984] 356–63).

[θεός] . . . περιεποιήσατο . . . τὴν ἐκκλησίαν . . . διὰ τοῦ αἵματος τοῦ ἰδίου ("[God] . . . obtained . . . the church . . . through his own [Son's?] blood") is a unique statement in Acts,[293] but the idea that God is the author of salvation and the authority over the church is consistent with the assumptions and declaration of the other speeches.[294]

(3.3) Paul's exhortation to alertness in v. 31 contains the hyperbolic phrase νύκτα καὶ ἡμέραν ("night and day"), which occurs again in speech in 26:7 to emphasize the magnitude of an activity. Moreover, the words ἕνα ἕκαστον, "everyone" (elsewhere: εἷς ἕκαστος) appear in speeches in 17:27; 20:31 and emphasize the universal relevance of the gospel.

(4.0) The closing lines of the speech combine blessing and exhortation. (4.1) Again, the shift in the tone and focus comes with the temporal phrase καὶ τὰ νῦν ("and now"; see 3:17). The blessing comes through God's word of grace (τῷ λόγῳ τῆς χάριτος, "the message of his grace"; on λόγος, "word," for the Christian message, see 5:32); χάρις ("grace") repeats the language and thought of v. 24. Moreover, the reference to those experiencing salvation with the phrase ἐν τοῖς ἡγιασμένοις ("the ones who are sanctified") recurs in 26:18. (4.2) As the speech recalls Paul's labors, the striking word χρεία ("need") echoes the language of the apostles' speech to the Jerusalem community in 6:3.[295] (4.3) Verse 35 contains the important word δεῖ ("it is necessary"), probably indicating divine necessity (see 1:16). Finally, in 11:16 in Peter's speech to the circumcision party a similar phenomenon occurs with a reference to "the word of the Lord" and a quotation of the word—although in 11:16 one reads τοῦ ῥήματος τοῦ κυρίου ("the word of the Lord"), and here: τῶν λόγων τοῦ κυρίου Ἰησοῦ ("the words of the Lord Jesus").

Agabus's Speech in Caesarea (21:11b–c)

Paul and the Ephesian elders prayed together before their sad parting. Paul and his companions then sailed on to Tyre, where they remained for seven days in the company of other disciples who διὰ τοῦ πνεύματος ("through the Spirit") saw Paul's forthcoming experiences in Jerusalem and warned him against going there. Subsequently Paul and his associates took leave of these disciples after prayer together. They came by ship ultimately to Caesarea and stayed with Philip. While there, a prophet named Agabus came and spoke for the Holy Spirit dramatically declaring what would happen to Paul in

293. For a new, different, dubious manner of translating this phrase, see K. G. Dolfe, "The Greek Word of 'Blood' and the Interpretation of Acts 20.28," *SEÅ* 55 (1990) 64–70.
294. See K. N. Giles, "Luke's Use of the Term ΕΚΚΛΗΣΙΑ with Special Reference to Acts 20.28 and 9.31," *NTS* 31 (1985) 136–37.
295. Schneider, *Apostelgeschichte*, 2:298.

Jerusalem. Agabus's statement (and Paul's ensuing declaration) is a stirring public pronouncement that is best considered in relation to the other speeches in Acts despite its brevity.

Agabus's speech makes no proposal and calls for no action, so that it is essentially *epideictic* rhetoric. In outline it appears this way:

1.0 Introductory Formula (v. 11b)
2.0 Prophetic Declaration (v. 11c)

Analysis. (1.0) In comparison with the other speeches, Agabus's pronouncement is remarkable in that it not only mentions the Holy Spirit but portrays the Spirit as speaking through Agabus (see 2:32–33). Thus, the speech is one of those referring to the Holy Spirit (see 1:16), and it shows clearly the theme of divine authority, especially in relation to divine awareness or control of the future.

Paul's Speech to the Disciples in Caesarea (21:13b–c)

When the disciples heard Agabus's revelatory remark, they urged Paul not to go to Jerusalem. He, however, declared his determination to go. Again, the speech is *epideictic* rhetoric and may be outlined as follows:

1.0 Paul's Objection to the Disciples' Plea (v. 13b)
2.0 Paul's Firm Intention (v. 13c)

Analysis. (2.0) This brief speech contains one of the seven overt references in the speeches to early Christian concern with τοῦ ὀνόματος τοῦ κυρίου Ἰησοῦ, "the name of the Lord Jesus" (see 2:38).

The Speech of James and the Jerusalem Elders (21:20b–25)

Some time later Paul and friends, including disciples from Caesarea, went to Jerusalem, where they lodged with Mnason of Cyprus, who, Luke reports, was an early disciple. The Jerusalem disciples received the group gladly, and on the next day Paul and the rest visited James and the elders, to whom Paul related what God had done among the Gentiles through his ministry. Luke reports that James and the elders glorified God and then spoke to Paul in the hearing of his associates.

The speech is simple *deliberative* rhetoric, comparable to the early speeches in Acts.[296] There are two sections to the speech, which may be outlined in the following manner:

296. Kennedy, *Interpretation*, 134.

1.0 Paul's Situation (vv. 20b–22)
   1.1 Address (v. 20b)
   1.2 Recognizing the Jewish Christians (v. 20c)
   1.3 The Report about Paul (v. 21)
   1.4 Recognizing the Situation (v. 22)
2.0 Proposal and Explanation (vv. 23–25)
   2.1 Participation in the Vow (vv. 23–24)
   2.2 Recalling the Judgment concerning Gentile Christians (v. 25)

Analysis. (1.1) The Jerusalem leaders address Paul with the word ἀδελφέ ("brother"), which is but the singular form of the frequently used ἀδελφοί ("brothers"; see 1:16). (1.2) In speaking of the Jewish Christians, James and his colleagues say πάντες ζηλωταὶ τοῦ νόμου ὑπάρχουσιν ("they are all zealous for the law"), so that again a speech presents the issue of the law (see 7:53). (1.3) The subsequent report about Paul in v. 21 strikes three noticeable notes: First, the idea that Paul teaches diaspora Jews to abandon the law (ἀποστασία, "apostasy" [NRSV: "to forsake"]) will be heard in the next speech in 21:28. Second, the mention of Moses is a further reference to this prominent figure in speech (see 7:20). Third, the issue of circumcision appeared in Stephen's speech (see 7:8), and it may be the idea behind the words of 21:28.

(2.1) When James and the elders make their proposal to Paul, v. 24 states a concern with law observance (see 7:53). (2.2) The following statement in v. 25 is clearly related to 15:19–20 in terms of language and content. The restricted focus on Gentile Christians matches 15:19, and the four stipulated prohibitions match the items named in 15:20.

The Speech of the Jews from Asia (21:28)

Paul obviously agreed to the proposal, for Luke reports that he acted on it immediately. On the seventh day of a specified period Paul went to the Temple to complete the purification ritual. At that time some Jews from Asia recognized him, seized him, and started a riot by shouting.

The shouted speech is *judicial* rhetoric, leveling charges as it supplies information. In outline it appears as follows:

1.0 Address with Appeal for Assistance (v. 28b)
2.0 The Charges against Paul (v. 28c–d)
   2.1 Teaching against the People (v. 28c)
   2.2 Teaching against the Law (v. 28c)
   2.3 Teaching against the Temple (v. 28c)
   2.4 Defiling the Temple (v. 28d)

Analysis. (1.0) The address ἄνδρες ᾿Ισραηλῖται ("Men, Israelites") is one of several uses of this salutation in the speeches (see 2:22). (2.0) The charges in part echo the remarks of James and the elders in 21:21,[297] and even more one recalls the charges against Stephen in 6:13–14.[298] (2.1) The accusation that Paul teaches κατὰ τοῦ λαοῦ ("against the people") may reflect the earlier report in 21:21, μὴ περιτέμνειν αὐτοὺς τὰ τέκνα μηδὲ τοῖς ἔθεσιν περιπατεῖν ("not to circumcise their children or observe the customs"). (2.2) The indictment that Paul teaches κατὰ . . . τοῦ νόμου ("against the law") certainly relates to ἀποστασίαν διδάσκεις ἀπὸ Μωϋσέως ("you teach . . . to forsake Moses") in 21:21 and is similar to 6:13. (2.3) The complaint that Paul teaches κατὰ . . . τοῦ τόπου τούτου ("against this place") is without precedent in the earlier report, but it resembles the charge against Stephen in 6:13. (2.4) The charge that Paul κεκοίνωκεν τὸν ἅγιον τόπον τοῦτον ("has defiled this holy place") recurs in slightly different language in 24:6 (τὸ ἱερὸν ἐπείρασεν βεβηλῶσαι, "tried to profane the Temple").

Paul's Speech to the Jerusalem Jews (22:1, 3–21)

Following the cry of the Asian Jews, Luke explains why they thought Paul had brought Gentiles into the Temple. Then one reads that the crowd dragged Paul out of the Temple and beat him in an effort to kill him. The commotion came to the attention of the Roman tribune of the cohort, who led out troops to stop the disturbance. The tribune had Paul arrested, and when he could not find the cause of the chaos because of the persisting turmoil he ordered Paul to be carried into the barracks. But Paul identified himself to the tribune and was allowed to speak to the crowd.

Paul struck the pose of a Greek orator, standing and motioning with his hand (ἑστὼς . . . κατέσεισεν τῇ χειρί, "standing . . . he motioned with his hand"; compare 13:16; 26:1); and Luke reports that he spoke in Hebrew. The speech is *judicial* rhetoric, which simply narrates Paul's past, seeking through metastasis to transfer the responsibility for Paul's activities to God.[299] Luke inserts a narrative comment in v. 2, and the crowd makes it impossible for Paul to speak in v. 22, so that one regards the speech as incomplete; nevertheless, there are four well-defined sections to the speech which one may outline as follows:

1.0 From Birth to Damascus (vv. 1, 3–5)
    1.1 Address with an Appeal for a Hearing (v. 1)

297. Bruce, *Acts*, 449.
298. Haenchen, *Acts*, 617; Conzelmann, *Acts*, 183; Schneider, *Apostelgeschichte*, 2:313.
299. Kennedy, *Interpretation*, 134–35.

1.2 Birth and Upbringing (v. 3)
1.3 Persecution of the Way (vv. 4–5)
2.0 The Encounter with the Lord (vv. 6–11)
   2.1 Revelatory Confrontation (vv. 6–8)
   2.2 Perception of Paul's Companions (v. 9)
   2.3 Directions for Future Action (v. 10)
   2.4 Paul's Condition (v. 11)
3.0 Ananias and Paul (vv. 12–16)
   3.1 Restoration of Sight (vv. 12–13)
   3.2 Commission as a Witness (vv. 14–15)
   3.3 Directions for Baptism (v. 16)
4.0 Subsequent Vision in Jerusalem (vv. 17–21)
   4.1 Paul's Trance and the Lord's Instructions (vv. 17–18)
   4.2 Paul's Protest (vv. 19–20)
   4.3 The Commission to the Gentiles (v. 21)

Analysis.[300] (1.1)The speech opens with the familiar ἄνδρες ἀδελφοί ("Men, brothers"; see 1:16) coupled with καὶ πατέρες ("and fathers"; see 7:2 for this combination) and an appeal for a hearing, ἀκούσατε ("listen"; see 2:22), all of which together match the opening of Stephen's speech.[301] The line also includes a temporal qualifier, νυνί ("now"), which recurs in 24:13.[302] Moreover, the speech is characterized as an ἀπολογία ("apology" or "defense"), a word that appears in Festus's speech in 25:16.[303] (1.2) After Luke's narration in v. 2, the speech continues by telling of Paul's origins and raising. Verse 3 may be compared with 24:14–15; 26:4–5. In form several speeches open in such a way as to emphasize Paul's good reputation (22:3; 23:1, 6; 24:10–11; 26:4–5; also 22:5; 26:10, 12).[304] Moreover, the speech is one that includes the topic of the law (see 7:53). (1.3) One may compare the recalling of Paul's previous persecution of the church in vv. 4–5 with 26:9–12.

(2.0) The account of the encounter of Σαούλ ("Saul") with the raised Jesus in vv. 6–11 may be compared as a whole and in detail with the speech report

---

300. On the general context and themes of this address, see P. Schubert, "The Final Cycle of Speeches in the Book of Acts," *JBL* 87 (1968) 5, 8.

301. Conzelmann points out, however, that the address is the same but the audience being addressed is different (*Acts*, 186).

302. Schneider, *Apostelgeschichte*, 2:320.

303. Noting this parallel, Krodel goes further and observes that the verb ἀπολογεῖσθαι occurs in 24:10; 25:8; 26:1, 2, 24 (*Acts*, 412).

304. Krodel (*Acts*, 411), modifying the work of J. Neyrey ("The Forensic Defense Speech and Paul's Trial Speeches in Acts 22–26," in *Luke-Acts: New Perspectives from the SBL Seminar* [ed. C. H. Talbert; New York: Crossroad, 1984] 210–24).

in 26:12–18 and with Luke's earlier narration of these happenings in 9:1–19.[305] In general, the way in which the raised Jesus intervenes in Paul's life, disables him, and converts him clearly shows the operation of divine authority and direction. (2.1) Verses 6–8 are comparable to 26:13–15. The speech here assumes the resurrection and ascension of Jesus (see 1:11). In form, such information in speeches aims at proving the validity of Paul's activities (22:6–8, 9, 12–16; 26:14, 19–23).[306] Moreover, the salutation the stricken Saul uses in reply to the voice, κύριε ("Lord"), is the form of prayerful address employed in other speeches (see 1:24). Implicit in this address is reference to the theological identity of Jesus (see 2:36), and the heavenly Jesus' manner of naming himself, Ἰησοῦς ὁ Ναζωραῖος ("Jesus the Nazorean"), is the way he is named in other speeches (see 2:22). (2.2) The report of Paul's companions' perception of these occurrences is comparable to 26:14; (2.3) the directions given to Paul in v. 10 are comparable to 26:16–18; and (2.4) the report of Paul's condition is not mentioned in the subsequent speech, but see 9:8.

(3.0) One does not find the report of Ananias's visit to Paul in the speech before King Agrippa in Acts 26, though the story is narrated in 9:10–19. (3.1) There is a further mention of the law in v. 12 (see 7:53). (3.2) The commissioning of Paul as a "witness" for the Lord Jesus in vv. 14–15 may be compared with 26:16–18.[307] Several features of these verses are noteworthy. First, the phrase ὁ θεὸς τῶν πατέρων ἡμῶν ("the God of our fathers") occurs in other speeches as a designation for God (see 5:30). Second, the explicit mention of God's θέλημα ("will") is the equivalent of references to God's plan (see 1:8) and shows that God has authority and works deliberately for a purpose. Third, the reference to Jesus as ὁ δίκαιος ("the Righteous One") repeats a title encountered in 3:14; 7:52, which is one of the declarations in the speeches of Jesus' theological identity (see 2:36). Fourth, that Paul will be a μάρτυς αὐτῷ πρὸς πάντας ἀνθρώπους ὧν ἑώρακας καὶ ἤκουσας ("witness to him to all people of what you have seen and heard") both sounds the "witness" theme (see 1:8) and highlights the universal relevance of the Christian message. (3.3) The directions concerning baptism in v. 16 also contain striking items. First, the words καὶ νῦν ("and now") indicate the significance of the moment (see 3:17). Second, the statement is one of the several calls in speeches to baptism (see

---

305. On the genuine distinctions and yet complementary nature of the three accounts of Saul's conversion, see C. W. Hedrick, who ably moves past being fixed on the frictions among the stories to see and show how they work together to give the reader a fuller version of the events as Luke saw them than could be imparted by a single account ("Paul's Conversion/Call: A Comparative Analysis of the Three Reports in Acts," *JBL* 100 [1981] 415–32).

306. Krodel (*Acts*, 411) with reference to Neyrey (see n. 304).

307. P. B. Mather examines the development of the image of Paul as Christ's witness, showing the pivotal role of this theme in Acts, especially as it relates to Paul ("Paul in Acts as 'Servant' and 'Witness,'" *BR* 3 [1985] 23–44).

2:38). Third, the directions refer to the washing away (forgiveness) of sins, thus implicitly recognizing the need for repentance (for both see 2:38). And fourth, the instructions that Paul is to do all this ἐπικαλεσάμενος τὸ ὄνομα αὐτοῦ ("calling on his name") is similar to statements about "the name of Jesus Christ" (see 2:38).

(4.0) The account of the subsequent vision in Jerusalem in vv. 17–21 is without parallel, though the verses contain elements that are comparable to other items in Acts.[308] (4.1) In vv. 17–18 Paul's experience of a vision while at prayer recalls the lines of the citation of Joel in Peter's Pentecost speech (see 2:17). (4.2) In the report of the plea Paul uttered in response to the directions to leave Jerusalem (vv. 19–20), one finds the address κύριε ("Lord"; see 1:24); and Stephen is described as the Lord's μάρτυς ("witness"), again echoing the "witness" theme (see 1:8). (4.3) In the final line, v. 21, the information is comparable to 26:16–18. The verb here for "sending" (ἐξαποστέλλειν) regularly refers to divine commissioning (see 7:12). Moreover, the language seems both to sound and to echo the idea of the universal significance of the Christian message, for εἰς ἔθνη μακράν ("far away to the Gentiles") recalls εἰς μακράν ("far away") in 2:39.[309] "Paul's objection is rejected by Jesus, who definitively commands. . . ."[310] And "only the heavenly command . . . has now led Paul . . . to the Gentile mission"[311] — a clear demonstration of divine authority.

After the report of Jesus' words, the crowd explodes. This pattern of interruption, although the speech seems complete, occurs repeatedly (see 2:36–37).

Paul's Speech before the Council (23:1b, 3, 5, 6b)

With the crowd once again in an uproar, the tribune had Paul taken into the barracks, and he ordered that Paul be examined by scourging. Before this process began, however, Paul revealed his Roman citizenship, so that the order was not carried out. The tribune still wanted to know why the Jews brought charges against Paul, so he called the chief priests and the council together and brought the now unbound Paul before them. With no prompting Paul spoke.

Through Luke's narration and reports of statements by others, Paul's speaking is constantly interrupted. Thus, there are four statements by him. They

308. O. Betz makes a case for reading this report in relation to Isa 6:1–13 ("Die Vision des Paulus in Temple von Jerusalem," in *Verborum Veritas: Festschrift für G. Stählin zum 70. Geburtstag* [ed. O. Böcher and K. Haacker; Wuppertal: Theologischer Verlag Rolf Brockhaus, 1970] 113–23). While there may be some slight similarities between these passages, the form and content of the two accounts are so different as to speak against connecting these two Temple-vision commissionings.

309. Schneider, *Apostelgeschichte*, 2:323.

310. Krodel, *Acts*, 418.

311. Haenchen, *Acts*, 628.

are *judicial* rhetoric, alternating from self-defense to condemnation to self-defense. In the sequence of their occurrence one observes:

1.0 Statement of Paul's Good Reputation (v. 1b)
2.0 Paul's Rebuke of the High Priest (v. 3)
3.0 Paul's Profession of Ignorance (v. 5)
4.0 Paul's Statement concerning Resurrection (v. 6b)

Analysis. (1.0) The speech begins as Paul addresses the assembly with the salutation ἄνδρες ἀδελφοί ("Men, brothers"), which recurs in v. 6 (see 1:16). The statement is one of the remarks in Paul's speeches in Acts 22–26 that are intended to emphasize Paul's good reputation (see 22:3). Such statements about Paul's zeal for the things of God occur in 22:14–15; 23:1; 24:16. In this particular comment Schneider notes the temporal phrase ἄχρι ταύτης τῆς ἡμέρας ("up to this day"), which appears in speeches in 2:29; 23:1; 26:22 to stress the idea of constancy or continuity.[312] Implicit in this remark is the idea that human life is lived before God, whose standards determine the validity or invalidity of human life; that is, God holds ultimate authority in divine–human relations.

(2.0) After the high priest ordered Paul struck on the mouth, Paul reprimanded him with a powerful and colorful remark. The language of the statement sounds "biblical" and the image of a deceptively enhanced wall occurs in Ezek 13:10–15; although as Bruce remarks, "There is probably no special biblical allusion here."[313] The rejoinder makes overt reference to the law (see 7:53).

(3.0) In turn, when Paul was scolded for inappropriately chiding the high priest, he attributes his behavior to ignorance. He addresses the audience a second time, now with the word ἀδελφοί ("brothers"; see 3:17). Then the speech cites scripture to illustrate Paul's awareness of the incorrectness of such criticism. The statement refers to scripture overtly, γέγραπται γάρ ("for it is written"; see 1:20) before quoting Exod 22:27 LXX in a slightly altered manner. Thus, Paul uses the text to declare himself to be observant of the law.[314]

(4.0) In v. 6a Luke explains that Paul noticed the mixture of Sadducees and Pharisees, so that in v. 6b he again addresses the assembly, ἄνδρες ἀδελφοί ("Men, brothers"; see 1:16), to declare that his Pharisaic belief in the resurrection is the cause of his being on trial. Kennedy compares Paul's "diversionary tactic" to a similar phenomenon in Greek oratory.[315] Moreover,

312. Schneider, *Apostelgeschichte*, 2:331.
313. Bruce, *Acts,* 464.
314. Conzelmann, *Acts,* 192.
315. Kennedy, *Interpretation,* 135.

comparable personal information comes in 26:5 and similar statements explaining the reason Paul is on trial in 24:15, 21; 26:6–8; 28:20. This reference to the resurrection is an important element of many speeches (see 1:22b), and the specific use of ἀνάστασις ("resurrection") occurs in 22:6; 24:15, 21. In commenting on this statement, Schubert suggests that v. 6b is "the shortest, but centrally important speech of Paul," and he notes that this declaration about the resurrection is linked in the overall story with the subsequent vision of the Lord (v. 11), which speaks of Paul's activity saying, "Take courage, for as you have testified about me in Jerusalem, so you must bear witness also in Rome."[316] In sum, this portion of Acts strongly emphasizes the themes of resurrection, witness, and divine necessity in conjunction with one another.[317]

The Pharisees' Speech in the Council (23:9c–d)

Following Paul's declaration about the resurrection of the dead Luke explains the difference between Sadducees and Pharisees and reports that the council fell into lively dissension. Then some scribes of the party of the Pharisees stood and spoke. Their striking speech is *judicial* rhetoric in that it pronounces their verdict concerning Paul. The brief speech has two parts:

1.0 Verdict (v. 9c)
2.0 Explanation (v. 9d)

Analysis. (1.0) The declaration that the scribes of the Pharisees found nothing wrong with Paul is the first of several statements referring to Paul's apparent innocence (23:9; 25:18–20, 25; 26:31, 32; also 23:29). (2.0) The rhetorical question that follows the declaration offers an explanation of the verdict. The question seems to refer to Paul's earlier speech report of his encounter with the raised Jesus on the road to Damascus (see 22:6–11), but it is not impossible that this question refers to the earlier reported Temple vision (see 22:17–21). The mention of πνεῦμα ("spirit") with neither an article nor the adjective ἅγιον ("holy") may have the sense of "the Holy Spirit," given the information supplied in v. 8 (see 1:16).

316. Schubert, "Final Cycle," 5–6.
317. On the sense and function of Paul's statements about resurrection here and in 24:15–16; 26:6–7; 28:20, see K. Haacker, who views the statements in relationship to the Old Testament and the hope/eschatology of segments of first-century Judaism ("Das Bekenntnis des Paulus zur Hoffnung Israels nach Apostelgeschichte des Lukas," *NTS* 31 [1985] 437–51).

Tertullus's Speech (24:2b-8)

The uproar in the council continued, so the tribune removed Paul from the potential violence. Later in the barracks Paul experienced a nocturnal visit by the Lord, who told him he must bear witness to him in Rome as he had in Jerusalem (Θάρσει· ὡς γὰρ διεμαρτύρω τὰ περὶ ἐμοῦ εἰς Ἰερουσαλήμ, οὕτω σε δεῖ καὶ εἰς Ῥώμην μαρτυρῆσαι, "Keep up your courage! For just as you have testified for me in Jerusalem, so you must bear witness also in Rome"). Then Luke tells of events concerning a plot against Paul by certain Jews who intended to ambush and kill him. Paul's nephew, however, informed the tribune of the conspiracy; and so the tribune wrote a letter (23:26-30) to M. Antonius Felix the governor and sent it by night with Paul and a large number of Roman soldiers to Antipatris and then to Caesarea. There Paul and the letter were delivered to Felix, who determined to hear the case. After five days Luke reports that the high priest Ananias, some elders, and a rhetor named Tertullus arrived. Tertullus delivered a speech bringing charges against Paul. The brief speech is *judicial* rhetoric and it proceeds in three movements:

1.0 Flattering Introduction (vv. 2b-4)
2.0 The Charge (vv. 5-6)
    2.1 Paul's Identity (v. 5)
    2.2 Paul's Activity (v. 6)
3.0 Appeal for Felix's Examination of Paul (v. 8)[318]

Analysis. (1.0) The opening of the speech is a *captatio benevolentiae,* a pure rhetorical convention. (2.0) Interpreters debate whether all the information in vv. 5-6 or simply that in v. 6 is to be understood as charges.[319] (2.1) Tertullus's initial statement concerning Paul identifies him as an undesirable character (λοιμός, "a pestilent fellow"). Implicit in the phrase πᾶσιν τοῖς Ἰουδαίοις τοῖς κατὰ τὴν οἰκουμένην ("all the Jews throughout the world"), however, is a recognition of the worldwide character of Christian faith; and the description of Paul as πρωτοστάτην . . . τῆς τῶν Ναζωραίων αἱρέσεως ("a ringleader . . . of the sect of the Nazoreans") employs language reminiscent of the references in speeches to Jesus as Ἰησοῦς ὁ Ναζωραῖος ("Jesus the Nazorean"; see 2:22). (2.2) The report of Paul's alleged attempt to profane the Temple repeats the charge of the Asian Jews in 21:28, although the language is different.[320] (3.0) The speech ends by suggesting that Felix may

318. Verse 7 is poorly attested and not original. See Metzger, *Textual Commentary,* 490.
319. E.g., Bruce (*Acts,* 476) contends there are three charges here, but Schneider (*Apostelgeschichte,* 2:346) finds merely one.
320. Here: τὸ ἱερὸν ἐπείρασεν βεβηλῶσαι; but there: κεκοίνωκεν τὸν ἅγιον τόπον τοῦτον.

investigate the case. The verb used for the act of interrogating, ἀνακρίνειν ("to examine"), occurs in speeches in reference to the official questioning of Christians (see 4:9).

Paul's Speech before Felix (24:10b–21)

When Tertullus spoke, Luke reports that οἱ 'Ιουδαῖοι ("the Jews") were affirming his accusations, and when he finished speaking the governor signaled to Paul to speak. The reply is *judicial* rhetoric in which Paul simply denies the accuracy of the charges through statement of facts without offering any evidence. The speech has several distinct parts:

1.0 Introductory Statement (v. 10b)
2.0 Denial of Charges (vv. 11–13)
3.0 Paul's Involvement with the Way (vv. 14–15)
4.0 Declaration of Paul's Scruples (v. 16)
5.0 Explanation of Paul's Presence in the Temple (vv. 17–18)
6.0 Objections to Accusations (vv. 19–20)
7.0 Reiteration of Earlier Resurrection-Declaration (v. 21)

Analysis. (1.0) The speech begins with a *captatio benevolentiae* which uses the verb ἀπολογεῖσθαι ("to make a defense") in reference to Paul's speaking. This verb occurs in speeches in 24:10; 25:8; 26:1, 2, 24. Haenchen refers to ἀπολογεῖσθαι as "the real catchword of these last chapters."[321]

(2.0) Verses 11–13 simply and directly deny the validity of the accusations, narrating the facts over against the charges. In v. 11 the words δυναμένου σου ἐπιγνῶναι ("you can find out") are similar to the words of Tertullus's appeal to Felix in 24:8, so that the speech is clearly intended as a rebuttal. In v. 13 the unusual temporal qualifier νυνί ("now") occurs as previously in 22:1.

(3.0) In the next segment of the speech Paul's remarks echo 22:3 and offer another statement of Paul's good reputation. As Schneider observes, vv. 14–15 are entirely theocentric.[322] Several items merit attention. First, the distinctive verb λατρεύειν for "worship" is a feature of other speeches (see 7:7). Second, the phrase τῷ πατρῴῳ θεῷ ("the God of the fathers") is remarkable in form, but it is the equivalent of ὁ θεὸς τῶν πατέρων ("the God of the fathers"), which occurs frequently in the speeches (see 3:13). Third, references to the law occur throughout the speeches (see 7:53). Fourth, the mention of the law is coupled with τοῖς ἐν τοῖς προφήταις γεγραμμένοις ("the things written in the prophets"), which recalls other explicit references both to the prophets (see 2:16) and to "what is written" (see 1:20). Fifth, the mention of the resurrection in v. 15,

321. Haenchen, *Acts,* 654.
322. Schneider, *Apostelgeschichte,* 2:348.

using ἀνάστασις ("resurrection"), echoes 23:6 and will be repeated in v. 21 (see 1:22b).

(4.0) The declaration of Paul's scruples recalls the idea that he is zealous for the things of God (22:14–15; 23:1) and recognizes God's authority. This statement also enhances Paul's good reputation (see the discussion at 22:3).

(5.0) The explanation of why and how Paul was in the Temple contrasts sharply with Tertullus's accusations (24:5–6) and points to Paul's law-observance. Verses 17–18 allude to a broad segment of the previous account in Acts, but especially to 21:26–29.

(6.0) In vv. 19–20 Paul's objections to the charges and to the absence of the Asian Jews employ two striking words. First, in v. 19 one finds δεῖ ("it is necessary"), but it is unlikely that the word in this context connotes anything more than practical necessity. Second, in v. 20 the technical term ἀδίκημα ("crime") signifies a legal violation which Paul denies he had committed; the word occurred in Gallio's speech to the Corinthian Jews also naming something not done (see 18:14b).

(7.0) The speech ends with v. 21 overtly referring to and repeating Paul's previous statement in 23:6b concerning the resurrection. Again the word ἀνάστασις ("resurrection") appears (see 1:22b).

Paul's Speech before Festus (25:8b, 10b–11)

Felix passed no judgment but said he would decide the case when Lysias the tribune arrived. Paul remained incarcerated but with some freedom. Later Felix and his wife, Drusilla, a Jewess, talked with Paul περὶ τῆς εἰς Χριστὸν Ἰησοῦν πίστεως ("concerning faith in Christ Jesus"). But as Paul elaborated the matter Luke reports that Felix became anxious and dismissed Paul. Luke also reports that although Felix spoke subsequently and frequently with Paul, for ignoble reasons he kept him imprisoned for two years. Finally Felix's term of office expired and he was succeeded by Porcius Festus.

When Festus took office, he visited Jerusalem, where Paul's opponents renewed their charges and even reactivated the plot to ambush Paul. Festus denied a request to have Paul sent to Jerusalem and instead called for the accusers to appear in Caesarea. There Festus heard the bogus charges, and Paul spoke in defense of himself. Festus interrupted Paul with a question (v. 9) that sent Paul's speech in a new direction.

Paul's initial remark is *judicial* rhetoric, but after Festus's question the speech becomes a combination of *judicial* and *deliberative* rhetoric as Paul continues his defense and then makes an appeal to Caesar. The speech appears as follows in outline:

1.0 Denial of Any Wrongdoing (v. 8b)
2.0 Denials and Appeal (vv. 10b–11)

2.1 Recognition of Caesar's Authority (v. 10b)
2.2 Denial of Wronging the Jews (v. 10c)
2.3 Willingness to Accept Justice (v. 11a)
2.4 Further Denial of Wrongdoing (v. 11b)
2.5 Appeal to Caesar (v. 11c)

Analysis. (1.0) Paul's opening remark in v. 8b mentions two topics given attention in other speeches. First, the denial that Paul had done anything against the law refers immediately back to 21:21; 21:28, and it is part of the larger network of statements in the speeches about the law (see 7:53). Second, the denial that Paul had done anything against the Temple replies directly to the charge in 21:28 and 24:6 that he had sought to profane the Temple, and the statement recalls the situation faced in Acts 6–8 by Stephen. Paul's declaration of innocence (see 18:6) includes a new item when he denies having done anything against Caesar. This denial may be developed from Tertullus's earlier statement in 24:5, which cast Paul as a troublemaker, λοιμός ("a pestilent fellow"),[323] and it anticipates the forthcoming focus of vv. 10–11.

(2.1) Following Festus's question, Paul's speech resumes with a statement recognizing Caesar's authority (v. 10b). This declaration, however, employs δεῖ ("it is necessary"), which now strongly suggests that it is because of divine necessity that Paul "must" go to Rome.[324] The raised Jesus has already informed Paul of the divine plan for his testimony in Rome (23:11). (2.2) The declaration in v. 10c is a strong reiteration of Paul's plea of innocence. (2.3) The following statement about Paul's willingness to accept a just death sentence implicitly demonstrates Paul's good character (see the discussion at 22:14–15). (2.5) The final part of v. 11 makes the appeal to Caesar, which moves toward the fulfillment of the prophecies of 19:21; 23:11, and later when Paul arrives in Rome there is a reference to this appeal in his speech to the Roman Jews (28:19).

Festus's Speech (25:14c–21, 24–27)

Festus promptly acknowledged Paul's appeal to Caesar. Then Luke reports developments that occurred with the arrival of King Agrippa and his sister Bernice, who came to Caesarea to call on the new procurator. During their stay Festus presented Paul's case to the king, first privately and, at Agrippa's

323. Bruce, *Acts*, 487.
324. On this verse Schneider writes, "In dem δεῖ läßt Lukas zugleich den Gedanken der von Gott verfügten Notwendigkeit anklingen, daß Paulus nach Rom gehen wird (19,21; 23,11). Der Plan Gottes beginnt sich zu erfüllen: Paulus wird auch in Rom Zeugnis ablegen" (*Apostelgeschichte*, 2:359).

request, later publicly. Thus, there are two sections of Festus's remarks to Agrippa. Both parts simply narrate the situation. As Festus's telling invites Agrippa to assist him in determining what to write to Caesar about Paul, the speech takes on the tones of *judicial* rhetoric. In outline the two sections of the speech appear as follows:

1.0 Festus's Informing Agrippa about Paul (vv. 14c–21)
    1.1 The Situation Facing Festus (vv. 14c–15)
    1.2 Festus's Initial Position (v. 16)
    1.3 Festus's Report of the Hearing (vv. 17–21)
        1.3.1 Festus's Call for a Trial (v. 17)
        1.3.2 The Charges against Paul (vv. 18–19)
        1.3.3 Festus's Dilemma (v. 20)
        1.3.4 Paul's Appeal and Festus's Response (v. 21)

Agrippa asked to hear Paul's case. Luke reports that on the next day a splendid procession led to an assembly at which Festus again spoke.

2.0 Festus's Public Presentation of the Situation (vv. 24–27)
    2.1 Address and Introductory Remarks (v. 24)
    2.2 Festus's Finding (v. 25a)
    2.3 Paul's Appeal and Festus's Decision (v. 25b)
    2.4 The Purpose of Presenting the Case (vv. 26–27)

Analysis. (1.0) Verses 14c–21 basically retell in direct speech the earlier narrative of Acts 25:1–12 with noticeable, but appropriate, variation. (1.2) In the retelling of Festus's denial of the request simply to condemn Paul, the word ἀπολογία ("defense") names the necessary speech one made in one's defense at a trial (see 21:1). (1.3.2) The position attributed to those leveling charges against Paul is a feature related to other speeches (see 2:14). Further, the information in v. 19 is particularly remarkable, since in the previous speech before Festus Paul said nothing about Jesus or the resurrection; indeed, in the statements about resurrection before the Jewish Council (23:6) and before Felix (24:15, 21) the speeches said nothing of Jesus' resurrection. This striking declaration relates to the larger system of statements in the speeches about resurrection (see 1:22b). (1.3.3) Festus's report of bafflement at how to investigate the charges against Paul is an indirect recognition of Paul's innocence, and it anticipates the more direct statement in v. 25a. (1.3.4) The report of Paul's appeal and Festus's response repeats 25:10–12 and this same information comes again in v. 25b.

(2.0) Verses 24–27 present the broad currents of Acts 21:27–25:12 in direct speech. (2.1) After addressing King Agrippa personally, Festus's salutation addresses πάντες οἱ συμπαρόντες ἡμῖν ("all here present with us") with the simple word ἄνδρες ("men"; see 14:15). In Festus's introduction of Paul δεῖ ("it is necessary") appears, but here the word indicates nothing more than practical necessity. (2.2) Festus's report of his findings in v. 25a is one of the several overt statements of Paul's innocence (see 23:9). (2.4) In v. 26 one observes the word ἀνάκρισις ("examination"), which is related to the verb ἀνακρίνειν ("to examine"), which appears in other speeches recognizing that Christians are being formally examined in relation to some charge (see 4:9).

Paul's Speech before King Agrippa (26:2–23, 25–27, 29)

With Festus's stage-setting speech completed, Luke reports that Agrippa addressed Paul directly giving him permission to speak. In good rhetorical form — as Haenchen notes, despite the chains[325] — Paul made the gesture of an orator. The speech continues through vv. 2–23 before the interruption by Festus in v. 24 states his astonishment at Paul's declarations. Paul's answer, however, shifts the focus back to Agrippa, to whom the speech continues to be directed, although now the rhetoric becomes quite aggressive. Thus, there is an interruption in v. 28 by Agrippa, but a reply from Paul follows in v. 29 so that one understands he said all he had to say. These interruptions actually allow Paul's speech to offer an epilogue as vv. 25–26 recapitulate something of Paul's defense and vv. 27, 29 state Paul's beliefs and purposes in an effort to stir the audience (and the reader!) to action.

The *judicial* rhetoric largely narrates and explains, although the reference to scripture in v. 22 offers a kind of evidence. The speech, however, ultimately seeks through metastasis to transfer the responsibility for Paul's manner of living to God as is clear from the reference to the Hebrew voice and the recitation of the statements by the raised Jesus in vv. 14–18.[326] Moreover, although this speech comes in a clearly judicial setting and Luke repeatedly defines it as an apology (26:1, 2, 24), the speech simultaneously advances testimony to Christ that almost transforms it into a "missionary sermon" on the resurrection of Jesus (vv. 6–8, 22–23).[327] As Conzelmann observes, "The thrust of the speech leads from the apology, addressing the situation, to a missionary appeal."[328] Thus, there are strong elements of *deliberative* rhetoric through portions of the speech and especially at the end.

The speech has clearly defined parts, discernible through noticing transitional particles and temporal phrases. In outline it appears as follows:[329]

---

325. Haenchen, *Acts,* 682.

326. See Kennedy, *Interpretation,* 137–38.

327. Schneider, *Apostelgeschichte,* 2:369–70.

328. Conzelmann, *Acts,* 209.

329. I am especially indebted to the work of R. F. O'Toole (*Acts 26: The Christological Climax of Paul's Defense (Ac 22:1–26:32)* [AnBib 78; Rome: Biblical Institute Press, 1978]), whose own suggestions I have modified through additions and expansion in composing this outline. As O'Toole

1.0 Flattering Address with Appeal for a Hearing (vv. 2–3)
2.0 Paul's Background and Convictions (vv. 4–8)
    2.1 Background (vv. 4–5)
    2.2 The Resurrection-Hope (vv. 6–8)
        2.2.1 Commitment and Consequences (vv. 6–7)
        2.2.2 Rhetorical Confrontation (v. 8)
3.0 Paul's Experience and Testimony (vv. 9–23)
    3.1 Previous Persecution of the Church and Encounter with the Raised Jesus (vv. 9–21)
        3.1.1 Activity as Persecutor (vv. 9–11)
        3.1.2 The Revelatory Encounter (vv. 12–18)
        3.1.3 Paul's Obedience (vv. 19–20)
        3.1.4 The Consequences (v. 21)
    3.2 Paul's Testimony (vv. 22–23)
        3.2.1 Divine Support and Consistency with Scripture (v. 22)
        3.2.2 Christological Kerygma (v. 23)
4.0 Epilogue through Dialogue (vv. 25–27, 29)
    4.1 Comments after Festus's Interruption (vv. 25–27)
        4.1.1 Reply with Explanatory Reference to Agrippa (vv. 25–26)
        4.1.2 Question and Assertion to Agrippa (v. 27)
    4.2 Reply to Agrippa Stating Paul's Purpose (v. 29)

Analysis. (1.0) Paul's speech addresses Agrippa personally with a title (βασιλεῦ 'Αγρίππα, "King Agrippa") and a statement of appreciation (ἥγημαι ἐμαυτὸν μακάριον ἐπὶ σοῦ μέλλων σήμερον ἀπολογεῖσθαι, "I consider myself fortunate that it is before you . . . I am to make my defense today") which v. 3 explains. In general this opening is comparable to 24:10b, which is another *captatio benevolentiae.* In v. 2 (and v. 7) one observes the rare verb ἐγκαλεῖν for "bringing legal charges" (see 19:40), and the verb ἀπολογεῖσθαι ("to make a defense") defines what this speech attempts (see 24:10). Finally, the speech makes a formal appeal for a hearing using the verb ἀκούειν ("to listen"; see 2:22).

(2.1) The description of Paul's background in vv. 4–5 presents information similar to that at 22:3; 23:6; 24:14–15. This material intends to emphasize Paul's good reputation (see 22:3). (2.2) Verses 6–8 treat the resurrection, a familiar topic from several other speeches (see 1:22). Similar information

---

states his own understanding of the structure, "This position sees 26:2–3 as a *captatio benevolentiae,* but not a mere formality. The rest of the speech falls into two major divisions, 26:4–8, 9–23, each introduced by *men oun.* Each of these major divisions is made up of two parts; the first of these (26:4–5, 9–21) reports experiences from the life of Paul; the second (26:6–8, 22–23), the consequence of Paul's experiences formulated in terms of the Scriptural promises, especially the resurrection. Therefore, after the *captatio benevolentiae,* the speech . . . is made up of two panels which parallel and develop one another" (p. 28).

appeared in Paul's previous defense speeches (see 23:6) (2.2.1) Here the temporal phrase καὶ νῦν ("and now") underscores the gravity of the moment (see 3:17). The speech connects Paul's belief in the resurrection with the promise of God, a connection demonstrating continuity and that God works with a plan.[330] In this statement the last of the fourteen occurrences of the phrase οἱ πατέρες ἡμῶν ("our fathers") occurs in the speeches (see 7:11). Moreover, in v. 7 the magnitude of the hope is registered with the dramatic phrase νύκτα καὶ ἡμέραν ("night and day"; see 20:31), which is used in relation to the striking verb λατρεύειν for "worship" (see 7:7). (2.2.2) Finally, in the confronting question of v. 8 one sees the stark conviction that God has power and authority over human life and death, wherein the reference to God's activity of raising the dead is stated using ἐγείρειν ("to raise up"; see 1:22).

(3.1.1) The next section of the speech reports Paul's former persecution of the church. The material in vv. 9–11 is generally comparable with 22:4–5. The use of the verb δεῖ ("it is necessary") in this context probably connotes divine necessity, but its use signals a false understanding of God's will. Moreover, Paul's report explained the persecution saying that he thought it necessary to do many things against τὸ ὄνομα 'Ιησοῦ τοῦ Ναζωραίου ("the name of Jesus the Nazorean"). In this statement one recognizes both the theme of "the name of Jesus" (see introductory discussion to 3:12–26) and the pattern of naming him as 'Ιησοῦς ὁ Ναζωραῖος ("Jesus the Nazorean"; see 2:22).

(3.1.2) One may compare the recollection in vv. 12–18 of the Damascus road experience with information given in Paul's speech at 22:6–11, 14–15, 21. In vv. 13–15 this report agrees with the group of speeches that explicitly refer to or implicitly assume the resurrection and ascension of Jesus (see 1:11). Moreover, the use of that information in defense of Paul's behavior occurs elsewhere (22:6–8), so that Haenchen comments, "Paul is completely in the power of Jesus."[331] Thus, these verses acknowledge divine authority over humanity. Along that line, Paul's address to the raised Jesus, κύριε ("Lord"), repeats a form of prayerful address (see 1:24) that implicitly declares the theological identity of Jesus (see 2:36).

In turn, the words of Jesus' commission to Paul are filled with significant language and thoughts. Paul is appointed a μάρτυς ("witness").[332] Thus, one

330. Advocating this understanding is not, however, to agree with Conzelmann, who writes, "The conception of promise and fulfillment is expressed more clearly than before: The true Jew must become a Christian, in order to remain a Jew" (*Acts*, 21). Indeed, the speech casts the promise as a revelatory declaration in which Paul trusted and by which he lived, not merely as a promise or prophecy waiting to be fulfilled so that it will have significance.

331. Haenchen, *Acts*, 685.

332. J. J. Kilgallen shows in detail how this speech (1) summarizes Luke's editorial concerns regarding the presentation of Paul and (2) delivers one of the key kerygmatic proclamations of the book ("Paul before Agrippa [Acts 26,2–23]: Some Considerations," *Bib* 69 [1988] 170–95). Thus, Paul gives witness to himself and the gospel. Seeing the second dimension of this speech should warn against compartmentalizing the addresses for study.

finds both the "witness" theme (see 1:8) and Jesus' acting with divine authority in the appointment of witnesses (see 1:8; 6:2b–4). Moreover, in v. 17 the declaration that the raised Jesus delivered Paul from and sent Paul to the people and the Gentiles recognizes divine authority and the universal scope of the Christian mission, as well as the extension of that mission according to a divine plan. Thus, the simple statement ἐγὼ ἀποστέλλω σε ἀνοῖξαι ὀφθαλμοὺς αὐτῶν ("I am sending you to open their eyes") in vv. 17–18 demonstrates divine direction in the experience of salvation! Furthermore, the language and thought of these two verses are remarkably similar to 13:46–47; 22:21; 28:28. Moreover, the dramatic results of Jesus' sending Paul, described in v. 18 strike several important notes. The coupling of the call to repentance with the promise of forgiveness is the fourth instance of this combination (see 3:19b), and the forgiveness of sins alone is mentioned in other speeches (see 2:38). In turn, ἐν τοῖς ἡγιασμένοις ("among those who are sanctified") echoes 20:32, and the phrase πίστει τῇ εἰς ἐμέ ("by faith in me") explicates the statement in 15:9 and relates to the subject of Paul's conversations with Felix and Drusilla reported in the narrative in 24:25, namely, περὶ τῆς εἰς Χριστὸν Ἰησοῦν πίστεως ("concerning faith in Christ Jesus").

(3.1.3) The report of Paul's obedience in vv. 19–20 again addresses "King Agrippa," so that one recognizes a new focus. The scheme of proclamation delineated in these verses is on the familiar pattern of "to the Jews first."[333] Haenchen recognized v. 19 as the crux of Paul's defense, for here Paul explains that it was impossible to resist the heavenly command.[334] Verse 20 implicitly recognizes the need for repentance (see 2:38) and formulates a dramatic twofold call to repentance (μετανοεῖν καὶ ἐπιστρέφειν, "to repent and to turn to") that echoes 3:19a. The language of "turning to God" (ἐπιστρέφειν ἐπὶ τὸν θεόν) recalls 14:15; 15:19; 26:18.

(3.1.4) In v. 21 the statement of the consequences of Paul's obedience is the second of only two New Testament uses of the striking verb διαχειρίζεσθαι ("to kill"). This use echoes 5:30.

(3.2.1) Paul's testimony opens with an acknowledgment of God's support of his labors. With the temporal phrase ἄχρι τῆς ἡμέρας ταύτης ("to this day"; see 23:1) the speech emphasizes that every aspect of the effects of the revelatory encounter reported in vv. 19–23 extend to the very moment in which Paul addressed Agrippa.[335] Moreover, the occurrence of μαρτυρεῖν ("to bear witness") strikes the chord of the "witness" theme (see 6:3; 1:8). In turn, the explicit reference to the prophets sounds a regular note (see 2:16), although the reference without a subsequent quotation is part of a distinct subgroup of statements concerning the prophets (see 3:18); and, more particularly still,

333. Similarly, Conzelmann, Acts, 211.
334. Haenchen, Acts, 686.
335. Similarly, Schubert, "Final Cycle," 8.

similar sweeping references occur in 3:24; 10:43. In addition, the mention of Moses is another regular detail of the speeches (see 7:20); indeed, in 3:22–24 one finds a report of the content of the testimony of Moses and the prophets stated explicitly as Peter speaks in the temple. Finally, Paul speaks of ὧν τε οἱ προφῆται ἐλάλησαν μαλλόντων γίνεσθαι καὶ Μωϋσῆς ("what the prophets and Moses said would take place"). The idea behind the use of γίνεσθαι ("to take place") here is that God revealed a plan and acted on it with divine authority.

(3.2.2) Verse 23 is christological kerygma. Jesus has already been named explicitly as the raised Lord who spoke to Paul from heaven, and now the outlines of Paul's proclamation are sketched. The reference to Χριστός ("Christ") is an explicit declaration of the theological identity of Jesus (see 2:36). The manner of speaking about his "passion" or "suffering" (παθητής) casts the cross not as a scandal but as part of the divine plan (see 2:23), and in this case the often-repeated reference to the resurrection from the dead uses ἀνάστασις ("resurrection"; see 1:22). Moreover, the language here concerning proclamation of light (φῶς μέλλει καταγγέλλειν, "he would proclaim light") recalls similar statements in 1:8; 13:47; and the mention of both the people and the Gentiles (τῷ τε λαῷ καὶ τοῖς ἔθνεσιν, "both to our people and to the Gentiles") emphasizes the universal relevance of salvation and the universal significance of the message.

At this point Paul's speech is interrupted. Kennedy notes that this interruption comes at exactly the same point that Paul was interrupted in 22:21/22, namely, after the mention of the proclamation to the Gentiles.[336] The speech is interrupted in both 26:23/24 and 26:28/29 (see 2:36/37).

(4.0) An epilogue to Paul's speech comes in vv. 25–27, 29. (4.1.1) The reply to Festus contains three striking items. First, in v. 25 the word ῥήματα ("words") may refer to the gospel message using a technical term (see 5:32). Second, Paul declares his boldness in v. 26 using the verb παρρησιάζεσθαι ("to speak boldly"), which recalls the boldness and power of Christian proclamation elsewhere in Acts (see 1:8). Third, interpreters suggest that the phrase οὐ γάρ ἐστιν ἐν γωνίᾳ πεπραγμένον τοῦτο ("for this was not done in a corner") is programmatic for Luke.[337] The phrase indicates the worldwide significance, boldness, power, and purpose of the events that are now proclaimed. (4.1.2) Paul's jabbing question provides still another reference to the prophets (see 2:16). (4.2) Finally, in the telling statement in v. 29 one sees the coalescence of important elements of the speech that have already been analyzed: commitment (vv. 6–7) and obedience (vv. 19–20) in relation to the universally relevant message of the forgiveness of sins through faith in the crucified and raised Lord Jesus Christ (vv. 16–18, 22–23).

336. Kennedy, *Interpretation*, 137.
337. Haenchen, *Acts*, 689, 691–92; Conzelmann, *Acts*, 212. Furthermore, on the background and probable apologetic function of this phrase, see A. J. Malherbe, "'Not In a Corner': Early Christian Apologetic in Acts 26:26," *Second Century* 5 (1985–86) 193–210.

Paul's Speech(es) during the Sea Voyage to Rome
(27:10b, 21b–26, 31b, 33b–34)

Following Paul's speech, Agrippa, Bernice, and company arose and withdrew, acknowledging among themselves Paul's innocence. Agrippa stated this conclusion to Festus, but, with the appeal having been made to Caesar, Paul was now out of Festus's jurisdiction. Chapter 27, then, tells of the sea voyage and shipwreck of Paul and the others with him.

When sailing became difficult, Paul spoke, warning of costly impending danger (v. 10b), but the centurion in charge of Paul, the captain, the owner, and the majority aboard the ship determined to sail ahead toward Phoenix of Crete attempting to find a suitable winter harbor. The vessel was struck by a violent storm that required drastic emergency measures. After days of difficulty Paul addressed those on board, encouraging them despite the circumstances (vv. 21b–26). Later, as the ship came perilously close to land, some sailors prepared to abandon ship, and Paul spoke against the plan to escape (v. 31b). Shortly thereafter Paul spoke a final time, again encouraging those on the ship (vv. 33b–34).

Paul's comments form a cluster, focusing on one situation, and may be viewed together to see their cumulative effect. The rhetoric is varied: vv. 10b; 21b–26; 31b are *epideictic;* and vv. 33b–34 are *deliberative.* In sequence and detail the speech statements appear as follows:

1.0 Warning against Further Sailing (v. 10b)
2.0 Rebuke and Encouragement (vv. 21b–26)
    2.1 Rebuke (v. 21b)
    2.2 Hortatory Revelation (vv. 22–24)
        2.2.1 Exhortation (v. 22a)
        2.2.2 Promise (v. 22b)
        2.2.3 Evidence in Support of the Promise (vv. 23–24)
    2.3 Another Exhortation (v. 25)
        2.3.1 Call to Courage (v. 25a)
        2.3.2 Paul's Confidence (v. 25b)
    2.4 Directions (v. 26)
3.0 Strong Warning against Abandoning Ship (v. 31b)
4.0 Final Encouragement (vv. 33b–34)
    4.1 The Situation (v. 33b)
    4.2 Encouragement to Eat (v. 34a–b)
    4.3 Encouraging Promise (v. 34c)

Analysis. Interpreters debate both the historicity and the meaning of Acts 27. Careful comparison of the speech(es) by Paul through the course of the story supplies insight into the latter of these concerns.

(1.0) Paul's initial statement was a warning against sailing in the circumstances being faced. The address ἄνδρες ("Men") is a simple salutation occurring in several speeches (see 14:15a). Further, Schneider notes that ψυχή is used here with the sense of "life," as it is in other speeches by Paul in 20:24; 27:10, 22.[338]

(2.0) The narrative introduction to the longest segment of speech has Paul σταθείς ("standing") as a Greek orator (see 2:14) and locates him, even on shipboard, ἐν μέσῳ ("in the middle"; see introductory discussion to 1:16–22, 24–25). (2.1) Paul's rebuke employs δεῖ ("it is necessary"), which may, even in this context, carry the sense of divine necessity. The likelihood of this understanding is increased through the combination of δεῖ ("it is necessary") and πειθαρχεῖν ("to obey" [NRSV: "to listen to"]), which appeared together in 5:29 when the issue was whether to obey divine directives or human will. With characteristic astuteness Schubert argues,

> The final and climactic obstacle which Paul has to overcome before his arrival at Rome . . . is not brought about by the forces of nature but by the human decision to carry out the wrong plan for the voyage (vss. 9–12), a plan devised by the centurion, the captain, the owner of the ship, and the majority of the ship's company (ἔθεντο βουλὴν ἀναχθῆναι, vs. 12). It is a clearly articulated Lukan motif, especially in the speeches, to distinguish sharply between human and the divine βουλή and to make the former subservient to the latter (Acts 2:22–23, 3:17f., 5:38f., 13:37; see also Luke 7:30 and 23:51)."[339]

(2.2.1) The temporal phrase καὶ τὰ νῦν ("and now") registers the importance of the exhortation in v. 22a, marking a moment of significance (see 3:17). (2.2.2) Then the speech states a promise that reduces the severity of Paul's reported perception in v. 10b, and, as one sees from the following lines, the change in expectation resulted from divine revelation. (2.2.3) From vv. 23–24 one learns that Paul now knows the future with clarity because of the nighttime visit from the angel of God. This evidence in support of the previous promise illustrates the conviction that events occur according to divine will and direction. Two particular features of this offer of evidence are noteworthy. First, in v. 23 there is another occurrence of the striking verb λατρεύειν in reference to "worship" (see 7:7). Second, in v. 24 δεῖ ("it is necessary") occurs in the report of the statement by the angel, so that there is no doubt that the word signifies divine necessity[340] (see 1:16b–17). "Paul's arrival in Rome to

338. Schneider, *Apostelgeschichte*, 2:388.

339. Schubert, "Final Cycle," 8–9. Although others understand the line less theologically, e.g., Schneider writes, "Das Imperfekt ἔδει bezeichnet einen Zustand, der existieren sollte, aber nicht existiert . . ." (*Apostelgeschichte*, 2:392 n. 66).

340. On the portrait of God as a saving deity in Paul's speech(es) in 27:21–26, 33–38, see the incisive analysis by S. M. Praeder ("Acts 27:1–28:16: Sea Voyages in Ancient Literature and the Theology of Luke-Acts," *CBQ* 46 [1984] 683–706, esp. 695–700).

bear his witness there 'in the presence of Caesar' was divinely decreed and could not be frustrated. . . ."[341]

(2.3) Paul delivers another word of exhortation in v. 25. (2.3.1) This is the sixth and final use of ἄνδρες ("men"; see 14:15). (2.3.2) The basis of Paul's confidence is sheer faith in God, stated explicitly πιστεύω γὰρ τῷ θεῷ ("for I have faith in God"). Regarding Paul's statement of confidence, Schneider compares οὕτως . . . καθ' ὃν τρόπον λελάληταί μοι ("that it will be exactly as I have been told") with οὕτως . . . ὃν τρόπον ("in the same way") at 1:11 and notes that οὕτως ("thus") refers to the realization of divine promises in these instances and in 3:18; 7:8; 27:25; 27:44 (not in speech).[342]

Concerning v. 25 Haenchen states, "Here Luke makes plain above all Paul's trust in God's faithfulness. . . ."[343] Yet one wonders whether Haenchen has the correct focus. Given that the statement occurs in the context of the entire Acts account, not merely as an independent statement in an independent story, it would be more reasonable to argue that here "Luke makes plain through Paul's statement that God is faithful."

(2.4) In v. 26 the declaration εἰς νῆσον δέ τινα δεῖ ἡμᾶς ἐκπεσεῖν ("but we will have to run aground on some island") again employs δεῖ ("it is necessary"), probably with the sense of divine necessity (see 1:16b–17). Bruce, however, suggests, "This was a statement of faith . . . but it was a slender hope indeed."[344] Yet, given the profound theological dimensions of Paul's speech at this point, Haenchen seems correct when he argues, "Verse 26 does not report a private conjecture by Paul, but rather the δεῖ introduces a prophetic prediction. . . ."[345]

(3.0) The warning against abandoning ship in v. 31b continues to speak from a theological point of view. Now, Bruce has the wrong focus, commenting, "Paul shows outstanding presence of mind, not for the first time in this narrative. Had the sailors made good their escape in the dinghy, there would not have been enough skilled hands left to work the ship."[346] This explanation seems inadequate in relation to the context of the whole story. Paul has already been told through angelic annunciation that God has granted him the lives of all on board. Should they now leave the sphere of God's purpose, they would defy the plan of God. The speech makes this understanding clear by the use of σῴζειν ("to save") in the passive voice (see 4:12). The promise and the power to save are God's, and Paul's statement to the centurion and the soldiers is based on his faith in God's faithfulness.

(4.0) In Paul's final declarations, vv. 33b–34, there may also be hints of

341. Bruce, Acts, 521. On this verse, Schneider remarks, "Mit δεῖ (vgl. 19,21; 23,11; 25,10) wird die gott-verfügte Notwendigkeit ausgedrückt" (Apostelgeschichte, 2:393).

342. Schneider, Apostelgeschichte, 2:394.

343. Haenchen, Acts, 705.

344. Bruce, Acts, 522.

345. Haenchen, Acts, 705.

346. Bruce, Acts, 524.

the thoroughly theological nature of the speech(es) on shipboard. (4.2) In the statement encouraging those on board to eat, one notices the word σωτηρία ("salvation"), which interpreters typically understand as "physical preservation from death" through the consumption of food.[347] Haenchen takes this line and observes, "σωτηρία means earthly deliverance only here and Hebr. 11.7. . . ." The word may well refer merely to physical health, but in the context of the other statements, especially in relation to σωθῆναι ("to be saved") in v. 31b, Paul's "urging" (παρακαλῶ, which occurs in descriptions of the actions of Christians in calling others to conversion; see 2:40) may somehow relate to the operation of God's plan to save those on ship with Paul. (4.3) Moreover, the promise that follows declares salvation overtly in metaphor. That God guarantees οὐδενὸς γὰρ ὑμῶν θρὶξ ἀπὸ τῆς κεφαλῆς ἀπολεῖται ("for none of you will lose a hair from your heads") is clear from Paul's previous report of the angel's declaration concerning God's plan.

Paul's Speech to the Roman Jewish Leaders
(28:17c–20, 25b–28)

After Paul's final words on shipboard, Luke reports that Paul prayed, broke bread, and ate; thus encouraged, the others joined him. When they had eaten, they threw the remaining provisions overboard to lighten the vessel. Then Luke reports the shipwreck, including the desire of the soldiers to kill the prisoners lest they escape; but the centurion stopped them in order to save Paul. All came to land safely and learned they were on the island of Malta, where the local population treated them kindly. Paul made quite an impression when being bitten by a snake he did not die; and subsequently many were cured as he ministered among them.

After three months Paul and companions set sail on a ship that had wintered at Malta. They sailed to Puteoli and traveled by land to Rome, encountering other Christians along the way. In Rome Paul was lodged privately with a guard, and after being there three days he called together the foremost Jews and spoke to them.

The speech recalls Paul's earlier judicial addresses, but in the informal setting the rhetoric is essentially *epideictic*. In outline the speech appears as follows:[348]

---

347. E.g., Schneider, *Apostelgeschichte,* 2:395–96.

348. I am indebted to the careful study by H. J. Hauser (*Strukturen der Abschlusserzählung der Apostelgeschichte (Apg 28,16–31* [AnBib 86; Rome: Biblical Institute Press, 1979] esp. 20, 35) for the recognition of the major divisions of Paul's speech(es) in Acts 28. Insufficient attention has been given to this excellent study and Hauser's case for viewing 28:16–31 as a unit.

1.0 Report of the Past (vv. 17c–19)
   1.1 Paul's Situation (vv. 17c)
   1.2 The Romans' Findings (v. 18)
   1.3 The Necessity of Paul's Appeal to Caesar (v. 19)
2.0 A Double Explanation to the Roman Jews (v. 20)
   2.1 The Reason for Calling Them (v. 20a)
   2.2 The Reason for Paul's Incarceration (v. 20b)

After Paul spoke, the Roman Jews reported they had no negative information from Judea about Paul, and they expressed their desire to hear Paul's views (παρὰ σοῦ ἀκοῦσαι ἃ φρονεῖς, "to hear from you what you think"), especially since they had heard negative reports about Christianity (τῆς αἱρέσεως ταύτης . . . πανταχοῦ ἀντιλέγεται, "this sect . . . everywhere it is spoken against"). Luke then reports that a time was set and great numbers of the Roman Jews listened to Paul as ἐξετίθετο διαμαρτυρόμενος τὴν βασιλείαν τοῦ θεοῦ πείθων τε αὐτοὺς περὶ τοῦ Ἰησοῦ ἀπό τε τοῦ νόμου Μωϋσέως καὶ τῶν προφητῶν ("he explained the matter to them, testifying to the kingdom of God and trying to convince them about Jesus both from the law of Moses and from the prophets"). This summary has at least seven vital points in common with elements of the speeches (witness, kingdom, God, Jesus, law, Moses, and the prophets). The results of Paul's efforts were mixed, and as they quarreled among themselves Paul had the last word, which he spoke to those who disbelieved. The speech is *epideictic* rhetoric with strong *judicial* tones and in outline it has this form:

3.0 Concluding Remarks (vv. 25b–28)
   3.1 Citation of Scripture (vv. 25b–27)
   3.2 Salvation and the Gentiles (v. 28)
      3.2.1 The Sending of Salvation (v. 28a–b)
      3.2.2 The Gentiles' Hearing (v. 28c)

Analysis. (1.0) Conzelmann observes that this speech is the final example of the pattern "to the Jews first."[349] (1.1) The address ἄνδρες ἀδελφοί ("Men, brothers") is the last occurrence of this salutation, which has opened speeches frequently since 1:16. Schneider notes that within the larger group of speeches employing this address in 2:29; 3:17; 7:2; 13:26, 38; 22:1; 23:1, 6 Jewish Christians hail Jews with ἄνδρες ἀδελφοί ("Men, brothers").[350] The denial of wrongdoing repeats Paul's protests in 25:8b, 10, 11. More specifically, the statement that Paul did οὐδὲν ἐναντίον . . . τῷ λαῷ ("nothing against our people") echoes 21:28 and resembles 25:10, and the claim that Paul did nothing ἐναντίον . . . τοῖς ἔθεσι τοῖς πατρῴοις ("against the customs of our fathers")

349. Conzelmann, *Acts*, 227.
350. Schneider, *Apostelgeschichte*, 2:414 n. 25.

echoes 21:21 and resembles 25:8b. Furthermore, Schneider notices a parallel
between a portion of Agabus's prophecy in 21:11 and Paul's statement (Agabus:
εἰς χεῖρας ἐθνῶν, "into the hands of the Gentiles"; Paul: εἰς τὰς χεῖρας τῶν
Ῥωμαίων, "into the hands of the Romans").[351]

(1.2) The report concerning the Romans' conclusion that Paul was innocent refers to 25:18–20; 26:31, 32. The verb ἀνακρίνειν ("to examine") once
again refers to Christians being examined in a legal setting regarding charges
filed against them (see 4:9). And the phrase μηδεμίαν αἰτίαν θανάτου ("no cause
for a sentence of death") repeats the words of a statement about Jesus made
in 13:28.

(1.3) Verse 19 states that it was necessary for Paul to appeal to Caesar.
This remark refers to 25:11 and gives additional information (οὐχ ὡς τοῦ ἔθνους
μου ἔχων τι κατηγορεῖν, "though I had no charge to bring against my nation")
to make clear the purely defensive nature of Paul's appeal. This statement
becomes ironic in relation to the ensuing blast in 28:25b–28.

(2.1) In v. 20a Paul's statement explains that he called the leaders of the
Roman Jewish community to him to give them the information imparted in
vv. 17c–19. (2.2) Then, v. 20b offers an additional explanation with respect
to the cause of Paul's incarceration. The remark echoes similar statements
about the reason for Paul's imprisonment or being on trial (see 23:6b).

(3.0) In form and function the concluding remarks, vv. 25b–28, are comparable to 13:46–47; 18:6,[352] but these verses are generally similar to other
polemical remarks made in speeches (see 7:4b).[353] (3.1) The opening declaration is reminiscent of statements in speeches that confront the audience
directly with their guilt (see 2:36). The mention of the Holy Spirit is the last
of many such references in the speeches (see 1:16). The citation of the prophet
Isaiah is one of the explicit references in the speeches to the prophets (see
2:16), and the passage cited is a very slightly altered version of Isa 6:9–10
LXX.[354]

(3.2.1) Verse 28a–b opens with a bold formula encountered previously in
speeches, γνωστὸν . . . ἔστω ("let this be known to you"; see 2:14). The declara-

---

351. Ibid., 2:414 n. 29.

352. D. P. Moessner compares these three pronouncements with three similar statements in
Luke's Gospel to point out the parallels between Jesus and Paul that show the believing portion
of Israel to be an eschatological remnant illustrating nonbelieving Israel's peril but also the continuing possibility of repentance and belief ("Paul in Acts: Preacher of Eschatological Repentance to Israel," NTS 34 [1988] 96–104). This interpretation attempts, rightly, to correct those
readings of Acts which find the door to salvation closed to Israel at the end of Acts.

353. F. Bovon has noticed the form of this "citation within a citation," to show how there the
past bears witness to the present, for both come from divine inspiration ("'Schön hat der heilige
Geist durch den Propheten Jesaja zu euren Vätern gesprochen' (Act 28,25)," ZNW 75 [1984]
226–32, esp. 230–32).

354. The passage is not as Bruce maintains, "a verbatim quotation" (Acts, 540).

tion per se refers to τοῦτο τὸ σωτήριον τοῦ θεοῦ ("this salvation of God"). Salvation is a crucial theme of the speeches (see 2:40b; 4:12), and the identification of the salvation as "God's" makes clear the divine authority and direction of the outworking of salvation on a universal scale according to the divine plan. Krodel finds echoes of 1:8 as well as 15:15 in this declaration.[355] (3.2.2) Finally, the statement concerning the Gentiles' willingness to accept God's salvation is very similar to 13:46–47; 22:21; 26:17–18.

355. Krodel, *Acts*, 505.

3 THE SPEECHES IN ACTS AND ANCIENT LITERATURE

S INCE AT LEAST the late nineteenth and early twentieth centuries
scholars have viewed the speeches in Acts in relation to the speeches
occurring in other ancient literature.[1] In this chapter, with the aid of
the information garnered from the previous analysis, I shall attempt to survey,
critique, and build on earlier comparative studies in order to appreciate more
fully the role of the speeches in Acts. In this work I shall consider the speeches
in Acts in relation to three somewhat artificially distinguished bodies of
literature. First, I shall reflect on the relationship of Acts to a selected body
of Greco-Roman historiography. Second, I shall relate Acts to selected portions
of the Septuagint. And, third, I shall relate Acts to selected pieces of literature
from Hellenistic Judaism. The artificiality of this division is that certain of
the writings of Hellenistic Judaism are found in the Septuagint. I am, however,
distinguishing original Hebrew and Aramaic texts that have been translated
into Greek from those documents in the Septuagint that were originally
composed in Greek. Thus, I shall consider the original Greek texts of the
Septuagint in conjunction with nonbiblical writings of the Hellenistic era.

Greco-Roman Historiography

Above all, M. Dibelius registered the significance of studying Acts, especially
the speeches, in relation to Greco-Roman historiography.[2] Critical scholars

1. See the bibliographical note by H. J. Cadbury ("Note XXXII: The Speeches in Acts," in
The Beginnings of Christianity: Part I, The Acts of the Apostles [ed. F. J. Foakes Jackson and K.
Lake; 5 vols.; London: Macmillan, 1920–33] 5:404–5 n. 2) referring to the interest of scholars
in the speeches in Acts in relation to classical studies or ancient historiography.
2. M. Dibelius, "The Speeches in Acts and Ancient Historiography," in *Studies in the Acts of*

of all stripes, from conservatives to extreme skeptics, recognize the importance of this aspect of comparative study,[3] although the use made of the comparisons and the conclusions drawn from such study vary greatly.

As noted in chapter 1, Dibelius separated the speeches into different groups — speeches analogous to those in Greco-Roman historiography and repetitive missionary speeches, which are in Dibelius's opinion not actually comparable to ancient history writing. Dibelius understood that Luke had traditions he freely used in composing the speeches, but what lay behind the so-called missionary speeches was a pattern of preaching typical of Luke's own day (ca. 90 C.E.).

In a *Habilitationsschrift* from 1958, revised and first published in 1961, U. Wilckens subjected Dibelius's contentions concerning the missionary speeches to rigorous scrutiny and concluded that the missionary speeches did not depend on a scheme of preaching from Luke's own time. Instead, Wilckens concluded that these speeches to Jews were completely the constructions of Luke's own theology and that the sermons to pagan audiences were composed in relation to a traditional pattern observable in 1 Thess 1:9–10 and Heb 5:11–6:2.[4]

Following Wilckens's denial that a pattern of preaching from Luke's day lay behind the missionary speeches in Acts, E. Plümacher regarded the

---

the Apostles (ed. H. Greeven; New York: Charles Scribner's Sons, 1956) 138–85. While Dibelius and those who follow and advance his style of criticism tend to reflect on Luke's creative purposefulness in the speeches, others such as F. F Bruce ("The Acts of the Apostles: Historical Record or Theological Reconstruction?" *ANRW* 2.25.3 [1985] 2569–2603, esp. 2582–88) view the speeches in relation to "the tradition of Greek historical writing" in order to defend their authenticity and to perceive the valuable historical sources behind their composition and inclusion in Acts.

3. See the discussion of Dibelius's contribution in chapter 1 above. For a sharply negative appraisal of Dibelius's work, see W. W. Gasque, "The Speeches of Acts: Dibelius Reconsidered," in *New Dimensions in New Testament Study* (ed. R. N. Longenecker and M. C. Tenney; Grand Rapids: Zondervan, 1974) 232–50.

4. U. Wilckens, *Die Missionsreden der Apostelgeschichte: Form- und traditionsgeschichtliche Untersuchungen* (WMANT 5; Neukirchen-Vluyn: Neukirchener Verlag, 1961; 2d ed. 1963). Wilckens schematizes 1 Thess 1:9–10 in this manner:

I πῶς ἐπεστρέψατε πρὸς τὸν θεὸν ἀπὸ τῶν εἰδώλων δουλεύειν θεῷ ζῶντι καὶ ἀληθινῷ,
II καὶ ἀναμένειν τὸν υἱὸν αὐτοῦ ἐκ τῶν οὐρανῶν,
III ὃν ἤγειρεν ἐκ τῶν νεκρῶν,
IV Ἰησοῦν τὸν ῥυόμενον ἡμᾶς ἐκ τῆς ὀργῆς τῆς ἐρχομένης.
And, in turn, he divides Heb 6:1b–2 as follows:
I μετανοίας ἀπὸ νεκρῶν ἔργων καὶ πίστεως ἐπὶ θεόν,
II βαπτισμῶν διδαχῆς,
III ἐπιθέσεώς τε χειρῶν,
IV ἀναστάσεως νεκρῶν
V καὶ κρίματος αἰωνίου.
In terms of tradition history Wilckens argues that these items are independent of one another but reflect a common pattern that is suited for liturgical purposes in Hebrews.

question of the relationship of the missionary speeches to conventions of Greco-Roman historiography to be reopened, and he wrote a dissertation investigating the matter. Plümacher is actually interested in all of Acts in relation to Hellenistic historiography, both the narrative and the speeches,[5] yet more than anyone else he has taken up and advanced the investigation of the speeches. His concern was to determine Luke's purpose(s) in composing the speeches and their function in the context of Acts. Plümacher compares the missionary speeches with speeches in Dionysius of Halicarnassus and Livy (as well as others) in order to make six amply illustrated points. In what follows I shall reiterate selected references from Acts and Greco-Roman historians to give basic illustration of Plümacher's argument, and in presenting this material I shall work freely to clarify and augment Plümacher's references.

First, following Dibelius, Plümacher observes that the speeches in Acts are similar to those in Greco-Roman historiography in that they are loosely fitted to the context in which they occur; indeed, at times they conflict with the surrounding narrative material.[6] For example, Acts 6:13–14 reports charges brought against Stephen, but one wonders what the long segment of the speech presenting the history of Israel (7:2–43) has to do with the situation Stephen faced; moreover, Acts 17:16 reports Paul's irritation with the idolatry of Athens, but in the speech in 17:22 one finds a *captatio benevolentiae* praising the piety of the Athenians; and in Acts 20:18–35, before an entirely friendly audience of the Ephesian elders, Paul repeatedly (vv. 20, 21, 27, 33–34) defends himself in an apologetic fashion that even goes beyond the defenses he makes in situations where he actually faces charges.

As parallels in Greco-Roman historiography, Plümacher cites the following places where one finds tensions or conflicts between portions of the account: (A) In *Ant.* 1.21.3 Josephus tells of the death and burial of Rachel at Hebron, but as he continues the story in *Ant.* 2.3.1 (eight paragraphs later) Josephus remarks that the plotted murder of Joseph by his brothers would have done great harm to a father and driven a mother into sorrow (ᾧ πατήρ τε ἀναιρουμένῳ συναδικεῖται καὶ μήτηρ εἰς πένθος, "whose destruction would entail grievous injury to a father and plunge a mother into mourning"). (B) In Appian's *Punic War* 9.64 there is

---

5. E. Plümacher, *Lukas als hellenistischer Schriftsteller: Studien zur Apostelgeschichte* (SUNT 9; Göttingen: Vandenhoeck & Ruprecht, 1972). Plümacher has reiterated and even expanded his analysis in articles in standard reference works, scholarly journals, and congress papers. See E. Plümacher, "Lukas als griechischer Historiker," PWSup 14 (1974) cols. 235–64; "Wirklichkeitserfahrung und Geschichtsschreibung bei Lukas: Erwägungen zu den Wir-Stücken der Apostelgeschichte," ZNW 68 (1977) 2–22; "Apostelgeschichte," TRE 3 (1979) 483–528; and "Die Apostelgeschichte als historische Monographie," in *Les Actes des Apôtres: Tradition, rédaction, théologie* (ed. J. Kremer; BETL 48; Gembloux: Duculot; Leuven: Leuven University Press, 1979) 457–66.

6. Plümacher, "Lukas," cols. 244–45.

a reference by the speaker Publius Cornelius to the speech which Scipio has made a little while previously in the camp before the envoys from Carthage. The speaker in Rome cannot, however, know of this speech yet! Moreover, Censorinus then makes a speech in the same place which, in [12.86], begins graciously but, in [13.90], after the resumption of the narrative, results in a threat.[7]

(C) In Dio's *Roman History* 38.36–46 one finds a speech by Caesar to his troops, who had fallen into deep dejection at the report of the great assembly of German forces against them. The speech as reported by Dio is a long, general deliberation about taking the right point of view regarding public interests, especially the justice of engaging in war. By contrast, Caesar himself portrays the speech as a far more pointed, pertinent address in *Gallic War* 1.40.

Second, speeches by governmental and military leaders are often powerful forces in Hellenistic historiography, frequently being the very cause of subsequent events in the account. Similarly, the speeches by early Christian leaders are compelling forces in the account of Christianity in Acts.[8] Thus, one encounters speeches in both Acts and ancient histories at decisive turning points in the narrative.[9] For example, the missionary activity of the church begins and makes its initial path among the Jews with Peter's speeches in 2:14–39 and 3:12–26. The general turning point of the proclamation of the gospel to the Gentiles comes, in turn, through Peter's speech in 10:34–43. Further, the preaching of Paul in 13:16–41 peaks with the last call to repentance addressed to the Jews, and their rejection results in the ensuing turning of the missionaries to the Gentiles.[10] Passages in Greco-Roman historiography illustrating the forceful function and crucial location of speeches in historical narratives include: (A) Dionysius of Halicarnassus remarks in *Roman Antiquities* 7.66.3 that he thought it necessary over all else to report speeches made by the heads of contending parties in instances of civil commotion—speeches by means of which incredible and amazing actions were accomplished (τοὺς λόγους δι' ὧν αἱ παράδοξοι καὶ θαυμασταὶ πράξεις ἐπετελέσωησαν, "the speeches by which the extraordinary and remarkable events were brought to pass"). (B) Plümacher presents Livy as the master reporter of such speeches. In historical narrative Livy (7.29.1–2) explains the significance and magnitude of the wars of the Romans against the Samnites, Pyrrhus, and the Carthaginians, declaring, "Quanta rerum moles!—How vast a series of events!" As Livy, then, goes on to report the great series of events, he includes a speech by the ambassadors of the Campanians before the senate

7. Dibelius, "Speeches," 177 n. 71.
8. Plümacher, *Lukas*, 33–38; "Lukas," cols. 247–48.
9. Plümacher, "Lukas," col. 247.
10. Plümacher refers in a general way to Wilckens in making observations about 13:16–41 ("Lukas," col. 247), so that he seems to follow Wilckens's lead in this interpretation. The reading of Acts in this fashion is full of problems, and it is not enough simply to cite a previous opinion as one repeats it in order to make a case. Exegesis is necessary.

(7.30) which called for Rome's entry into war in defense of the Campanians. The Roman response (7.31.2) and the Campanian reaction (7.31.3–4) are reported through speeches. Through the remainder of the account of the war(s) one finds speakers addressing critical issues at crucial points of development (e.g., 7.32.13–17, 7.33.10; 7.40.4–14, 15–19). Similarly, in narrating the Macedonian War, Livy records speeches at the crucial junctions of the story, so that the speeches themselves are regularly the causes of subsequent events. For example, Livy reports that Titus Quinctius Famininus's speech to Philip V of Macedonia and the Aetolians displeased them so much that "haec cum omnium sociorum adsensu dicta Aetolis non in praesentia modo gravia auditu, sed mox etiam belli causae magnarumque ex eo cladium iis fuerunt" ("these words were received with applause from all the allies, but to the Aetolians they were unpleasant to hear at the moment, and later on they were the cause of war, and as a result of the war, of great slaughter to the Aetolians") (33.13.13).

Third, like other ancient historians Luke brings speeches to an end by reporting either that the speaker said much more than was reported or that the speech was interrupted (a frequent device in Acts, but less frequent in other ancient histories).[11] For example, Acts 2:40 reports that Peter bore witness to the crowd on Pentecost by saying many more things than recorded; and at several places — for example, 4:1; 22:22 (and see the analysis of Acts 2:37 in chapter 2 for a full list) — speeches are ended by interruption. (A) In relation to the comment that the speaker could or did say more than recorded, Plümacher simply reproduces a list that Dibelius originally offered of such comments found in ancient historiography (Xenophon, *Hellenica* 2.4.42; Polybius 3.111.1; 21.14.4; Appian, *Samnite History* 10.6; idem, *Civil Wars* 3.63.257). To illustrate this point, however, consider the following: In Xenophon's *Hellenica,* after Pausanius disbanded the victorious "Spartan" army in Athens in 403 B.C.E., some of the soldiers mounted the Acropolis still armed and offered sacrifice. There, Xenophon records a speech to them by Thrasybulus in deliberative rhetoric (2.4.42). The speech is pointed, challenging, but brief. At the conclusion one reads, εἰπὼν δὲ ταῦτα καὶ ἄλλα τοιαῦτα . . . ("when he had said this and more to the same effect . . ."). (B) In turn, the infrequent device of interrupting a speech in Greco-Roman historiography occurs in speeches in the writing of Josephus (*Ant.* 16.11.5) and Xenophon (*Hellenica* 6.5.37).

Fourth, in Gamaliel's speech in Acts 5:36–37, one observes a standard rhetorical device found seldom in Acts but frequently in the speeches in Greco-Roman historiography, namely, the introduction of historical examples.[12] An excellent specimen of this rhetorical device in a speech in historiography comes in Tacitus's record of events in 48 C.E. (*Annals* 11.24). During the course

---

11. Plümacher, "Lukas," col. 249.
12. Ibid.

of a debate over allowing full Roman citizens without senatorial rank to become eligible for an official career, Tacitus reports a speech by the emperor, Claudius, in which repeated references to past events are introduced and interpreted in order to provide direction for making a crucial decision. Similarly, Plümacher lists speeches in Sallust (*Catilinarian War* 51.5–6) and Josephus (*J.W.* 5.9.4).

Fifth, Hellenistic historiography manifested a tendency toward Atticizing; that is, the authors imitated the style and ambience of the classical period in Greek. This device was popular and common. Similarly, as Luke writes Acts, especially in selected speeches, Plümacher contends he engaged in literary *mimesis* as he tended toward a Septuagintal style and flavor; thus, Luke seeks through the use of Septuagintalisms to cast the early era of the church as its classical period.[13] For example, (a) Acts 2:14 employs the Septuagintal phrase ἐπῆρεν τὴν φωνήν ("raised his voice"), which occurs in places such as Judg 2:4; 9:7; Ruth 1:9, 14; 2 Sam 13:36; Ps 92:3; (b) Acts 2:14 and 4:10 employ γνωστὸν ἔστω ("let it be known to you"), which occurs in Exod 33:16; 1 Esdr 6:8; Ezra 4:12; Wis 16:28; Isa 19:28; Ezek 36:32; and (c) Acts 3:17 and 20:22 employ καὶ νῦν ("and now"), which occurs in Tob 6:13; 1 Macc 4:10; Jdt 11:23; 1 Esdr 8:79. (Many other examples are possible.) The practice of "classical imitation" or literary mimesis is a well known and widely recognized phenomenon in ancient literature, including historiography.[14] Among the illustrations of this kind of imitation in Greco-Roman historiography that Plümacher offers is the speech by the Alban Mettius Fufetius to the Roman king Tullus Hostilius recorded in Dionysius of Halicarnassus's *Roman Antiquities* 3.7.2. The speech appears in its opening to copy the beginning of a speech in Thucydides (6.89.1) by Alcibiades to the Lacedaemonians. Compare:

Dionysius: Ἀναγκαῖον εἶναί μοι δοκεῖ τὰς αἰτίας πρῶτον ἐπιδεῖξαι . . . .
"It seems to me necessary to begin my speech by setting forth the reasons . . . ."

Thucydides: Ἀναγκαῖον περὶ τῆς ἐμῆς διαβολῆς πρῶτον ἐς ὑμᾶς εἰπεῖν . . .
"It is necessay first of all to speak to you about the prejudice against me . . . ."

Moreover, Plümacher illustrates a series of parallel points between the response-speech by Tullus Hostilius (*Roman Antiquities* 3.11.1–11) and other elements of speeches in Thucydides (e.g., *Roman Antiquities* 3.11.4 parallels

13. Plümacher, *Lukas*, 38–72, esp. 41–50; "Lukas," cols. 250–54.
14. See the copious bibliography regarding secondary literature on "classical imitation" in Plümacher, "Lukas," cols. 251–54. For a balanced, lucid, and concise discussion of Luke's imitation of the Septuagint, see H. J. Cadbury, *The Making of Luke-Acts* (London: Macmillan, 1927; reprint, London: S.P.C.K., 1961] 122–23).

Thucydides 2.37.1; and *Roman Antiquities* 3.11.5 parallels Thucydides 2.39.1). Plümacher gives further examples of this phenomenon by comparing elements of speeches in Dionysius with other speeches in Thucydides and still others in Demosthenes and Xenophon.[15]

Sixth, Plümacher observes a phenomenon similar to "classical imitation" in Greco-Roman historiography, namely, *archaizing*. Hellenistic historians deliberately included archaisms in their narratives in an effort to achieve the noble status of antiquity. Similarly, Plümacher suggests, while drawing on earlier tradition-historical investigations of Acts, that Luke included early Christian christological titles and kerygmatic formulas that seem intended to give the Acts account an archaic tone that casts the early period as an archetypal age.[16] Plümacher lists the following "older christological titles" that he understands to be incorporated into the speeches: (a) παῖς θεοῦ, "servant of God" (3:13, 26); (b) ὁ ἅγιος, "the Holy One" (3:14); (c) ὁ δίκαιος, "the Righteous One" (3:14); (d) ἀρχηγός, "the Author" or "the Leader" (3:15; 5:31); and (e) σωτήρ, "Savior" (5:31; 13:23). Furthermore he lists old forms of the passion and resurrection kerygma as occurring in 2:22–23, 36; 3:13–15; 10:40; 13:27–28; and 3:26; 13:30. Moreover, Plümacher understands that a "witness-formula" lies behind 2:32; 3:15; 10:41–42; and still other older traditional pieces are included in 3:20–21; 5:31. Plümacher finds that similar archaizing elements occur in Livy, in contrast to Dionysius, who does not employ such a device, because as Livy presents the early history of Rome he gives the reader the impression of that former time. He does so by incorporating stylistic devices such as archaic grammatical forms, cultic formulas, vows, and legal forms into the history. For example, in 1.17.10 Livy quotes a declaration concerning the "senate's" preparedness to certify the results of the citizens' election of a king as follower of Romulus; and in 1.18.9 he records the words of a prayer of an "augur" to "Father Jupiter" asking that the gods give a sign of their own approval of the chosen king. Other portions of the account that are thought to be archaizing touches include 1.24.4–8; 1.26.5–6; 1.32.6; 1.38.2.

In sum, Plümacher contends these characteristics are neither passive nor casual phenomena; they are Luke's deliberate techniques as a Hellenistic historian.[17] Plümacher's thesis is that Luke used the form and the style of Hellenistic historiography because of his own particular theological understanding of Christianity. The literary standards of Luke's day demanded a close-to-exact correspondence between the form and the content of a

---

15. Plümacher, *Lukas*, 52–55, 59–60. Plümacher acknowledges a special debt to the work of J. Fleirle (*Über Nachahmungen des Demosthenes, Thukydides und Xenophon in den Reden der Römischen Archäologie des Dionysius von Halicarnass* [Munich: Programm des Ludwigs-Gymnasiums München, 1890]).

16. Plümacher, *Lukas*, 72–78; "Lukas," cols. 254–55.

17. Plümacher, *Lukas*, 78–79.

composition. Thus, Luke wrote Acts in the style of Hellenistic history because he wanted to establish the worldwide or universal significance of the claims of Christianity. Through Acts itself Luke communicates to the reader that the leaders and the community of the early church were important at the level of world history; they were not merely provincial or obscure. Thus, one sees that Plümacher's analysis of the speeches along the lines observed above is a crucial element in his argument.

To Plümacher's credit, in arguing that Luke works as a Hellenistic historian, in addition to describing how the speeches in Acts are *like* those in Greco-Roman histories, he also notes ways in which the speeches in Acts are *different from* speeches in Hellenistic historiography.[18] First, the speeches in Acts are considerably shorter than typical speeches in Hellenistic histories. While there are brief addresses in almost all ancient historical accounts, such speeches are the exception, whereas speeches that last for pages on end are the rule. Second, the speeches in Acts never function as do clusters of speeches in Hellenistic historiography—that is, to give various perspectives on critical issues and events. The speeches in Acts present or defend one point of view and do not weigh matters before the eyes of the readers in a comparative fashion. Third, Plümacher suggests there is no deliberative element and little epideictic rhetoric in the speeches in Acts ("Auch innerhalb der Reden fehlt jedes deliberative Element [wir übrigens auch das epideiktische]).[19] Fourth, Luke did not seek, as Hellenistic historians frequently did, to use the speeches to characterize the particular speakers. The speakers in Acts sound alike, so that Peter can even employ "Pauline" terminology in Acts 15:7–11.

Plümacher's meticulously articulated case is, however, finally not fully persuasive; although one cannot deny some relationship between Acts, especially the speeches, and Hellenistic historiography. Among the problems with Plümacher's comparisons and findings I would list these items: First, the argument about Luke's purpose as discernible through the *form* of Acts is self-destructive, especially in conjunction with other observations that Plümacher himself makes. The case for Christianity's universal significance is not made by the historiographical form of Acts. If ancient readers expected a close correspondence between form and content and if historiography normally narrated the course of events of worldwide or universal significance, then Acts defies the expectations of ancient readers. The main characters are not people of preeminence in the social, political, or even religious world of antiquity. Moreover, the Septuagintal styling of parts of Acts would not win the account universal admiration; indeed, the strange Semitic tones of the Greek of Acts would be a cause for ridicule in the Hellenistic world at large. Paul's audience in Acts 17 calls him ὁ σπερμολόγος οὗτος ("this babbler") and Luke's most

18. Plümacher, "Lukas," cols. 248–49.
19. Ibid., col. 249.

cultured readers would likely use a similar designation for him. Second, as the analysis in the preceding chapter demonstrated, the speeches are a mixture of rhetorical styles, and there is much deliberative and epideictic rhetoric in Acts. Thus, the speeches as a whole are less apologetic or judicial and more urging and praiseful than Plümacher suggests. Third, the speeches do characterize the speakers more than Plümacher recognizes. Stephen's anti-Temple rhetoric defines his attitude in distinction from the majority of the other speakers; Peter employs a set of christological titles that other speakers do not share;[20] and the well-known Pauline concept of justification (δικαιοῦν, "to justify") occurs only in a speech by Paul in Acts 13:39, as does the note concerning freedom through (διά) Christ which was not previously a provision of Moses' law (ἀπὸ πάντων ὧν οὐκ ἠδυνήθητε ἐν νόμῳ Μωϋσέως δικαιωθῆναι, "from all which you could not be justified by the law of Moses"; see 13:38). Fourth, as the analysis of the speeches demonstrates, the use of the past is a far more complex phenomenon than Plümacher allows. For example, Gamaliel's speech certainly uses historical examples overtly, but numerous other forms of reference to the past occur in numerous other speeches in Acts. Fifth, Plümacher notes perhaps too many points of parallel between the speeches in Acts and those in ancient historiography. For example, it is not clear, despite the declarations of both Dibelius and Plümacher, that the speeches in ancient historiography were often poorly related to their narrative situations. The speeches in Hellenistic historiography may be vague and unnecessarily lengthy, but the speakers still speak *around* the central concern that led to the delivery of the speech. One may judge a speech in Hellenistic historiography to be verbose or tendentious, but the speakers do not raise new topics that completely alter the subject with which they are initially occupied. The speeches in Acts, however, often simply change the subject. Thus, the seemingly *irrelevant* material in a speech in Acts is conspicuous in comparison to the content of speeches in ancient historiography and, therefore, demands attention. Indeed, frequently in Acts the "new" material introduced by the speaker is exactly the portion of the speech that generates the strongest reaction from the audience in the narrative; and the content of the seemingly intrusive material is what one finds repeatedly in several speeches in Acts. In short, Plümacher pays inadequate attention to

20. Making this point says nothing about the "primitive" character of these titles, for as H. J. Cadbury observed long ago ("Speeches," in *Beginnings*, 5:402-27), the arguments about the primitive nature of the theological elements of certain speeches are circular and uninformed. The only sources available for identifying the assumed primitive theological elements of early Christianity are the speeches in Acts. Some commentators, therefore, read the early speeches in Acts and label the titles in these speeches "primitive," and then, with a list of purportedly primitive titles composed, the same or other commentators find that the early speakers in Acts employ "primitive" titles in their speeches. Indeed, the only surely primitive item in this kind of interpretation is the logic. Nevertheless, such argumentation goes on and on.

the content of the speeches in Acts in comparison with the content of speeches in Hellenistic historiography. Rather than attend to concerns that are implied by formal and stylistic elements of the speeches, one must recognize that the contents of the speeches make the concerns of the speakers explicit and thereby demand direct attention.[21] This point is made emphatically by the striking, highly unusual repetitive content of the speeches.

In conclusion, there is a clear relationship between the form and style of speeches in Hellenistic historiography and the form and style of the speeches in Acts, although there is no exact correspondence in these matters. Nevertheless, the contents of the speeches in Acts, especially in the portions of the speeches that completely or almost completely depart from the situation at hand, are quite distinct from the contents of speeches in Hellenistic historiography. Moreover, the steady repetition of nonsituational information is distinct from Hellenistic historiography. Thus, one must look to and beyond the speeches in Greco-Roman histories for a full appreciation of the speeches in Acts.

The Septuagint

The clear use of the Septuagint by the speakers in Acts in citations and probable allusions indicates some relationship between the speeches in Acts and the Septuagint. Moreover, the religious nature of the contents and Septuagintal flavor of the language of the speeches in Acts, especially in the highly repetitive portions that go beyond matters at hand, naturally commend a comparison of the speeches in Acts and the Septuagint. The pointed question for this portion of the current investigation is whether there are speeches in the Septuagint that may have influenced the form, style, content, and function of the speeches in Acts.

Three groups of speeches in the Septuagint merit comparison with the speeches in Acts. First, since the pioneering studies of M. Noth, scholars have recognized that the "great speeches" of the Deuteronomistic History, especially

---

21. A program of interpretation similar to Plümacher's comes from W. C. van Unnik, who works from the statements about history writing in Lucian of Samosata (*The Art of Writing History*, esp. chaps. 34–60) and Dionysius of Halicarnassus (*Epistle to Pompey*) to evaluate Acts in terms of two vital qualifications and ten key rules for ancient history writing ("Luke's Second Book and the Rules of Hellenistic Historiography," in *Les Actes des Apôtres: Tradition, rédaction, théologie* [ed. J. Kremer; BETL 48; Gembloux: Duculot; Leuven: Leuven University Press, 1979] 37–60). In van Unnik's evaluation Luke's work in Acts earns praise in terms of ancient standards.

With particular regard to the speeches, van Unnik found that Luke included them in a form (suitable to the speaker and the situation) and a style (lucid, with appropriate but not excessive rhetoric) typical of history writing. Thus, van Unnik also did not understand the speeches to be primarily concerned to present content.

as recognized in specific repeated items, unifies the presentation of the whole premonarchical period of Israel's history.[22] The "great speeches" offer focused narrative summaries and repeat the theme of the threat of divine retribution in the event of Israel's unfaithfulness to the Lord. The initial "great speech" is that of Moses, which runs from Deut 1:6 through 30:20. The speech initially recounts history (1:6–3:29) and gives a general introduction to the law (4:1–40); then, in speech, Moses delivers the Deuteronomic law (5:1–30:20).[23] The next "great speech" comes from Joshua in Joshua 23. There is a brief reference to the history of the occupation of Canaan, which attributes the taking of the land to the Lord God of Israel (23:3). Promises of God's further actions for Israel follow (23:5), and then, based on God's past and promised actions, the speech exhorts "all Israel" to be steadfast in observing *all* the law of Moses and repeatedly warns against unfaithfulness (23:6-23). As Noth remarks,

> [The Deuteronomist's] account is constructed in such a way that this speech marks the end of an historical epoch and, looking back to the great events now at an end, goes on to warn the people against the gods and cults of the land that has now been taken for a possession, and culminates in a threat of retribution. It cannot be accidental that this threat resembles in meaning and wording the threat at the end of that part of Moses' great speech composed by [the Deuteronomist] (Deut. 4:25–28. esp. v. 26).[24]

Then, in the course of the Deuteronomistic History one encounters the relatively lengthy story of Gideon (Judg 6:1–8:32). Noth judged this material to be an old tradition compiled from a variety of elements prior to the work of the Deuteronomist. Thus, Noth concluded that the Gideon story was incorporated into the Deuteronomistic History. Yet, even so, Noth observed the speech by an unnamed prophet in Judg 6:8–10, which again provided "a reflection upon the situation such as [the Deuteronomist] on occasion likes to put into his characters' mouths."[25] While this small speech is no "great speech," Noth found that it worked in the same manner and in relation to the "great speeches" to reiterate and thereby unify the overall history. Finally, at the end of the period of the judges in Israel's history (Judg 2:6–1 Sam 12:25) the Deuteronomist records the last "great speech," this one by Samuel. As Noth observed, there is a high degree of correspondence between this speech and that of Joshua in Joshua 23. And, once again, "this speech culminates in a threat of retribution similar to that in the speech by Joshua and in part of Moses' great speech written by [the Deuteronomist] (Deut 1:6–4:28)."[26]

22. M. Noth, *The Deuteronomistic History* (JSOTSup 15; Sheffield: JSOT Press, 1981; trans. of *Überlieferungsgeschichtliche Studien* [2d ed.; Tübingen: Niemeyer, 1957] 1–110).
23. See Noth, *History*, 34–35.
24. Ibid., 39–40.
25. Ibid., 45.
26. Ibid., 42.

As Noth summarized the matter, the Deuteronomist used speeches to portray the history of events, to create narrative flow, to circumscribe and to summarize epochs, and to unify the entire premonarchic period. When one compares the form, style, content, and function of these "great speeches" in the Deuteronomistic History with the speeches in Acts one observes certain similarities in style, content, and function, but in form the speeches in Acts are more like the form of speeches in Hellenistic historiography. Among the notable correspondences between the speeches of the Deuteronomistic History and Acts are the following: (A) In Acts 7:37 there is an explicit quotation from Deut 18:15, which indicates the possibility of further points of contact between the speeches in the Deuteronomistic History and the speeches in Acts. (B) The speeches by Moses, Joshua, and Samuel recount selected portions of the past — the sojourn of Israel in Egypt, the Exodus and the wilderness wanderings, and the occupation of Canaan — from a distinctively theological point of view. The same perspective on the same events occurs in Stephen's speech in Acts 7 and Paul's speech in Acts 13. Moreover, the theological perspective itself colors the majority of speeches in Acts, even when they are not recounting the history of Israel. Indeed, the assumption of divine authority articulated in the words ἐνώπιον κυρίου ("before the Lord") in 1 Sam 12:7 underlies the speeches of Acts (compare especially Acts 4:19–20). (C) The repeated threat against unfaithfulness or idolatry in Deut 4:25–28; Josh 23:15–16; Judg 6:8–10; 1 Sam 12:24–25 is echoed in Acts 7:41 and 17:29, although one cannot determine that there is deliberate imitation. Nevertheless, the way in which Deut 4:26 deliberates (διαμαρτύρομαι ὑμῖν σήμερον τόν τε οὐρανὸν καὶ τὴν γῆν, "I call heaven and earth to witness against you today") demonstrates the same concern with "witness" that one observes regularly in the speeches in Acts; and, similarly, 1 Kgdms 12:6 (Μάρτυς κύριος ὁ ποιήσας τὸν Μωυσῆν καὶ τὸν Ααρων, ὁ ἀναγαγὼν τοὺς πατέρας ἡμῶν ἐξ Αἰγύπτου, "The Lord is witness, who appointed Moses and Aaron and brought our fathers out of Egypt") refers to the Lord as "witness" and portrays the Lord working in relation to the same group (τοὺς πατέρας ἡμῶν, "our fathers") often referred to as the object of God's attention in the speeches in Acts. (D) The idea of "seeking God" in Deut 4:29 (καὶ ζητήσετε ἐκεῖ κύριον τὸν θεὸν ὑμῶν καὶ εὑρήσετε, ὅταν ἐκζητήσητε αὐτὸν ἐξ ὅλης τῆς καρδίας σου καὶ ἐξ ὅλης τῆς ψυχῆς σου ἐν τῇ θλίψει σου, "From there you will seek the Lord your God, and you will find him if you search after him with all your heart and soul in your distress") may, in part, supply the thought behind the declaration in Paul's speech in 17:27 (ζητεῖν τὸν θεόν, εἰ ἄρα γε ψηλαφήσειαν αὐτὸν καὶ εὕροιεν, "to search for God, and perhaps grope for him and find him").[27]

---

27. Compare B. Gärtner, *The Areopagus Speech and Natural Revelation* (ASNU 21; Lund: C. W. K. Gleerup, 1955) 152–58, esp. 156.

In conclusion, the use of Israel's history is strikingly similar to portions of speeches in Acts, as are the theological perspective of the statements, the ideas of witness and bearing witness, and the assumption of divine authority. Yet the most striking similarity is the repetition of history and threat in such a manner that the entire account is unified and given pointed emphasis. Nevertheless, the cast of the "great speeches" is different from that of the speeches in Acts. The Deuteronomist presents these speeches as past-time calls to faithfulness, but in the calls one observes a strong element of future prediction of unfaithfulness, punishment by God, reconciliation, and restoration. These future elements actually make these seemingly past-time calls active in the present, that is, in the postexilic period in which the Deuteronomist lived and wrote. In turn, the central concern articulated in these speeches is distinct from that found in the speeches in Acts. The "great speeches" call for faithfulness to God by means of the observance of God's law. This call is not controversial. The speeches advocate a particular belief and behavior, but one does not find opposition to the speakers in the form of denial or disbelief. Thus, in comparing the "great speeches" of the Deuteronomistic History and the speeches of Acts one sees that (1) there are sufficient similarities to indicate that the "great speeches" provided inspiration for *elements* of the speeches in Acts, but (2) there are differences between the two groups of speeches which mean that despite striking similarities the "great speeches" are not simply models for the speeches in Acts.

Second, U. Wilckens's ongoing examination of the speeches in Acts in relation to possible tradition-historical backgrounds suggests a pair of speeches in the Septuagint as possible models for the speeches in Acts. In the first two editions of his monograph on the *Missionsreden* in Acts, Wilckens defended the thesis that Luke composed the preaching to the Gentiles on the basis of a tradition perceptible behind 1 Thess 1:9–10 and Heb 6:1–2, but the preaching to the Jews was developed from Luke's own theology.[28] But in the third edition of his study, Wilckens articulated a different interpretation. Wilckens's change of mind came about through the influence of a study by O. H. Steck of the Deuteronomistic portrayal of "Israel and the violent fate of the prophets."[29] In a variety of Jewish and Christian literature Steck discerned a pattern of Deuteronomistic proclamation that registered guilt, pronounced judgment, called for repentance (implicitly or explicitly), and promised forgiveness. According to Steck, four elements are fairly constant (items A–D below), two others are occasional (E and F), and at times the order

28. See n. 4 above.

29. O. H. Steck, *Israel und das Gewaltsame Geschick der Propheten: Untersuchungen zur Überlieferung des deuteronomistischen Geschichtsbildes im Alten Testament, Spätjudentum und Urchristentum* (WMANT 23; Neukirchen-Vluyn: Neukirchener Verlag, 1967). Steck set forth his "detective work" primarily in pp. 60–195.

of the elements of the proclamation shifts. But, taken collectively in a kind of sequential logic, the pattern Steck detected is as follows:

A. In the course of the history of Israel since the occupation of the land, Israel has proved itself repeatedly to be disobedient and "stiff-necked" toward God.

B. The Lord sent the prophets again and again to Israel to call the people to repentance.

C. Nevertheless, Israel repeatedly rejected the prophets. (Items B and C are Steck's key to locating passages where the larger pattern occurs.)

D. Therefore, the Lord will now pass a terrible judgment on Israel.

E. Yet there is a "final" call to repentance and law-observance.

F. God promises forgiveness, a new relationship, and salvation to the repentant and obedient; but God also pronounces a curse over the wicked.

Working under the influence of Steck's study, Wilckens defended the theses that Luke knew this Deuteronomistic tradition as it was mediated to him by Hellenistic Jewish Christianity. In turn, Luke brought this pattern into Acts, above all in Stephen's speech; and then he developed this pattern further in composing the missionary speeches to Jews. According to Wilckens the most crucial passages from the Septuagint for Luke's work are Neh 9:26; Ezra 9:10–15; 2 Kgs 17:7–23; portions of Jeremiah and Zechariah;[30] and 2 Chr 36:14–16 (20).[31]

The highly subjective and forced nature of Steck's construction of the "Deuteronomistic-repentance-preaching" has been noticed by M. Rese, and the illogical character of Wilckens's tradition-historical argument is discussed by G. Schneider.[32] Nevertheless, by identifying the focus of portions of the Septuagint on a critique of the history of Israel that is coupled with a call to repentance, Steck and Wilckens locate passages that may, in some less-formal fashion, be related to certain of the speeches in Acts.

Examination of the passages listed by Wilckens discloses the following: (A) The texts in 2 Kings and 2 Chronicles are comparable. Neither passage, however, is a speech. Both narrate selected portions of Israel's past by decrying Israel's unfaithfulness to God and recalling God's judgment. The story of the past is told from a decidedly theological angle. In comparison with the speeches in Acts, there are no striking parallels; at most these segments of the Septuagint have a theological understanding of history in common with

---

30. Wilckens does not list these passages; rather, he refers his readers to Steck, *Israel*, p. 72 for the reference to Jeremiah and p. 74 n. 2 for the Zechariah texts.

31. Wilckens, *Missionsreden* (3d ed., 1974) 203.

32. M. Rese, "Einige Überlegungen zu Lukas XIII,31–33," in *Jésus aux origines de la christologie* (ed. J. Dupont; BETL 40; Leuven: Leuven University Press; Gembloux: Duculot, 1975) 201–25, esp. 206–7 n. 34; G. Schneider, *Die Apostelgeschichte* (HTKNT 5/1–2; Freiburg/Basel/Vienna: Herder, 1980–82) 1:100–101.

the speeches in Acts. (B) In Ezra one encounters a speech-prayer. Ezra is the speaker, and he confesses the guilt of Israel's disobedience to God. In the course of the prayer one observes Ezra referring to the possession of the land as a gift from God. This item and the other portions of the prayer-speech assume God's ultimate divine authority. Yet, in form, style, content, and function, there is minimal correspondence with the speeches in Acts. (C) The case is quite different with regard to Nehemiah. The verse upon which Steck and Wilckens focus (9:26) is but one line of a long prayer-speech by Ezra before the assembled people of Israel at Neh 9:6–38 (2 Esdr 19:6–20:1). A careful reading of the entire prayer-speech finds numerous parallels between this portion of the Septuagint and the speeches in Acts, most notably Acts 4:24–30; 7:2–53; 13:16–41, 46–47. Consider:

1. The address and ascriptions to God

2 Esdr 19:6   καὶ εἶπεν Εσδρας Σὺ εἶ αὐτὸς κύριος μόνος· σὺ ἐποίησας τὸν οὐρανὸν καὶ τὸν οὐρανὸν τοῦ οὐρανοῦ καὶ πᾶσαν τὴν στάσιν αὐτῶν, τὴν γῆν καὶ πάντα, ὅσα ἐστὶν ἐν αὐτῇ, τὰς θαλάσσας καὶ πάντα τὰ ἐν αὐταῖς, καὶ σὺ ζωοποιεῖς τὰ πάντα, καὶ σοὶ προσκυνοῦσιν αἱ στρατιαὶ τῶν οὐρανῶν.

Acts 4:24   οἱ δὲ ἀκούσαντες ὁμοθυμαδὸν ἦραν φωνὴν πρὸς τὸν θεὸν καὶ εἶπαν, Δέσποτα, σὺ ὁ ποιήσας τὸν οὐρανὸν καὶ τὴν γῆν καὶ τὴν θάλασσαν καὶ πάντα τὰ ἐν αὐτοῖς. . . .

2 Esdr 19:6   And Ezra said: "You are the Lord, you alone; you have made heaven, the heaven of heavens, with all their host, the earth and all that is on it, the seas and all that is in them. To all of them you gave life, and the host of heaven worships you.

Acts 4:24   When they heard it, they raised their voices together to God and said, "Sovereign, you who made the heaven and the earth, the sea, and everything in them. . . ."

2. God's choice of Abraham and Abraham's leaving Chaldea

2 Esdr 19:7   σὺ εἶ κύριος ὁ θεός· σὺ ἐξελέξω ἐν Αβραμ καὶ ἐξήγαγες αὐτὸν ἐκ τῆς χώρας τῶν Χαλδαίων καὶ ἐπέθηκας αὐτῷ ὄνομα Αβρααμ.

Acts 7:2–4   ὁ δὲ ἔφη, Ἄνδρες ἀδελφοὶ καὶ πατέρες, ἀκούσατε. Ὁ θεὸς τῆς δόξης ὤφθη τῷ πατρὶ ἡμῶν Ἀβραὰμ ὄντι ἐν τῇ Μεσοποταμίᾳ πρὶν ἢ κατοικῆσαι αὐτὸν ἐν Χαρράν καὶ εἶπεν πρὸς αὐτόν, Ἔξελθε ἐκ τῆς γῆς σου καὶ [ἐκ] τῆς συγγενείας σου, καὶ δεῦρο εἰς τὴν γῆν ἣν ἄν σοι δείξω. τότε ἐξελθὼν ἐκ γῆς Χαλδαίων κατῴκησεν ἐν Χαρράν.

2 Esdr 19:7   You are the Lord, the God who chose Abram and brought him out of the region of the Chaldeans and gave him the name Abraham.

Act 7:2–4   But he replied, "Men, brothers and fathers, listen. The God of glory appeared to our father Abraham when he was in Mesopotamia, before he lived in Haran and said to him, 'Leave your country and your relatives, and go to the land I will show you.' Then he left the country of the Chaldeans and settled in Haran."

3. God's covenant with and promise to Abraham

2 Esdr 19:8 καὶ εὗρες τὴν καρδίαν αὐτοῦ πιστὴν ἐνώπιόν σου καὶ διέθου πρὸς
αὐτὸν διαθήκην δοῦναι αὐτῷ τὴν γῆν τῶν Χαναναίων καὶ Χετταίων
καὶ Αμορραίων καὶ Φερεζαίων καὶ Ιεβουσαίων καὶ Γεργεσαίων καὶ
τῷ σπέρματι αὐτοῦ· καὶ ἔστησας τοὺς λόγους σου, ὅτι δίκαιος σύ.

Acts 7:5, 8 καὶ οὐκ ἔδωκεν αὐτῷ κληρονομίαν ἐν αὐτῇ οὐδὲ βῆμα ποδός καὶ
ἐπηγγείλατο δοῦναι αὐτῷ εἰς κατάσχεσιν αὐτὴν καὶ τῷ σπέρματι
αὐτοῦ μετ' αὐτόν, οὐκ ὄντος αὐτῷ τέκνου. . . . καὶ ἔδωκεν αὐτῷ
διαθήκην περιτομῆς. . . .

2 Esdr 19:8 And you found his heart faithful before you, and made with him
a covenant to give to him and to his seed the land of the
Canaanite, the Chettites, the Amorite, the Perizzite, the Jebusite,
and the Girgashite; and you have fulfilled your promise, for you
are righteous.

Acts 7:5, 8 And he did not give him an inheritance in it, not even a foot's
length, and he promised to give it to him as his possession and
to his seed after him, even though he had no child . . . and he
gave him the covenant of circumcision. . . .

4. God sees Israel's difficulties in Egypt and at the Red Sea

2 Esdr 19:9 καὶ εἶδες τὴν ταπείνωσιν τῶν πατέρων ἡμῶν ἐν Αἰγύπτῳ καὶ τὴν
κραυγὴν αὐτῶν ἤκουσας ἐπὶ θάλασσαν ἐρυθράν.

Acts 7:34, 36 ἰδὼν εἶδον τὴν κάκωσιν τοῦ λαοῦ μου τοῦ ἐν Αἰγύπτῳ καὶ τοῦ
στεναγμοῦ αὐτῶν ἤκουσα, καὶ κατέβην ἐξελέσθαι αὐτούς· καὶ νῦν
δεῦρο ἀποστείλω σε εἰς Αἴγυπτον . . . . οὗτος ἐξήγαγεν αὐτοὺς
ποιήσας τέρατα καὶ σημεῖα ἐν γῇ Αἰγύπτῳ καὶ ἐν Ἐρυθρᾷ Θαλάσσῃ
καὶ ἐν τῇ ἐρήμῳ ἔτη τεσσεράκοντα.

2 Esdr 19:9 And you saw the distress of our fathers in Egypt and heard their
cry at the Red Sea.

Acts 7:34, 36 I have surely seen the mistreatment of my people who are in
Egypt and have heard their groaning, and I have come down
to rescue them. Come now I will send you to Egypt. . . . He led
them out, having performed wonders and signs in Egypt, at the
Red Sea, and in the wilderness for forty years.

5. God's signs done in Egypt

2 Esdr 19:10 καὶ ἔδωκας σημεῖα ἐν Αἰγύπτῳ ἐν Φαραω καὶ ἐν πᾶσιν τοῖς παισὶν
αὐτοῦ καὶ ἐν παντὶ τῷ λαῷ τῆς γῆς αὐτοῦ, ὅτι ἔγνως ὅτι
ὑπερηφάνησαν ἐπ' αὐτούς, καὶ ἐποίησας σεαυτῷ ὄνομα ὡς ἡ ἡμέρα
αὕτη.

Acts 7:36 οὗτος ἐξήγαγεν αὐτοὺς ποιήσας τέρατα καὶ σημεῖα ἐν γῇ Αἰγύπτῳ
καὶ ἐν Ἐρυθρᾷ Θαλάσσῃ καὶ ἐν τῇ ἐρήμῳ ἔτη τεσσεράκοντα.

Acts 13:17 ὁ θεὸς τοῦ λαοῦ τούτου Ἰσραὴλ ἐξελέξατο τοὺς πατέρας ἡμῶν, καὶ
τὸν λαὸν ὕψωσεν ἐν τῇ παροικίᾳ ἐν γῇ Αἰγύπτου καὶ μετὰ βραχίονος
ὑψηλοῦ ἐξήγαγεν αὐτοὺς ἐξ αὐτῆς . . . .

2 Esdr 19:10 You demonstrated signs in Egypt to Pharaoh and all his servants
and all the people of his land, for you knew that they acted

insolently against them, and you made a name for yourself, which
remains to this day.

Acts 7:36 He led them out, having performed wonders and signs in Egypt,
at the Red Sea, and in the wilderness for forty years.

Acts 13:17 The God of this people Israel chose our fathers and made the
people great during their stay in the land of Egypt, and with
uplifted arm he led them out of it.

6. God's care for Israel in the wilderness

2 Esdr 19:12–15 καὶ ἐν στύλῳ νεφέλης ὡδήγησας αὐτοὺς ἡμέρας καὶ ἐν στύλῳ πυρὸς
τὴν νύκτα τοῦ φωτίσαι αὐτοῖς τὴν ὁδόν, ἐν ᾗ πορεύσονται ἐν αὐτῇ.
καὶ ἐπὶ ὄρος Σινα κατέβης καὶ ἐλάλησας πρὸς αὐτοὺς ἐξ οὐρανοῦ
καὶ ἔδωκας αὐτοῖς κρίματα εὐθέα καὶ νόμους ἀληθείας, προστάγματα
καὶ ἐντολὰς ἀγαθάς. καὶ τὸ σάββατόν σου τὸ ἅγιον ἐγνώρισας αὐτοῖς,
ἐντολὰς καὶ προστάγματα καὶ νόμον ἐνετείλω αὐτοῖς ἐν χειρὶ Μωυσῆ
δούλου σου. καὶ ἄρτον ἐξ οὐρανοῦ ἔδωκας αὐτοῖς εἰς σιτοδείαν αὐτῶν
καὶ ὕδωρ ἐκ πέτρας ἐξήνεγκας αὐτοῖς εἰς δίψαν αὐτῶν. καὶ εἶπας
αὐτοῖς εἰσελθεῖν κληρονομῆσαι τὴν γῆν, ἐφ' ἣν ἐξέτεινας τὴν χεῖρά
σου δοῦναι αὐτοῖς.

Acts 7:36 οὗτος ἐξήγαγεν αὐτοὺς ποιήσας τέρατα καὶ σημεῖα ἐν γῇ Αἰγύπτῳ
καὶ ἐν Ἐρυθρᾷ Θαλάσσῃ καὶ ἐν τῇ ἐρήμῳ ἔτη τεσσεράκοντα.

2 Esdr 19:12–15 And you led them by day with a pillar of cloud, and by night
with a pillar of fire, to give them light on the way in which they
should go. You came down also upon Mount Sinai, and spoke
with them from heaven, and gave them right ordinances and
true laws, statutes and good commandments. And you made
known your holy sabbath to them and gave them statutes and
a law by the hand of your servant Moses. And for their food you
gave them bread from heaven and water out of a rock for their
thirst. And you told them to go in to possess the land over which
you stretched out your hand to give to them.

Acts 7:36 He led them out, having performed wonders and signs in Egypt,
at the Red Sea, and in the wilderness for forty years.

7. God's activity at Mount Sinai

2 Esdr 19:13 καὶ ἐπὶ ὄρος Σινα κατέβης καὶ ἐλάλησας πρὸς αὐτοὺς ἐξ οὐρανοῦ
καὶ ἔδωκας αὐτοῖς κρίματα εὐθέα καὶ νόμους ἀληθείας, προστάγματα
καὶ ἐντολὰς ἀγαθάς.

Acts 7:38 οὗτός ἐστιν ὁ γενόμενος ἐν τῇ ἐκκλησίᾳ ἐν τῇ ἐρήμῳ μετὰ τοῦ ἀγγέλου
τοῦ λαλοῦντος αὐτῷ ἐν τῷ ὄρει Σινα καὶ τῶν πατέρων ἡμῶν, ὃς
ἐδέξατο λόγια ζῶντα δοῦναι ἡμῖν . . . .

2 Esdr 19:13 You came down also upon Mount Sinai, and spoke with them
from heaven, and gave them right ordinances and true laws,
statutes and good commandments.

Acts 7:38 He is the one who was in the congregation in the wilderness
with the angel who spoke to him at Mount Sinai, and with our
fathers; and he received living oracles to give us.

8. Israel's stiff-necked rebellion

2 Esdr 19:16–17 καὶ αὐτοὶ καὶ οἱ πατέρες ἡμῶν ὑπερηφανεύσαντο καὶ ἐσκλήρυναν τὸν τράχηλον αὐτῶν καὶ οὐκ ἤκουσαν τῶν ἐντολῶν σου· καὶ ἀνένευσαν τοῦ εἰσακοῦσαι καὶ οὐκ ἐμνήσθησαν τῶν θαυμασίων σου, ὧν ἐποίησας μετ' αὐτῶν, καὶ ἐσκλήρυναν τὸν τράχηλον αὐτῶν καὶ ἔδωκαν ἀρχὴν ἐπιστρέψαι εἰς δουλείαν αὐτῶν ἐν Αἰγύπτῳ. καὶ σὺ θεὸς ἐλεήμων καὶ οἰκτίρμων, μακρόθυμος καὶ πολυέλεος, καὶ οὐκ ἐγκατέλιπες αὐτούς.

Acts 7:39 ᾧ οὐκ ἠθέλησαν ὑπήκοοι γενέσθαι οἱ πατέρες ἡμῶν, ἀλλὰ ἀπώσαντο καὶ ἐστράφησαν ἐν ταῖς καρδίαις αὐτῶν εἰς Αἴγυπτον . . . .

Acts 7:51 Σκληροτράχηλοι καὶ ἀπερίτμητοι καρδίας καὶ τοῖς ὠσίν, ὑμεῖς ἀεὶ τῷ πνεύματι τῷ ἁγίῳ ἀντιπίπτετε ὡς οἱ πατέρες ὑμῶν καὶ ὑμεῖς.

2 Esdr 19:16–17 But they and our fathers acted presumptuously and stiffened their necks and did not obey your commandments; and they refused to obey, and were not mindful of the wonders that you performed among them; but they stiffened their necks and appointed a leader to return unto their slavery in Egypt. But you God are merciful and compassionate, slow to anger and abounding in steadfast love, and you did not forsake them.

Acts 7:39 Our fathers were unwilling to obey him; instead, they pushed him aside, and in their hearts they turned back to Egypt. . . .

Acts 7:51 You stiff-necked people, uncircumcised in heart and ears, you are forever opposing the Holy Spirit, just as your fathers used to do.

9. Israel's making of the calf

2 Esdr 19:18 ἔτι δὲ καὶ ἐποίησαν ἑαυτοῖς μόσχον χωνευτὸν καὶ εἶπαν Οὗτοι οἱ θεοὶ οἱ ἐξαγαγόντες ἡμᾶς ἐξ Αἰγύπτου· καὶ ἐποίησαν παροργισμοὺς μεγάλους.

Acts 7:40–41 εἰπόντες τῷ Ἀαρών, Ποίησον ἡμῖν θεοὺς οἳ προπορεύσονται ἡμῶν· ὁ γὰρ Μωϋσῆς οὗτος, ὃς ἐξήγαγεν ἡμᾶς ἐκ γῆς Αἰγύπτου, οὐκ οἴδαμεν τί ἐγένετο αὐτῷ. καὶ ἐμοσχοποίησαν ἐν ταῖς ἡμέραις ἐκείναις καὶ ἀνήγαγον θυσίαν τῷ εἰδώλῳ καὶ εὐφραίνοντο ἐν τοῖς ἔργοις τῶν χειρῶν αὐτῶν.

2 Esdr 19:18 And still they even made for themselves an image of a calf and said, "This is the God who brought us up out of Egypt," and they did great provocations.

Acts 7:40–41 . . . saying to Aaron, "Make gods for us who will lead the way for us; as for this Moses who led us out from the land of Egypt, we do not know what has happened to him." At that time they made a calf, offered a sacrifice to the idol, and reveled in the works of their hands.

10. God cares for/tolerates Israel forty years in the wilderness (contrasting views!)

2 Esdr 19:19–21 καὶ σὺ ἐν οἰκτιρμοῖς σου τοῖς πολλοῖς οὐκ ἐγκατέλιπες αὐτοὺς ἐν τῇ ἐρήμῳ· τὸν στῦλον τῆς νεφέλης οὐκ ἐξέκλινας ἀπ' αὐτῶν ἡμέρας

ὁδηγῆσαι αὐτοὺς ἐν τῇ ὁδῷ καὶ τὸν στῦλον τοῦ πυρὸς τὴν νύκτα
φωτίζειν αὐτοῖς τὴν ὁδόν, ἐν ᾗ πορεύσονται ἐν αὐτῇ. καὶ τὸ πνεῦμά
σου τὸ ἀγαθὸν ἔδωκας συνετίσαι αὐτοὺς καὶ τὸ μαννα σοῦ οὐκ
ἀφυστέρησας ἀπὸ στόματος αὐτῶν καὶ ὕδωρ ἔδωκας αὐτοῖς τῷ δίψει
αὐτῶν. καὶ τεσσαράκοντα ἔτη διέθρεψας αὐτοὺς ἐν τῇ ἐρήμῳ, οὐχ
ὑστέρησαν· ἱμάτια αὐτῶν οὐκ ἐπαλαιώθησαν, καὶ πόδες αὐτῶν οὐ
διερράγησαν.

Acts 7:42–43   ἔστρεφεν δὲ ὁ θεὸς καὶ παρέδωκεν αὐτοὺς λατρεύειν τῇ στρατιᾷ τοῦ
                   οὐρανοῦ καθὼς γέγραπται ἐν βίβλῳ τῶν προφητῶν, Μὴ σφάγια καὶ
                   θυσίας προσηνέγκατέ μοι ἔτη τεσσεράκοντα ἐν τῇ ἐρήμῳ, οἶκος
                   Ἰσραήλ; καὶ ἀνελάβετε τὴν σκηνὴν τοῦ Μολὸχ καὶ τὸ ἄστρον τοῦ
                   θεοῦ [ὑμῶν] Ῥαιφάν, τοὺς τύπους οὓς ἐποιήσατε προσκυνεῖν αὐτοῖς,
                   καὶ μετοικιῶ ὑμᾶς ἐπέκεινα Βαβυλῶνος.

Acts 13:18   καὶ ὡς τεσσερακονταετῆ χρόνον ἐτροποφόρησεν αὐτοὺς ἐν τῇ
                  ἐρήμῳ. . . .

2 Esdr 19:19–21   And you in your great mercies did not forsake them in the
                  wilderness; the pillar of cloud that led them in the way did not
                  leave them by day, nor the pillar of fire by night that gave them
                  light on the way by which they should go. And you gave your
                  good spirit to instruct them, and did not withhold your manna
                  from their mouth, and gave them water for their thirst. And forty
                  years you sustained them in the wilderness, they did not lack;
                  their clothes did not wear out and their feet did not split.

Acts 7:42–43   But God turned away from them and handed them over to
                  worship the host of heaven, as it is written in the book of the
                  prophets: "Did you offer to me slain victims and sacrifices forty
                  years in the wilderness, O house of Israel? No; you took along
                  the tent of Moloch, and the star of your god Rephan, the images
                  that you made to worship; so I will remove you beyond Babylon."

Acts 13:18   For about forty years he put up with them in the wilderness.

11. God gives Israel possession of the land

2 Esdr 19:22–24   καὶ ἔδωκας αὐτοῖς βασιλείας καὶ λαοὺς καὶ διεμέρισας αὐτοῖς, καὶ
                  ἐκληρονόμησαν τὴν γῆν Σηων βασιλέως Εσεβων καὶ τὴν γῆν Ωγ
                  βασιλέως τοῦ Βασαν. καὶ τοὺς υἱοὺς αὐτῶν ἐπλήθυνας ὡς τοὺς
                  ἀστέρας τοῦ οὐρανοῦ καὶ εἰσήγαγες αὐτοὺς εἰς τὴν γῆν, ἣν εἶπας τοῖς
                  πατράσιν αὐτῶν, καὶ ἐκληρονόμησαν αὐτήν. καὶ ἐξέτριψας ἐνώπιον
                  αὐτῶν τοὺς κατοικοῦντας τὴν γῆν τῶν Χαναναίων καὶ ἔδωκας αὐτοὺς
                  εἰς τὰς χεῖρας αὐτῶν καὶ τοὺς βασιλεῖς αὐτῶν καὶ τοὺς λαοὺς τῆς
                  γῆς ποιῆσαι αὐτοῖς ὡς ἀρεστὸν ἐνώπιον αὐτῶν.

Acts 13:19   καὶ καθελὼν ἔθνη ἑπτὰ ἐν γῇ Χανάαν κατεκληρονόμησεν τὴν γῆν
                  αὐτῶν. . . .

2 Esdr 19:22–24   And you gave them kingdoms and you divided the peoples to
                  them, and they took possession of the land of King Sihon of
                  Esebon and the land of King Og of Bashan. And you multiplied
                  their sons like the stars of heaven, and you brought them into
                  the land which you said to their fathers, and they inherited it.

And you subdued before them the inhabitants of the land, the Canaanites, and you gave them into their hands, both their kings and the peoples of the land, to do with them as they pleased.

Acts 13:19　After he had destroyed seven nations in the land of Canaan, he gave them their land as an inheritance. . . .

12. Israel's disobedience and killing of the prophets

2 Esdr 19:26　καὶ ἤλλαξαν καὶ ἀπέστησαν ἀπὸ σοῦ καὶ ἔρριψαν τὸν νόμον σου ὀπίσω σώματος αὐτῶν καὶ τοὺς προφήτας σου ἀπέκτειναν, οἳ διεμαρτύραντο ἐν αὐτοῖς ἐπιστρέψαι αὐτοὺς πρὸς σέ, καὶ ἐποίησαν παροργισμοὺς μεγάλους.

Acts 7:51–52　Σκληροτράχηλοι καὶ ἀπερίτμητοι καρδίαις καὶ τοῖς ὠσίν, ὑμεῖς ἀεὶ τῷ πνεύματι τῷ ἁγίῳ ἀντιπίπτετε ὡς οἱ πατέρες ὑμῶν καὶ ὑμεῖς. τίνα τῶν προφητῶν οὐκ ἐδίωξαν οἱ πατέρες ὑμῶν; καὶ ἀπέκτειναν τοὺς προκαταγγείλαντας περὶ τῆς ἐλεύσεως τοῦ δικαίου, οὗ νῦν ὑμεῖς προδόται καὶ φονεῖς ἐγένεσθε. . . .

2 Esdr 19:26　And they changed and rebelled against you and cast your law behind their bodies and killed your prophets, who gave witness among them in order to turn them back to you, and they did great provocations.

Acts 7:51–52　You stiff-necked people, uncircumcised in heart and ears, you are forever opposing the Holy Spirit, just as your fathers used to do. Which of the prophets did your fathers not persecute? They killed those who foretold the coming of the Righteous One, and now you have become his betrayers and murderers.

13. God's granting of "saviors" to Israel

2 Esdr 19:27　καὶ ἔδωκας αὐτοὺς ἐν χειρὶ θλιβόντων αὐτούς, καὶ ἔθλιψαν αὐτούς· καὶ ἀνεβόησαν πρὸς σὲ ἐν καιρῷ θλίψεως αὐτῶν, καὶ σὺ ἐξ οὐρανοῦ σου ἤκουσας καὶ ἐν οἰκτιρμοῖς σου τοῖς μεγάλοις ἔδωκας αὐτοῖς σωτῆρας καὶ ἔσωσας αὐτοὺς ἐκ χειρὸς θλιβόντων αὐτούς.

Acts 13:23　τούτου ὁ θεὸς ἀπὸ τοῦ σπέρματος κατ' ἐπαγγελίαν ἤγαγεν τῷ Ἰσραὴλ σωτῆρα Ἰησοῦν. . . .

2 Esdr 19:27　And you gave them into the hand of their enemies, and they made them suffer. And they cried out to you in a time of their suffering and you heard them from heaven, and in your great mercies you gave them saviors and you saved them from the hand of their enemies.

Acts 13:23　Of this man's seed God has brought to Israel a savior, Jesus, as he promised.

14. Israel's repeated disobedience

2 Esdr 19:28　καὶ ὡς ἀνεπαύσαντο, ἐπέστρεψαν ποιῆσαι τὸ πονηρὸν ἐνώπιόν σου· καὶ ἐγκατέλιπες αὐτοὺς εἰς χεῖρας ἐχθρῶν αὐτῶν, καὶ κατῆρξαν ἐν αὐτοῖς. καὶ πάλιν ἀνεβόησαν πρὸς σέ, καὶ σὺ ἐξ οὐρανοῦ εἰσήκουσας καὶ ἐρρύσω αὐτοὺς ἐν οἰκτιρμοῖς σου πολλοῖς.

Acts 7:51　Σκληροτράχηλοι καὶ ἀπερίτμητοι καρδίαις καὶ τοῖς ὠσίν, ὑμεῖς ἀεὶ τῷ πνεύματι τῷ ἁγίῳ ἀντιπίπτετε, ὡς οἱ πατέρες ὑμῶν καὶ ὑμεῖς.

2 Esdr 19:28   And as they rested, they turned to do evil before you; and you
                abandoned them to the hands of their enemies, and they had
                dominion over them. And again they cried to you, and you heard
                from heaven and according to your mercies you rescued them
                many times.

Acts 7:51   You stiff-necked people, uncircumcised in heart and ears, you
                are forever opposing the Holy Spirit, just as your fathers used
                to do.

15. God's work with Israel through the Spirit and the prophets

2 Esdr 19:30   καὶ εἵλκυσας ἐπ' αὐτοὺς ἔτη πολλὰ καὶ ἐπεμαρτύρω αὐτοῖς ἐν
                πνεύματί σου ἐν χειρὶ προφητῶν σου· καὶ οὐκ ἠνωτίσαντο, καὶ ἔδωκας
                αὐτοὺς ἐν χειρὶ λαῶν τῆς γῆς.

Acts 7:51–52   Σκληροτράχηλοι καὶ ἀπερίτμητοι καρδίαις καὶ τοῖς ὠσίν, ὑμεῖς ἀεὶ
                τῷ πνεύματι τῷ ἁγίῳ ἀντιπίπτετε ὡς οἱ πατέρες ὑμῶν καὶ ὑμεῖς.
                τίνα τῶν προφητῶν οὐκ ἐδίωξαν οἱ πατέρες ὑμῶν; καὶ ἀπέκτειναν
                τοὺς προκαταγγείλαντας περὶ τῆς ἐλεύσεως τοῦ δικαίου, οὗ νῦν ὑμεῖς
                προδόται καὶ φονεῖς ἐγένεσθε. . . .

2 Esdr 19:30   Many years you were patient with them, and testified to them
                by your spirit through the hand of your prophets; and they did
                not heed, and you gave them into the hand the peoples of the
                lands.

Acts 7:51–52   You stiff-necked people, uncircumcised in heart and ears, you
                are forever opposing the Holy Spirit, just as your fathers used
                to do. Which of the prophets did your fathers not persecute?
                They killed those who foretold the coming of the Righteous One,
                and now you have become his betrayers and murderers.

16. Israel's persistent disobedience despite God's repeated warnings

2 Esdr 19:33–34 καὶ σὺ δίκαιος ἐπὶ πᾶσι τοῖς ἐρχομένοις ἐφ' ἡμᾶς, ὅτι ἀλήθειαν
                ἐποίησας, καὶ ἡμεῖς ἐξημάρτομεν. καὶ οἱ βασιλεῖς ἡμῶν καὶ οἱ
                ἄρχοντες ἡμῶν καὶ οἱ ἱερεῖς ἡμῶν καὶ οἱ πατέρες ἡμῶν οὐκ ἐποίησαν
                τὸν νόμον σου καὶ οὐ προσέσχον τῶν ἐντολῶν σου καὶ τὰ μαρτύριά
                σου, ἃ διεμαρτύρω αὐτοῖς.

Acts 7:51   Σκληροτράχηλοι καὶ ἀπερίτμητοι καρδίαις καὶ τοῖς ὠσίν, ὑμεῖς ἀεὶ
                τῷ πνεύματι τῷ ἁγίῳ ἀντιπίπτετε ὡς οἱ πατέρες ὑμῶν καὶ ὑμεῖς.

2 Esdr 19:33–34 And you are righteous in all that has come upon us, for you acted
                truly and we have acted wickedly; our kings, our leaders, our
                priests, and our fathers did not do your law and did not heed
                your commandments and your testimonies that you witnessed
                to them.

Acts 7:51   You stiff-necked people, uncircumcised in heart and ears, you
                are forever opposing the Holy Spirit, just as your fathers used
                to do.

Beyond particular elements, one notices that the *form* of the addresses in
2 Esdras 19 and Acts 4 are similar, as are the *form* of historical narrative in
2 Esdras 19 and Acts 7 and 13 (in part). The *style* of the Septuagint passages

and the texts from Acts are also similar in that there are both linguistic and rhetorical parallels. Even more, the *contents* of the passages from 2 Esdras 19 and Acts 4 (in part), 7, and 13 (in part) are strikingly similar. The *functions* of the various texts are, however, distinct. The prayer-speech in 2 Esdras is a confession of sins and a petition for mercy that closes with a promise of faithfulness. The prayer in Acts 4 is a prayer of praise and a petition for courage. Stephen's speech in Acts 7 confronts the audience with its guilt for rejecting "the Righteous One" and draws an analogy to the history of Israel to make the point ὡς οἱ πατέρες ὑμῶν καὶ ὑμεῖς ("as your fathers also you"). This confrontation precedes and prepares for the pointed christological declarations that follow the main body of the speech in 7:56a, 59b, 60b. Paul's speech in Acts 13 declares salvation, issues christological kerygma, warns the audience against rejecting the message, and finally explains the turning of the missionaries to the Gentiles. Nevertheless, the bold repetition of God's faithfulness over against Israel's disobedience in 2 Esdras 19 forms a striking parallel to the remarkable repetitions of the speeches in Acts. While this speech from the Septuagint does not account for all matters of form, style, content, and function of the speeches in Acts, there are sufficient parallels to suggest some relationship between Ezra's prayer-speech and at least the three speeches in Acts noted above.[33]

Third, in 1 Maccabees, the account of the Hasmonean family's activities from approximately 167 B.C.E. to 134 B.C.E., one encounters a series of speeches. The speeches emphasize the piety of Judas Maccabeus and "provide a theological evaluation of the events which are narrated, events in which God's delivering hand is seen to be at work as it was of old."[34] While the form and frequency of the speeches in 1 Maccabees put one in mind of the regular occurrence of speeches in Acts, the contents and the functions of the speeches in 1 Maccabees and Acts are distinct. In 1 Maccabees one finds deliberative

33. E. J. Richard examines the possible relationship between Stephen's speech and "histories of Israel" that briefly and selectively recapitulate Hebrew history in the Septuagint (*Acts 6:1–8:4: The Author's Method of Composition* [SBLDS 41; Missoula, MT: Scholars Press, 1978] 141–45). Richard judges Jdt 5:16–18 to be the "closest historical analogue" (p. 143) to Stephen's speech, although he notes the similarities of "terminology" between Acts 7 and 2 Esdras 19. Richard's conclusion, however, is that the speech by Stephen draws directly from the full biblical narratives of the Septuagint rather than from any of the historical summaries. In my opinion Richard's careful work underestimates the parallels between Stephen's speech and Ezra's prayer; indeed, in his analysis Richard actually brought only 2 Esdr 19:9–10 into comparison with Acts 7. He ignored the rest of Ezra's prayer and did not consider Acts 4 and 13 at all. On the other hand, the materials Richard examines from Judith 5 (vv. 7, 10–11) are actually part of a larger speech in Jdt 5:5–21. Both in the three verses Richard considers and in the entire speech, there are numerous unparalleled details; so that only broad story lines are comparable between Jdt 5:5–21 or Jdt 5:7, 10–11 and Stephen's speech.

34. H. W. Attridge, "Historiography," in *Jewish Writings of the Second Temple Period* (ed. M. Stone; CRINT 2/2; Assen: Van Gorcum; Philadelphia: Fortress, 1984) 172.

rhetoric cast as a call to law observance or to confidence in God that gives courage for waging war against foreign adversaries. Thus, the speakers speak to the point at hand, not beyond it. The single speech that in form and content is most comparable to speeches in Acts occurs in 1 Macc 2:49–68. There Mattathias delivers a testamentary address to his sons. As a farewell speech, the form is similar to Paul's speech to the Ephesian elders in Acts 20; but in terms of content, the speech recalls selected moments of the history of Israel, so that it is comparable to Acts 7 and 13. Moreover, the function of the speech is similar to other addresses in 1 Maccabees; that is, it calls Mattathias's children to law observance and to courage in the fight against the Gentile enemies. Furthermore, careful examination of the survey of Israel's history in Mattathias's speech finds little that is actually comparable to the surveys of history in Acts. The history is recalled by focusing on heroic figures: Abraham, Joseph, Phinehas, Joshua, Caleb, David, Elijah, Hannaniah, Azariah, Mishael, and Daniel. The majority of these figures are not mentioned in Acts, and those who are included in both 1 Maccabees and Acts (Abraham, Joseph, Joshua, and David) are recalled and described quite differently in the two works. Clearly, then, 1 Maccabees is not a model for Acts. But in 1 Maccabees one does see a Jewish writing from the Hellenistic period that employs the historiographic genre to express a theological interpretation of history.[35]

Conclusions concerning the Septuagint

The overt citation of the Septuagint in the speeches in Acts indicates a relationship between the Septuagint and Acts. Moreover, the "great speeches" of the Deuteronomistic History *function* by means of repetition to unify the larger account in which they occur. At one level the speeches in Acts function similarly. In turn, the pointed recapitulation of history in 2 Esdras 19 shows sufficient parallels in form, style, and content to suggest that Ezra's prayer may have provided inspiration for elements of certain speeches in Acts — especially Acts 7, but also Acts 4 and 13. Finally, 1 Maccabees illustrates the use of historiography for the presentation of a theological understanding of events. Yet, despite these noticeable similarities, the Septuagint materials are still different from the speeches in Acts; for there is nothing controversial

---

35. Above all others, B. Gärtner argues that 1 Maccabees is the most immediate background for viewing Acts (*Areopagus Speech*). Gärtner estimates that speeches comprise one-sixth of 1 Maccabees, and he judges the recourse to speeches in 1 Maccabees to be closer to the use of speeches in the Old Testament than to their occurrence in Greek historiography. Gärtner's points of comparison are, however, quite general: view of history, particular composition of speeches, and underlying purpose of the words. Gärtner correctly emphasizes the similarities between Acts and selected documents of Hellenistic Judaism, but he overstates the distinctiveness of Acts and the Hellenistic Jewish literature in comparison with Greco-Roman historiography.

about the repetition of history in the Septuagint. The speeches in the Septuagint are not made in controversial situations comparable to the events in Acts, and the speeches in the Septuagint do not address controversies as do certain of the speeches in Acts. In short, there is no truly apologetic dimension to the Septuagint speeches, whereas one detects such a tone in almost all the speeches in Acts.

Hellenistic Jewish Literature

In recent New Testament scholarship there is a marked tendency to declare that Acts and the literature of Hellenistic Judaism are similar. In making this comparison there is regular reference to the apologetic literature preserved in fragments from Hellenistic Jewish historians, 2 Maccabees, and Josephus. Thus, M. Hengel refers to Luke's writings, especially Acts, in relation to Josephus and, above all, 2 Maccabees and declares that comparison shows Luke's "particular proximity to Jewish Hellenistic historiography."[36] As Hengel explains the comparison,

> The historical views of Herodotus, the first great Greek historian (fifth century B.C.), are based on his conviction of the absolute sway of inexorable destiny which no mortal man can escape, in which the gods cause misfortune to follow excessive good fortune and well-deserved punishment to follow hybris. . . . In contrast to [the] very varied views of history among Greek and Hellenistic-Roman historians, the distinguishing feature of history-writing in the Old Testament and Judaism was the certain faith that the God who chose Israel was the sole Lord of history and guided it in judgment and in grace. . . . Despite all the differences, the New Testament narrators are closest to this Old Testament and Jewish picture of history.[37]

Similarly, in a review of E. Plümacher's *Lukas als hellenistischer Schriftsteller*, E. Schüssler Fiorenza writes:

> A . . . weakness of P.'s study is that he only rarely (and then only in passing or in footnotes) refers to the missionary apologetic literature of hellenistic Judaism. A more careful comparison of the literary style of Luke and that of the Jewish hellenistic religious propaganda literature would have not only proved fruitful but would have also clarified his main thesis.[38]

When scholars offer essentially abstract descriptions of the historiographic techniques and the theological perspectives of Hellenistic Jewish literature

36. M. Hengel, *Acts and the History of Earliest Christianity* (Philadelphia: Fortress, 1980) 51–52.
37. Ibid., 50–51.
38. E. Schüssler Fiorenza, *CBQ* 37 (1975) 145–46; quotation from p. 146.

one easily makes comparisons with Acts.[39] For example, in summarizing the theology of the Hellenistic Jewish *Missionsliteratur,* P. Dalbert points to three crucial characteristics: monotheism, spiritualized revelation, and the election of Israel.[40] In explaining these dimensions of this literature Dalbert points out that because absolute monotheism presented one God (ὁ θεός), not a god among the gods, this neutral designation necessitated "naming" this God in such a way that pagans could understand the identity of this God. Thus, God was named "Creator," "Pantocrator," "Lord over the world," "King of kings," and "the all-powerful One." God was not only all powerful but also wise, righteous, transcendent; yet God was involved with creation and concerned with humanity as was evident from God's giving the law to Israel to set the Jews apart from other humans in order to demonstrate the universal relevance of the law. In Acts one finds an array of titles for God and Christ. Moreover, because God was transcendent, Hellenistic Judaism avoided anthropomor-phisms in reference to God's will and activity. Instead, God's interaction with creation and, in particular, humans was cast as coming through mediators — angels and prophets — and dreams. God's power was understood to be revealed in miraculous events, although there was no notion of present theophanies. Earlier anthropomorphisms were allegorized into abstractions. For Hellenistic Judaism, the Temple, the cult, and the law were actually incarnations of God.[41] In the speeches in Acts one finds the same tendencies and points of concern, although there are noticeable differences. Finally, despite the attempt of Hellenistic Judaism to be connected with the larger Hellenistic world, there was a strong sense of "election" on the part of the Hellenistic Jews. Dalbert illustrates that the past, the present, and the future all came into play in Israel's consciousness of election.[42] Hellenistic Judaism understood that God called and cares for Israel, so that God was Helper, Leader, Protector, and Giver of the Promises. In this strong sense of election, Hellenistic Judaism under-stood that Israel was God's people chosen to demonstrate God's power; Temple, cult, and law are eternally valid evidence of God's saving will.[43] The speeches in Acts demonstrate a similar sense of both election and necessity of service on the part of the early Christian speakers.

Thus we see that in summary descriptions of Hellenistic Jewish literature one finds many points that seem relevant for comparison and contrast with

39. See, e.g., the concise and insightful critical summaries of fragments of Hellenistic historians by Attridge ("Historiography," 160–71).

40. P. Dalbert, *Die Theologie der hellenistisch-jüdischen Missionsliteratur unter Ausschluss von Philo und Josephus* (TF 4; Hamburg-Volksdorf: H. Reich/Evangelischer Verlag, 1954) 124–43.

41. Dalbert states: "Es besteht kein Zweifel, daß die meisten der hellenistisch-jüdischen Schrift-steller den Tempel in Jerusalem, seinen Kult und das Gesetz als Inkarnationen Gottes betrachtet haben" (*Theologie,* 136).

42. Ibid., 137.

43. Ibid., 139–43.

the materials in the speeches in Acts. But, in fact, when one moves to examine carefully the fragments from the Hellenistic Jewish historians,[44] Josephus, and 2 Maccabees, there is little or nothing concrete upon which to base comparisons. There are no speeches in the historical fragments; rather, the historians simply use historiography as a genre to present, advocate, and defend Judaism in the larger context of Hellenism. In turn, as B. Gärtner demonstrates, Josephus and Acts are quite distinct in terms of methods, aims, understandings of history, and even the authors' abilities.[45] While Josephus is dedicated to a favorable presentation of Judaism, he nevertheless is essentially concerned with historical cause and effect.[46] Finally, 2 Maccabees is an abbreviating work in a concise style that makes very little use of speeches.[47] In 2 Maccabees 7 one does find speeches by the seven brothers and their mother, who are being tortured to death. These speeches are highly repetitious, and through the repetition one encounters a strong doctrine of future resurrection as the speeches express and inspire an absolute confidence in

44. Here I have in mind specifically a cluster of authors whom J. J. Collins classifies in three groups: (1) faithful chroniclers—Demetrius, Aristeas, and Philo the Elder; (2) the historical romances—Artapanus, Pseudo-Eupolemus, Thallus, Cleodemus, Eupolemus, and Pseudo-Hecataeus; and (3) the epic poets—Philo the Epic Poet and Theodotus (*Between Athens and Jerusalem: Jewish Identity in the Hellenistic Diaspora* [New York: Crossroad, 1983] 27, 38). I would judge Acts in terms of contents and form to fall somewhere between the wooden, mechanical style of Demetrius and the imaginative, romantic flair that characterizes Artapanus.

45. Gärtner, *Areopagus Speech*, 20–26.

46. H. W. Attridge remarks, "Whether his particular form of hellenized Judaism is representative of any wider group of Jews is difficult to determine. The fact that personal factors loom so large in the forces operating on the biblical paraphrase may suggest that what we find in the *Antiquities* is a very individual production" (*The Interpretation of Biblical History in the* Antiquitates Judaicae *of Flavius Josephus* [HDR 7; Missoula, MT: Scholars Press, 1976] 184).

In another context Attridge describes Josephus's tendencies in *Jewish War*: (1) to flatter himself and to blame revolutionary leaders who were brigands and tyrants for the revolt that brought Jerusalem's destruction; (2) generally to absolve the Roman leadership, especially Titus; (3) to blame humans, but to explain that the outcome was determined by God's will; (4) to isolate responsibility and to arouse sympathy for Jewish people as a whole ("Josephus and His Work," in *Jewish Writings of the Second Temple Period* [ed. M. Stone; CRINT 2/2; Assen: Van Gorcum; Philadelphia: Fortress, 1984] 185–232). In turn, Attridge describes Josephus's tendencies in *Antiquities* as being chiefly theological: "To express this divine governance of affairs Josephus relies primarily on the Greek term *pronoia*, which, for the most part, replaces the more deterministic language of fate and destiny used prominently in the *War*" (p. 217).

Remarkably, the most recently published study of Luke-Acts in relation to ancient historiography, a magisterial monograph by G. E. Sterling (*Historiography and Self-Definition: Josephos, Luke-Acts and Apologetic Historiography* [NovTSup 64; Leiden/New York/Cologne: Brill, 1992] 393) concludes by observing, "The apex of Hellenistic Jewish historiography reached in the *Antiquitates Judaicae* of Josephos is complemented by Luke-Acts which not only marks the end of the same tradition, but serves as the beginning of another." I regret that this excellent study came to my attention only during the final editing of the current work.

47. See the excellent summary description of 2 Maccabees by Attridge ("Historiography," 176–83).

God. Yet, beyond the fact of repetitions and the references to resurrection and God, one does not find points for comparison with the speeches in Acts. In 2 Maccabees one observes a Jewish writing from the Hellenistic era that uses historiography to present, defend, and advocate the validity or superiority of Judaism; so that again one recognizes the availability and use of historiography in relation to the expression of religious concerns.

In conclusion, despite the claims of many contemporary scholars, upon scrutiny one finds practically no specific points for comparison of the speeches in Acts with the literature of Hellenistic Judaism. Yet the lack of specific points for comparison should not cause one to miss the general similarity between Acts, especially the speeches, and Hellenistic Jewish literature. On the one hand, Acts and this literature demonstrate the use of the genre of historiography for the presentation, defense, and advocation of religious concerns. On the other hand, the existence of wisdom literature and overt apologetic writings indicates that there were other avenues available for presenting, defending, and advocating particular religious concerns. Therefore, in the Hellenistic era, one sees that both the early Christian author Luke and several authors from Hellenistic Judaism deemed historiography the suitable genre for the articulation of their concerns. Thus, the form of the speeches in Acts is clearly related to Greco-Roman historiography, and the language and themes of the speeches seem most comparable to portions of the Septuagint; but that Luke wrote history—including especially the speeches—in relation to religious convictions and the debate over such convictions makes Acts perhaps most comparable to Hellenistic Jewish literature. Despite genuine distinctions, in Acts and the literature of Hellenistic Judaism one finds the combination of Greco-Roman forms with Jewish (LXX) language and themes as historiography functions to present, defend, and advocate particular religious convictions.

Summary

In form and rhetoric one can see that the speeches in Acts are often parallel to speeches in Greco-Roman historiography. In content, however, the speeches of Acts are more like portions of the Septuagint than comparable to Greco-Roman historiographical addresses. Yet, in their purpose—that is, in the use of Greco-Roman historiographical forms in religious compositions for the basic instruction of adherents of a particular religious conviction[48]—

---

48. As Collins observes concerning the works of the Hellenistic Jewish historians, "In fact, the Greeks paid little attention to any of the writings of the native orientals, but many Jewish writers did express themselves in forms which might have been accessible to the Greeks. Even if they failed to make any significant impact on the gentile audience they surely helped satisfy the self-understanding of the increasingly Hellenized Jewish community" (*Between Athens and*

the speeches in Acts are most like the work of the fragmentary writings of Hellenistic Jewish historians. Nevertheless, in sheer repetitiveness the speeches in Acts stand apart. One can say that the most distinctive feature of the speeches is repetition — of forms and of content.

Jerusalem, 26). Later, Collins remarks, "Such propaganda is directed to both gentile and Jew, with complementary objectives of inspiring respect from without and self-respect from within" (p. 36).

4 OVERVIEW AND CONCLUSIONS

T HE SHEER MAGNITUDE of the material in the analysis done above in chapter 2 necessitates a summary that allows one to see the main lines of the speeches in an abbreviated form. The following presentation sketches the themes and prominent rhetorical features of the speeches, giving minimal attention to matters of vocabulary. The style and value of this kind of summarizing of speeches, in order to see beyond the particular elements to major patterns, structures, and even themes, were demonstrated above all by the careful study of Herodotean narrative and discourse by M. L. Lang.[1] In the following epitomes I have not, however, followed Lang's lead in reducing the speeches into codes; for, as will be apparent, in this study repetition of central themes is more important in the speeches in Acts than recurring structures. A section of reflections on the substance of the speeches follows the presentation of their contents.

Sketches of the Contents of the Speeches

The Words of the Risen Jesus and the Angels
to the Apostles (1:4b–5, 7–8, 11)

1.0 Use of the past: John the Baptist
     Holy Spirit
2.0
2.1 Divine authority

---

1. M. L. Lang, *Herodotean Narrative and Discourse* (Martin Classical Lectures 28; Cambridge, MA: Harvard University Press, 1984).

2.2   Holy Spirit
       Implicit recognition of divine authority
       Witness
       Universal significance of salvation
3.0   Address: ἄνδρες Γαλιλαῖοι ("Men, Galileans")
       Recognition of the situation
       Ascension

Peter's Speech and the Disciples' Prayer
Prior to the Enrollment of Matthias (1:16–22, 24b–25)

1.0
1.1   Address: ἄνδρες ἀδελφοί ("Men, brothers")
1.2   Divine necessity
       Holy Spirit
       David
1.3
1.4   Use of the past: scripture quotation
2.0
2.1   Use of the past: scripture quotation
       Implicit statement of divine necessity
2.2
2.2.1 Eyewitness
       Use of the past: John the Baptist
2.2.2 Witness
       Resurrection
and
1.0   Address: σὺ κύριε ("You, Lord")
2.0   Implicit recognition of divine authority
3.0   Implicit recognition of divine authority and divine necessity

Peter's Speech at Pentecost (2:14b–36, 38–39, 40b)

1.0
1.1   Address: ἄνδρες 'Ιουδαῖοι ("Men, Jews")
       Call for a hearing: γνωστὸν ἔστω ("let it be known to you")
1.2   Situation: misunderstanding
       Use of the past: reference to the prophets
1.3   Use of the past: scripture quotation
       ὅραμα, τέρατα, σημεῖα ("visions," "wonders," "signs")
       Universal character of the gospel

2.0–2.1
2.1.1 Address: ἄνδρες Ἰσραηλῖται ("Men, Israelites")
      Appeal: ἀκούσατε ("listen")
2.1.2 Christological kerygma
          Ἰησοῦν τὸν Ναζωραῖον ("Jesus the Nazorean")
          ἀνήρ ("a man")
          τέρατα and σημεῖα ("wonders" and "signs")
          Divine authority
          ἡ βουλὴ θεοῦ + ὁρίζειν ("the plan of God" + "to determine")
          Cross not a scandal
          "Lawless" did the will of the Jerusalem Jews in executing
              Jesus
          Christological contrast scheme
          Resurrection
2.1.3 Use of the past: scripture quotation
      David
2.2
2.2.1 ἄνδρες ἀδελφοί ("Men, brothers")
2.2.2 David
      David's heir on the throne
      Resurrection
2.2.3 Christological kerygma
          Divine authority
          Resurrection and exaltation
          Witness
          Holy Spirit
2.2.4 David
      Use of the past: scripture quotation
2.2.5 Divine authority
          κύριος + χρίστος ("Lord" + "Christ")
          Guilt of the hearers
Interruption
3.0
3.1   Call to repentance
      Call to baptism
      Name of Jesus
      Forgiveness of sins
3.2   Holy Spirit as a gift
3.3   Universal character of the gospel
4.0   Call to "be saved"
      Implicit recognition of divine authority

Peter's Speech in Solomon's Portico of the Temple (3:12–26)

1.0
1.1 Address: ἄνδρες Ἰσραηλῖται ("Men, Israelites")
     Situation: misunderstanding
1.2 Divine authority
     παῖς ("Servant")
     Guilt of the hearers
     Pilate served the will of the Jerusalem Jews in permitting the
         execution of Jesus
     Christological contrast scheme
     Resurrection
     ὁ δίκαιος ("the Righteous One")
1.3
1.3.1 Witness
1.3.2 Name of Jesus
2.0
2.1 καὶ νῦν ("and now")
     Address: ἀδελφοί ("brothers")
     Ignorance
2.2 Divine authority
     Implicit recognition of God's plan
     Use of the past: reference to the prophets without a citation
2.3
2.3.1 Double call to repentance (μετανοήσατε . . . ἐπιστρέψατε,
     "repent" . . . "turn")
2.3.2 Forgiveness of sins
2.3.3 Divine authority (via Christ)
2.4
2.4.1 Moses
     Use of the past: scripture quotation
     "Prophet like Moses"
2.4.2 Use of the past: reference to Samuel and the prophets
     Covenant
     Situation: τὰς ἡμέρας ταύτας ("these days")
     Use of the past: reference to the prophets without a citation
2.5 Divine authority
     Resurrection
     Repentance

Peter's Speech to the Jewish Authorities
after His and John's Arrest (4:8b–12, 19b–20)

1.0
1.1   Address: ἄρχοντες τοῦ λαοῦ καὶ πρεσβύτεροι ("leaders of the people and elders")
1.2   Situation: ἀνακρίνειν ("to examine")
1.3   Call for a hearing: γνωστὸν ἔστω ("let it be known to you")
1.3.1 Name of Jesus
       Ἰησοῦς ὁ Ναζωραῖος ("Jesus the Nazorean")
       Christological contrast scheme
       Resurrection
       Implicit call to repentance
1.3.2 Possible use of the past: possible allusion to scripture
       Contrast scheme
1.3.3 Name of Jesus
       Universal nature of salvation
       Divine necessity
2.0
2.1   Implicit recognition of divine authority
2.2   Witness
       Implicit recognition of divine authority

The Prayer of the Apostles and Their Friends (4:24b–30)

1.0
1.1   Address: δέσποτα, σύ ("Sovereign, you")
1.2   Creator God
1.3   David
       Holy Spirit
       Use of the past: scripture quotation
       Divine authority (Revealer God)
1.4   παῖς ("Servant")
       Divine authority
       Herod + Pontius Pilate
       The plan of God
2.0
2.1   καὶ τὰ νῦν ("and now")
       κύριε ("Lord")
2.2   Divine authority
       Witness

σημεῖα καὶ τέρατα ("signs and wonders")
Name of Jesus
παῖς ("Servant")

The Speech of Peter and the Apostles
to the Council (5:29b–32)

1.0 Divine necessity and authority
2.0
2.1 Christological contrast scheme
     Resurrection
     ξύλον ("tree") = use of the past: allusion to scripture
2.2 Divine authority
     ἀρχηγός + σωτήρ ("Leader" + "Savior")
     Exaltation
     Repentance and forgiveness
     Divine necessity
3.0
3.1 Witness
     ῥῆμα ("word")
     Holy Spirit

Gamaliel's Speech to the Council (5:35b–39)

1.0 Address: ἄνδρες 'Ισραηλῖται ("Men, Israelites")
2.0 Warning: προσέχετε ἑαυτοῖς ("keep watch over yourselves")
3.0 Use of the past: two historical illustrations
3.1
3.2
4.0
4.1 καὶ τὰ νῦν ("and now")
4.2 A plan (here: human?)
4.3 The plan of God
     Divine authority and necessity
4.4 Divine authority

The Speech by the Twelve Prior to the Appointment
of the Seven (6:2b–4)

1.0 λόγος ("word")
2.0

2.1   Charge: ἐπισκέπτεσθαι ("to select")
       Address: ἀδελφοί ("brothers")
2.2
2.2.1 Indirect reference to "witness"
2.2.2 Holy Spirit
2.2.3
3.0   λόγος ("word")
       Implicit reference to "witness"
       Implicit recognition of divine necessity

Stephen's Speech (7:2–53, 56, 59b, 60b)

1.0
1.1   Address: ἄνδρες ἀδελφοί καὶ πατέρες ("Men, brothers and fathers")
       Appeal: ἀκούσατε ("listen")
1.2
1.2.1 Divine authority
       Abraham
       Use of the past: scripture quotation
1.2.2 Divine authority
1.2.3 Polemic against hearers
1.2.4 Use of the past: scripture quotation
       λατρεύειν ("to worship")
       Divine authority + implicit recognition of the divine plan
1.2.5 Covenant
       Divine authority
1.3–1.3.3
1.4   Polemical tone of the narrative
1.4.1 Possible use of the past: possible allusion to scripture
1.4.2 Possible use of the past: possible allusions to scripture
       Polemical tone of the narrative
1.4.3 Possible use of the past: possible allusion to scripture
1.4.4 Possible use of the past: possible allusion to scripture
       ἐξαποστέλλειν ("to send forth")
       Divine authority and implicit recognition of the divine plan
1.4.5 Possible use of the past: possible allusions to scripture
       Divine authority
1.5   Divine necessity and authority
1.5.1 Use of the past: apparent scripture quotation
1.5.2 Moses
       Divine authority

1.5.3 Moses' determination: ἐπισκέπτεσθαι
σωτηρία ("salvation")
Divine authority
Use of the past: scripture quotation
Human guilt
Implicit recognition of ignorance
1.5.4 Possible use of the past: possible allusion to scripture
Use of the past: scripture quotations
καὶ νῦν ("and now")
Divine authority
1.5.5 Use of the past: scripture quotation
Divine authority
τέρατα καὶ σημεῖα ("wonders and signs")
1.5.6 Use of the past: scripture quotation
Possible use of the past: possible allusion to scripture
1.5.7 Use of the past: scripture quotation
1.5.8 Divine authority
Use of the past: reference to the prophets + scripture quotation
1.6
1.6.1 Possible use of the past: possible allusion to scripture
Witness
"Not without a witness"
Divine authority (plan?)
1.6.2 David
Divine authority
1.6.3 Temple (here "house")
1.6.4 Polemical remarks
Use of the past: reference to the prophets + scripture quotation
Divine authority
2.0 Guilt of the hearers
2.1 Holy Spirit
Polemical remarks
2.2 Use of the past: reference to the prophets
Divine purposes (plan?)
ὁ δίκαιος ("the Righteous One")
Guilt of the hearers
Law observance
Interruption
3.0
3.1 Jesus raised and exalted
ὁ υἱὸς τοῦ ἀνθρώπου ("the Son of Man")
3.2 κύριε Ἰησοῦ ("Lord Jesus")
Implicit recognition of Jesus as savior

3.3   κύριε ("Lord")
Forgiveness
Divine authority

Peter's Speech in Cornelius's House (10:28b–29, 34b–43, 47)

1.0   Divine authority
Address: ὑμεῖς ("you")
Appeal to the knowledge of the hearers
2.0
2.1   Universal character of salvation
2.2   Divine authority
3.0   Christological kerygma
3.1   λόγος ("word")
Possible use of the past: possible allusions to scripture
God's authority shown via Christ
Jesus Christ = κύριος ("Lord")
Universal significance of the gospel
3.2   Address: ὑμεῖς ("you")
Use of the past: John the Baptist
3.3   Divine authority seen in God's action in relation to Jesus
'Ιησοῦν τὸν ἀπὸ Ναζαρέθ ("Jesus, the one from Nazareth")
Holy Spirit
3.4   Divine authority
4.0   Witness
5.0   Christological contrast scheme
ξύλον ("tree") = use of the past: allusion to scripture
Resurrection
Divine authority
6.0   Witness
Divine authority (plan?)
7.0   Witness
Divine authority
Allusion to God's plan
Raised Jesus = Judge
8.0   Use of the past: reference to the prophets without a citation
Witness
Forgiveness of sins
Name of Jesus
Implicit call to repentance
Universal significance of the gospel

Interruption
9.0   Implicit call to baptism
       Holy Spirit
       Universal nature of God's work

Peter's Speech to the Circumcision Party (11:5–17)

1.0   ὅραμα ("visions")
       κύριε ("Lord")
       Divine authority
2.0   Holy Spirit
       Divine authority
3.0   ῥήματα ("words")
       Salvation
       Holy Spirit
       Divine authority
4.0   ῥήμα ("word")
       Use of the past: John the Baptist
5.0   Holy Spirit as a gift
       Universal significance of the gospel
       Divine authority

Paul's Speech at Antioch of Pisidia (13:16b–41, 46–47)

1.0
1.1   Address: ἄνδρες 'Ισραηλῖται καὶ οἱ φοβούμενοι τὸν θεόν ("Men,
       Israelites and others who fear God")
       Appeal: ἀκούσατε ("listen")
1.2   Possible use of the past: possible allusions to scripture
1.2.1 Divine authority
1.2.2 Divine authority
1.2.3 Divine authority
1.2.4 Divine authority
1.2.5 Polemical remark
1.2.6
1.2.7 Divine authority
       David
       Witness
       Use of the past: scripture quotation
       Divine authority (plan?)

1.2.8 Christological kerygma
'Ιησούς ("Jesus") = σωτήρ ("savior")
Divine authority
1.3
1.3.1 Use of the past: John the Baptist
1.3.2 Witness
2.0   Divine authority
2.1   Address: ἄνδρες ἀδελφοί ("Men, brothers") + God-fearers
Abraham
λόγος ("word")
σωτηρία ("salvation")
Divine authority (ἐξαποστέλλειν, "to send forth")
2.2   Christological kerygma
Polemical tone
Christological contrast scheme
Guilt of the Jerusalemites
Ignorance
Use of the past: reference to the prophets without a citation
Pilate did the will of the Jerusalem Jews
Use of the past "what was written" without a citation
ξύλον ("tree") = use of the past: allusion to scripture
Cross not a scandal, God's plan
Resurrection
Divine authority
2.3   Witness
2.4   Resurrection
Use of the past: scripture quotations
Jesus = Son
Use of the past: scripture quotation
David
ἡ βουλὴ τοῦ θεοῦ ("the plan of God")
3.0
3.1   Call for a hearing: γνωστὸν . . . ἔστω ("let it be known to you")
Address: ἄνδρες ἀδελφοί ("Men, brothers")
3.2   Forgiveness of sins
Divine authority
Implicit call to repentance
Law
Moses
Universal significance of the gospel
4.0   Polemic against the hearers
Use of the past: reference to the prophets with scripture quotation
5.0

5.1 λόγος ("word")
Polemic against the hearers
5.2 Use of the past: reference to the prophets with scripture quotation
Universal significance of the gospel
Divine authority

The Speech of Barnabas and Paul at Lystra (14:15–17)

1.0 Address: ἄνδρες ("Men")
Situation: misunderstanding
2.0 Call to repentance
Implicit recognition of divine authority
3.0 Kerygma
3.1 Creator God
Possible use of the past: possible allusion to scripture
Universal character of salvation
Divine authority
3.2 Divine authority and necessity
Ignorance
3.3 Witness
"Not without a witness"
Divine authority

Peter's Speech at the Jerusalem Gathering (15:7b–11)

1.0
1.1 Address: ἄνδρες ἀδελφοί ("Men, brothers")
Appeal to the knowledge of the hearers
1.2 Divine authority
λόγος . . . εὐαγγελίου ("word . . . of good news")
1.3 Implicit recognition of divine authority
Witness
Divine authority
Holy Spirit
Universal character of the gospel
1.4 Universal nature of salvation
Divine authority
2.0 νῦν ("now")
Law (-observance)
3.0 κύριος 'Ιησοῦς ("Lord Jesus")
σωθῆναι ("to be saved")
Divine authority

James's Speech at the Jerusalem Gathering (15:13b–21)

1.0
1.1   Address: ἄνδρες ἀδελφοί ("Men, brothers")
      Appeal: ἀκούσατέ μου ("listen to me")
1.2   Divine authority
1.3   Use of the past: scripture quotations
      λόγος ("word")
      Divine authority
      David
      Name of the Lord
      Divine plan (?)
2.0
2.1   Repentance
2.2   Implicit denunciation of idolatry
3.0   Moses

Paul's Speech in the Middle of the Areopagus (17:22–31)

1.0
1.1   Address: ἄνδρες 'Αθηναῖοι ("Men, Athenians")
1.2   Indirect allusion to "ignorance"
1.3
1.3.1 Divine authority
      Possible use of the past: possible allusion to scripture
1.3.2 Creator God
      Divine authority
1.3.3 God = κύριος ("Lord")
1.3.4 Divine generosity (authority)
1.3.5 Divine authority
      Divine plan (?)
1.3.6 Use of the past: reference to and citation of pagan poets
      "Not without a witness"
2.0
2.1   Critique of idolatry
2.2   Ignorance
      Call to repentance (implicit recognition of hearers' guilt)
      τὰ νῦν ("now")
      Universal character of salvation
2.3
2.3.1 Jesus = ἀνήρ ("a man")

Jesus = Judge
Divine authority
Divine plan (?)
2.3.2 Resurrection
Implicit recognition of Jesus' being exalted
Divine authority
Interruption (?)

Paul's Speech to the Corinthian Jews (18:6b–d)

1.0   Polemic against the hearers
Divine plan (?)
2.0   Paul's innocence
3.0   ἀπὸ τοῦ νῦν ("from now on")
Universal character of the gospel

Gallio's Speech to the Corinthian Jews (18:14b–15)

1.0   Address: ὦ 'Ιουδαῖοι ("O Jews")
2.0   λόγος ("word")
Law

Demetrius's Speech (19:25b–27)

1.0   Address: ἄνδρες ("Men")
Appeal to the knowledge of the hearers
2.0   Reference to critique of idolatry
Implicit recognition (in the critique) of divine authority
3.0   Temple (here = pagan)

The Speech of the Ephesian Town Clerk (19:35b–40)

1.0   Address: ἄνδρες 'Εφέσιοι ("Men, Ephesians")
2.0
3.0
3.1   Innocence of Christians
3.2
3.3   ἐγκαλεῖν ("to choose")
4.0   Behavior signifies ignorance and guilt (civic)

Paul's Speech to the Ephesian Elders (20:18b–35)

1.0
1.1   Address: ὑμεῖς ("you")
       Appeal to the knowledge of the hearers
1.2   Divine authority
       Witness
       Repentance
       Implicit call to repentance
2.0
2.1
2.1.1 καὶ νῦν ("and now")
       Divine authority
       Holy Spirit
2.1.2 Witness
       τὸ εὐαγγέλιον ("the good news")
       Divine authority
2.2
2.2.1 καὶ νῦν ("and now")
2.2.2 Witness
       Paul's innocence
       ἡ βουλὴ τοῦ θεοῦ ("the plan of God")
3.0
3.1   Warning: προσέχετε ἑαυτοῖς ("keep watch over yourselves")
       Holy Spirit
       Divine authority
3.2
3.3   Universal significance of the gospel
4.0
4.1   καὶ τὰ νῦν ("and now")
       λόγος ("word")
       Divine authority
4.2
4.3   Divine necessity: δεῖ ("it is necessary")
       λόγοι τοῦ κυρίου Ἰησοῦ ("the words of the Lord Jesus")

Agabus's Speech in Caesarea (21:11b–c)

1.0   Holy Spirit
       Divine authority (plan?)
2.0

Paul's Speech to the Disciples in Caesarea (21:13b–c)

1.0
2.0   Name of the Lord Jesus

The Speech of James and the Jerusalem Elders (21:20b–25)

1.0
1.1   ἀδελφέ ("brother")
1.2   Law
1.3   Law
       Moses
       Circumcision (?)
1.4
2.0
2.1   Law-observance
2.2   Implicit critique of idolatry

The Speech of the Jews from Asia (21:28)

1.0   ἄνδρες 'Ισραηλῖται ("Men, Israelites")
2.0
2.1   Paul teaches κατὰ τοῦ λαοῦ ("against the people")
2.2   Paul teaches κατὰ τοῦ νομοῦ ("against the law")
2.3   Temple
2.4   Temple

Paul's Speech to the Jerusalem Jews (22:1, 3–21)

1.0
1.1   ἄνδρες ἀδελφοὶ καὶ πατέρες ("Men, brothers and fathers")
       Appeal: ἀκούσατε ("listen")
       νυνί ("now")
       Situation: ἀπολογία ("defense")
1.2   Paul's origins
       Paul's good reputation
       Law
1.3   Previous persecution of the church

2.0   Divine authority
      "Vision"
2.1   Implicit reference to resurrection, ascension, exaltation
      κύριε ("Lord")
      'Ιησοῦς ὁ Ναζωραῖος ("Jesus the Nazorean")
2.2–4
3.0
3.1   Law
3.2   Witness
      Divine authority
      Divine plan: θέλημα ("will")
      Jesus = ὁ δίκαιος ("the Righteous One")
      Universal significance of the gospel
3.3   καὶ νῦν ("and now")
      Baptism
      Forgiveness of sins
      Implicit call to repentance
      Name of [Jesus Christ]
4.0
4.1   "Vision" in the temple
4.2   κύριε ("Lord")
      Witness
4.3   Divine authority (ἐξαποστέλλειν, "to send forth")
      Universal significance of the gospel
      Divine authority
Interruption

Paul's Speech before the Council (23:1b, 3, 5, 6b)

1.0   Address: ἄνδρες ἀδελφοί ("Men, brothers")
      Paul's good reputation
      Implicit recognition of divine authority
2.0   Law
3.0   Address: ἀδελφοί ("brothers")
      Use of the past: scripture quotation
      Law-observance
4.0   Address: ἄνδρες ἀδελφοί ("Men, brothers")
      Why Paul is on trial: resurrection
      Implicit recognition of "witness" and "divine necessity"

The Pharisees' Speech in the Council (23:9c–d)

1.0   Paul's innocence
2.0   "Spirit"

Tertullus's Speech (24:2b–8)

1.0
2.0
2.1   Implicit recognition of worldwide character of Christianity
2.2   Temple
3.0   Situation: ἀναχρίνειν ("to examine")

Paul's Speech before Felix (24:10b–21)

1.0   Situation: ἀπολογεῖσθαι ("to make a defense")
2.0   νυνί ("now")
3.0   Paul's good reputation
      Divine authority
      λατρεύειν ("to worship")
      Law
      Use of the past: reference to the prophets without a citation
      Why Paul is on trial: resurrection
4.0   Divine authority
      Paul's good reputation
5.0   Law-observance
6.0   Paul's innocence
7.0   Why Paul is on trial: resurrection

Paul's Speech before Festus (25:8b, 10b–11)

1.0   Law
      Temple
      Paul's innocence
2.0
2.1   Divine necessity: δεῖ ("it is necessary")
2.2   Paul's innocence
2.3   Paul's good character
2.4–5

Festus's Speech (25:14c–21, 24–27)

1.0
1.1
1.2   Situation: ἀπολογία ("defense")
1.3
1.3.1
1.3.2 Jesus' resurrection
1.3.3 Implicit recognition of Paul's innocence
1.3.4
2.0
2.1   Address: ἄνδρες ("Men")
2.2   Paul's innocence
2.3
2.4   Situation: ἀνάκρισις ("examination")

Paul's Speech before King Agrippa (26:2–23, 25–27, 29)

1.0   Address: βασιλεῦ 'Αγρίππα ("King Agrippa")
       Situation: ἐγκαλεῖν . . . ἀπολογεῖσθαι ("to bring legal charges . . .
          to make a defense")
       Appeal: ἀκούειν ("to listen")
2.0
2.1   Paul's good reputation
2.2
2.2.1 καὶ νῦν ("and now")
       Why Paul is on trial: resurrection
       God's promise = plan
       λατρεύειν ("to worship")
2.2.2 Divine authority
       Resurrection
3.0–3.1
3.1.1 Paul's previous persecution of the church
       Divine necessity (δεῖ, "it is necessary" — negative force)
       Name of Jesus
       'Ιησοῦ τοῦ Ναζωραίου ("Jesus the Nazorean")
3.1.2 Paul's "vision" on the Damascus road
       Divine authority
       κύριε ("Lord")
       Witness
       Divine authority

Universal significance of the gospel
Divine plan (?)
Metaphorical reference to salvation
Call to repentance
Promise of forgiveness
Faith
3.1.3 Divine authority
Implicit recognition of need for repentance
3.1.4
3.2
3.2.1 Divine authority
Witness
Use of the past: reference to the prophets without a citation
Moses
Divine plan (?)
Divine authority
3.2.2 Christological kerygma
Χριστός ("Christ")
Cross not a scandal, part of divine plan
Resurrection
Universal significance of salvation and the gospel
Interruption
4.0–4.1
4.1.1 ῥήματα ("words")
Bold "witness"
Universal significance of the gospel
4.1.2 Use of the past: reference to the prophets without a citation
4.2   Implicit call to repentance

Paul's Speech(es) during the Sea Voyage to Rome
(27:10b, 21b–26, 31b, 33b–34)

1.0   Address: ἄνδρες ("Men")
2.0
2.1   Possible reference to "divine necessity": δεῖ ("it is necessary")
2.2
2.2.1 καὶ τὰ νῦν ("and now")
2.2.2 Implicit recognition of divine authority
2.2.3 Divine authority
λατρεύειν ("to worship")
Divine necessity: δεῖ ("it is necessary")
2.3

2.3.1 Address: ἄνδρες ("Men")
2.3.2 Implicit recognition of divine authority
2.4   Divine necessity: δεῖ ("it is necessary")
3.0   Divine authority
      Salvation
4.0–4.1
4.2   σωτηρία ("salvation" [?])
4.3   Metaphorical declaration of salvation
      Implicit recognition of divine plan (?)

Paul's Speech to the Roman Jewish Leaders
(28:17c–20, 25b–28)

1.0
1.1   Address: ἄνδρες ἀδελφοί ("Men, brothers")
      Paul's innocence
1.2   Paul's innocence
1.3
2.0–2.1
2.2   Why Paul is on trial: resurrection
3.0   Polemic against the hearers
3.1   Guilt of the hearers
      Holy Spirit
      Use of the past: scripture quotation
3.2
3.2.1 Call for a hearing: γνωστὸν . . . ἔστω ("let it be known to you")
      Salvation
      Divine authority
      Universal significance of salvation
      Divine plan (?)
3.2.2

Considering the Substance of the Speeches

By scanning the foregoing summaries one begins to perceive how Luke
used the speeches in Acts to create the overall *unity* of the account.[2] At the

---

2. I am indebted in many ways in what follows to the discussion of unity in Herodotus and
the Old Testament by J. Van Seters (*In Search of History: Historiography in the Ancient World
and the Origins of Biblical History* [New Haven/London: Yale University Press, 1983] 31–40).

most basic level the regularly repeated act of speaking[3] unifies the narrative through the phenomenon of repetition.[4] Luke's literary technique itself shows the arrangement of materials through the principle of analogy, as one after another of the characters in the story makes a speech. In turn, examination of the themes or subjects of the speeches shows that an identifiable set of topics or concerns recur in the speeches either explicitly or implicitly with striking regularity. Here, again, through the principle of analogy Luke weaves speeches into the narrative of Acts and creates *emphasis* so that the speeches articulate a distinct worldview. In the remainder of this chapter I shall examine the main lines of the worldview expressed in the speeches in Acts. Clear comprehension of this worldview promotes a better understanding of the role of the speeches in Acts and the place and purpose of Acts in the context of the ancient world. Along with recognizing the way the speeches create unity and bring didactic emphasis to the account, I shall comment on the *expectation* created through the speeches. Thus, in what follows I am primarily concerned with the repetitions in the speeches and their coherence, although it is instructive to notice that certain speeches serve more to advance the action of the narrative than to unify or to emphasize a point of view.

3. According to the analysis of "major speeches" in Acts by G. H. R. Horsley ("Speeches and Dialogue in Acts," *NTS* 32 [1986] 609–14), the density of speeches in Acts is twice that found in Tacitus's *Annals* or Herodotus's *Histories*, four times that in Josephus's *Jewish War*, eight times that in Thucydides' *History*, and sixteen times that in Polybius's *Histories*. Horsley deals, however, only with the major speeches, not all of them, so that the frequency of speeches in Acts is even greater than he recognizes.

4. Citing O. Ducrot and T. Todorov (*Encyclopedic Dictionary of the Science of Language* [trans. C. Porter; Baltimore/London: Johns Hopkins University Press, 1979] 278), T. B. Dozeman writes, "Repetition can be defined simply as 'a re-use of the same word or group of words'" (*God on the Mountain: A Study of Redaction, Theology and Canon in Exodus 19–24* [SBLMS 37; Atlanta: Scholars Press, 1989] 147–48). Dozeman continues: "The moment that we pursue a more extended definition problems arise, because repetition is two-sided in its function: it simultaneously unifies and creates difference in literature. . . . Repetition is a basic unifying device within literature. In fact it not only unifies literature in general, it also is meant to build emphasis. . . . On the other hand, repetition also creates difference within literature. Bruce Kawin succinctly states this problem in his book, *Telling it Again and Again:* 'The growth of a work, even from one identical line to another, makes exact repetition impossible. . . .' [B. F. Kawin, *Telling It Again and Again: Repetition in Literature and Film* (Ithaca: Cornell University Press, 1972) 7]. What this means for a study of repetition is that even though it is meant to unify literature and to create emphasis, contrast — or perhaps more appropriately, difference — is inherent in the trope. At best we can only discuss near-repetition in literature." As is clear, the following discussion attempts to come to terms with the unifying function of repetition that creates emphasis. Most often the *differences* between "near repetitions" in biblical literature have been studied in order to discern the history of the biblical traditions; yet the biblical writings as final-form documents unify tradition(s) and emphasize central concerns through "near-repetition."

Divine Authority

The speeches in Acts tell of a transcendent but active God who relates to the world, especially to humans, in order to bring to fruition God's own divine will. One after another of the speeches articulates a view of the world characterized by the conviction that God intervenes in life in this world to initiate relationships, to give directions for present or future actions, and to reverse the course of events by undoing certain effects which result from particular humanly initiated causes that are inconsistent with God's own purposes.

The idea of God's supreme will, realized primarily by God's own activities (often explicitly through human agents), recurs regardless of the speaker, the situation, or the species of the rhetoric of the speech. One finds both reports of God's actions and references to God's will in a variety of ways. The raised Jesus declares God's divine authority to the disciples (1:7). Peter speaks of divine necessity to the assembly of disciples prior to Matthias's enrollment among the twelve apostles (1:16b–17, 20b), and the subsequent prayer recognizes God's authoritative, active will (1:24b, 24c–25). Further, as the analysis of the speeches shows, other statements concerning God's ultimate authority occur in at least the following speeches: Peter's speech at Pentecost (2:22b–24, 32–33, 36, 40b); Peter's speech in Solomon's portico of the Temple (3:13–15, 18, 20–21, 26); Peter's speech to the Jewish authorities after his and John's arrest (4:12, 19b, 20); the prayer of the apostles and their friends (4:25–26, 27–28, 29b–30); the speech of Peter and the apostles to the council (5:29b, 31); Gamaliel's speech to the council (5:39); the speech by the Twelve prior to the appointment of the Seven (6:4); Stephen's speech (7:2c–3, 4a, 6–7, 8a, 12–13, 14–16, 20–22, 23–29, 30–34, 35–36, 42–43, 44, 45–46, 48–50, 52–53, 60b); Peter's speech in Cornelius's house (10:28b–29, 35, 36, 38a–b, 38c–d, 39b–40, 41, 42); Peter's speech to the circumcision party (11:5–10, 11–12, 13–15, 17); Paul's speech at Antioch of Pisidia (13:17, 18, 19–20a, 20b, 22, 23, 26, 27–30, 32–37, 38b–39, 47); the speech of Barnabas and Paul at Lystra (14:15b, 15c, 16, 17); Peter's speech at the Jerusalem gathering (15:7b, 8, 9, 11); James's speech at the Jerusalem gathering (15:14, 15–18); Paul's speech in the middle of the Areopagus (17:23b, 24a, 24b–25a, 25b, 26–27, 31a, 31b); Paul's speech to the Corinthian Jews (18:6b [?]); Demetrius's speech (19:26 — doubtful); Paul's speech to the Ephesian elders (20:18c–21, 22–23, 24, 26–27, 28, 32, 35); Agabus's speech in Caesarea (21:11b); Paul's speech to the Jerusalem Jews (22:6–11, 14–15, 21); Paul's speech before the council (23:1b, 6b); Paul's speech before Felix (24:14–15, 16); Paul's speech before Festus (25:10b); Paul's speech before King Agrippa (26:6–7, 8, 9–11 [?], 12–18, 19–20, 22, 23 [?]); Paul's speech(es) during the sea voyage to Rome (27:21b [?], 22b, 23–24, 25b, 26, 31b, 34c [?]); and Paul's speech to the Roman Jewish leaders (28:28a–b).

Recognition of the central importance of the idea of God's supreme divine authority is not a new insight into the substance of Luke's writings. As H. J. Cadbury wrote in 1927, "One feature of Luke's whole work [Luke-Acts] that might be conscious intention, quite as well as traditional *motif* or subconscious conviction, is the evidence of divine guidance and control that pervades it. The divine intervention is one of the credentials of the Christian movement."[5] Since Cadbury, much interpretive energy has gone into the attempt to understand "divine necessity," especially in terms of the word δεῖ ("it is necessary"), in relation to its correct background in antiquity.[6] Recently scholars have found that the ideas of "divine necessity" and "the plan of God" would have been intelligible to a variety of audiences in Luke's world.[7] Indeed, the recent studies have shown that the concept of divine necessity and the operation of this idea as a theme in Luke-Acts actually occur at the level of an assumption rather than an assertion.[8] This insight provides additional nuance for the incisive comments of Cadbury and even calls into question whether one should regard the theme of divine necessity or intervention as "one of the credentials of the Christian movement." Rather, Acts presents the credentials of early Christianity in the particular manner that the speeches declare that God's plan has been and is being brought to realization. Because divine necessity was a widespread assumption of people in the world from which Acts comes, the speeches do not so much advance as assume the idea of God's divine controlling will; moreover, the speeches in Acts use the assumption of God's divine

---

5. H. J. Cadbury, *The Making of Luke-Acts* (London: Macmillan, 1927; reprint, London: S.P.C.K., 1958, 1961) 303.

6. The interpretive debate is summarized and criticized by C. H. Cosgrove ("The Divine ΔΕΙ in Luke-Acts: Investigations into the Lukan Understanding of God's Providence," *NovT* 26 [1984] 168–90). Cosgrove focuses on the work of E. Fascher ("Theologische Beobachtungen zu δεῖ," in *Neutestamentliche Studien für Rudolf Bultmann zu seinem siebzigsten Geburtstag am 20. August 1954* [ed. W. Eltester; BZNW 21; Berlin: A. Töpelmann, 1954] 228–54), which advocates an interpretation of δεῖ in relation to the Old Testament and Paul and the work of S. Schulz ("Gottes Vorsehung bei Lukas," *ZNW* 54 [1963] 104–16), which argues that δεῖ and the other language of "divine necessity" in Luke-Acts "ist nicht mehr alttestamentlich-spätjüdisch-judenchristlich verstandene Erwählungs-, sonders hellenistisch-römisch interpretierte Vorsehungsgeschichte" ("Vorsehung," 111). Pointing to the artificiality of the distinction of "Old Testament/Jewish" and "Hellenistic" in relation to first-century Judaism, Cosgrove continues by showing that δεῖ is not a *terminus technicus* in Luke-Acts; rather it functions in a variety of ways: (1) to express rootedness in God's plan, (2) to summon to obedience, and (3) to express God's own guarantee.

7. J. T. Squires, "The Plan of God in Luke-Acts" (Ph.D. dissertation, Yale University, 1987); C. H. Talbert, "Once Again: The Gentile Mission in Luke-Acts," in *Der Treue Gottes Trauen: Beiträge zum Werk des Lukas für Gerhard Schneider* (ed. C. Bussmann and W. Radl; Freiburg/ Basel/Vienna: Herder, 1991) 99–109, esp. 102–5.

8. See Cosgrove, who refers to "the unreflective nature of the Lukan conception" ("Divine ΔΕΙ ," 185–86, 189–90; quotation from p. 185) and Talbert, who writes that "Mediterranean culture assumed a divine plan behind the events of history" ("Gentile Mission," 102–5; quotation from p. 105).

authority in order to articulate an assertion about the particular manner in which God's plan is fulfilled. In turn, seeing the level at which the idea of divine necessity occurs in the speeches leads to the consideration of the elements of the particular assertions made concerning God's plan.

Theology and Christology

What gives the understanding and presentation of God's will and divine necessity a special cast in the speeches in Acts is the regular focusing of statements in the speeches about God's will and work in terms of Christology. Within the worldview assumed by the speeches in Acts one finds the distinctive, repeated, and debated bold assertion that God's will and work for salvation are brought to realization in Jesus Christ. This element occurs in the speeches in a variety of ways.

The clearest evidence of the crucial nature of this christological pointing of assertions about God's activity is seen in statements in the speeches that explicitly declare that ἡ βουλὴ τοῦ θεοῦ is realized in Jesus Christ. Early in Acts, Peter's speech at Pentecost declares: 'Ἰησοῦν τὸν Ναζωραῖον, ἄνδρα ἀποδεδειγμένον ἀπὸ τοῦ θεοῦ εἰς ὑμᾶς δυνάμεσι καὶ τέρασι καὶ σημείοις οἷς ἐποίησεν δι' αὐτοῦ ὁ θεὸς ἐν μέσῳ ὑμῶν καθὼς αὐτοὶ οἴδατε, τοῦτον τῇ ὡρισμένῃ βουλῇ καὶ προγνώσει τοῦ θεοῦ ἔκδοτον διὰ χειρὸς ἀνόμων προσπήξαντες ἀνείλατε, "Jesus the Nazorean, a man attested to you by God with deeds of power, wonders, and signs that God did through him among you, as you yourselves know—this man, handed over to you according to the definite plan and foreknowledge of God, you crucified and killed by the hands of the lawless" (2:22c–23). Then, later in the prayer of the apostles and their friends one reads, συνήχθησαν γὰρ ἐπ' ἀληθείας ἐν τῇ πόλει ταύτῃ ἐπὶ τὸν ἅγιον παῖδά σου 'Ἰησοῦν ὃν ἔχρισας, Ἡρῴδης τε καὶ Πόντιος Πιλᾶτος σὺν ἔθνεσιν καὶ λαοῖς 'Ἰσραήλ, ποιῆσαι ὅσα ἡ χείρ σου καὶ ἡ βουλὴ [σου] προώρισεν γενέσθαι, "For in this city, in fact, both Herod and Pontius Pilate, with the Gentiles and the peoples of Israel, gathered together against your holy servant Jesus, whom you anointed, to do whatever your hand and your plan had predestined to take place" (4:27–28). Both statements are clear indications that the plan of God was at work in the events transpiring in relation to Jesus Christ. Similarly, portions of certain speeches use δεῖ to express the theme of divine necessity with explicit reference to Jesus Christ. In Peter's speech in the portico of the temple one hears of τὸν προκεχειρισμένον ὑμῖν Χριστόν, 'Ἰησοῦν, ὃν δεῖ οὐρανὸν μὲν δέξασθαι ἄχρι χρόνων ἀποκαταστάσεως πάντων ὧν ἐλάλησεν ὁ θεὸς διὰ στόματος τῶν ἁγίων ἀπ' αἰῶνος αὐτοῦ προφητῶν, "the Messiah appointed for you, that is, Jesus, who must remain in heaven until the time of universal restoration that God announced long ago through his holy prophets" (3:20b–21); and in Peter's subsequent remarks to the Jewish authorities after he and John were arrested one reads, καὶ οὐκ ἔστιν ἐν ἄλλῳ οὐδενὶ ἡ σωτηρία, οὐδὲ γὰρ ὄνομά ἐστιν ἕτερον ὑπὸ τὸν οὐρανὸν τὸ δεδομένον ἐν ἀνθρώποις ἐν ᾧ δεῖ σωθῆναι ἡμᾶς, "There is salvation in no one else, for there is no other name under heaven given among humans by which we must be saved" (4:12). From these explicit statements (and the many similar remarks in other speeches) one sees clearly that the plan of God moves by divine necessity toward realization in Jesus Christ.

The Operation of God's Plan

The network of statements concerning both ἡ βουλὴ τοῦ θεοῦ ("the plan of God") and divine necessity, as indicated by the use of δεῖ ("it is necessary"), are not exhausted by the explicit references to God's plan, will, and work in relation to Jesus Christ. For example, in Paul's speech in Antioch of Pisidia one learns that, before Jesus, David served the plan of God (Δαυὶδ μὲν γὰρ ἰδίᾳ γενεᾷ ὑπηρετήσας τῇ τοῦ θεοῦ βουλῇ ἐκοιμήθη καὶ προσετέθη πρὸς τοὺς πατέρας αὐτοῦ καὶ εἶδεν διαφθοράν, "For David, after he had served the purpose of God in his own generation, died, was laid beside his fathers, and experienced corruption," 13:36), although this declaration leads to a statement of contrast that bridges from David to Jesus and explains that God's will and work are seen in a realized form in Jesus Christ rather than in David (ὃν δὲ ὁ θεὸς ἤγειρεν, οὐκ εἶδεν διαφθοράν, "but he whom God raised up experienced no corruption," 13:37). Later in Acts, however, as Paul addresses the Ephesian elders, his statement indicates that the plan of God has breadth beyond the will and work of God in history in relationship to Jesus alone (οὐ γὰρ ὑπεστειλάμην τοῦ μὴ ἀναγγεῖλαι πᾶσαν τὴν βουλὴν τοῦ θεοῦ ὑμῖν, "for I did not shrink from declaring to you the whole purpose of God," 20:27). Thus, one sees that the activity of the members of the early church — apparently in bearing testimony to God's plan, especially at work in Jesus Christ — is part of the ongoing operation of God's plan.

Furthermore, as δεῖ ("it is necessary") occurs in the speeches indicating divine necessity, one learns that events other than those related exclusively to Jesus Christ transpire because of God's will. For example, Peter explains both Judas's end (ἔδει πληρωθῆναι τὴν γραφὴν ἣν προεῖπεν τὸ πνεῦμα τὸ ἅγιον διὰ στόματος Δαυὶδ περὶ Ἰούδα . . . , "the scripture had to be fulfilled, which the Holy Spirit through David foretold concerning Judas," 1:16) and the selection of his successor (δεῖ οὖν τῶν συνελθόντων ἡμῖν ἀνδρῶν ἐν παντὶ χρόνῳ ᾧ εἰσῆλθεν καὶ ἐξῆλθεν ἐφ' ἡμᾶς ὁ κύριος Ἰησοῦς, "It is necessary that one of the men who have accompanied us during all the time that the Lord Jesus went in and out among us," 1:21) to the members of the early Christian community in terms of divine necessity. Later, when Peter and the apostles stand before the high priest and the council, they say, Πειθαρχεῖν δεῖ θεῷ μᾶλλον ἢ ἀνθρώποις, "It is necessary to obey God rather than humans" (5:29b); so that one sees divine necessity continuing to operate in relation to the activities of the members of the church. This continuing operation of divine necessity beyond God's work in relation to Jesus Christ is even clearer in Paul's report at sea of the words of the angel concerning the divine necessity of Paul's standing before Caesar (Μὴ φοβοῦ, Παῦλε, Καίσαρί σε δεῖ παραστῆναι, "Do not be afraid, Paul; you must stand before the emperor," 27:24).

Thus, one sees that ἡ βουλὴ τοῦ θεοῦ ("the plan of God") operating by divine necessity was not merely completed in Jesus Christ. God's plan existed and was in operation both prior to Jesus and after his ascension. The statements in the speeches do, however, indicate the crucial, definitive nature of God's work in relation to Jesus Christ, since the continuing activity of the Christian community is always somehow related to God's work in and through Jesus Christ. For example, the reply of the apostles to the high priest and the council (5:29b) is followed by a remark that explains the necessity of the apostles defying the instruction of the council: ὁ θεὸς τῶν πατέρων ἡμῶν ἤγειρεν 'Ιησοῦν ὃν ὑμεῖς διεχειρίσασθε κρεμάσαντες ἐπὶ ξύλου· τοῦτον ὁ θεὸς ἀρχηγὸν καὶ σωτῆρα ὕψωσεν τῇ δεξιᾷ αὐτοῦ [τοῦ] δοῦναι μετάνοιαν τῷ 'Ισραὴλ καὶ ἄφεσιν ἁμαρτιῶν. καὶ ἡμεῖς ἐσμεν μάρτυρες τῶν ῥημάτων τούτων καὶ τὸ πνεῦμα τὸ ἅγιον ὃ ἔδωκεν ὁ θεὸς τοῖς πειθαρχοῦσιν αὐτῷ, "The God of our fathers raised up Jesus, whom you had killed by hanging him on a tree. God exalted him at his right hand as Leader and Savior that he might give repentance to Israel and forgiveness of sins. And we are witnesses to these things, and so is the Holy Spirit, whom God has given to those who obey him" (5:30–32). The apostles do God's will because of God's having raised and exalted Jesus. Moreover, the resurrection and the exaltation of Jesus establish him as Leader and Savior, so that through him God gives repentance to Israel for the forgiveness of sins. Finally, the apostles declare that their obedience to God is both the gift and the demand of their being Spirit-empowered witnesses to God's work in and through Jesus Christ. Effectively this brief answer to the council makes clear that the plan of God is grounded on or rooted in God's actions relative to Jesus Christ, so that the plan continues to be realized by divine necessity in the obedient witness of the apostles — and, as Acts shows, the other members of the early church. Thus, one should understand that the decisive activity of God in relation to Jesus Christ inaugurated the ongoing testimony to God's saving work. As Luke writes in the prologue to Acts, "the first book" (the Gospel according to Luke) treated πάντων . . . ὧν ἤρξατο ὁ 'Ιησοῦς ποιεῖν τε καὶ διδάσκειν, all that Jesus did and taught from the beginning" (1:1). And, as I have stated in another context,

> In Acts (2:17; 3:22), it becomes apparent that the Passion of Jesus *inaugurated* the penultimate eschatological era of the Last Days. Following the Passion, Jesus resides in heaven until the time for the establishment of all that God plans,[9]

9. The phrase "inaugurated eschatology" is borrowed from W. S. Kurz, "Acts 3:19–26 as a

although he continues what he began by working in and through his disciples . . . .
Luke can say at Acts 9:34 that Jesus Christ heals and at 26:22–23 that Christ
proclaims light to his own people and to the Gentiles. Thus the patterns of human
response to Jesus that were seen throughout his earthly ministry, and which
culminated in the events of the Passion, continue after Jesus' death and resurrection; for, while Jesus is exalted into heaven, humanity continues to accept
or reject him as he ministers among and through the disciples.[10]

One sees that the time of Jesus is not merely a past event to be looked back
to by the members of the church. Thus, one should not separate the time
of Jesus from the time of the church.[11] The last days began with Jesus, and,
according to the speeches in Acts, they are the era in which the church lives
(2:17). Moreover, the speeches suggest a vital anticipation of the *last day,*
that is, a day of final judgment appointed by God through Jesus Christ
(17:31).[12] God's work in Jesus Christ sets boundaries on an era in which the
speakers in Acts contend they live and give testimony. Indeed, the repetitions in the speeches work to unify time so that history cannot be regarded
as a mere linear evolution. In Acts there is no chain of causes and effects
where causes produce effects that themselves become causes for subsequent
effects. Acts knows and repeats one cause — God's work in Jesus Christ. Far
from producing a theology of history, Luke writes Acts in such a manner that
time spirals, moving ahead only as it reaches back and brings into the present
the crucial reality of God's work in Jesus Christ. Thus, Israel's past is recalled
in Acts as it is related to Jesus Christ, and the church's present and future
both have their meaning in relation to God's work in Jesus Christ, which
determines the character and course of every new moment.

Test Case of the Role of Eschatology in Lukan Christology," in *Society of Biblical Literature
1977 Seminar Papers* (Missoula, MT: Scholars Press, 1977) 309–23.

10. M. L. Soards, *The Passion according to Luke: The Special Material of Luke 22* (JSNTSup
14; Sheffield: JSOT Press, 1987) 111 and 159.

11. This point, of course, runs against one of the major contentions in the interpretation of
Luke's program in Luke and Acts as understood by H. Conzelmann (*Die Mitte der Zeit: Studien
zur Theologie des Lukas* [BHT 17; 6th ed.; Tübingen: J. C. B. Mohr (Paul Siebeck), 1977]). The
criticisms of Conzelmann are so well known that it is superfluous to go on repeating them. See,
above all, W. C. Robinson, Jr., *Der Weg des Herrn: Studien zur Geschichte und Eschatologie im
Lukas-Evangelium: Ein Gespräch mit Hans Conzelmann* (TF 36; Hamburg-Bergstedt: H. Reich,
1964) 45–67; and see J. A. Fitzmyer (*The Gospel according to Luke* [AB 28; Garden City, NY:
Doubleday, 1981] 171–92) for a compact discussion of the matter.

12. An elaborate case for the reality and importance of eschatological expectation in Luke-
Acts comes from A. J. Mattill, Jr. (*Luke and the Last Things — a perspective for understanding
Lukan thought* [Dillsboro, NC: Western North Carolina Press, 1979]). While Mattill claims
more than he proves, through overstatement he is able to demonstrate that eschatological
expectation is more than a faint or marginal issue, as though it were a residue, in Luke-
Acts.

The Marking of the Time

In several of the speeches temporal words or phrases function to recognize the nature of the time or times. In the order of their first occurrence in Acts these temporal designations are καὶ νῦν ("and now") τὰς ἡμέρας ταύτας ("these days"), καὶ τὰ νῦν ("and now"), νῦν ("now"), τὰ νῦν ("now"), ἀπὸ τοῦ νῦν ("from now on"), and νυνί ("now"). These words and phrases work in three basic ways to mark the moments in which the speakers recognize or address the situation faced by themselves and their audiences. First, in some instances they recognize the critical nature of the time in which the speaker speaks. For example, in the prayer of the apostles and their friends, the assembly calls upon the Lord to grant them boldness in bearing witness despite the threats of those opposed to Jesus and his followers (καὶ τὰ νῦν, κύριε, ἔπιδε ἐπὶ τὰς ἀπειλὰς αὐτῶν καὶ δὸς τοῖς δούλοις σου μετὰ παρρησίας πάσης λαλεῖν τὸν λόγον σου, "and now, Lord, look at their threats, and grant to your servants to speak your word with all boldness," 4:29). Gamaliel's advice to the council marks the moment in which he and they stand as a time of potential crisis requiring prudent action (καὶ τὰ νῦν λέγω ὑμῖν, ἀπόστητε ἀπὸ τῶν ἀνθρώπων τούτων καὶ ἄφετε αὐτούς, "And now, I tell you, keep away from these men and let them alone," 5:38). In Peter's speech at the Jerusalem gathering a temporal marker recognizes the time of the gathering as a crucial moment mandating affirmation of God's saving activity in relation to the Gentiles (νῦν οὖν τί πειράζετε τὸν θεόν ἐπιθεῖναι ζυγὸν ἐπὶ τὸν τράχηλον τῶν μαθητῶν ὃν οὔτε οἱ πατέρες ἡμῶν οὔτε ἡμεῖς ἰσχύσαμεν βαστάσαι; ἀλλὰ διὰ τῆς χάριτος τοῦ κυρίου Ἰησοῦ πιστεύομεν σωθῆναι καθ᾽ ὃν τρόπον κἀκεῖνοι, "Now therefore why are you putting God to the test by placing on the neck of the disciples a yoke that neither our fathers nor we have been able to bear? On the contrary, we believe that we will be saved through the grace of the Lord Jesus, just as they will," 15:10–11). Temporal words and phrases that function similarly are found in 20:22 (καὶ νῦν, "and now"), 20:32 (καὶ τὰ νῦν, "and now"), 22:1 (νυνί, "now"), 24:13 (νυνί, "now"), 26:6 (καὶ νῦν, "and now"), and 27:22 (καὶ τὰ νῦν, "and now").

Second, in other instances temporal phrases create a contrast between the past and the present moment of the speech. For example, in 3:17 in Peter's speech in Solomon's portico of the Temple, καὶ νῦν separates the moment in which Peter speaks from the foregoing time in which the audience acted in ignorance in opposition to the will of God, specifically in relationship to Jesus (καὶ νῦν, ἀδελφοί, οἶδα ὅτι κατὰ ἄγνοιαν ἐπράξατε, ὥσπερ καὶ οἱ ἄρχοντες ὑμῶν, "And now, brothers, I know that you acted in ignorance, as did also your rulers"). Then, later in the same speech, the phrase τὰς ἡμέρας ταύτας creates a contrast between the time from Samuel and the prophets up to "these days" with "these days" themselves (καὶ πάντες δέ οἱ προφῆται ἀπὸ Σαμουὴλ καὶ τῶν καθεξῆς ὅσοι ἐλάλησαν καὶ κατήγγειλαν τὰς ἡμέρας ταύτας, "And all the prophets, as many as have spoken, from Samuel and those after him, also predicted these days," 3:24). Strikingly, in Stephen's speech in the recollection of God's direction to Moses concerning the deliverance of Israel out of Egypt, a temporal phrase contrasts the time of bondage with the moment in which God spoke, a moment that was itself the time of God's decisive saving activity (ἰδὼν εἶδον τὴν κάκωσιν τοῦ λαοῦ μου τοῦ ἐν Αἰγύπτῳ καὶ τοῦ στεναγμοῦ αὐτῶν ἤκουσα, καὶ κατέβην ἐξελέσθαι αὐτούς· καὶ νῦν δεῦρο ἀποστείλω σε εἰς Αἴγυπτον, "I have surely seen the mistreatment of my people who are in Egypt and have heard their groaning, and I have come down to rescue them. And now come, I will send you to Egypt," 7:34). Other contrasts between the past and the present moment of the speech occur in 17:30 (τὰ νῦν, "now"), 18:6 (ἀπὸ τοῦ νῦν, "from now on"), 20:25 (καὶ νῦν, "and now"), and 22:16 (καὶ νῦν, "and now").

Third, a function of the temporal phrases that is closely related to the second use occurs when the speaker signals a call to repentance and forgiveness. One explicit example of this function is in Paul's speech in the middle of the Areopagus (τοὺς μὲν οὖν χρόνους τῆς ἀγνοίας ὑπεριδὼν ὁ θεός, τὰ νῦν παραγγέλλει τοῖς ἀνθρώποις πάντας πανταχοῦ μετανοεῖν, "While God has overlooked the times of ignorance, now he commands all people everywhere to repent," 17:30).

These small but crucial markers show us one vital function of the speeches in Acts. The speakers recognize the critical nature of the moments in which they and their audience stand, and with their very words the speakers effect a contrast between past and present that exposes the real character of the human situation.[13] Formerly humans lived and acted in ignorance. The speeches acknowledge this ignorance and attribute it to both Jews (3:17: καὶ νῦν, ἀδελφοί, οἶδα ὅτι κατὰ ἄγνοιαν ἐπράξατε, ὥσπερ καὶ οἱ ἄρχοντες ὑμῶν, "And now, brothers, I know that you acted in ignorance, as did also your rulers"; 7:25: ἐνόμιζεν δὲ συνιέναι τοὺς ἀδελφοὺς [αὐτοῦ] ὅτι ὁ θεὸς διὰ χειρὸς αὐτοῦ δίδωσιν σωτηρίαν αὐτοῖς· οἱ δὲ οὐ συνῆκαν, "He supposed that his brothers would understand that God through him was rescuing them, but they did not understand"; and 13:27: οἱ γὰρ κατοικοῦντες ἐν Ἰερουσαλὴμ καὶ οἱ ἄρχοντες αὐτῶν τοῦτον ἀγνοήσαντες καὶ τὰς φωνὰς τῶν προφητῶν τὰς κατὰ πᾶν σάββατον ἀναγινωσκομένας κρίναντες ἐπλήρωσαν, "Because the residents of Jerusalem and their leaders did not recognize him or understand the words of the prophets that are read every Sabbath, they fulfilled those words by condemning him") and Gentiles (14:16: ὃς ἐν ταῖς παρῳχημέναις γενεαῖς εἴασεν πάντα τὰ ἔθνη προεύεσθαι ταῖς

---

13. While focusing on the *Missionsreden* E. Plümacher notes a similar function for this category of speeches (*Lukas als hellenistischer Schriftsteller: Studien zur Apostelgeschichte* [SUNT 9; Göttingen: Vandenhoeck & Ruprecht, 1972] 38). According to Plümacher they are distinct from the other speeches in Acts in that "sie führen dem Leser die geschichtsbestimmenden Kräfte zwar ebenfalls vor Augen, doch so, daß sie sich selbst, nämlich eben in ihrer Eigenschaft als Reden bzw. Predigten, als das erweisen, was die Geschichte jeweils vorangebracht hat." Plümacher reiterates this point in "Lukas als griechischer Historiker," PWSup 14 (1974) col. 247. But the force of the moment is registered in more than the so-called *Missionsreden*.

ὁδοῖς αὐτῶν, "In past generations he allowed all the nations to follow their own ways"; 17:23: διερχόμενος γὰρ καὶ ἀναθεωρῶν τὰ σεβάσματα ὑμῶν εὗρον καὶ βωμὸν ἐν ᾧ ἐπεγέγραπτο, ᾿Αγνώστῳ θεῷ. ὃ οὖν ἀγνοοῦντες εὐσεβεῖτε, τοῦτο ἐγὼ καταγγέλλω ὑμῖν, "For as I passed through and looked carefully at the objects of your worship, I found among them an altar with the inscription, 'To an unknown god.' What therefore you worship as unknown, this I proclaim to you"), as well as to all persons alike (17:30: τοὺς μὲν οὖν χρόνους τῆς ἀγνοίας ὑπεριδὼν ὁ θεός, τὰ νῦν παραγγέλλει τοῖς ἀνθρώποις πάντας πανταχοῦ μετανοεῖν, "While God has overlooked the times of ignorance, now he commands all people everywhere to repent"). Nevertheless, to both Jews and Gentiles, the speakers declare that even in the former time of ignorance God was not without a witness (to Jews: 7:44; to Gentiles: 14:17; 17:25b–28).

Yet, as the speeches repeatedly recognize, the past is behind the speaker and the hearers. The former time of ignorance which God permitted is no longer tolerable, as is recognized by the overt statements already examined and by the many additional explicit and implicit calls to repentance in the speeches (explicit: 2:38; 3:19; 14:15; 17:30; implicit: 3:26; 4:10; 5:31; 10:42–43; 13:38; 26:20–23, 29; and references to repentance and reports of calls to repentance: 15:19; 20:21; 26:20). The time of ignorance is brought to an end by the work of God in Jesus Christ, especially as Christ's witnesses testify to God's salvific activity. In order to understand more fully the shift of the times in relation to the working out of the plan of God, it is necessary to turn to the theme of witness in the speeches.

Witness[14]

Throughout the speeches and in the narrative of Acts Luke uses words belonging to the μαρτ-stem group.[15] The importance of this usage becomes immediately apparent from a survey and an analysis of the relative frequency with which the words occur in Acts in comparison with other New Testa-

14. A variety of significant studies have thrown much light on the importance of "witness," "witnesses," and "witnessing" in Luke's theology. E.g., N. Brox, Zeuge und Märtyrer: Untersuchungen zur frühchristlichen Zeugnis-Terminologie (SANT 5; Munich: Kösel, 1961) esp. 43–69; C. Burchard, Der dreizehnte Zeuge: Traditions- und kompositionsgeschichtliche Untersuchungen zu Lukas' Darstellung der Frühzeit des Paulus (FRLANT 103; Göttingen: Vandenhoeck & Ruprecht, 1970) esp. 130–35; J. Beutler, Martyria: Traditionsgeschichtliche Untersuchungen zum Zeugnisthema bei Johannes (FTS 10; Frankfurt a. M.: J. Knecht, 1972) esp. 188, 192; E. Nellessen, Zeugnis für Jesus und das Wort: Exegetische Untersuchungen zum lukanischen Zeugnisbegriff (BBB 43; Cologne: P. Hanstein, 1976); and A. A. Trites, The New Testament Concept of Witness (SNTSMS 31; Cambridge: Cambridge University Press, 1977) esp. 128–53, 222–30.

15. J. Beutler refers to Luke's development of a characteristic "Zeugen-Begriff," which presented the passion of Jesus as being in accordance with scripture, declared his resurrection, and proclaimed forgiveness ("μάρτυς," EWNT 2:971–72).

ment writings. In the order of their frequency from most to least they are the following:[16]

1. Μάρτυς ("witness") occurs thirteen times in Acts and thirty-five times in the New Testament. Two of the twenty-two uses of μάρτυς outside of Acts are in the Gospel according to Luke. After Acts, μάρτυς occurs most frequently in Revelation (five times); no other New Testament writing uses the word more than twice, although in the seven so-called undisputed letters of Paul μάρτυς appears six times. Μάρτυς occurs in the speeches in Acts in 1:8, 22; 2:32; 3:15; 5:32; 10:39, 41; 13:31; 22:15, 20; 26:16; and in the narrative at 6:13; 7:58.

2. Μαρτυρεῖν ("to bear witness") occurs eleven times in Acts and seventy-six times in the New Testament. One of the sixty-five uses of μαρτυρεῖν outside of Acts is in Luke. By comparison, the Gospel according to John employs μαρτυρέω thirty-three times, and 1 and 3 John use the verb a total of ten times.[17] Μαρτυρεῖν occurs eight times in Hebrews, four times in Revelation, twice in Romans, and never more than once in any other New Testament writing. Μαρτυρεῖν occurs in the speeches of Acts in 6:3; 10:43; 13:22; 15:8; 22:5, 12; 26:5, 22; in the narrative in 10:22; 14:3; 16:2; and in the report of a short statement in 23:11.

3. Διαμαρτύρεσθαι ("to witness" or "to testify") occurs nine times in Acts and fifteen times in the New Testament. One of the six uses of διαμαρτύρεσθαι outside of Acts is in Luke. 1 and 2 Timothy use the verb a total of three times, and it occurs once in both 1 Thessalonians and Hebrews. This verb occurs in speeches of Acts in 10:42; 20:21, 23; in the narrative in 2:40; 8:25; 18:5; 28:23; and in the report of a short statement in 23:11.

4. Μαρτύρεσθαι ("to witness" or "to testify") occurs twice in Acts and five times in the New Testament. Outside of Acts the verb is used in Galatians, Ephesians, and 1 Thessalonians. Both uses in Acts occur in speeches: 20:26; 26:22.

5. Μαρτύριον ("witness") also occurs twice in Acts, once in a speech in 7:44 and once in the narrative in 4:33. Outside of Acts μαρτύριον occurs seventeen times in the New Testament: three times each in Matthew, Mark, and Luke; and once in 1 Corinthians, 2 Corinthians, 2 Thessalonians, 1 Timothy, 2 Timothy, Hebrews, James, and Revelation.

6. Ἀμάρτυρος ("without a witness") occurs once in the New Testament in a speech in Acts 14:17.

7. Μαρτυρία ("witness") occurs once in Acts in the report of a statement

---

16. The following data are drawn from K. Aland, ed., *Vollständige Konkordanz zum Griechischen Neuen Testament. Band II: Spezialübersichten* (Berlin/New York: W. de Gruyter, 1978).

17. Interpreters regularly recognize and treat μαρτυρεῖν as a key term and concept in Johannine theology. See J. Beutler, "μαρτυρέω, διαμαρτύρομαι, μαρτύρομαι," *EWNT* 2:958–64.

of the risen Lord to Paul in 22:18. Outside of Acts the word occurs in the New Testament thirty-six times, once in the Gospel according to Luke.[18]

In order to appreciate the special emphasis brought to Acts by this cluster of crucial words it is necessary to consider two items: (A) the manner in which Luke ends the Gospel and begins (and continues) Acts using this language and (B) the identity of the "witnesses." By focusing on these items one comes to see that Acts is a story filled with speeches, wherein one may say that every speaker speaks *as, for,* or *against* a witness or the witnesses and their witness. Through repetition Luke unifies the picture of early Christianity, creates emphasis, and delivers a more complex total testimony than would be possible by means of any one speech. Thus, Luke tells the story of the early church's bearing witness to God's will and work in Jesus Christ in such a way that the witness itself is offered in the speeches.

The End of Luke and the Beginning of Acts

Three texts, two from Luke and one from Acts, cohere in such a way that one perceives both the coherence and the spiraling development of Luke's two-part account. First, in the version of Jesus' "little apocalypse" in Luke 21:5–36 Jesus speaks in 21:13 about the μαρτύριον ("witness") that his disciples would later bear. The larger statement is 21:12–19, which has parallels in Matt 10:17–22 and Mark 13:9–13. The differences among Luke, Matthew, and Mark are striking; yet clearly one encounters here three versions of the same saying(s). Through comparison of the passages one discovers the distinctive accents given to the material by each of the evangelists. More particularly, it is instructive to compare Luke 21:12–13; Matt 10:17–18; and Mark 13:9:

Luke 21:12–13	πρὸ δὲ τούτων πάντων ἐπιβαλοῦσιν ἐφ' ὑμᾶς τὰς χεῖρας αὐτῶν καὶ διώξουσιν, παραδιδόντες εἰς τὰς συναγωγὰς καὶ φυλακάς, ἀπαγομένους ἐπὶ βασιλεῖς καὶ ἡγεμόνας ἕνεκεν τοῦ ὀνόματός μου· ἀποβήσεται ὑμῖν εἰς μαρτύριον.
Matt 10:17–18	προσέχετε δὲ ἀπὸ τῶν ἀνθρώπων· παραδώσουσιν γὰρ ὑμᾶς εἰς συνέδρια καὶ ἐν ταῖς συναγωγαῖς αὐτῶν μαστιγώσουσιν ὑμᾶς· καὶ ἐπὶ ἡγεμόνας δὲ καὶ βασιλεῖς ἀχθήσεσθε ἕνεκεν ἐμοῦ εἰς μαρτύριον αὐτοῖς καὶ τοῖς ἔθνεσιν.
Mark 13:9	βλέπετε δὲ ὑμεῖς ἑαυτούς· παραδώσουσιν ὑμᾶς εἰς συνέδρια καὶ εἰς συναγωγὰς δαρήσεσθε καὶ ἐπὶ ἡγεμόνων καὶ βασιλέων σταθήσεσθε ἕνεκεν ἐμοῦ εἰς μαρτύριον αὐτοῖς.

18. By contrast, μαρτυρία is an important word in Johannine thought about "witness." It occurs fourteen times in the Gospel according to John, a total of seven times in 1 and 3 John, and nine times in Revelation. Otherwise the word is used three times in Mark, and once each in 1 Timothy and Titus.

Luke 21:12–13   But before all this occurs, they will arrest you and persecute you; they will hand you over to synagogues and prisons, and you will be brought before kings and governors because of my name. This will give you an opportunity to testify.

Matt 10:17–18   Beware of them, for they will hand you over to councils and flog you in their synagogues; and you will be dragged before governors and kings because of me, as a testimony to them and the Gentiles.

Mark 13:9   As for yourselves, beware; for they will hand you over to councils; and you will be beaten in synagogues; and you will stand before governors and kings because of me, as a testimony to them.

Through comparison one sees that Matthew and Mark are more similar than are Luke and Matthew or Luke and Mark. Mark's version is the shortest and, seemingly, the simplest. Then, on the one hand, Matthew's version is longer both because it is more detailed and there seems to be a heightening of specific polemical elements.[19] On the other hand, Luke's version of the material opens with a temporal qualifier that seems to distance the time of difficulty to be experienced by the disciples from the tribulations at the end of all time (πρὸ δὲ τούτων πάντων, "before all this"). Then the lines tell of the delivery to synagogues, but there is no mention of "councils" (συνέδρια); rather the disciples are told they will be imprisoned. The phrases ἐπιβαλοῦσιν ἐφ' ὑμᾶς τὰς χεῖρας αὐτῶν καὶ διώξουσιν, παραδιδόντες εἰς . . . φυλακάς ("they will arrest you and persecute you, they will hand you over to . . . prisons") anticipate the experiences of the apostles—particularly Peter, John, and James—Silas, and Paul in Acts (e.g., 4:3; 5:18–25; 8:3; 12:1, 3–6; 16:23). The disciples will appear before kings and governors for the sake of Jesus' name (ἕνεκεν τοῦ ὀνόματός μου, "because of my name"), a promise finding repeated emphasis in the speeches in Acts.[20] This reference to Jesus' name is broader than the mere ἕνεκεν ἐμοῦ ("because of me") of both Matthew and Mark, and as we have seen through analysis of the speeches, there are repeated references to the name of Jesus. Finally, the words εἰς μαρτύριον ("as a testimony"), which appear in identical prepositional phrases in Matthew and Mark (ἕνεκεν ἐμοῦ εἰς μαρτύριον αὐτοῖς, "because of me, as a testimony to them"), occur in Luke in an independent clause (ἀποβήσεται ὑμῖν εἰς μαρτύριον, "this will give you an opportunity to testify") that heightens the importance of the "witness" to be born by the disciples.[21]

19. The opening in Matthew 10:17 warns against other humans rather than merely calling for awareness and prudence. The statement seems aimed against the συνέδρια and the συναγωγαί through the use of αὐτῶν as a qualifier for the synagogue and the stronger, pointedly Jewish word μαστιγοῦν for the beating (see D. J. Harrington, *The Gospel of Matthew* [Sacra Pagina 1; Collegeville, MN: M. Glazier/Liturgical Press, 1991] 145). Furthermore, the longer ending (καὶ τοῖς ἔθνεσιν) probably reflects Matthew's interest in the Gentile mission of the church.
20. Consult the analysis of Acts 2:38 in chapter 2 above.
21. Referring to Luke 21:13, L. T. Johnson remarks that Jesus' words are "literally carried

Second, near the end of the Gospel, in 24:48, Luke recalls the declaration of Jesus to the Eleven, at least in the hearing of τοὺς σὺν αὐτοῖς, "the ones with them" (24:33), which informs them that they are witnesses.[22] Specifically Jesus says, ὑμεῖς μάρτυρες τούτων ("you are witnesses of these things"). In context Luke 24:48 refers to Luke's narration and Jesus' statements in 24:44–47, and the further word in 24:49 builds upon the words concerning witness. In a summary fashion these verses give the outline of the witness of the Eleven:

Εἶπεν δὲ πρὸς αὐτούς, Οὗτοι οἱ λόγοι μου οὓς ἐλάλησα πρὸς ὑμᾶς ἔτι ὢν σὺν ὑμῖν, ὅτι δεῖ πληρωθῆναι πάντα τὰ γεγραμμένα ἐν τῷ νόμῳ Μωϋσέως καὶ τοῖς προφήταις καὶ ψαλμοῖς περὶ ἐμοῦ. τότε διήνοιξεν αὐτῶν τὸν νοῦν τοῦ συνιέναι τὰς γραφάς· καὶ εἶπεν αὐτοῖς ὅτι Οὕτως γέγραπται παθεῖν τὸν Χριστὸν καὶ ἀναστῆναι ἐκ νεκρῶν τῇ τρίτῃ ἡμέρᾳ, καὶ κηρυχθῆναι ἐπὶ τῷ ὀνόματι αὐτοῦ μετάνοιαν εἰς ἄφεσιν ἁμαρτιῶν εἰς πάντα τὰ ἔθνη, ἀρξάμενοι ἀπὸ Ἰερουσαλήμ. ὑμεῖς μάρτυρες τούτων. καὶ [ἰδοὺ] ἐγὼ ἀποστέλλω τὴν ἐπαγγελίαν τοῦ πατρός μου ἐφ᾽ ὑμᾶς· ὑμεῖς δὲ καθίσατε ἐν τῇ πόλει ἕως οὗ ἐνδύσησθε ἐξ ὕψους δύναμιν.[23]

Then he said to them, "These are my words that I spoke to you while I was still with you—that everything written about me in the law of Moses, the prophets, and the psalms must be fulfilled." Then he opened their minds to understand the scriptures, and he said to them, "Thus it is written, that the Messiah is to suffer and to rise from the dead on the third day, and that repentance and forgiveness of sins is to be proclaimed in his name to all nations, beginning from Jerusalem. You are witnesses of these things. And see, I am sending upon you what my Father promised; so stay here in the city until you have been clothed with power from on high."

Regarding these verses, J. A. Fitzmyer writes, "One is not surprised to see *metanoia*, 'repentance,' or *aphesis hamartiōn*, 'forgiveness of sins,' surface here . . . but the theme of 'testimony' now begins, and it will be picked up in the programmatic verse of Acts (1:8) and used often thereafter. . . ."[24]

Third, in Acts 1:8 Jesus speaks τοῖς ἀποστόλοις . . . οὓς ἐξελέξατο ("to the apostles whom he had chosen"), telling them they shall be his witnesses: ἀλλὰ λήμψεσθε δύναμιν ἐπελθόντος τοῦ ἁγίου πνεύματος ἐφ᾽ ὑμᾶς καὶ ἔσεσθέ μου μάρτυρες ἔν τε Ἰερουσαλὴμ καὶ [ἐν] πάσῃ τῇ Ἰουδαίᾳ καὶ Σαμαρείᾳ καὶ ἕως ἐσχάτου τῆς γῆς ("But you will receive power when the Holy Spirit has come upon you; and you will be my witnesses in Jerusalem, in all Judea and Samaria, and to the end of the earth"). This statement is a near parallel to the more elaborate

out in Acts 3:15; 4:33; 5:32; 20:26; 26:22" (*The Gospel of Luke* [Sacra Pagina 3; Collegeville, MN: M. Glazier/Liturgical Press, 1991] 322).

22. Compare the discussion by Burchard (*Zeuge*, 130–32).

23. The punctuation here is mine. In agreement, see J. A. Fitzmyer, *The Gospel According to Luke (X–XXIV)* (AB 28A; Garden City, NY: Doubleday, 1985) 1578–85.

24. Fitzmyer, *Luke (X–XXIV)*, 1579. As we have seen, however, the crucial theme of "witness" actually surfaced or began in Luke 21. Thus, the mention of witness in Luke 24 is the first of many repetitions which bring emphasis and give additional meaning to the theme.

lines in Luke 24.[25] Now, however, the earlier phrase τὴν ἐπαγγελίαν τοῦ πατρός μου ἐφ' ὑμᾶς ("upon you what my father promised") is specified as δύναμιν ἐπελθόντος τοῦ ἁγίου πνεύματος ἐφ' ὑμᾶς ("power when the Holy Spirit has come upon you"), and the previous mention of Jerusalem is elaborated by the addition of καὶ [ἐν] πάσῃ τῇ 'Ιουδαίᾳ καὶ Σαμαρείᾳ καὶ ἕως ἐσχάτου τῆς γῆς ("and in all Judea and Samaria, and to the end of the earth"). The other information in Luke 24:44–49 seems to be presupposed by this partial repetition.

From examining these three passages (Luke 21:11–13; 24:44–49; Acts 1:8) one sees an important element by which Luke held the two volumes of his work together. One notices especially that as Luke concluded the Gospel and began Acts that the crucial theme of "witness" emerges dramatically and deliberately. Moreover, in the Gospel the group to whom Jesus speaks about witness is somewhat ambiguous. The eleven apostles are in view, but others stand in the background and at least hear Jesus' statements.[26] As Acts begins, however, Jesus speaks to "the apostles" (1:8), and as the story unfolds it is initially clear that the witnesses are the Eleven, who are joined by Judas's replacement, Matthias (1:15–26). As the story continues in Acts, those referred to as witnesses and those overtly bearing witness prove to be more than the Twelve. Thus, one gains additional clarity concerning witness, witnesses, and witnessing by considering "who are the witnesses?"

The Identity of the Witnesses in Acts

The designation μάρτυς ("witness") is applied overtly in Acts to five distinct groups or persons: (A) the apostles — that is, the Eleven, the Eleven and Judas's replacement, and the Twelve (1:8, 22; 2:32; 3:15; 5:32; 10:39, 41; 13:31 [?]; (B) the Holy Spirit (5:32); (C) Paul (22:15; 26:16); (D) Stephen (22:20); and (F) the obviously *false* "witnesses" against Stephen (6:13; 7:58). The last group, the false witnesses, are not to be associated with the other witnesses named in Acts, but it is remarkable that the same language can describe both the risen Jesus' protagonists and those who are opposed to them.

The verbs μαρτυρεῖν ("to bear witness"), διαμαρτύρεσθαι ("to testify" or "to declare"), and μαρτύρεσθαι ("to declare" or "to testify") are used in reference to the activity of seven groups or persons: (A) the Twelve or members of the Twelve (διαμαρτύρεσθαι, 2:40; 8:25; 10:42); (B) "all the prophets" (μαρτυρεῖν, 10:43); (C) God (μαρτυρεῖν, 13:22); (D) "the Lord," most likely referring to

---

25. See Burchard, *Zeuge*, 133–34.

26. As Fitzmyer recognizes, "Eyewitnesses are to become testifiers, and indeed 'ministers of the word' (1:2) (*Luke [X–XXIV]*, 1580). Though this becomes one of the criteria for the member who will replace Judas in the Twelve (Acts 1:21–22), it is not limited to such a member, as this episode [Luke 24:44–49] makes clear, in that the commission is addressed to 'the Eleven and all the others' (24:9, 33)."

Christ[27] (μαρτυρεῖν, 14:3); (E) Paul (μαρτυρεῖν, 23:11; 26:22; διαμαρτύρεσθαι, 18:5; 20:21, 24; 23:11; 28:23; μαρτύρεσθαι, 20:26; 26:22); (F) the Holy Spirit (διαμαρτύρεσθαι, 20:23); and (G) some of Paul's opponents from among the Jerusalem Jews (μαρτυρεῖν, 22:5; 26:5). Again, the last group is not to be directly associated with the activity of the others, for statements by Paul merely report that his opponents could "bear witness" to his former good standing in Judaism. But, again, it is striking that the same verb can name the actions of Christ's witnesses and those who oppose them.

The nouns μαρτύριον ("witness" or "testimony") and μαρτυρία ("witness" or "testimony") occur a total of three times as designations for the witness given by persons or the Twelve. (A) In the narrative in 4:33 Luke uses μαρτύριον in reference to the "witness" or "testimony" of the apostles to the resurrection of the Lord Jesus. (B) Then, in Stephen's speech in 7:44 μαρτύριον occurs in the phrase ἡ σκηνὴ τοῦ μαρτυρίου. While the language may reflect the Septuagint, "the tent of testimony" refers to God's divine self-witness.[28] (C) Finally, in Paul's speech to the Jerusalem Jews Paul reports a short statement made by the risen Jesus to him. Μαρτυρία names Paul's testimony about the risen Jesus (22:18), which the same Jesus says the Jerusalem Jews will not accept.[29] Thus, the Twelve, God, and Paul are said to bear witness.

A final item of vocabulary that is helpful for identifying those who are witnesses or those who give witness in Acts is the adjective ἀμάρτυρος ("without a witness") in 14:17. One learns that in relation to idolatrous pagans God οὐx ἀμάρτυρον αὐτὸν ἀφῆκεν . . . ("has not left himself without a witness . . ."). This negatively cast statement reiterates the idea that God bears witness or that God is a witness.

---

27. As G. Krodel recognizes, "The Lord who bore witness to Paul and Barnabas is either God (in 20:32 'the word of his grace' clearly refers to God) or Christ (in Luke 4:22 'the words of grace' proceed from Jesus)" (Acts [Augsburg Commentary on the New Testament; Minneapolis: Augsburg, 1986] 252–53). He concludes, "While either identification is possible and a choice between them difficult, I would lean toward identifying 'the Lord' with Jesus. But this difficulty also reveals the inseparability of Jesus Christ from the God of Israel." E. Haenchen takes the prudent course by remarking, "We cannot tell whether κύριος here means God or Christ" (The Acts of the Apostles: A Commentary [Philadelphia: Westminster, 1971; from the 14th German ed., 1965; German original, 1956] 420 n. 7). Nevertheless, G. Schneider, among others, takes this verse as a statement about God (Die Apostelgeschichte [HTKNT 5/1–2; Freiburg/Basel/Vienna: Herder, 1980–82] 1:151).

28. F. F. Bruce, The Acts of the Apostles: Greek Text with Introduction and Commentary (3d ed.; Grand Rapids: Eerdmans; Leicester: Apollos, 1990) 205.

29. Beutler notes the manner in which the word μαρτυρία occurs in Acts observing, correctly, that the word has no technical force (as it does in Johannine thought), rather it simply clusters with the other words of the μαρτ-stem group (Martyria, 188).

Further Observations on the "Witness" Theme

First, through examination of the vocabulary explicitly related to the theme of witness in Luke-Acts, one learns that a cast of characters either is called witnesses or they bear witness. In the order of their being referred to as witnesses in Acts, these are the apostles or the Twelve, the Holy Spirit, God, all the prophets, the Lord, Paul, and Stephen. These "witnesses" repeatedly bear witness or defend the witness that is given. Indeed, one encounters the theme of Spirit-empowered witness from the beginning (1:8) to the end (28:23) of Acts and all along the way, so that the speeches either articulate this witness, attack the witness (as testimony or person), or affirm some dimension of the validity of the witness. Thus, the role of the speeches in Acts is to tell the story of the witness — of its articulation, acceptance, or rejection — and to do so in such a way that through repetition the unified witness is emphasized and articulated in a manner greater than the capacity of any single speech. That God, the Holy Spirit, Christ, and "all the prophets" are said to be witnesses shows the divine character of the fulfillment of God's plan in Jesus Christ and the witness given to God's work through him.

Second, in encountering this language about "witness" one should recognize the *legal* cast given to the declarations about God's plan being realized in Jesus Christ and the witnesses' testimony to him.[30] The μαρτ-stem group comes from the language of the courtroom in secular Greek literature, although the word group came to be used in Greek historiography for the firm establishment of facts.[31] Moreover, in certain speeches in Acts the use of such words as ἀνακρίνειν ("to examine," 4:9; 24:8), ἀπολογία ("defense," 22:1; 25:16), ἀπολογεῖσθαι ("to make a defense," 24:10; 26:2), and ἀνάκρισις ("examination," 25:26) make clear the specifically judicial character of the witness and the situation in which the witness is given. Thus, the language of "witness" indicates that the Spirit-empowered testimony to all nations of divine salvation in repentance and forgiveness of sins in Christ's name occurs in a charged time and setting. Therefore, Luke may designate Stephen's accusers as "witnesses" and Paul can remark that his opponents could give testimony if they so desired.

30. Trites comments on the appropriateness of such language in early Christianity (*Concept,* 129–30). He writes: "The situation in which the apostles found themselves after the crucifixion and resurrection is worth pondering. Their Master had been 'committed for trial and repudiated in Pilate's court' (παρεδώκατε καὶ ἠρνήσασθε κατὰ πρόσωπον Πιλάτου, Acts 3:13, N.E.B.). He had been condemned by the Jews as a criminal and sentenced to die on the charges of blasphemy (cf. Mk 14:63 pars.; Jn 18:30; 19:7). After the resurrection the trial of Jesus, in effect, is reopened and fresh evidence is presented by the apostles to get the Jews to change their verdict." Whether or not one agrees with Trites's understanding of the Jewish involvement in Jesus' condemnation, the insight related to the early Christian response to Jesus' condemnation is helpful in understanding the language of witness in Acts.

31. Trites, *Concept,* 4–15.

The naming of the witnesses against Stephen and the capacity of Paul's opponents should warn against attempting to define "witness" as a *terminus technicus* in Acts.[32]

Third, in general the witnesses testify to God's plan moving toward realization. Of central importance in this testimony is the declaration that God's plan moved toward realization in Jesus Christ, specifically in his suffering, especially in his resurrection,[33] and in a vital way in the subsequent testimony to these events. At times the recognizable christological contrast scheme juxtaposes human rejection of Jesus against the divine affirmation of resurrection, but at times the speeches move directly to declare the resurrection as the evidence of God's plan moving to realization. Remarkably in the witness given in the speeches in Acts, other than in 1:21–22; 2:22; 10:39, there is no reference to the earthly ministry of Jesus. This lack of testimony certainly cannot be taken as a sign of Luke's lack of concern with Jesus ministry, for after all Luke did devote the greater portion of the Gospel he wrote to giving an account of that ministry. Perhaps the speeches simply presuppose a familiarity with the Gospel that would make further repetition of information about Jesus' ministry unnecessary. In any case, the witnesses in Acts are centrally concerned with the decisive act of God in relation to Jesus Christ, which necessitates, in the words of Luke 24:47, "to be preached in his name repentance unto forgiveness of sins unto all the nations."[34]

Two Features of the Repetition

In order to appreciate more fully the manner in which the speeches deliver an authoritative witness in Acts, it is helpful to consider two striking features of the speeches that recur with regularity.

The Various Uses of the Past

Repeatedly the speakers bring the past into play as they make their speeches. Perhaps what is most striking in this phenomenon is the several ways in which the past is employed. In the foregoing analysis each of the uses of the past was noted; in the following reflection on this feature of the speeches I shall recognize the different ways in which the past is used in the speeches, illustrate the particular kinds of uses, and catalogue the places in which one encounters each particular kind of use of the past.

32. Brox (*Zeuge*, 43) notes also at Luke 11:48 a use of μάρτυς which is "profane."
33. Brox (*Zeuge*, 45) calls the witness to the resurrection the *Mittelpunkt* of the testimony.
34. Nellessen (*Zeugnis*, 278) astutely observes, "*Gegenstand* des Zeugnisses ist der verherrlichte Herr Jesus, sein Wort und sein Wirken. Dabei ist die Inhaltsangabe des Zeugnisses bei den verschiedenen Zeugen oder Zeugengruppen etwas variiert."

First, the most frequent and perhaps most noticeable way in which the past is used in speeches is through the citation of scripture. Certainly this manner of using the past has received the most attention from scholars,[35] but the treatment of the scripture quotations in the speeches is typically done in isolation from the full range of uses of the past in the speeches — with the exception of some studies which hold the scripture quotations together with apparent allusions to scripture in the speeches. As scholars identify and isolate the quotations of scripture in the speeches, they typically engage in debates about "proof-from-prophecy" or "promise-and-fulfillment."[36] This debate goes on and remains unresolved in part because the scripture quotations (and allusions) are not understood and viewed as but one of several different uses of the past. When one considers the function of *the past* in the speeches in Acts one finds that a prophecy-and-fulfillment interpretation of the scripture quotations is too restricted a perspective for understanding the role of the past, especially the scripture quotations, in the speeches. Rather than a mere linear prophecy-fulfillment scheme, one should see that the past, especially the quotations of scripture, is used in the speeches to establish the continuity of the past, the present, and even the future.[37] Thus, the past works in relation to the assumption of the plan of God, which itself is an overarching and controlling entity in relation to the course of events. Moreover, *continuity* is registered in order to bring clarity and understanding. The citation of scripture in the speeches *proves* very little indeed; rather, the citations illuminate the points that various speakers mean to make. One should recognize that Luke is not Matthew, and one should allow Luke to be Luke. By far the clearest indication of the function of the past in the speeches in Acts, including especially the quotations of scripture, is given in a statement by Peter in Acts 10:43, τούτῳ πάντες οἱ προφῆται μαρτυροῦσιν ἄφεσιν ἁμαρτιῶν λαβεῖν διὰ τοῦ ὀνόματος αὐτοῦ πάντα τὸν πιστεύοντα εἰς αὐτόν ("All the prophets testify about him that everyone who believes in him receives forgiveness of sins through his name"). As Peter's speech states, all the prophets *bear witness* or *testify*. Testimony

---

35. On the subject in general, see the helpful summary by G. Schneider (*Apostelgeschichte*, 1:232–38) and the monograph by T. Holtz (*Untersuchungen über die alttestamentlichen Zitate bei Lukas* [TU 104; Berlin: Akademie-Verlag, 1968).

36. Against this interpretation, see M. Rese, *Alttestamentliche Motive in der Christologie des Lukas* (SNT 1; Gütersloh: G. Mohn, 1969); and C. H. Talbert, "Promise and Fulfillment in Lukan Theology," in *Luke-Acts: New Perspectives from the Society of Biblical Literature* (ed. C. H. Talbert; New York: Crossroad, 1984) 91–103. In defense of this understanding of Luke-Acts, see P. Schubert, "The Structure and Significance of Luke 24," in *Neutestamentliche Studien für Rudolf Bultmann* (ed. W. Eltester; BZNW 21; Berlin: W. de Gruyter, 1954) 165–86; E. E. Ellis, *Prophecy and Hermeneutic in Early Christianity* (WUNT 18; Tübingen: J. C. B. Mohr [Paul Siebeck], 1978) esp. 129–44 and 147–72; and D. L. Bock, *Proclamation from Prophecy and Pattern: Lucan Old Testament Christology* (JSNTSup 12; Sheffield: JSOT Press, 1987) esp. 13–53 and 155–279.

37. Similarly, Talbert emphasizes *continuity* as a crucial concern of Luke's program in Luke-Acts ("Promise").

seeks to clarify and, so, to confirm the veracity of a particular declaration, interpretation, or understanding. Testimony is not presented here as predictive or anticipatory. After the fact of Jesus—his life, passion, resurrection, and exaltation—the speakers in Acts turn to "the prophets" and scripture (and other elements of the past) in order to comprehend and communicate the meaning of Jesus and particularly of God's work in relation to him.[38] By citing scripture to establish the continuity of the past and the present, the speakers in Acts clarify the meaning of the present in terms of God's own purposes. Thus, in Acts 1:20, the Psalms interpret Judas's fate and indicate God's will for the early Christian community to seek his replacement. Likewise, in Acts 2:17 the passage from Joel tells the real meaning of the striking events of Pentecost. Then, in Acts 2:25–28 Peter can cite Ps 15:8–11 LXX, taking David's words as the words of the Messiah, in order to clarify and confirm the messianic identity of the raised Jesus.[39] Acts 2:34–35 also cites David as evidence or testimony to Jesus' identity as κύριος ("Lord"). Other speeches in Acts quote the scriptures explicitly in order to testify to the validity of particular understandings or declarations in 3:22–23; 4:25–26; 7:3, 6–7, 18, 27–28, 32, 33–34, 35, 37, 40, 42–43, 49–50; 13:22, 33, 34, 35, 41, 47; 15:16a, 16b–17b, 17c–18; 23:5; 28:26–27.

Second, other speeches seem to bring the past into play in order to establish continuity for comprehension by simply alluding to segments of scripture. While it may be impossible to recognize every case in which speeches allude to scripture, at the following places in the speeches the allusions seem clear: 4:11; 5:30; 7:9a, 9b–10, 11, 12–13, 14–16, 30–34, 37–38, 44; 10:36–39; 13:17–23, 29; 14:15; 17:23.[40]

Third, in several speeches the speakers refer to the prophets. One encounters, however, neither a citation of scripture nor an identifiable allusion. Rather, the reference to the prophets functions to identify testimony to the validity of the speaker's point(s). Such references occur in 3:18, 24–25; 7:52–53; 10:43; 13:27; 24:14; 26:22, 27. Again, validity is established as continuity is recognized.

Several other minor manners of using the past in speeches recognize

---

38. Here I am closest to Rese's understanding of the Old Testament quotations as "hermeneutical devices" (Motive). See also M. Rese, "Die Funktion der alttestamentlichen Zitate und Anspielungen in den Reden der Apostelgeschichte," in Les Actes des Apôtres: Tradition, rédaction, théologie (ed. J. Kremer; BETL 48; Gembloux: Duculot; Leuven: Leuven University Press, 1979) 61–79.

39. See Rese, "Funktion," 69–70, 73–76.

40. On Luke's technique of weaving scripture or scriptural language into his composition, see E. Richard, who steadily argues for understanding Luke's work, particularly in the speech by Stephen, as a masterful reworking of portions of the Septuagint (Acts 6:1–8:4: The Author's Method of Composition [SBLDS 41; Missoula, MT: Scholars Press, 1978]). Yet, as the analysis of Holtz (Untersuchungen) shows, one needs caution in attempting to determine whether Luke knew such language from a text or from tradition(s).

continuity, bring clarity for comprehension, and confirm particular claims or understandings; these include: fourth, references to John the Baptist in 1:5, 22; 10:37; 11:16; 13:24; fifth, references to scripture without any citation in 13:29; 24:14; sixth, recollection of the words of Jesus in 11:16; 20:35; seventh, Gamaliel's recitation of two historical fiascoes in 5:36–37; and eighth, an overt reference to and citation of pagan poets in 17:28.

Beyond these particular manners of using the past, one encounters at least two other, more general uses of the past that still function in a similar way. These are, on the one hand, references to a host of prominent personalities from Israel's history—for example, David, Moses, Abraham, Joseph and family, Saul, Samuel, and even Pharaoh, Pharaoh's daughter, Pilate, Herod, and others. On the other hand, the speakers sometimes refer to the past by focusing on their own personal experiences in order to verify particular patterns of understanding and specific behavior. Here one thinks immediately of speech statements by Peter (11:5–17; 15:7–11) and Paul (20:18–35; 22:1, 3–21; 23:1, 3, 5–6; 24:10–21; 25:8, 10–11; 26:2–23, 25–27, 29; 28:17–20); but also James (15:13–21; 21:20–25) and even Demetrius (19:25–27) and the Ephesian town clerk (19:35–40).[41]

Speaking beyond the Situation at Hand

Without being frivolous, one may observe that another remarkable phenomenon among the repetitions in the speeches in Acts is the tendency of speakers to get off the subject; that is, the speakers tend to speak about matters not directly related to the situations that led to their speaking.[42] As the speakers depart from the subject at hand, they regularly raise a standard set of topics which include five striking items: first, christological kerygma—found in many places and various ways, but prominent in 2:22b–24, 32–33; 3:13–15a; 4:10–12, 27–28, 29b–30; 5:30–31; 7:52–53 (?), 56, 59b, 60b; 10:36–38; 13:23, 27–30; 26:23; second, Jesus' resurrection or resurrection per se (see the

---

41. One should recall that in the inaugural address of Jesus in Nazareth in the Gospel according to Luke—a speech particular to Luke's Gospel—that Jesus himself speaks by referring to the past, finding testimony in the past to God's true manner of relating to humanity; so that the past is a hermeneutical device, not a mere proof or promise.

42. Dibelius gave a negative cast to the recognition and interpretation of this phenomenon when he wrote, "Luke has inserted speeches which do not necessarily fit the occasion but which have an obvious function in the book as a whole . . ." ("The Speeches in Acts and Ancient Historiography," in *Studies in the Acts of the Apostles* [ed. H. Greeven; New York: Charles Scribner's Sons, 1956] 175–76). Dibelius's original words in German were even more pointed, ". . . auch Lukas hat an großen Wendepunkten der Gemeindegeschichte Reden eingeschaltet, die der augenblicklichen Situation nicht immer angepaßt sind . . ." ("Die Reden der Apostelgeschichte und die antike Geschichtsschreibung," in *Aufsätze zur Apostelgeschichte* [ed. H. Greeven; 5th ed.; Göttingen: Vandenhoeck & Ruprecht, 1968] 120–62; quotation from 151).

analysis of 1:22b in chapter 2 for a listing of occurrences);[43] third, repentance and forgiveness, or repentance, or forgiveness (see the analysis of 2:38a in chapter 2 for a listing of occurrences); fourth, the universal significance of God's salvation—found in many places and various ways, but prominent in 1:8; 2:17–21, 39; 10:36, 43, 47; 11:17; 13:38b–39, 47; 14:15c; 15:8–9; 17:30; 18:6d; 20:31; 22:14–15, 21; 24:5 (?); 26:12–18, 23, 25–26; 28:28; and fifth, the Holy Spirit (see the analysis of 1:16b–17 in chapter 2 for a listing of occurrences).

Concluding Observations

The foregoing analysis of the connections between elements of the speeches in Acts has focused above all on repetitions as a key to perceiving the *unity* and *emphases* of the Acts account. Unity and emphasis clearly function together in service to Luke's didactic purposes, for as themes or elements recur in the speeches the reader of Acts learns of the coherence and concerns of the early church as Luke presents it.

While the analysis aimed at comprehensiveness through the inclusive scope of the study, it remained, despite its breadth, an essentially *synchronic*[44] study, since the speeches and the repeated elements of the speeches were viewed as points in the narrative rather than as steps or stages in Luke's story. In addition to *unity* and *emphasis* repetition can and does function to create *expectation* as a story unfolds with repetitions occurring. Thus, as a final word with regard to Luke's purposes in Acts, especially in and through the speeches, I shall consider the *diachronic* dimension of *expectation* created by the repetitions of certain statements in Acts. This reflection allows one to think in a more complex fashion about the *motive* of Acts.

The story in Acts begins with the Spirit directing the early Christian community into a universal mission. This direction is not overt; rather it is implicit in certain elements of speeches—for example, in Jesus' declaration that the

43. Recently C. H. Talbert examined the various functions of resurrection in Luke-Acts ("The Place of the Resurrection in the Theology of Luke," *Int* 44 [1992] 19–30). He shows how Luke's repeated references to the resurrection have theological, christological, soteriological, ecclesiological, and missiological ramifications *and* that these various dimensions of resurrection-emphasis work together to deliver a complex but unified message.

44. O. Ducrot (Ducrot and Todorov, *Encyclopedic Dictionary,* 137–44) comments on the "relative" nature of the distinction between *synchrony* and *diachrony* and concludes, "The adjectives *synchronic* and *diachronic* qualify less the phenomena themselves than the viewpoint adopted by the linguist." In light of that observation, Ducrot offers the following definitions, which inform my use of these terms, "A linguistic phenomenon is said to be synchronic when all the elements and factors that it brings into play belong to one and the same moment and of one and the same language (that is, to a single language state). It is diachronic when it brings into play elements and factors belonging to different states of development of a single language" (p. 137).

apostles would receive power when the Holy Spirit came upon them and that they would be his witnesses ἕως ἐσχάτου τῆς τῆς, "to the end of the earth" (1:8); and in Peter's Pentecost speech the citation of Joel 3:1–5 LXX ends with the statement καὶ ἔσται πᾶς ὃς ἂν ἐπικαλέσηται τὸ ὄνομα κυρίου σωθήσεται, "and everyone who calls on the name of the Lord shall be saved" (2:21). The story itself, however, shows the early church engaging in a mission only to the Jews, albeit on a broad scale (see Acts 2:9–11). As the story progresses one learns that the Spirit directed certain early Christian leaders into a mission to marginal Jews—specifically, Philip converted and baptized Queen Candice of Ethiopia's eunuch minister of the treasury (8:26–40).[45] But this innovative work went essentially unnoticed by the majority of the church, especially as one observes the work of its leadership.[46] Nevertheless, the work of the Holy Spirit continued, so that finally through the dramatic events associated with Peter's preaching in the house of the Gentile centurion Cornelius the central portion of the Jerusalem congregation and its leadership recognized the will of God in relation to a universal mission (10:1–11:18).

In turn, one sees a pattern of Spirit-directed preaching to Jews and Gentiles at once (e.g., 11:19–26; 13:16–47; 14:1). As the account continues, one observes that a portion of the Jewish hearers of the preaching rejected the message (e.g., 13:44–45; 17:5, 13; 18:6; 19:9; 28:24–25). In reaction to this rejection the preachers declared their intention to turn to the Gentiles directly,

---

45. Commentators routinely state that the eunuch was a Gentile, but that understanding is a questionable assumption. R. E. Brown recently pointed out to me that "the most sensible" understanding of the eunuch is that he is a Jew. The eunuch is depicted in Acts 8:26–40 as (1) going to Jerusalem to worship and (2) reading Isaiah. The behavior is normal behavior for a Jew, so that the eunuch was not merely a God-fearer, but an Ethiopian Jew. Indeed, confirmation for Brown's sensible understanding comes in what seems to be the oldest statement about the eunuch's identity. In the account of the life of Cyprian (200–258 C.E.) by his deacon Pontius, one finds the following comments in the course of a discussion concerning withholding baptism from "novices." "For although in the Acts of the Apostles the eunuch is described as at once baptized by Philip, because he believed with his whole heart, this is not a fair parallel [to the argument for baptizing novices]. For he was a Jew . . . ." See ANF 5:268 §3.

46. Regarding Acts 8:26–40 Haenchen comments, "Luke cannot and did not say that the eunuch was a Gentile; otherwise Philip would have forestalled Peter, the legitimate founder of the Gentile mission! For that reason Luke leaves the eunuch's status in a doubtful light" (Acts, 314). The problem Haenchen identifies is perhaps unreal, and his solution is untenable. In Luke's presentation the Gentile mission occurs by divine necessity according to the willful plan of God. If there is a "founder" of the Gentile mission, it is God or the Holy Spirit. Luke could easily have placed a slightly different version of this account of Philip's work between 11:20 and 11:21 if he regarded the eunuch as a Gentile and he were concerned to protect Peter's status. But in the present location of the story in Acts one sees human, specifically Christian, lack of perception and that the Holy Spirit, not an innovative disciple, inaugurated and directed the universal mission of the early church.

if not exclusively (13:46–48; 18:6; 28:28).[47] Subsequently Paul and companions engage Gentiles directly (e.g., 14:8–18; 16:11–15). Nevertheless, the preachers returned again and again to preach to Jewish hearers (e.g., 14:1; 17:1–4, 10–12, 16–17; 18:1–4; 19:8; 22:1, 3–21; 28:17–20). This pattern repeats itself in story and in speech. Thus, the primary protagonist of the final portion of Acts, Paul, preached to and defended himself before Jews and Gentiles alike.

At the end of Acts one observes the final report of Paul's preaching to Jews (28:17–20, 25–28). One learns that the hearers reacted in a mixed manner. It is crucial to notice that *some* believed (28:24a), so that at the end of Acts the reaction by Jewish hearers is no more absolute than it has been throughout the narrative. In the face of this final report of rejection (28:24b–25a) Paul once again — for the final time in Acts — states his intention to turn to the Gentiles (28:28). Interpreters make much of this statement,[48] often arguing that the ending of Acts depicts the end of the mission to the Jews. Yet neither the imperfect ἠπίστουν ("refused to believe") in reference to this particular act of disbelieving (28:24) nor the second aorist ἀπεστάλη ("has been sent")[49] in reference to the sending of the message to the Gentiles (28:28) requires such an understanding. Twice previously (13:46–47; 18:6) Paul declared his intention to turn to the Gentiles, and following both declarations he again preached to the Jews (14:1; 19:8) in new locations.[50] Indeed, the *expectation*

---

47. C. H. Talbert argues that the relative silence of Acts concerning the Gentile rejection of the gospel heightens, by contrast, the seemingly disproportionate attention give to Jewish rejection ("Once Again: The Gentile Mission," 105–8). In fact, Talbert observes that, as Acts reports, for Jews and Gentiles alike "some believe and some do not" (p. 106). Talbert sets aside interpretations of Acts that label this phenomenon "anti-Semitic" or anti-Jewish. Rather, he reads the pattern of "the Lukan focus on Jewish rejection and Gentile acceptance of the gospel . . . [as] yet another part of the general theme of reversal connected with eschatological fulfillment and its inauguration" (p. 106). Talbert contends this theme is ironic and intends to highlight Luke's understanding of salvation as *universal*.

48. E.g., R. Maddox focuses on the ending of Acts and notes Luke's "complete silence" about Paul's trial and "slight regard" for the Roman Christians, arguing that the final episode draws attention to the importance of the Gentile mission and perhaps even more highlights "the negative theme, that the Jews are excluded" which "is also most important to Luke" (*The Purpose of Luke-Acts* [FRLANT 126; Göttingen: Vandenhoeck & Ruprecht, 1982] 42–43). Maddox refers to Paul's "final repetition of the 'turning to the Gentiles,'" but he considers only "where Luke lets the emphasis fall" and gives no thought to the *expectation* created by repetition.

See, furthermore, Conzelmann's baffling remarks in relation to 28:17 (*Acts*, 227), which simply read into the narrative what it needed to draw the conclusions Conzelmann presents. It is telling that in interpreting 28:17–19 Conzelmann refers to 23:29; 25:8, 25; 26:31; 25:9–25, but he completely ignores 24:9; 25:7. In turn, he ignores the previous patterns of repetition.

49. F. Stagg, "The Abused Aorist," *JBL* 91 (1972) 222–31.

50. M. Rese surveys the lively discussion and disagreement concerning whether or not Luke-Acts is to be understood as "anti-Jewish" ("'Die Juden' im lukanischen Doppelwerk: Ein Bericht über eine längst 'neuere' Diskussion," in *Der Treue Gottes Trauen: Beiträge zum Werk des Lukas für Gerhard Schneider* [ed. C. Bussmann and W. Radl; Freiburg/Basel/Vienna: Herder, 1991] 61–79). Rese notes that often the expressions about "the Jews" in Luke-Acts are simply ignored

created by the repetitions in the speeches and narrative of Acts is that Paul (and others?) will have increasing success among the Gentiles but that, as before, the preachers will certainly return to preach to the Jews. If one considers the ending of Acts in relation to the patterns of repetition in the entire account, one is safe to conclude that while Luke writes Acts to explain an increasingly Gentile church to itself, through repetition he also creates an *expectation* of an ongoing mission to the Jews.[51] Whether Luke sought simply to explain this work or to motivate such a mission with Paul's statement at the ending of Acts is, of course, a matter of guesswork.[52] What is certain is

---

by interpreters, that those reflecting on the subject of Luke's possible "anti-Judaism" disagree. He suggests that a way forward in the discussion may be to consider the topic of possible "anti-Judaism" in relation to the issues of the author's identity and the goal of Luke's double work. Rese insists one must stick to the text of Luke-Acts and not fly into hypothetical presumptions.

51. To move past this observation and speak of the needs of Luke's readers is a purely hypothetical step. M. Rese ("'Die Juden,'" 77 n. 43) cites F. Overbeck (*Kurze Erklärung der Apostelgeschichte* [Kurzgefasstes exegetisches Handbuch zum Neuen Testament von W. M. L. de Wette 1/4; 4th rev. ed.; Leipzig: S. Hirzel, 1870] XVII [*sic*; rather, XXVII]) regarding such "interpretations" "Das Problem des Inhalts der AG. erklären mit den Bedürfnissen der Leser des Buchs . . . heisst Dunkles mit Dunklem zu erhellen."

The most detailed examination of the "rejection by Jews and turning to Gentiles" is an essay by R. C. Tannehill ("Rejection by Jews and Turning to Gentiles: The Pattern of Paul's Mission in Acts," in *Luke-Acts and the Jewish People* [ed. J. B. Tyson; Minneapolis: Augsburg, 1988] 83–101). Tannehill recognizes that Luke presents two fundamental points that are in tension with each other: "a persistent concern with the realization of scriptural promises which . . . apply first of all to the Jewish people, and the stinging experience of rejection of the message that the hope of Israel is now being fulfilled. . . . Acts offers no solution except the patient and persistent preaching of the gospel in hope that the situation will change" (p. 101). To this point Tannehill understands Acts correctly, but as he continues to reason in relation to the present situation faced by Christians and Jews today, Tannehill thinks in terms Luke would not understand. Tannehill writes, "The situation has not changed. . . . it is now necessary to recognize the diverse ways in which different groups will find [God's] salvation and express its meaning for their lives" (p. 101). Luke does not think that humans find God's salvation; rather, God in Christ, and now God through Christ's witnesses, finds and proclaims the good news of God's grace whereby God is saving humanity. If one believes that God did work and continues to work through Jesus Christ for the salvation of humanity, then Luke would not understand how or why one who believes would not bear witness to that truth.

52. The seemingly harsh declaration in Acts 28:26–27 requires that attention be given to my interpretive suggestion concerning the creation of expectation through repetitions. Two observations support my conclusion. First, the quotation in 28:26–27 comes from Isa 6:9–10 LXX. These verses from the Septuagint are found in Matt 13:14–15 and Mark 4:12, but the parallel passage in Luke 8:10 offers a much less harsh statement. Luke has a well-known practice of omitting material from one context and then using it later in another story. (I have discussed this phenomenon in "Tradition, Composition, and Theology in Luke's Account of Jesus before Herod Antipas," *Bib* 66 [1985] 344–64; "A Literary Analysis of the Origin and Purpose of Luke's Account of the Mockery of Jesus, *BZ* 31 [1987] 110–16; and *Passion*, passim.) If Luke did know this line originally as Jesus-material, he also knew that after Jesus uttered these words he certainly continued his ministry to the Jews. Second, equally harsh, absolute-sounding warnings occur in Acts 13:40–41, 46–47. In vv. 40–41 Paul cites Hab 1:5 LXX, and in v. 47 Paul and Barnabas

that the open-ended ending of Acts suggests that the message of God's saving work in Jesus Christ would continue in a significant way.

---

quote Isa 49:6. Here, the Jews are scolded, denounced, and the future turn to the Gentiles is declared. We read that the announcement delighted the Gentiles and that the Jews brought persecution on Paul and Barnabas. Yet the very next story in Acts tells of the work of Paul and Barnabas in a Jewish synagogue in Iconium. A similar pattern unfolds in Acts 18 and 19. Given the evidence from Acts, the burden of proof lies with those who read the ending of Acts as a declaration of the end of the mission to the Jews rather than on those who understand that Luke wants the readers to expect the mission to the Jews to continue.

INDEX OF
MODERN AUTHORS

INDEX OF ANCIENT
TEXTS AND AUTHORS

Please note: Because the Psalms are numbered differently in the LXX and the Hebrew Bible the list of Psalms below indicates whether the references above are to the Greek or Hebrew numbering, and I have given the corresponding numbers for ease in looking up the materials in English, Hebrew, or Greek. Moreover, because the references to Acts are so numerous and are regularly catalogued in various ways above, I have not included Acts in the index of ancient literature.

Old Testament and Septuagint

Genesis	82
12	61
12:1	61
12:1	60 n. 139
12:7	61
15:13–14	60 n. 139, 62
17	62
17:8	62, 62 n. 144
21	62
22:18	43, 60 n. 139
23	64
26:4	43, 60 n. 139
33	64
37–50	62
37:11	63
37:28	63
39:10	63
39:21	63, 74
41	63
41–42	63

42	63
45	63
46:27	63, 63 n. 151
49–50	64
Exodus	
1	64
1:7	64
1:8	61, 64
1:10–11	64
2	64–65
2:14	60 n. 139, 65
3	65
3:5	60 n. 139, 65
3:6	40, 40 n. 80, 60 n. 139, 65
3:7–8	60 n. 139, 65
3:10	60 n. 139, 65
3:12	60 n. 139, 62
3:15	40, 40 n. 80
6	82
20:11	48, 89
22:27	61 n. 139, 115